W9-BAN-724

MacBook®

FOR

DUMMIES®

4TH EDITION

MacBook® FOR DUMMIES®

4TH EDITION

by Mark L. Chambers

WILEY

John Wiley & Sons, Inc.

MacBook® For Dummies®, 4th Edition

Published by
John Wiley & Sons, Inc.
111 River Street
Hoboken, NJ 07030-5774
www.wiley.com

For general information on our other products and services, please contact our Customer Care Department within the U.S. at 877-762-2974, outside the U.S. at 317-572-3993, or fax 317-572-4002.

For technical support, please visit www.wiley.com/techsupport.

Wiley publishes in a variety of print and electronic formats and by print-on-demand. Some material included with standard print versions of this book may not be included in e-books or in print-on-demand. If this book refers to media such as a CD or DVD that is not included in the version you purchased, you may download this material at http://booksupport.wiley.com. For more information about Wiley products, visit www.wiley.com.

Library of Congress Control Number: 2012950497

ISBN 978-1-118-20920-2 (pbk); ISBN 978-1-118-22868-5 (ebk); ISBN 978-1-118-23139-5 (ebk); ISBN 978-1-118-26597-0 (ebk)

Manufactured in the United States of America

10 9 8 7 6 5 4 3 2 1

WILEY

About the Author

Mark L. Chambers has been an author, a computer consultant, a BBS sysop, a programmer, and a hardware technician for almost 30 years — pushing computers and their uses far beyond "normal" performance limits for decades now. His first love affair with a computer peripheral blossomed in 1984 when he bought his lightning-fast 300 BPS modem for his Atari 400. Now he spends entirely too much time on the Internet and drinks far too much caffeine-laden soda.

With a degree in journalism and creative writing from Louisiana State University, Mark took the logical career choice: programming computers. However, after five years as a COBOL programmer for a hospital system, he decided there must be a better way to earn a living, and he became the Documentation Manager for Datastorm Technologies, a well-known communications software developer. Somewhere in between writing software manuals, Mark began writing computer how-to books. His first book, *Running a Perfect BBS,* was published in 1994 — and after a short 15 years or so of fun (disguised as hard work), Mark is one of the most productive and best-selling technology authors on the planet.

His favorite pastimes include collecting gargoyles, watching St. Louis Cardinals baseball, playing his three pinball machines and the latest computer games, supercharging computers, and rendering 3D flights of fancy — and during all that, he listens to just about every type of music imaginable. Mark's worldwide Internet radio station, *MLC Radio* (at www.mlcbooks.com), plays only CD-quality classics from 1970 to 1979, including everything from Rush to Billy Joel to the Rocky Horror Picture Show.

Mark's rapidly expanding list of books includes *iMac For Dummies,* 7th Edition; *MacBook All-in-One For Dummies,* 2nd Edition; *Mac OS X Mountain Lion All-in-One For Dummies; Macs for Seniors For Dummies,* 2nd Edition; *Build Your Own PC Do-It-Yourself For Dummies; Building a PC For Dummies,* 5th Edition; *Scanners For Dummies,* 2nd Edition; *CD & DVD Recording For Dummies,* 2nd Edition; *PCs All-in-One For Dummies,* 5th Edition; *Mac OS X Tiger: Top 100 Simplified Tips & Tricks; Microsoft Office v. X Power User's Guide; BURN IT! Creating Your Own Great DVDs and CDs; The Hewlett-Packard Official Printer Handbook; The Hewlett-Packard Official Recordable CD Handbook; The Hewlett-Packard Official Digital Photography Handbook; Computer Gamer's Bible; Recordable CD Bible; Teach Yourself VISUALLY iMac; Running a Perfect BBS; Official Netscape Guide to Web Animation;* and *Windows 98 Troubleshooting and Optimizing Little Black Book.*

His books have been translated into 15 different languages so far — his favorites are German, Polish, Dutch, and French. Although he can't read them, he enjoys the pictures a great deal.

Mark welcomes all comments about his books. You can reach him at mark@mlcbooks.com, or visit MLC Books Online, his website, at www.mlcbooks.com.

Author's Acknowledgments

It hit me right in the middle of this project — while writing a book about Apple's well-designed Macintosh laptops and software — that I had the "best-designed" people in the technology publishing business working alongside me! These folks made sure that what you read is accurate, funny, and easy to understand.

Coincidence? I think not. That's the Wiley Way.

First, I'd like to thank my technical editor (and good friend) Dennis Cohen, whose expert knowledge of Apple hardware and software ensured that I didn't get Thunderbolt mixed up with FireWire 800.

As with every book I've written, I'd like to thank my wife, Anne, and my children, Erin, Chelsea, and Rose, for their support and love — and for letting me follow my dream!

Finally, I need to send my heartfelt thanks to two wonderful editors at Wiley: my superb project editor, Susan Pink, and my long-standing acquisitions editor, Bob Woerner. A book like this wouldn't be possible without the patience, guidance, and hard work that Susan and Bob provide . . . and they're great friends as well. It's win-win!

Publisher's Acknowledgments

We're proud of this book; please send us your comments at http://dummies.custhelp.com. For other comments, please contact our Customer Care Department within the U.S. at 877-762-2974, outside the U.S. at 317-572-3993, or fax 317-572-4002.

Some of the people who helped bring this book to market include the following:

Acquisitions and Editorial

Project Editor: Susan Pink

Acquisitions Editor: Bob Woerner

Copy Editor: Susan Pink

Technical Editor: Dennis Cohen

Editorial Manager: Jodi Jensen

Editorial Assistant: Leslie Saxman

Sr. Editorial Assistant: Cherie Case

Cover Photo: © kristian sekulic/iStockphoto

Cartoons: Rich Tennant (www.the5thwave.com)

Composition Services

Project Coordinator: Katherine Crocker

Layout and Graphics: Jennifer Creasey, Corrie Niehaus, Laura Westhuis

Proofreaders: Lindsay Amones, Cynthia Fields

Indexer: Sherry Massey

Publishing and Editorial for Technology Dummies

 Richard Swadley, Vice President and Executive Group Publisher

 Andy Cummings, Vice President and Publisher

 Mary Bednarek, Executive Acquisitions Director

 Mary C. Corder, Editorial Director

Publishing for Consumer Dummies

 Kathleen Nebenhaus, Vice President and Executive Publisher

Composition Services

 Debbie Stailey, Director of Composition Services

Contents at a Glance

Table of Contents

Introduction

Laptop owners are special people.

You see, a laptop owner demands everything from a computer that a desktop owner does: reliability, performance, expandability, and ease of use. Owners of Mac Pro, Mac mini, or iMac desktop computers can draw the line right there because their computers are designed for a stationary existence. But you and I are laptop owners. We also need that same computer to be an inch thick (or less). We demand that it run for hours on a single battery charge. We require that it be light as a feather. We want to conquer the coffee shop, the library, and even a lecture hall or two!

Today's Apple laptops deliver all that, and more. If you've bought one of these modern masterpieces — or you're thinking about it right now — I applaud your good taste, common sense, and discerning eye. Apple laptops have everything: super performance, a top-shelf LED screen, rugged reliability, and a trouble-free, powerful operating system. Heck, your Intel-based Apple laptop can even run . . . wait for it . . . Windows 7 or 8. (If you absolutely have to, the option is there.)

I wrote this book for myself — and for every other Apple laptop owner who desires to become a laptop techno-wizard. In these pages, you find a guide to both your laptop's hardware and OS X Mountain Lion, the latest version of Apple's superb operating system. After I cover the basics that every laptop owner should know, you find out how to accomplish all sorts of cutting-edge audio, visual, and Internet projects. (Oh, and if you already have another of my books, you know that I don't skimp on the power-user tips and tricks that save you time, effort, *and* money.)

Like my 30-or-so other *For Dummies* titles, I respect and use the same English language you mastered in school, avoiding jargon, ridiculous computer acronyms, and confusing techno-babble whenever possible. (Plus, I try to bring out the humor that's hidden inside every computer. Finding out how to use your MacBook should be fun — not a chore!)

What's Really Required

If you're *not* an engineer with a degree in Advanced Thakamology — imagine that — you don't need to worry! Here's a reasonably complete list of what's *not* required to use this book.

- I make no assumptions about your previous knowledge of computers — laptop or otherwise — and software. I start at the beginning, which is where every book should start.

- Still considering buying a MacBook Pro, MacBook Air, or MacBook Pro Retina? Heck, you don't even need the computer to benefit from this book! If you're evaluating whether a Mac laptop is right for you, this book is a great choice. I introduce you to both the hardware and software you'll get, so you can easily determine whether a MacBook is the machine for you. (It is. Trust me.)

- Upgrading from the monster that is Windows? I have tips, tricks, and entire sections devoted to the hardy pioneers called *switchers!* You discover the similarities and differences between the two operating systems, how you can make the switch as easily and quickly as possible, and how to run Windows on your new laptop, if you absolutely must.

- If your friends and family have told you that you're going to spend half your savings on software — or that no decent software is available for Mac computers — just smile quietly to yourself! These are two persistent myths about Mac computers, and those same folks are going to be blown away by the images, music, movies, and documents you produce. (Oh, by the way, Mac laptops come complete with a ton more software than any other PC desktop or laptop, and the iLife suite of applications is better than anything available on a PC!) To sum up: *You can do virtually everything in this book with the software that came with your MacBook!*

So what *is* required? Only a Mac laptop and the desire to become a power user — someone who produces the best work in the least amount of time and has the most fun doing it!

I should note that this book was written using the latest MacBook Air computer, so owners of older Mac laptops who aren't running Intel processors (or those folks who can't run OS X Mountain Lion) might not be able to follow along with everything I cover.

About This Book

Each chapter in this book is written as a reference on a specific hardware or software topic. As fruit of the hard work of my editors, you can begin reading anywhere you like because each chapter is self-contained. However, if you want to get the most out of this tome (and your MacBook experience), nothing's wrong with reading this book from front to back. I warn you, however, that Tom Clancy and Stephen King have nothing to fear from my "no-frills" prose.

Conventions Used in This Book

Even with a minimum of techno-speak, this book needs to cover the special keys you have to press or menu commands you have to choose to make things work. Hence, this short list of conventions.

Stuff you type

I may ask you to type a command in OS X. That text usually appears in bold-face, like this:

Type me.

You usually have to press Return before anything happens.

Menu commands

I list menu commands in this format:

Edit⇨Copy

This example of a shorthand menu instruction indicates that you should click the Edit menu and then choose the Copy item.

Web addresses

No up-to-date book on a computer is complete without a bag full of web addresses for you to check out. When you see these addresses in the text, they look like this — www.mlcbooks.com.

(By the way, that website does exist. You're always welcome to check out my little acre of web space!) If you bought the e-book version of this tome, you'll find that you can click (or tap) on these web addresses to visit the pages directly. Convenience is A Good Thing!

For the technically curious

Your MacBook is an elegant and sophisticated machine — and as easy to use as a computer can be — but from time to time, you may be curious about the technical details that surround your hardware and software. (You probably disassembled alarm clocks as a kid, like I did.) Techie stuff is formatted as a sidebar, like this one, and you don't have to read it unless you want to know what makes things tick. (Pun by sheer accident.)

How This Book Is Organized

After careful thought (read that "flipping a coin"), I divided this book into seven major parts — plus an index, just because you deserve one. For your convenience, cross-references to additional coverage of many topics are sprinkled liberally throughout the book.

The Seven Parts Shall Be As Follows:

Part I: Tie Myself Down with a Desktop? Preposterous!

Part I introduces you to the important features of your laptop — like finding out where all the cables connect — and helps you set up your system. I also introduce *OS X Mountain Lion,* which is the Apple operating system that comes preinstalled on your MacBook Pro, MacBook Air, or MacBook Pro Retina.

Part II: Shaking Hands with OS X

It's time to familiarize you with Mountain Lion (don't worry, this cat won't bite). In Part II, you find out how to take care of mundane chores (such as moving your stuff) as well as how to customize and personalize your system until it fits like the proverbial glove. Switchers from the PC world will be especially interested in understanding the ins and outs of OS X — and friends, *it ain't hard.* The Mac started out easier to use than a Windows PC, and *nothing* has changed.

Part III: Connecting and Communicating

In Part III, it's time to jump into the one application you're likely to use every day: your Safari web browser! You also find out more about Apple's iCloud service as well as how to connect your laptop for printing, sharing information with your tablet or cellphone, and even videoconferencing. (I told you this thing was powerful, didn't I?)

In this part, I also discuss how to share your Mac laptop among a group of people and how to connect your Mac to a network. (Wired or wireless, it makes no difference to me!)

Part IV: Living the iLife

Ah, readers, you can begin humming happily to yourself right this second! Yep, Part IV provides complete coverage of the latest iLife release, with the names that are the envy of the Windows crowd: iTunes, iPhoto, iMovie, and GarageBand. You find out how to turn your mobile monster computer into the hub for all your digital media. Whether you listen to it, display it, compose it, or direct it, this part of the book explains it.

Part V: Getting Productive with iWork

Part V is dedicated to the iWork productivity suite, which you can purchase as individual applications for your MacBook using the App Store. You find out how to produce works of office art: spreadsheets, presentations, and printed documents that deliver your message with aplomb.

Part VI: Necessary Evils: Troubleshooting, Upgrading, Maintaining

In Part VI, I cover the stuff you need to know to upgrade your MacBook Pro with more memory, or outfit any MacBook with all sorts of external hardware. If you need to troubleshoot a problem with your hardware or software, check out my should-be-patented troubleshooting guide. Finally, I describe what you can do to help keep your laptop running as fast and as trouble-free as the day you took it out of the box!

Part VII: The Part of Tens

The two chapters in Part VII — the famous "Part of Tens" section — contain advice on a specific laptop or Macintosh topic. Each chapter has ten concise tips, and one or two readers have told me that they make excellent tattoos. (Personally, I'm not *that* much of a Mac guru.)

Bonus chapters: Bluetooth and Boot Camp

In two free bonus chapters available on www.dummies.com/go/MacBookFD4e (and on my website, www.mlcbooks.com), I cover how to share data and stream music among wireless devices by using Bluetooth technology and how to run Windows 7 or 8 on your MacBook using Mountain Lion's Boot Camp feature. Enjoy!

Icons Used in This Book

Like other technology authors, I firmly believe that important nuggets of wisdom should **stand out** on the page! With that in mind, this *For Dummies* book includes a number of margin icons for certain situations.

The most popular icon in the book, you find it next to suggestions I make that save you time and effort — and once or twice, even cash!

These are my favorite recommendations — in fact, I'll bet just about any laptop power user would tell you the same. Follow my maxims, and you'll avoid the quicksand and pitfalls that I've encountered with all sorts of Macs for over two decades!

You don't have to know this stuff, but the technologically curious love high-tech details. (Of course, we're great fun at parties, too.)

Always read the information for this icon first! I'm discussing something that could harm your hardware or throw a plumber's helper into your software.

This is the highlighter stuff — not quite as universally accepted (or as important to the author) as a Mark's Maxim, but a good reminder! I use these icons to reinforce That Which Should Be Remembered.

This icon denotes stuff that's new in OS X Mountain Lion and other Apple software.

Where to Go from Here

My recommendations on how to proceed? I just happen to have three:

- ✔ If you're thinking about buying a new MacBook Pro, MacBook Air, or MacBook Pro Retina, the box is still unopened in your living room, or you'd like help setting things up, start with Part I.

- ✔ If you're already on the road with your laptop but you'd like guidance with running OS X — Hey, you Windows switchers! Take note! — start with Part II.

- ✔ For all other concerns, use the index or check out the table of contents to jump straight to the chapter you need.

Occasionally, Wiley has updates to their technology books. If this book does have technical updates, they will be posted at www.dummies.com/go/macbookfdupdates.

A Final Word

I thank you for buying my book, and I hope that you find _MacBook For Dummies,_ 4th Edition, invaluable! With this fearless guide in hand, I believe that you and your Mac will bond as I have with mine. (That sounds somewhat wrong, but it's really not.)

Time for the first Mark's Maxim in this book:

 Take your time — after all, finding out how to use your computer isn't a race — and don't worry if you're not a graphic artist, professional photographer, or video editor. With your Mac laptop and its software, you don't have to be!™

Part I

Tie Myself Down with a Desktop? Preposterous!

The 5th Wave

By Rich Tennant

"I'm not saying I believe in anything. All I know is since it's been there my MacBook is running 50% faster."

In this part . . .

Your journey as a Mac road warrior — pun intended — begins with a description of your laptop itself as well as the details you need to know when unpacking and setting up your newest family member. You'll also find an introduction to OS X Mountain Lion, the latest version of Apple's super-popular operating system.

I also talk about the differences among the MacBook models as of this writing: the powerful MacBook Pro, the visually dazzling MacBook Pro Retina, and the incredibly thin MacBook Air.

Chapter 1

Hey, It Really Does Have Everything I Need

Most action films have one scene in common: I call it the "gear up" scene, where the good guys strap on their equipment in preparation for battle. (It doesn't matter what era: You see "gear up" scenes in *Gladiator, Aliens,* and virtually every movie Arnold has made.) You're sure to see lots of clicking straps and equipping of offensive weapons (and sometimes even a dash of war paint). The process usually takes a minute or so, all told with whiplash camera work and stirring martial music in the background.

Well, fellow Macintosh road warrior, it takes only *two seconds* and *one move* for you to gear up: closing the lid. That's because your MacBook is a self-contained world, providing virtually everything you'll find on a desktop iMac, Mac mini, or Mac Pro. This is indeed the decade of the laptop, meshing nicely with your cellphone and that wireless connection at your local coffee shop. You have selected the right companion for the open road.

Unlike some of Apple's other designs, such as the Mac mini or the iMac, your MacBook looks similar to a PC laptop running Windows. (In fact, an Intel-based Mac laptop can run Windows, if you absolutely must.) But your laptop holds a number of pleasant surprises that no PC laptop can offer — and, in the case of the MacBook Air and MacBook Pro Retina, you'll lose pounds and inches from your chassis! In this chapter, I introduce you to the hardware and all the major parts of the machine — you even find out how to unpack and connect your computer. And, as frosting on the cake, I preview the software of which Apple is so proud, as well as the accessories that you should buy now rather than later.

Welcome to your Mac laptop, good reader. Gear up!

An Overview of Your Mac Laptop

Sure, your MacBook Pro might be less than an inch thin (a MacBook Air and a MacBook Pro Retina are even more svelte than that — I get to that later in the chapter), but a lot of superb design lives inside, and you'll encounter the same parts that you'd find in a desktop machine. In the following sections, I discuss those important parts — both the stuff you can see and the stuff shoehorned within.

The parts you probably recognize

Every laptop requires some of the same gizmos. Figure 1-1 helps you track them down. Of course, as you'd expect, a computer has a body of sorts in which all the innards and brains are stored, a display screen, a keyboard, a trackpad or other pointing device, and ports for powering and exchanging data with outside toys.

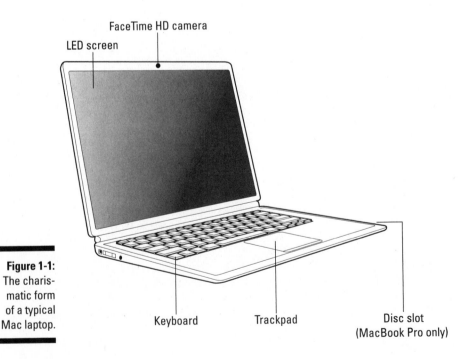

Figure 1-1: The charismatic form of a typical Mac laptop.

FaceTime HD camera

LED screen

Keyboard

Trackpad

Disc slot (MacBook Pro only)

Feeling outdated? Never!

Are you using an older MacBook? It seems that Apple's product line changes every time you tear a page from your 12-month calendar. In addition, every new generation of laptops includes new whiz-bang features. Sometimes you can add those features separately to your older machine — such as an external video camera — but you can't update some things, such as your MacBook's motherboard. Sigh.

Here's my take on this situation: If your older laptop does what you need at a pace you can accept, there's *no need* to upgrade it.

Skeptical? Here's the proof: Before my upgrade to a MacBook Air, yours truly was lugging a pristine iBook G3, which booted OS X Tiger and did absolutely everything that I demanded. (A little more patience was required, certainly, but technology authors are simply *brimming* with

patience.) The moral: Avoid the upgrade fever unless you really need a new companion!

If you're the proud owner of an older MacBook, as long as it can run OS X Mountain Lion you can still enjoy this book and discover new tips and tricks from it! Unless the current breed of Intel-based Mac laptops has a feature that you absolutely can't use on your MacBook (such as USB 3.0 support), you can sail on with your current computer, fiercely proud of The Bitten Apple that appears on the cover. (In fact, older MacBooks have features that no longer appear on some current models, such as optical drives and built-in Ethernet ports.) Although this book was written with the MacBook Pro, MacBook Air, and MacBook Pro Retina lines in mind, virtually everything you read here still applies to your older laptop. Unless it's steam-driven, of course.

That magnificent screen

What a view you have! Today's Mac laptops feature a 13- or 15-inch LED display. Most displays are available in glossy or antiglare finish: The former is a good choice for the brightest colors and deepest blacks, and the latter is a good choice where reflections might be a problem.

LED screens use far less electricity than their antique CRT ancestors do, and they emit practically no radiation.

Apple's laptop screens offer a *widescreen* aspect ratio (the screen is considerably wider than it is tall), which augurs well for those who enjoy watching DVD movies. (A favorite editor of mine loves it when I use the antique word *augur,* meaning *to predict or foretell.*)

That reminds me: Throw away your printed dictionary! You won't need it because OS X Mountain Lion includes the fantastic Dictionary widget, which uses the Internet to retrieve definitions from the online Oxford American Dictionary site (and yes, it does contain *augur*). More on widgets in general in Chapter 5.

The keyboard and trackpad

Hey, here's something novel for your laptop. Unlike the external input devices on a standard desktop computer, your Mac has a built-in keyboard and track-pad (which does the job of a mouse). The keyboard is a particular favorite of mine for a few reasons:

- ✔ You can control the volume or mute all that noise completely.
- ✔ You can use your MacBook's illuminated keyboard, which is perfect for darkened dorm rooms and airplane flights.
- ✔ A handy-dandy Media Eject key on the MacBook Pro keyboard lets you eject a CD or DVD.

The disc slot

You'll notice a long groove on the right side of your MacBook Pro. No, it's not for your credit card. This slot accepts CDs and DVDs into your optical drive. If the drive is empty, loading a disc is as simple as sliding it in an inch or so; the drive sucks in the disc automatically. Note that this drive only accepts standard-sized CD and DVD discs — don't try to load a minidisc or an odd credit-card-shaped optical disc into your drive.

Neither the MacBook Air nor the MacBook Pro Retina has an internal optical drive (more on both models later in this chapter). You use either the CD & DVD Sharing feature in Mountain Lion to read discs remotely (from another Mac or PC on your network), or you can pick up an external optical drive from Apple for about $80. (Such is the price you pay for super-thin and super-light.)

"Luke, the printed label side of the disc should always be *facing you* when you load a disc. Always."

Food for your ears

A machine this nice had better have great sound, and the Mac doesn't disap-point. You have a couple of options for Mac laptop audio:

- ✔ All Mac laptops sport built-in stereo speakers (and a microphone to boot).
- ✔ Use the built-in audio Line Out jacks to connect your Mac's audio to a pair of headphones, a more powerful (and expensive) external speaker system, or a home stereo system.

The power cable

Sorry, you can't get a wireless power system . . . yet. (Apple's working hard on that one.) However, the MacBook Pro was the first major release of a laptop with a magnetic power connector; the MacBook Air followed suit soon after. The MagSafe 2 connector reduces the chances of your pride and joy being yanked off a desk when someone trips over the power cord, because the magnetic closure pops off under significant strain. Now that's *sassy*.

When you connect your power cable, an amber light on the cable connector indicates that your battery is charging; a green light indicates that the battery is fully charged.

Many MacBook owners ask me whether they should disconnect the power cable after the battery is fully charged or leave the power cable connected. I leave the cable connected — it won't cause any damage to your MacBook, and you can continue to use your laptop while it's charging. (Oh, and road warriors prefer a laptop's battery that's always topped off when it's time to go mobile!)

The power button

Yep, you have a power button, too. It's at the upper-right corner of the keyboard, bearing the familiar "circle with a vertical line" logo.

The FaceTime HD camera

Check out that tiny square lens above your screen. That's a built-in FaceTime HD camera, which allows you to chat with others in a videoconferencing environment by using Mountain Lion's Messages and FaceTime features. You can even take photos with the camera, using the Photo Booth software that comes with your laptop, or set up a travelin' webcam. (If you need a higher-resolution camera — or one that can be easily turned or tilted — check out the discussion of a favorite of mine later in this chapter.)

The battery

Apple's current MacBook computers do not include user-replaceable batteries — the battery is sealed inside the case and can be replaced only by an Apple technician. However, you should get several years of trouble-free operation from your MacBook's battery.

Although your laptop can display in OS X Mountain Lion the remaining battery power, you can also monitor the battery level on a MacBook Pro from outside the case! A series of tiny LED lights on the left side of the case indicate the remaining battery charge — push the charge button, and you'll see a number of lights that correspond to the approximate charge remaining.

The holes called ports

The next stop on your tour of Planet Laptop is Port Central — those rows of holes on the sides of your computer. Each port connects a different type of cable or device, allowing you to easily add all sorts of functionality to your computer.

Each of these stellar holes is identified by an icon to help you identify it. Here's a list of what you'll find and a quick rundown on what these ports do.

The following connections are used for external devices and networking:

- **Thunderbolt port:** The Thunderbolt port is the expansion racehorse for today's MacBooks, offering the fastest data transfer rates and the capability to add all sorts of peripherals, from external hard drives to monitors to wired Ethernet connections! (A *peripheral* is another silly techno-nerd term that means a separate device you connect to your computer.) Thunderbolt devices are far more expensive than their FireWire and USB cousins, but prices are dropping as more Thunderbolt peripherals arrive on the market.

  Although Thunderbolt-compatible monitors are available, they're significantly more expensive than a standard display. Luckily, you can also buy an adapter for this port that allows you to send the video signal from your laptop to another VGA or DVI monitor.

- **FireWire port:** These ports can connect external hard drives and optical drives, as well as peripherals such as your digital video (DV) camcorder. If you have a current MacBook Pro model, you have a fast FireWire 800 port. (The MacBook Air and MacBook Pro Retina models don't have a FireWire port.)

- **USB port(s):** Short for *Universal Serial Bus,* the familiar USB port is the jack-of-all-trades in today's world of computer add-ons. Most external devices that you want to connect to your laptop (such as portable hard drives, scanners, and digital cameras) use a USB port, including the iPod. Depending on the model of laptop, you'll have either two or three USB 3.0 ports available. USB 3.0 connections are much faster than the old USB 2.0 standard, but they still accept USB 2.0 devices running at the slower speed.

  Get the lowdown on Thunderbolt, FireWire, and USB ports in Chapter 22.

- **Ethernet port:** Today's MacBook Pro laptops include a standard 10/100/1000 Ethernet port, so the laptop is ready to join your existing wired Ethernet network. (Alternatively, you can go wireless for your network connection; more on that in the next section and in Chapter 12.) Because both the MacBook Air and the MacBook Pro Retina are designed to be completely wireless, they don't have a wired Ethernet port; if necessary, you can add a Thunderbolt-to-Gigabit-Ethernet adapter to add a wired network port to your Air or Retina. (Apple sells one for about $30.)

✔ **SD/SDXC card slot:** All MacBook models include an SD (Secure Digital) or SDXC (Secure Digital Extended Capacity) card slot, allowing you to plug SD or SDXC memory cards from digital cameras, cellphones, and portable devices directly into your laptop.

The connections that follow are used for external video and audio:

✔ **HDMI port:** The MacBook Pro Retina includes an HDMI port, allowing a direct connection between your laptop and high-definition displays and TVs.

✔ **Headphone/Optical Output port:** You can send the high-quality audio from your rectangular beast to a set of standard headphones or an optical digital audio device such as a high-end home theater system.

✔ **Audio Line In jack:** Last (but certainly not least) is the Audio Line In jack on the 15-inch MacBook Pro, which allows you to pipe the signal from another audio device into your laptop. This connector comes in particularly handy when you record MP3 files from your old vinyl albums or when you want to record loops in GarageBand.

Don't forget the parts you can't see

When you bought your new digital pride and joy, you probably noticed a number of subtle differences between the low-end MacBook Air and the über-expensive, top-end MacBook Pro and MacBook Pro Retina models. I call these differences the *Important Hidden Stuff* (or IHS, if you're addicted to acronyms already), and they're just as important as the parts and ports that you can see.

Internal storage devices are as follows:

✔ **CPU:** Today's Mac laptops feature the latest Intel Core i5 and i7 processors. Of course, the faster the processor, the better. (Definitely *not* rocket science.)

✔ **Storage:** Today's MacBook models are equipped with either traditional magnetic hard drives or solid-state drives. The drive capacities are different across the entire MacBook product line, but only the MacBook Pro can be ordered from Apple with either magnetic hard drives or solid-state storage.

The MacBook Pro Retina and MacBook Air, on the other hand, are available only with solid-state drives, which have a number of advantages over traditional magnetic hard drives: You'll find no moving parts in a solid-state drive, and it offers better performance than a standard hard drive. Think of the solid-state drive as an internal USB flash drive, which uses RAM chips rather than magnetic platters to hold your data! Pricey compared to a magnetic hard drive, but *super sweet*.

✔ **Optical drive:** Okay, I'm cheating a little here. I mention the optical drive in an earlier section, but all you can see is the slot, so it qualifies as an IHS item. Depending on your MacBook, your computer includes one of the following:

- *No built-in optical drive*

  The MacBook Air and MacBook Pro Retina can be equipped with an external SuperDrive, or you can use another computer's drive remotely over your network (both wired and wireless, although wired is faster and far more reliable).

- *A DVD-R/CD-RW SuperDrive, which can play and record both CDs and DVDs*

  If you prefer to burn Blu-ray discs on your MacBook Pro, don't give up hope of recording! Thanks to those handy FireWire and USB ports, it's child's play to add an external Blu-ray recorder.

Wireless communications devices include the following:

✔ **Wireless Ethernet:** "Look, Ma, no wires!" As I mention earlier, you can connect your laptop to an existing wireless Ethernet network. All current Mac laptops have built-in AirPort Extreme hardware. With wireless connectivity, you can share documents with another computer in another room, share a single high-speed Internet connection betwixt several computers, or enjoy wireless printing. Truly *sassy!*

Although Apple would want you to build your wireless wonderland with an Apple AirPort Extreme Base Station or a Time Capsule unit — go figure — you can use your Mac with any standard 802.11 wireless network. And yes, PCs and Macs can intermingle on the same wireless network without a hitch. (Scandalous, ain't it?)

✔ **Bluetooth:** Let's get the old "digital pirate" joke out of the way: "Arrgh, matey, I needs me a wireless parrot." (Engineers again . . . sheesh.) Although strangely named, Bluetooth is another form of wireless connectivity. This time, however, the standard was designed for accessories such as your keyboard and mouse and devices such as a personal digital assistant (PDA) and a cellphone.

Here's the video display device:

> ✔ **Video card:** If your applications rely heavily on high-speed 3-D graphics, you'll be pleased as punch to discover that today's MacBook Pro and MacBook Pro Retina laptops can be ordered with the muscle-bound NVIDIA GeForce GT 650M. This card is well suited to 3-D modeling, video editing, and well, honestly, blasting the enemy into small smoking pieces with aplomb.

Meet the MacBooks

So far in this chapter, I've discussed the common hardware shared by today's MacBook models, but it's time to compare the MacBook Air, MacBook Pro, and MacBook Pro Retina with an eye to selecting the right one for you. (Unless you decide to pick up one of each — certainly an elegant choice, but not everyone has that option!)

For example, consider the least expensive (and lightest) MacBook: The MacBook Air is unique for both its size and weight (see Figure 1-2). And yet the Air is just like the MacBook Pro and the MacBook Pro Retina. Well, mostly.

Figure 1-2:
Behold the MacBook Air.

"Hold on, Mark. How can it be so singular and yet share so much with its road warrior siblings?" I answer that question in the following sections, which discuss the many similarities and the handful of striking differences between the three laptops in the MacBook line. If you're considering buying a MacBook, these sections can help you decide whether you'd like to go ultra-thin or stick with the more powerful laptop crowd.

One thing's for sure — Apple *never* creates a mundane design!

Comparing 'twixt MacBooks

Do you remember when Apple introduced those first iMacs? Although they shared the same basic components as any computer — a monitor, keyboard, ports, speakers, and cables — the iMac was revolutionary because it was completely self-contained. And it came in colors. And it didn't have a floppy drive. In fact, Apple had redesigned the common computer with the focus on *style* and *ease of use,* and had scrapped the floppy drive (and rightly so, seeing as how floppies had become practically useless and were unreliable, to boot).

I consider both the MacBook Air and the MacBook Pro Retina to be extensions of the iMac revolution. With these designs, Apple has focused this time on *physical dimensions* and *weight,* and has tossed anything that isn't absolutely necessary for the lecture hall, boardroom, or city park. However, I'm happy to note that these ultralight MacBooks are no toys, nor are they bare-bones netbooks. You'll find the MacBook Pro Retina as powerful as the standard MacBook Pro, and the Air even shares some of the features of the MacBook Pro.

What are the MacBook similarities?

Consider the similarities between the MacBooks:

- ✔ **Widescreen display:** Each MacBook model sports a widescreen LED backlit display — the Air offers either an 11-inch or a 13-inch display, and the MacBook Pro can be ordered with a 13-inch or 15-inch display. The superb Retina display on the MacBook Pro Retina is the star of the show, however, with the highest resolution available on any MacBook. (It's available only in a 15-inch display.).

- ✔ **Intel Core i5 and i7 processor:** All three MacBooks can be ordered from Apple with Core i5 or i7 power.

- ✔ **Keyboard and trackpad:** All three MacBooks share the same backlit keyboard and use the same Multi-Touch trackpad. (Read more about Multi-Touch in Chapter 4.)

- ✔ **Mountain Lion:** All current MacBooks run the latest version of OS X with aplomb.

- ✔ **FaceTime HD:** Every MacBook is video ready, using the same FaceTime HD camera. You can record audio with the built-in microphone as well — in fact, the Retina has two microphones. (Read more about video chatting and FaceTime in Chapter 13.)

✔ **Sealed battery:** You can't swap batteries with any of Apple's current MacBook line because the battery is sealed inside. (Think iPod.)

✔ **Wireless support:** Each MacBook has both built-in AirPort Extreme hardware (802.11n) and built-in Bluetooth hardware. (Read more about AirPort Extreme in Chapter 12.)

I think most Apple laptop owners would agree that these major MacBook features show there's no underpowered pushover in the lineup!

So what's so flippin' radical?

I'm glad you asked! Here's the checklist of striking differences that set the Air apart from the MacBook Pro and MacBook Pro Retina:

✔ **Physical dimensions:** Apple doesn't call this machine the Air for nothing! The current Air laptop measures a mere 0.68 inches in height (at its tallest point) when closed, 11.8 inches in width (for the 11-inch display model), and 7.56 inches in depth. Oh, and hold on to your chair for this one: Our lightweight champ weighs in at less than 2 ½ pounds! (That's a couple of pounds you won't be carrying around all day at that convention expo. Take it from this traveler: You *will* feel the refreshing difference in just an hour or two.) The MacBook Pro Retina, on the other hand, weighs in at almost 4½ pounds, while the more powerful MacBook Pro is over 5½ pounds.

✔ **Cost:** At the time of this writing, two versions of the laptop are available. An entry-level 11-inch MacBook Air will set you back $999, and the top-of-the-line 13-inch Air is $1,499. The more expensive Air is equipped with a higher-capacity larger screen, a more capacious solid-state drive, and a faster CPU. By comparison, the 15-inch MacBook Pro is $1,799 and the Retina display pushes the cost of the MacBook Pro Retina to a whopping $2,199 in its base configuration.

✔ **Ports:** The Air offers only a handful of ports: two USB 3.0 ports, an Audio Line Out jack, and a Thunderbolt port for connecting an external monitor or high-speed drive. Note that I didn't mention a FireWire port, which can be a big problem for Apple old-timers like me. I have a huge collection of FireWire devices. The Retina also has no FireWire port (but it does include an HDMI port for connecting the laptop to a high-definition TV or external display). Both the Air and the Retina also lack a wired Ethernet port, so you'll need the Thunderbolt-to-Gigabit-Ethernet adapter from Apple. Rats.

✔ **Sealed case:** You can't add or replace RAM modules on the Air or the Retina — if you haven't ordered your laptop yet, it's a *very* good idea to configure your MacBook with the maximum RAM it can carry, because you won't be able to add more in the future. On the other hand, the

MacBook Pro can be upgraded to 16GB of RAM by upgrading the RAM modules.

✔ **No built-in optical drive:** *Whoa, Nellie!* This difference is a big one, and it applies to both the Air and the Retina. Apple decided that owners of these slimmer, trimmer laptops are likely to use a wireless connection for transferring files and media. But what if you have to reinstall applications available only on disc? If you need to read or burn discs, you can buy a separate external USB SuperDrive for about $80, or you can use the Remote Disc feature and share the drive on another computer. (More on Remote Disc in the section "Sharing a CD or DVD drive," later in this chapter.)

As you can see, these striking differences make the choice between a MacBook Air, a MacBook Pro, and a MacBook Pro Retina easy indeed. To wit:

✔ The Air is designed for the traveler who appreciates minimum weight and size. These folks see the MacBook Air as a race car: nimble, with reduced weight and no unnecessary frills. (Think of a typical NASCAR entry: Who needs an expensive stereo or air conditioning?)

✔ The MacBook Pro Retina is all about the brilliant Retina display, of course, but it's also designed to be somewhat slimmer and lighter than a standard MacBook Pro — and, of course, it's considerably faster than the Air. The Retina appeals to presenters, graphics professionals, and video editors who will appreciate the higher-resolution display and the direct HDMI output.

✔ I highly recommend that you stick with the more conventional MacBook Pro if you don't mind the extra weight and prefer its additional versatility, including the standard set of ports and built-in optical drive.

Look, Ma, no moving parts!

You're probably familiar with the common species of *usbius flashimus* — more commonly called the USB Flash drive. With one of these tiny devices, you get the equivalent of a 4–256GB hard drive that plugs into a USB 2.0 or 3.0 port, allowing you to pack your data with you as you jet across the continents. But have you ever asked yourself, "Self, why don't they make internal drives that use this same technology?"

Actually, dear reader, solid-state drives have been around for a number of years now (think iPod shuffle and iPod nano). Unfortunately, however, the solid-state memory used in today's flash drives gets pretty expensive as capacity increases. In fact, the cost has been the limiting factor, as a solid-state drive offers a number of advantages that set it apart from a conventional magnetic hard drive:

✔ **No moving parts:** Unlike a typical magnetic hard drive, you find no read-write heads and no magnetic platter — just gobs of happy silicon memory chips. In effect, a solid-state drive works along the same lines as your MacBook's system RAM. Unlike your Mac's RAM, though, a solid-state drive doesn't lose the data it stores when you turn off your laptop. As you can imagine, no moving parts on a computer in motion is superior on two levels:

- The solid-state drive never wears out or needs replacing.

- If your laptop is accidentally abused (think, gets knocked off your desk), it's far less likely that you'll lose a hard drive's worth of priceless data when it hits the ground.

✔ **Speed:** Oh, my goodness, is this thing fast! Your MacBook will boot, restart, or awaken in far less time, and everything you do on your laptop will benefit from the speed boost. A solid-state drive can read data far faster than a conventional magnetic hard drive.

✔ **Power usage:** Forget your hard drive spinning up from sleep mode. The solid-state drive uses far less power than a conventional hard drive, resulting in significantly longer battery life.

✔ **Blessed silence:** The solid-state drive is completely silent. (No more of that gargling noise while the disk is accessed. *Sweet.*)

Both the MacBook Air and the Retina are available only with a solid-state drive, but do you need the solid-state drive option for your MacBook Pro? The answer lies in your bank account (as well as your need for elbow room). If you can afford the extra expense of the solid-state drive and you can fit all your applications and data into the 128GB drive (or the even more expensive 256GB and 512GB drives), I heartily recommend that you consider joining Buck Rogers with the storage device of the future.

If you'd rather save that coin for something else, or you need a larger internal hard drive to hold things such as digital video and a massive collection of digital images, stick with the tried-and-true magnetic hard drive.

What if I need that pesky optical drive?

Can a laptop survive in the jungle that is Real Life without a DVD drive? The terse answer is *no*. I'll be honest here: Ripping an audio CD or watching a DVD movie without an optical drive is impossible. (Rather like a cheap tank of gas.) And the wonders of digital media are a big part of the iWorld. So what was Apple thinking?

First, a bit of explanation. Today's DVD drives are thin, but not Air and Retina thin. To create these stunning designs with truly revolutionary dimensions, Apple engineers had to leave out the drive. However, if you own a MacBook Air or MacBook Pro Retina, you have two choices when it comes to reading the contents of a CD or DVD: Go external, or find out how to share.

The external USB route

I have no problem toting around an external USB DVD burner with a MacBook Air. Heck, half the time, you're likely to leave it at home because most of us don't install software every day. The folks at Cupertino want you to download your movies from the iTunes Store and your software from the App Store, so if you follow the Apple Path, you still don't need an optical drive!

A USB SuperDrive from Apple costs a mere $80, and it can read and write DVDs as well as the built-in SuperDrive you find in the MacBook Pro.

You can also use any third-party USB DVD drive that's compatible with Apple's laptops and OS X Mountain Lion.

Sharing a CD or DVD drive

The other option for installing software or reading a DVD on the MacBook Air and MacBook Pro Retina is Mountain Lion's built-in CD/DVD Sharing feature. Sharing is an option if you have a wired or wireless network (see Chapter 12) with at least one of the following:

  ✔ A Macintosh running OS X Tiger, Leopard, Snow Leopard, Lion, or Mountain Lion

  ✔ A PC running Windows XP, Vista, 7, or 8 (and a Windows application supplied by Apple with your MacBook).

You can *only read from a shared optical drive.* You can't write data to the remote drive, even if that drive is a DVD recorder.

On the Macintosh with the optical drive, open System Preferences, click the Sharing icon, and then select the DVD or CD Sharing check box. Note that you can set whether the Mac will request your permission when another computer attempts to share the drive.

On a PC, display the Control Panel, click the DVD or CD Sharing icon, and then select the Enable DVD or CD Sharing check box. Again, you can specify that permission is required if security is a concern.

After you set up the shared drive, just load the disc and select the Remote Disc item in any Finder sidebar. (Remote Disc appears under the Devices heading in the sidebar.) Now you can access the drive as if it were directly connected to your MacBook Air or Retina. Ah, technology!

Location, Location, Location!

If you choose the wrong spot to park your new laptop, I can *guarantee* that you'll regret it. Some domiciles and office cubicles don't offer a choice — you have one desk at work, for example, and nobody's going to hand over another one — but if you can select a home for your MacBook, consider the important placement points in this section:

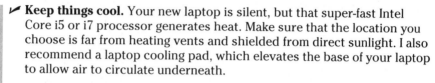

✔ **Keep things cool.** Your new laptop is silent, but that super-fast Intel Core i5 or i7 processor generates heat. Make sure that the location you choose is far from heating vents and shielded from direct sunlight. I also recommend a laptop cooling pad, which elevates the base of your laptop to allow air to circulate underneath.

✔ **Outlets are key!** Your computer needs a minimum of at least one nearby outlet, and perhaps as many as three:

- A standard AC outlet (using a current adapter if you're traveling abroad, if necessary)

- A telephone jack (if you have an external USB modem for connecting to the Internet or sending and receiving faxes)

- A nearby Ethernet jack (if you use the MacBook Pro's built-in Ethernet port for connecting to a wired Ethernet network)

  If you prefer to send your data over the airwaves, consider wireless networking for your Mac — I discuss everything you need to know in Chapter 12.

✔ **Don't forget the lighting.** Let me act as your mom. (I know that's a stretch, but bear with me.) She'd say, "You can't possibly expect to work without decent lighting! You'll go blind!" She's right, you know. You need a desk lamp or floor lamp at a minimum if you need to refer to books or documents often in your work.

✔ **Plan to expand.** If your laptop hangs out on a desk, allow an additional foot of space on each side. That way, you have room for external peripherals, more powerful speakers, and an external keyboard and mouse if you need one.

If you want to keep an external keyboard handy, consider using a laptop shelf. These Plexiglas or metal stands elevate your laptop several inches above the desk, putting the screen at a better ergonomic position and allowing you to park your keyboard and external mouse underneath.

Unpacking and Connecting Your Laptop

You're going to love the following sections. They're short and sweet because the configuration of a laptop on your desktop is a piece of cake. (Sorry about the cliché overload, but this really *is* easy.)

Unpacking for the road warrior

Follow these guidelines when unpacking your system:

- ✔ **Check for damage.** I've never had a box arrive from Apple with shipping damage, but I've heard horror stories from others (who claim that King Kong must have been working for That Shipping Company).

  Check all sides of your box before you open it. If you find significant damage, take a photograph (just in case).

- ✔ **Search for all the parts.** When you're removing those chunks o' foam, make certain that you've checked all sides of each foam block for parts snuggled therein or taped for shipment.

- ✔ **Keep all packing materials.** Do *not* head for the trash can with the box and packing materials. Keep your box and all packing materials for at least a year, until the standard Apple warranty runs out. If you have to ship the laptop to an Apple service center, the box and the original packing are the only way for your machine to fly.

  And now, a dramatic Mark's Maxim about cardboard containers:

  Smart computer owners keep their boxes far longer than a year. If you sell your laptop or move across the country, for example, you'll want that box. *Trust me on this one.*™

- ✔ **Store the invoice for safekeeping.** Your invoice is a valuable piece of paper, indeed.

  Save your original invoice in a plastic bag, along with your computer's manuals, original software, and other assorted hoo-hah. Keep the bag on your shelf or stored safely in your desk, and enjoy a little peace of mind.

- ✔ **Read the Mac's manual.** "Hey, wait a minute, Mark. Why do I have to read the manual from Apple along with this tome?" Good question, and here's the answer: The documentation from Apple might contain new and updated instructions that override what I tell you here. (For example, *"Never* cut the red wire. Cut the blue wire instead." Or something to that effect.) Besides, Apple manuals are rarely thicker than a restaurant menu.

You can always download the latest updated manuals for Apple computers in electronic format from Apple's website. (Adobe's PDF format is the standard for reading documents on your computer, and Mountain Lion can open and display any PDF document by using the Preview application or the QuickLook feature.) I always keep a copy of the PDF manual for my MacBook Air on my drive, just in case.

Connecting Cables 101

Your laptop makes all its connections simple, but your computer depends on you to get the outside wires and thingamabobs where they go.

The absolutely essential connection

After your new Mac is resting comfortably in its assigned spot (I assume that's a desktop), you need to make just one required connection: the power cable! Plug the cable into the corresponding MagSafe 2 socket on the MacBook first, and then plug 'er into that handy AC outlet. (After your battery is completely charged, of course, you can go mobile at a moment's notice.)

Adding the Internet to the mix

If you have Internet access or a local computer network, you need to make at least one of the following connections described in this section.

If you get on the Internet by dialing a standard phone number and your laptop has an external USB modem, just make two more connections:

1. **Plug one of the telephone cable's connectors into your external modem.**

2. **Plug the other telephone cable connector into your telephone line's wall jack.**

After you get your account information from your ISP, Chapter 12 has the details on configuring your modem and Internet settings for dial-up access.

If you have high-speed Internet service, or if you're in an office or a school with a local computer network, you can probably connect through your MacBook Pro's built-in Ethernet port (or by using the Thunderbolt-to-Gigabit-Ethernet adaptor with your MacBook Air or Retina). You make two connections:

1. **Plug one end of the Ethernet cable into the Ethernet port on the MacBook.**

2. **Plug the other end of the Ethernet cable into the Ethernet port from your network.**

   Your network port is probably one of the following: an Ethernet wall jack, an Ethernet hub or switch, or a cable or DSL Internet router (or sharing device).

Will you be joining a wireless network? If so, you find the information you need on configuring Mountain Lion for wireless networking in Chapter 12.

Great, a Lecture about Handling My Laptop

Proper handling of your laptop is important, so take a moment to cover the Rules of Proper Laptop Deportment. Okay, perhaps I'm lecturing a bit, but a little common sense goes a long way when handling *any* computer equipment, and your laptop is no different. (Scolding mode off.)

Keep these rules in mind while opening and carrying your laptop:

- **The cover is your friend.** Open your laptop's cover slowly, without jerking or bending it.

- **Close it before you move it.** By closing your laptop, you put your OS X operating system into sleep mode, and (if your MacBook uses a magnetic hard drive for storage) the hard drive automatically spins down, making it safer to move. The laptop is still on, and will spring back to life after you open the cover.

- **Don't stack stuff on your laptop.** You'd be surprised how many horror stories I've heard about laptop owners piling a stack of books or other heavy stuff on top of their computers. Remember that LED display? Made of glass?

- **Be nice to your keyboard.** Don't press too hard on those keys! Use the same amount of pressure that you use with a desktop computer keyboard.

- **Keep food and drinks far away.** Care to turn your laptop into a very expensive doorstop? Then go ahead and park your soda next to it. (Oh, and crumbs are perfect if you're interested in buying replacement keyboards.)

- **Keep your laptop as level as possible.** Using your laptop while it's tilted too far in any direction can eventually cause problems with your magnetic hard drive. I kid you not. (If you choose a solid-state hard drive, of course, this rule no longer applies!)

An Overview of Mac Software Goodness

The following sections answer the most common of all novice computer questions: "What the heck will I *do* with this thing?" You find additional details and exciting factoids about the software that you get for free, software you'll want to buy, and stuff you can do on the Internet.

What comes with my laptop?

Currently, Apple laptops ship with the following major software applications installed and ready to use:

- ✔ **OS X Mountain Lion:** Naturally, your MacBook comes preloaded with Mountain Lion.

- ✔ **The iLife suite:** You know you want these applications! They turn your Mac into a digital hub for practically every kind of high-tech device on the planet, including camcorders, digital cameras, portable music players, and even cellphones.

  Chapters 14–17 focus on the major iLife applications that will appeal to MacBook owners: iTunes, iPhoto, iMovie, and GarageBand.

- ✔ **Photo Booth and FaceTime:** You discover more about these applications elsewhere in the book. For now, suffice it to say that Photo Booth works with your laptop's FaceTime HD camera, as does FaceTime (the video-chatting application that can connect you with iPad, iPhone, and iPod touch owners).

The installed software on your MacBook might change as new programs become available.

Connecting to the Internet from your lap

What is a modern computer without the Internet? Apple gives you great tools to take full advantage of every road sign and off-ramp on the Information Superhighway right out of the box:

- ✔ **Web surfing:** I use Mountain Lion's Apple Safari web browser every single day. It's faster and better designed than Internet Explorer, with features such as tabbed browsing and Facebook and Twitter sharing.

  If *tabbed browsing* sounds like ancient Aztec to you, don't worry. Chapter 9 is devoted entirely to Safari.

✔ **Web searches:** Dashboard widgets can search the entire Internet for stocks, movie listings, airline schedules, dictionaries, and foreign language translations. I explain the Dashboard in Chapter 5.

✔ **Instant messaging:** *Messages* lets you use your MacBook to chat with others around the world for free on the Internet — by keyboard, voice, or full-color video. This is awesome stuff straight out of Dick Tracy and Buck Rogers. If you've never seen a video chat, you'll be surprised by just how good your friends and family look!

Always wear a shirt when videoconferencing.

✔ **E-mail:** Soldier, Apple has you covered. The Mail application is a full-featured e-mail system, complete with defenses against the torrent of junk mail awaiting you. (Imagine a hungry digital mountain lion with an appetite for spam.) Send pictures and attached files to everyone on the planet, and look doggone good doing it.

Applications that rock

Dozens of small applications are supplied with OS X. I mention them in later chapters, but here are three good examples to whet your appetite:

✔ **DVD Player:** Put all that widescreen beauty to work and watch your favorite DVD movies with DVD Player! You have all the features of today's most expensive stand-alone DVD players, too, including a spiffy on-screen control that looks like a remote.

✔ **Contacts:** Throw away that well-thumbed collection of fading addresses on paper. Use the Mountain Lion Contacts application to store, search, and recall just about any piece of information on your friends, family, and acquaintances.

✔ **Chess:** Ah, but this isn't the chessboard your dad used! Play the game of kings against a tough (and configurable) opponent — your MacBook — on a beautiful 3-D board. Heck, your Mac even narrates the game by speaking the moves!

You can use the data you store in your Contacts in other Apple applications included with Mountain Lion, such as Apple Mail and Messages.

Boot Camp For Dummies

OS X Mountain Lion includes one particularly exciting feature for Windows switchers: You can use the Apple Boot Camp utility and your licensed copy of Windows 7 or 8 to install and boot Windows on your Intel-based Mac laptop!

Boot Camp creates a Windows-friendly *partition* (or section) on your hard drive, where all your Windows files are stored. Other than the slightly strange key assignments you'll have to remember, Boot Camp is reliable and easy to use. However, I strongly urge you to back up your laptop on a regular basis; inviting Windows to your Mac laptop also invites potential viruses as well.

Apple's Boot Camp Assistant provides step-by-step instructions, making it easy to configure your laptop for Windows. To run the Boot Camp Assistant, click the Launchpad icon in the Dock, click the Utilities folder icon, and then click the Boot Camp Assistant application icon. You can also download a free bonus chapter from the www.dummies.com/go/MacBookFD4e website (or my website, www.mlcbooks.com) that explains how to use Boot Camp in more detail.

Other Stuff That Nearly Everyone Wants

No man is an island, and no computer is either. I always recommend the same set of stuff for new PC and Mac owners. These extras help keep your new computer clean and healthy (and some make sure that you're happy as well):

✔ **A laptop sleeve or case:** Most laptop owners eschew the traditional bulky laptop bag, because a bag broadcasts the fact that you're carrying a valuable MacBook (and adds yet another item to carry on your trip). On the other hand, if you pack your MacBook in a briefcase, book bag, or backpack, you *need* to provide protection from bumps and scratches. That's where a laptop sleeve or thin case comes in. I use the very cool *BookBook* hardback leather case from Twelve South (www.twelve south.com), which looks — you guessed it — exactly like an old-fashioned leather-bound book from the outside! (I think it makes me appear scholarly while disguising my MacBook.) The BookBook (shown in Figure 1-3) is available for all sizes of MacBooks, costs about $80, and provides long-lasting, cushioned protection for your expensive road warrior.

✔ **An external camera:** Sure, your MacBook has a built-in FaceTime HD camera, but many folks prefer a stand-alone external camera that they can pan, tilt, and point where they like (especially those moviemakers who need high-resolution video clips of whatever's happening around them). I carry the stylish steel aGent V6 HD webcam from Liquid Digital Solutions (www.liquiddigital.com.au), shown in Figure 1-4, with my MacBook Air — it provides full 1080p high-definition recording in iMovie and connects to a USB port. You can choose to clip the webcam to your MacBook or use the desktop stand on any flat surface. The video quality is excellent, with auto exposure and low-light compensation for environments with less-than-perfect illumination. The aGent V6 HD webcam costs about $100.

Figure 1-3:
The
BookBook
case
provides
protec-
tion and
camouflage
for your
MacBook.

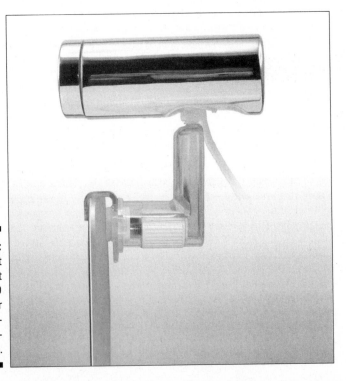

Figure 1-4:
Break out
your aGent
V6 HD
webcam for
on-the-
spot movie-
making.

✔ **Surge suppressor:** Even an all-in-one computer like your laptop can fall prey to a power surge. I recommend using one of these:

- *A basic surge suppressor* with a fuse can help protect your MacBook from an overload.

- *A UPS (uninterruptible power supply)* costs a little more but does a better job of filtering your AC line voltage to prevent brownouts or line interference from reaching your computer.

  Of course, your laptop's battery immediately kicks in if you experience a blackout, so a UPS is less important for your computer. However, any computer tech will tell you that filtered AC current is far better for your laptop, and your UPS can also provide power for external devices that *don't* have a battery.

✔ **Screen wipes:** Invest in a box of premoistened screen wipes to keep your screen pristine. Your MacBook's screen can pick up dirt, fingerprints, and other unmentionables faster than you think.

Make sure that your wipes are especially meant for LED, LCD, or laptop computer screens.

✔ **Blank CDs and DVDs:** If you're using a MacBook with an internal or external optical drive — and the type of media you're recording, such as computer data CDs, DVD movies, or audio CDs — you'll want blank discs for

- CD-R (record once) and CD-RW (record multiple times)

- DVD-R (record once) and DVD+RW (record multiple times)

✔ **Cables:** Depending on the external devices and wired network connectivity you'll be using, these are

- A standard Ethernet cable (for wired networks or high-speed Internet)

- FireWire, Thunderbolt, or USB cables for devices you already have

✔ **Restraining cable:** For those who are a little more security conscious or tend to use their laptops in public places, a standard Kensington laptop lock slot is provided on the MacBook Pro case. (Sorry, MacBook Air and Retina owners, but your case is too thin to sport a lock slot.) The principle is the same as a bicycle cable lock: If your laptop is secured by a cable to a sturdy fixture, it's nearly impossible for it to walk off with someone else.

✔ **Wrist rest:** You might have many reasons to buy a new Mac laptop, but I know that a bad case of carpal tunnel syndrome is not one of them. Take care of your wrists by carrying a keyboard wrist rest in your laptop bag.

Chapter 2

Turning On Your Portable Powerhouse

*I*n Chapter 1, you got as far as unpacking your Mac laptop and connecting a number of cables to it, but unless you bought this computer solely as a work of modern art, it's time to turn *on* your MacBook and begin living The Good Life. (Plus, you still get to admire that Apple design while using iTunes.) After you get your new beauty powered on, I show you how to run an initial checkup of your laptop's health. Then I wax enthusiastic on maintaining (and even augmenting) your laptop battery.

I also familiarize you with the initial chores that you need to complete — such as using the OS X Setup Assistant and moving the data and settings from your existing computer to your MacBook Pro, MacBook Air, or MacBook Pro Retina — before you settle in with your favorite applications.

In this chapter, I assume that OS X Mountain Lion was preinstalled on your Mac or that you just completed an upgrade to Mountain Lion from OS X Lion.

Tales of the On Button

Your MacBook's power switch is located on the right side of the keyboard. Press it now to turn on your laptop, and you will hear the pleasant start-up tone that's been a hallmark of Apple computers for many years. Don't be alarmed if you don't immediately see anything on-screen because it takes a few seconds for the initial Apple logo to appear.

In my experience, sometimes a simple quick press of the power button on some Mac laptop models just doesn't do it. Rather, you have to hold down the button for a count of two or so before the computer turns on. However, if your Mac laptop ever locks up tight (and you can't quit an application, as I demonstrate in Chapter 4), the power button gives you another option: Hold it down for a count of five or so (depending on your counting speed), and your Mac shuts off completely — even if your laptop is locked up tight.

As the Apple logo appears, you see a twirling, circular, high-tech progress indicator that looks like something from a *James Bond* movie. That indicator is the sign that your MacBook is loading Mountain Lion and checking the internal hardware for problems. Sometimes the twirling circle can take a bit longer to disappear. As long as it's twirling, though, something good is happening — your laptop is busy loading certain file-sharing, networking, and printing components (and so on). This process won't take long.

At last, your five to ten seconds of patience is rewarded, and after a short (but neat) video, you see the Mountain Lion Setup Assistant.

Mark's Favorite Signs of a Healthy Laptop

Before you jump into the fun stuff, don't forget an important step — a quick prelim check of the signs that your new mobile Mac survived shipment intact and happy.

If you can answer "yes" to each of these questions, your MacBook likely made the trip without serious damage:

1. **Does the laptop's chassis appear undamaged?**

   It's pretty easy to spot damage to your MacBook's svelte design. Look for scratches and puncture damage.

2. **Does the LED screen work, and is it undamaged?**

   Does the cover open smoothly? Are any individual dots (or *pixels*) on your LED screen obviously malfunctioning? Bad pixels appear black or in a different color than everything surrounding them. (Techs call these irritating anarchists *dead pixels.* A 13-inch MacBook screen has over a million pixels, and unfortunately, some new LED screens include one or two dead ones.

3. **Do the keyboard and trackpad work?**

   Check your MacBook's built-in trackpad by moving your finger across its surface; the cursor should move on your screen. To check the keyboard, press the Caps Lock key on the left and observe whether the Caps Lock light turns on and off.

If you do notice a problem with your laptop (and you can use your Safari browser and reach the web), you can make the connection to an Apple support technician at `www.apple.com`. If your MacBook Pro remains dead — like an expensive paperweight — and you can't get to the Internet, you can check your phone book for a local Apple service center, or call the AppleCare toll-free number at 1-800-275-2273. Chapter 21 also offers troubleshooting information.

You're Not Going to Lecture about Batteries, Are You?

No, this is not going to be a lecture. In fact, the only lecture I put you through in this book concerns backing up (ahem, which *you should do*). Instead, consider these tips as your rules of the road for monitoring and charging your battery:

- **Recharge your laptop in sleep mode or when powered off.** Your battery recharges faster when your laptop is off or in sleep mode. (I go into more detail on sleep mode in Chapter 6.)

- **Keep your laptop plugged into an AC socket (or a car inverter, which plugs into your cigarette lighter) when possible.** I take every opportunity to top off my laptop's battery, and so should you.

  If you don't have much time to charge your battery before you're away from an AC socket — say, half an hour — don't use your MacBook while it's plugged in and charging.

- **Save your juice.** For the most juice you can scavenge, here are some easy tricks:

    - *Turn off your laptop or leave it in sleep mode.*

    - *Turn off unnecessary hardware.* To conserve battery power as much as possible, disconnect any unnecessary USB, Thunderbolt, or FireWire devices, and turn off your Wi-Fi and Bluetooth wireless hardware if you're not connected to a network. (I cover Wi-Fi wireless networking in Chapter 11.)

- *Reduce the brightness of your display from your laptop's keyboard, using the F1 key.*

- *Remove CDs and DVDs from the optical drive. (MacBook Air and MacBook Pro Retina owners: Don't go hunting for a built-in optical drive because your laptop doesn't have one.)*

✔ **Monitor your battery level from the Finder menu.** I love Mountain Lion's battery-monitoring system! Your laptop's battery life can be displayed in the Finder menu in several different views — my favorite is as a percentage of power remaining (with a fully charged battery registering at 100%). To display the percentage, click the battery icon in the Finder menu and choose Show⇨Percentage.

Keep in mind that the percentage shown is estimated by using your current System Preferences settings and power usage, so if you change your Energy Saver settings or remove a USB device that draws power from your laptop, you'll see that change reflected in the battery meter. Figure 2-1 illustrates the battery meter in Percentage view.

✔ **Calibrate your battery.** You can "train" your battery to provide the maximum charge by calibrating it, which Apple recommends doing monthly. The process is a snap:

a. *Charge your battery until the Finder menu battery meter indicates that the unit is fully charged, at 100%.*

b. *Keep your laptop connected to an AC socket for another two hours to ensure a maximum charge.*

c. *Disconnect the power cord and use your laptop on battery power until it is fully discharged and automatically switches to sleep mode.*

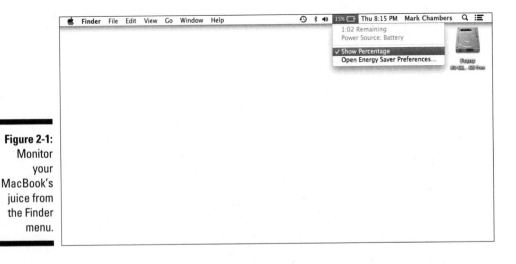

Figure 2-1:
Monitor
your
MacBook's
juice from
the Finder
menu.

Make sure that you close all your applications when you see the low battery warning dialog box so that you don't lose anything.

d. *Allow your laptop to sleep (or turn it off) for a full five hours.*

e. *Reconnect the AC cord and fully charge your battery.*

✔ **Invest in an external battery.** If you often find yourself running out of battery power on the road without an AC socket handy, consider buying an external battery! These handy units are especially designed to charge your MacBook and other USB-powered devices when no other power source is available. I use the HyperJuice external battery from Sanho Corporation (`www.hypershop.com`). The rechargeable HyperJuice battery can power and charge your MacBook, as well as an iPhone and other USB devices. And to make things easier, it adjusts automatically to the voltage requirements of any MacBook model and displays the remaining power with its own built-in meter. The HyperJuice costs between $170 and $450, depending on the battery's capacity.

If your battery is no longer holding a charge — in other words, if you fully charge it and unplug the AC adapter, only to discover that you have only a few minutes of battery life — it's time to invest in a replacement battery. If you use an older Mac laptop with a replaceable battery, you can buy a new battery (from Apple or an online vendor) and install it yourself. Unfortunately, owners of current MacBook models must bring their computers in for servicing. Today's Mac laptop is a sealed unit, and you can't replace the battery yourself.

Hot patootie, is my laptop steam-powered?

Laptops generate heat. Today's super-fast multicore processors can work up a head of steam (pun intended) while you're using them, and some of that heat is simply radiated from the bottom of the computer — even though all current MacBook models have a fan.

What you might not realize, however, is just how *much* heat your MacBook Air or MacBook Pro can produce! No, you won't be scalded if you shift your MacBook from a desk to your lap (Apple dislikes lawsuits as much as the next company), but that laptop will be uncomfortably hot if you've been using it for hours!

To avoid that burning sensation, buy a laptop stand or cooling pad for your desk. These nifty metal or Plexiglas pedestals raise your laptop off your desk, allowing air to flow under the bottom of the computer for better cooling. Also, a laptop stand elevates the screen to a more ergonomic position. (The keyboard might suddenly be harder to use, naturally, but that's yet another reason why I recommend an external keyboard when you're using your Mac laptop at a semipermanent desk location. The other reasons are that an external keyboard saves wear and tear on your laptop keyboard, and you get the ease of using a full-size keyboard.)

Setting Up and Registering Your Laptop

After your MacBook is running and you give it the once-over for obvious shipping damage, your next chore is to set up your laptop. I won't cover the setup process step by step, unlike other tasks in this book. Apple continuously tweaks the questions that you see during setup on a regular basis, and the questions are easy to answer. Everything is explained on-screen, complete with on-screen Help if you need it.

However, I do want you to know what to expect, as well as what information you need to have at hand. I also want you to know about support opportunities, such as Apple's iCloud service. Hence, this section: Consider it a study guide for whatever your MacBook's setup procedure throws at you.

Setting up OS X Mountain Lion

After you start your computer for the first time — or if you just upgraded from OS X Lion — your laptop will likely launch Mountain Lion Setup automatically. (Note that some custom install options, such as the Archive and Install option, might not launch the setup procedure.) The setup process takes care of a number of tasks:

✔ **Setup provides Mountain Lion with your personal information.** As I mention in Chapter 1, your Mac ships with a bathtub full of applications, and many of those use your personal data (such as your address and telephone number) to automatically fill out your documents.

If that stored personal information starts you worrying about identity theft, I congratulate you. If you're using your common sense, sharing your personal data at any time *should* make you uneasy. However, in this case, Apple doesn't disseminate this information anywhere else, and the applications that use your personal data won't send it anywhere, either. And Safari, the Apple web browser, fills out forms on a web page automatically *only* if you give your permission.

✔ **Setup creates your user account.** You're prompted for a username and password, which Setup uses to create your administrator-level account.

✔ **Setup configures your language and keyboard choices.** OS X is a truly international operating system, so you are offered a chance to configure your laptop to use a specific language and keyboard layout.

✔ **Setup configures your e-mail accounts in Apple Mail.** If you already have an e-mail account set up with your ISP, keep handy the e-mail account information that the ISP provided to answer these questions.

The info should include your e-mail address and your login name and password. Mountain Lion can even automatically configure your e-mail account for you (including many web-based e-mail services such as Google Mail, Yahoo! Mail, and Hotmail) if you supply your account ID and password. *Sweet.*

✔ **Setup allows you to open an iCloud account.** Apple's iCloud service just plain rocks — especially the free storage. Take my word for it: Join up, trooper, and create your Apple ID during setup. The standard iCloud service is free, and upgrading to additional space is a breeze if you decide you like the service benefits. I go into these benefits in detail in Chapter 10, but for now, just sign up (or sign in, if you already have an existing iCloud account) and take the opportunity to feel smug about owning an Apple computer.

✔ **Setup sends your registration information to Apple.** As a proud owner of a Mac laptop, take advantage of the year of hardware warranty support and the free 90 days of telephone support. All you have to do is register to use 'em. Rest assured that all this info is confidential.

✔ **Setup launches Migration Assistant.** This assistant guides you through the process of *migrating* (an engineer's term for *moving*) your existing user data from your old Mac or PC to your new laptop. Naturally, if your MacBook is your first Macintosh computer, you can skip this step with a song in your heart! (Read more on Migration Assistant in the section "Importing Stuff from Another Mac," later in this chapter.)

Your Apple ID is your friend

Remember when you were offered the chance to create an Apple ID during the initial setup of Mountain Lion? (If you already had an Apple ID from using OS X Lion, or you created an ID while using your iPad or iPhone, you skipped ahead without a second thought.) If you're careful about your online travels and you decided not to supply your personal data, however, you may have passed up the chance to immediately create your Apple ID during Mountain Lion setup, thinking that you could probably take care of it later.

Unfortunately, you've probably realized by now that all sorts of OS X features and applications hinge on your Apple ID: your iCloud account, the App Store, Messages, the iTunes Store, and FaceTime come to mind. If you haven't created your Apple ID yet, take care of the chore now! It's free and painless, and marks you as one of the In Crowd.

When you're prompted for an Apple ID by one of Mountain Lion's applications, click the Create Apple ID button to start the ball rolling — the application will lead you through the process step-by-step. You can also create your ID through the App Store or the iTunes Store — click the Account link in either application's window and you'll be prompted to create your Apple ID.

Registering your MacBook

I'll be honest here: Many of us, myself included, don't register every piece of computer hardware we buy. For example, I didn't register the wireless Bluetooth adapter that I bought for my older iBook because the expenditure was only around $40, the gizmo has no moving parts, and I'm never likely to need technical support to use it or get it fixed.

However, your MacBook is a different kettle of fish altogether, and I *strongly* recommend that you register your purchase with Apple during the setup process. You spent a fair amount on your computer, and your investment has a significant number of very expensive parts.

Even the hardiest of techno-wizards would agree with this important Mark's Maxim:

If you don't register your new laptop, you can't receive support.™

And rest assured that Apple is not one of those companies that constantly pesters you with e-mail advertisements and near-spam. I've registered every Apple computer I've owned, and I've never felt pestered. (And I have an extremely low tolerance for pester.)

Importing Stuff from Another Mac

If you're upgrading from an older Mac running OS X to your new MacBook or MacBook Pro, I have great news for you: Apple includes *Migration Assistant,* a utility application that can help you copy (whoops, I mean, *migrate*) all sorts of data from your old Mac to your new machine, via your laptop's wired or wireless Ethernet network connection, a FireWire or Thunderbolt cable, or an existing Time Machine backup on an external hard drive.

To use Migration Assistant to copy your system from your older Mac using FireWire or Thunderbolt, you need the corresponding cable to connect the computers. If you don't already have the cable, you can pick one up at your local Maze o' Wires electronics store or at your computer store. (This cable will probably come in handy in the future as well, so it's not a one-use wonder.)

If you're a MacBook Pro Retina or MacBook Air owner, you might be scratching your head looking for a FireWire port on your new laptop. Let me save you the trouble: You don't have one. Therefore, you can use only a Thunderbolt connection. However, you *can* use a wired or wireless Ethernet network connection between computers (assuming, of course, that both your MacBook and your older Mac can communicate over your home or office network). You can even transfer over your network a limited amount of data from Windows on your old PC to your new MacBook!

As I mention earlier, Setup launches Migration Assistant automatically if you indicate that you want to transfer stuff during the setup process, but you can always launch Migration Assistant manually at any time. Simply open Launchpad, click the Utilities folder, and then click the Migration Assistant icon.

The list of stuff that gets copied includes the following:

- ✔ **User accounts:** If you set up multiple user accounts (so that more than one person can share the computer), the utility ports them all to your new Mac.

- ✔ **Network settings:** Boy, howdy, this is a real treat for those with manual network settings provided by an ISP or a network administrator! Migration Assistant can re-create the entire network environment of your old Mac on your new laptop.

- ✔ **System Preferences settings:** If you're a fan of tweaking and customizing OS X to fit you like a glove, rejoice. Migration Assistant copies all the changes that you've made in System Preferences on your old Mac! (Insert sound of angelic chorus: *Hallelujah!*)

- ✔ **Documents:** The files in your Documents folder(s) are copied to your new Mac.

- ✔ **Applications:** Migration Assistant tries its best to copy over third-party applications you've installed in your Applications folder on the older Mac. I say "tries its best" because you might have to reinstall some applications, anyway. Some developers create applications that spread all sorts of files across your hard drive, and Migration Assistant just can't keep track of those nomadic files. Other applications make the trek just fine, but you might have to reenter their serial numbers.

By far, the easiest (and most popular) method of using Migration Assistant is over a wired or wireless Ethernet network (a wired connection is much faster), and that's the procedure I describe here. Follow these steps to use Migration Assistant to transfer data to your new MacBook:

1. **If Migration Assistant isn't already open, open Launchpad and click the Utilities folder, then click the Migration Assistant icon.**

2. **Click From a Mac, PC, Time Machine backup, or other disk.**

3. **Click Continue.**

Migration Assistant prompts you for the account name and password that you create during the setup procedure, as shown in Figure 2-2. Your account is an *admin account,* meaning that you have a higher security level that allows you to change things in Mountain Lion. (See Chapter 11 for much more detail on user accounts.)

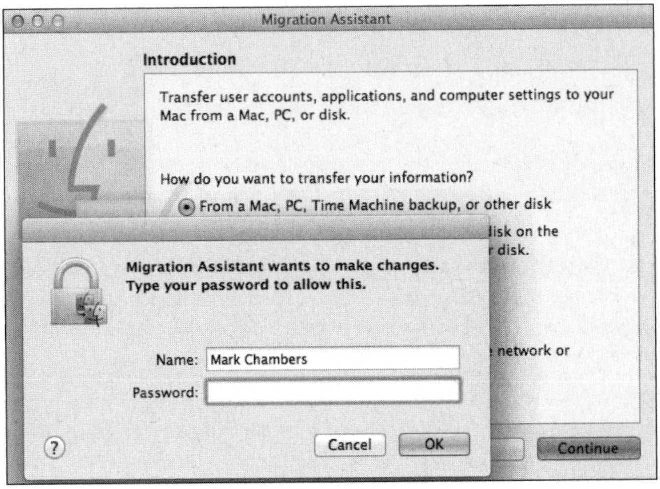

Figure 2-2:
Enter your
admin pass-
word to use
Migration
Assistant.

4. **Type your account name and password, and then click OK.**

   Characters in your password are displayed as bullet characters for security. After you successfully enter your admin account name and password, this dialog disappears, and you get to play in the real Migration Assistant dialog.

5. **Select the From a Mac or PC radio button and then click Continue.**

6. **Launch Migration Assistant on the other computer.**

   Your MacBook searches for available computers using your wired or wireless Ethernet network. MacBook Air owners, as well as owners of the current generation of MacBook Pro Retina laptops, will have to use either a wireless network connection or a Thunderbolt-to-Gigabit-Ethernet adapter (for a wired Ethernet network). If you're migrating data from a PC, you must download and install the Windows Migration Assistant (www.apple.com/migrate-to-mac).

7. **Select the computer with the data from the list, and then click Continue.**

8. **Select the check boxes next to the user accounts that you want to transfer from your older machine.**

   Migration Assistant displays how much space is required to hold the selected accounts on your new laptop's hard drive.

9. **Select the check boxes next to the applications and files that you want to copy.**

10. **Select the check boxes next to the settings that you want to transfer.**

    Normally, you want to migrate all settings groups.

11. **Click Continue.**

    Migration Assistant may take an hour (over a wired connection) or even several hours (over a wireless connection) to complete, depending on the amount of data to be moved.

Importing Stuff from Windows (If You Must)

If you're a Windows-to-Mac *Switcher,* you made a wise choice, especially if you're interested in the creative applications in the iLife suite! Although you could choose to start your Apple computing life anew, you probably want to migrate some of your existing documents and files from that tired PC to your bright, shiny, new MacBook.

As I mention in the preceding section, Windows Migration Assistant can transfer much of the Windows data you want to take with you. If you find that some files were left behind, you can move stuff manually as well! You can copy your files to a USB flash drive or over a network. To make this manual move more manageable, Table 2-1 covers a number of typical Windows file locations and their Mountain Lion counterparts.

Table 2-1   Moving Media and Documents betwixt Computers

File Type	Windows Location	OS X Location	Mac Application
Music files	My Music folder	Music folder	iTunes
Video and movie files	My Videos folder	Movies folder	QuickTime, DVD Player, iTunes
Digital photos	My Pictures folder	Pictures folder	iPhoto
Office documents	My Documents folder	Documents folder	Mac Office, OpenOffice, iWork

Switching from a PC to . . . an Apple PC?

With the Mountain Lion Boot Camp feature, you can actually create a full Windows 7 or 8 system on your Intel-based Mac laptop. Yup, Windows and Mountain Lion coexist peacefully *on the same computer.* However, you'll have to reboot your computer to use your MacBook as a Windows system.

This possibility brings a whole new meaning to the term *Switcher* because some Mac owners are moving their stuff from Windows (running on their old PC) to . . . well, Windows (running on

their new MacBook) rather than Mountain Lion. If you decide to create a Windows system on your MacBook with Boot Camp, the files and folders on your existing PC can be copied directly by using the Files and Settings Transfer Wizard (in Windows XP) or the Windows Easy Transfer utility (in Windows Vista, 7, and 8). In effect, you're copying your settings and data between your old PC and your new Apple-based PC! (That sounds a little skewed, but die-hard Apple apostles will have to forgive me.)

The OS X Help system contains an entire subsection on specific tricks you can use when switching from Windows to Mac, including how to connect to a Windows network and how to directly connect the two computers.

Manually moving existing Windows applications (such as PaintShop Photo Pro) to your laptop's drive usually doesn't work even with *Boot Camp* — Apple's dual-boot feature that allows you to run both Mountain Lion and Windows 7 or 8 on your MacBook. Most Windows software installs all sorts of necessary files in several folders across your drive, and manually moving applications won't put those files where they should go. Instead, you have to install Windows 7 or 8 on your Mac laptop (using Boot Camp) and then reinstall your Windows applications.

If you decide to run Windows on your laptop (using Boot Camp or an application that creates a virtual computer), visit www.dummies.com/go/MacBookFD4e or my website, www.mlcbooks.com, and download the PDF bonus chapter "Running Windows on Your Mac" — you'll be glad you did!

Chapter 3

The Laptop Owner's Introduction to OS X

In This Chapter

▶ Introducing OS X Mountain Lion

▶ Appreciating the UNIX core underlying Mountain Lion

▶ Recognizing similarities between Windows and Mountain Lion

▶ Getting help while learning about Mountain Lion

*I*n the other books that I've written about OS X Mountain Lion, I use all sorts of somewhat understated phrases to describe my operating system of choice, such as *elegantly reliable, purely powerful,* and *supremely user friendly.*

But *why* is Mountain Lion such a standout? To be specific, why do creative professionals and computer techno-wizards across the globe hunger for the very same OS X that runs your MacBook? Why is Mountain Lion so far ahead of Windows 7 and 8 in features and performance? Good questions, all!

In this chapter, I answer those queries and satisfy your curiosity about your new big cat. I introduce the main elements of the Mountain Lion desktop, and I show you the fearless UNIX heart that beats beneath Mountain Lion's sleek exterior. I also point out the most important similarities between Mountain Lion and Windows, and I outline the resources available if you need help with OS X.

Oh, and I promise to use honest-to-goodness English in my explanations, with a minimum of engineer-speak and indecipherable acronyms. (Hey, you have to boast about Mountain Lion in turn to your family and friends. Aunt Harriet might not be as technologically savvy as we are.)

Your Own Personal Operating System

Mountain Lion is a special type of software called an *operating system* (or *OS,* as in *OS X*). That means that Mountain Lion essentially runs your MacBook and also allows you to run all your other applications, such as iTunes or Photoshop. It's the most important computer application — or *software* — that you run.

Think of a pyramid, with Mountain Lion as the foundation and other applications running on top.

You're using the OS when you aren't running a specific application, such as these actions:

- ✔ Copying files from a USB flash drive to your drive
- ✔ Navigating through files and folders on your drive
- ✔ Choosing a different screen saver

Sometimes, Mountain Lion even peeks through an application while it's running. For example, application actions such as these are also controlled by Mountain Lion:

- ✔ The Open, Save, and Save As dialogs that you see when working with files in Photoshop
- ✔ The Print dialog that appears when you print a document in Microsoft Word

In the following sections, I escort you around the most important hotspots in Mountain Lion, and you meet the most interesting on-screen thingamabobs that you use to control your laptop. (I told you I wasn't going to talk like an engineer!)

The Mountain Lion Desktop

The Mountain Lion desktop isn't made of wood, and you can't stick your gum underneath. However, this particular desktop does indeed work much like the surface of a traditional desk. You can store things there, organize things into folders, and take care of important tasks such as writing and drawing (using tools called *applications*). Heck, you even have a clock and a trash can.

Gaze upon Figure 3-1 and follow along as you venture to your desktop and beyond.

Finder menu   Finder window

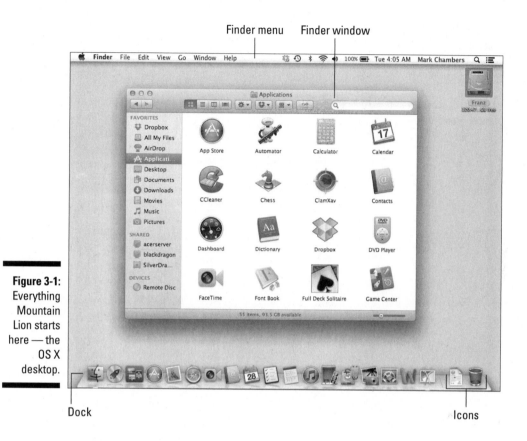

Figure 3-1:
Everything
Mountain
Lion starts
here — the
OS X
desktop.

Dock   Icons

Meet me at the Dock

The Dock is a versatile combination: one part organizer, one part application launcher, and one part system monitor. From the Dock, you can launch applications, see what's running, and display or hide the windows shown by your applications.

Each icon in the Dock represents one of the following (many of which are proudly displayed in Figure 3-2):

- ✔ An application that you can run (or is running)
- ✔ An application window that's *minimized* (shrunk)
- ✔ A web page URL link
- ✔ A document or folder on your system
- ✔ A network server, shared document, or shared folder
- ✔ Your Trash

I cover the Dock in more detail in Chapter 5.

Running application   Trash

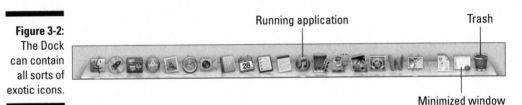

Figure 3-2:
The Dock
can contain
all sorts of
exotic icons.

Minimized window

The Dock is highly configurable:

✔ It can appear at different edges of the screen.

✔ It can disappear until you move your mouse pointer to the edge to call it forth.

✔ You can resize it.

Dig those crazy icons

By default, Mountain Lion always displays at least one icon on your desktop: your Mac's internal drive. To open a drive and view or use the contents, you double-click the icon. Other icons that might appear on your desktop include

✔ CDs and DVDs

✔ An iPod

✔ External hard drives, solid-state drives, or USB flash drives

✔ Applications, folders, and documents

✔ Files and folders

✔ Network servers you access

Chapter 4 provides the good stuff on icons and their uses in Mountain Lion.

There's no food on this menu

The menu bar isn't found in a restaurant. You find it at the top of the desktop, where you can use it to control your applications. Virtually every application that you run on your laptop has a menu bar.

To use a menu command, follow these steps:

1. Click the menu title (such as File or Edit).

2. Choose the desired command from the list that appears (see Figure 3-3).

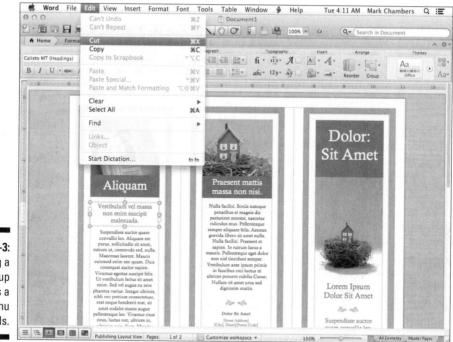

Figure 3-3:
Clicking a
menu group
displays a
list of menu
commands.

Virtually every Macintosh application has some menus, such as File, Edit, and
Window. You're likely to find similar commands within these menus. However,
only two menus are in *every* OS X application:

   ✔ The *Apple menu* (which is identified with that jaunty Apple Corporation
   icon,).

   ✔ The *Application menu* (which always bears the name of the active application). For instance, the DVD Player menu group appears when you run
   the Mountain Lion DVD Player, and the Word menu appears when you
   launch Microsoft Word.

I cover these two common menus in more detail in Chapters 4 and 5.

You can also display a shortcut menu — which regular human beings call a
right-click menu — by right-clicking your Mountain Lion desktop, an application, a folder, or a file icon. I get into the shortcut menu in detail in Chapter 4.
(Because your MacBook is equipped with a trackpad, you can right-click by
tapping the trackpad with two fingertips.)

It's Apple to the rescue!

UNIX is the established, super-reliable OS that powers most of the high-performance servers that make up the Internet. UNIX has built-in support for virtually every hardware device ever wrought by the Hand of Man (including all the cool stuff that came with your MacBook), is well designed, and is highly efficient.

Unfortunately, standard UNIX looks as hideous as DOS, complete with a confusing command line, so ease of use for normal human beings like you and me goes out the door. Enter the genius types at Apple, who understood several years ago that all UNIX needed was a state-of-the-art, novice-friendly interface! To wit:

OS X was developed with a UNIX foundation (or *core*), so it shares the same reliability and performance as UNIX. However, the software engineers at Apple (who know a thing or two about ease of use) made it good looking and easy to use.

If you're interested in all the details about what makes OS X tick, as well as its settings and features, I can heartily recommend another of my books, the bestselling (and extremely heavy) *OS X Mountain Lion All-in-One For Dummies* (Wiley). It comprehensively covers everything Mountain Lion — over 700 pages devoted entirely to OS X and its companion applications!

There's always room for one more window

You're probably already familiar with the ubiquitous window itself. Both Mountain Lion and the applications that you run use windows to display things such as

- ✔ The documents that you create
- ✔ The contents of your drive

For example, the window in Figure 3-1 is a Finder window, where Mountain Lion gives you access to the applications, documents, and folders on your system.

Windows are surprisingly configurable. I cover them at length in Chapter 4.

Why get so excited by Mountain Lion?

How the core of an operating system is designed makes more of a difference than all the visual bells and whistles, which tend to be similar between Windows 8, Windows 7, Vista, and OS X Mountain Lion (and Linux as well, for that matter). Time for a Mark's Maxim:

Sure, Mountain Lion's elegant exterior is a joy to use, but OS X is a *better* OS than Windows because of the unique UNIX muscle that lies underneath!™

So what should you and I look for in an OS? Keep in mind that today's computer techno-wizard demands three requirements for a truly high-powered software wonderland — and OS X Mountain Lion easily meets all three:

- ✔ **Reliability:** Your OS has to stay up and running reliably for as long as necessary — I'm talking *nonstop* here — without lockups or error messages. If an application crashes, the rest of your work should remain safe, and you should be able to shut down the offending software.

- ✔ **Performance:** If your computer has advanced hardware, your OS must be able to use those resources to speed things up big-time. The OS must be highly configurable, and it has to be updated often to keep up with the latest in computer hardware.

"Mark, what do you mean by advanced hardware?" Well, if you're knowledgeable about state-of-the-art hardware, you might recognize these examples:

- • True 64-bit computing

- • Multiple processors (such as the multicore Intel chip in your MacBook)

- • A huge amount of RAM (anywhere from 2–8GB in today's MacBooks)

- • Support for an external RAID array

If all that sounds like ancient Sumerian, gleefully ignore this technical drivel and keep reading.

- ✔ **Ease of use:** All the speed and reliability in the world can't help an OS if it's difficult to use.

Like Windows done right

You may have heard of the *Windows switcher:* a uniquely intelligent species that's becoming more and more common these days. Switchers are former PC owners who have abandoned Windows and bought a Macintosh, thereby joining the Apple faithful running OS X. (Apple loves to document this migration on its website.) Because today's Macintosh computers are significantly easier to use than their PC counterparts — and you get neat software, such as Mountain Lion and the iLife suite when you buy a new Mac — switching makes perfect sense.

Switchers aren't moving to totally unfamiliar waters. Windows 7 and 8 and Mountain Lion share a number of important concepts. Familiarizing yourself with Mountain Lion takes far less time than you might think.

Here's an overview of the basic similarities between the two operating systems:

✔ **The desktop:** The Mountain Lion desktop is a neat representation of a real physical desktop, and Windows uses the same idea:

  • You can arrange files, folders, and applications on your desktop to help keep things handy.

  • Application windows appear on the desktop.

✔ **Drives, files, and folders:** Data is stored in files on your drive(s), and those files can be organized in folders. Both Mountain Lion and Windows use the same file-and-folder concept.

✔ **Specific locations:** Both Windows and Mountain Lion provide every user with a set of folders to help keep various types of files organized. For example, the My Videos folder that you can use in Windows 7 corresponds to the Movies folder that you find in your Home folder in Mountain Lion.

✔ **Running programs:** Both Mountain Lion and Windows run programs (or applications) in the same manner:

  • Double-clicking an application icon launches that application.

  • Double-clicking a document runs the corresponding application and then automatically loads the document.

✔ **Window control:** Yep, both operating systems use windows, and those windows can be resized, hidden (or minimized), and closed in similar fashions. (Are you starting to see the connections here?)

✔ **Drag-and-drop:** One of the basics behind a GUI (a ridiculous acronym that stands for *graphical user interface*) such as Windows and Mountain Lion is the capability to drag documents and folders around to move, delete, copy, and load them. Drag-and-drop is one of the primary advantages of both of these operating systems because copying a file by dragging it from one window to another is intuitive and easy enough for a kid to accomplish.

✔ **Editing:** Along the same lines as drag-and-drop, both Mountain Lion and Windows offer similar cut-and-paste editing features. You've likely used cut, copy, and paste for years, so this is familiar stuff.

And Just in Case You Need Help . . .

You can call on the resources described in this section if you need additional help while you're discovering how to tame the Mountain Lion.

Some of the help resources are located on the Internet, so your Safari web browser will come in handy when searching for answers.

The Mountain Lion built-in Help system

Sometimes the help you need is as close as the Help menu on the Finder menu bar. You can get help for either of the following:

- **A specific application:** From the application, just click Help. Then, click in the Search box and type a short phrase that sums up your query (such as *startup keys*). You see a list of help topics on the menu. Just click a topic to display more information.

- **General topics:** Click a Finder window and then click Help on the menu bar. Again, you see the Search box, and you can enter a word or phrase to find in the Help system. To display the Help Center window, click the Help Center item under the Search box.

The Apple web-based support center

Apple has online product support areas for every hardware and software product that it manufactures. Visit www.apple.com and click the Support tab at the top of the web page.

The Search box works just like the OS X Help system, but the knowledge base that Apple provides online has a *lot* more answers.

Magazines

Many magazines and publications (both in print and online) offer tips and tricks on using and maintaining OS X Mountain Lion.

My personal online favorites are Macworld (www.macworld.com) and the Wiley *For Dummies* website (www.dummies.com).

Mac support websites

A number of private individuals and groups offer support forums on the web, and you can often find help from other Mac owners on these sites within a few hours of posting a question.

I'm very fond of CNET's MacFixIt (www.macfixit.com) and Mac OS X Hints (http://forums.macosxhints.com).

Local Mac user groups

I'd be remiss if I didn't mention your local Mac user group. Often, a user group maintains its own website and discussion forum. If you can wait until the next meeting, you can even ask your question and receive a reply from a real-live human being . . . quite a thrill in today's web-riffic world!

Part II
Shaking Hands with OS X

In this part . . .

*I*t's time to delve deeper into the workings of OS X Mountain Lion. Here, I show you how to perform all sorts of common tasks as well as how to customize your system, how to change settings in System Preferences, where your personal files are stored, and how to use Apple's Spotlight search technology to find virtually *anything* you've stored on your MacBook Pro, MacBook Pro Retina, or MacBook Air!

Chapter 4

Opening and Closing and Tapping and Such

. . . .

. . . .

A h, the Finder — many admire its scenic beauty, but don't ignore its unsurpassed power nor its many moods. And send a postcard while you're there.

Okay, so Mountain Lion's Finder might not be *quite* as majestic as the mighty Mississippi River, but it's the basic toolbox that you use every single day while piloting your MacBook. The Finder includes the most common elements of OS X: window controls, common menu commands, icon fun (everything from launching applications to copying files), network connections, keyboard shortcuts, and even emptying the Trash. In fact, one could say that if you master the Finder and find how to use it efficiently, you're on your way to becoming a power user! (My editor calls this the Finder "window of opportunity." She's a hoot.)

That's what this chapter is designed to do: This is your Finder tour guide, and we're ready to roll.

Using the All-Powerful Finder

This is a hands-on tour, with none of that, "On your right, you'll see the historic Go menu" for *my* readers! Time to get off the bus and start the tour with Figure 4-1, where I show you around the most important elements of the Finder. (In the upcoming section, "Performing Tricks with Finder Windows," I give you a close-up view of window controls.)

The popular attractions include

✔ **The Apple menu (🍎):** This is a special menu because it appears both in the Finder menu bar and the menu bar in every application that you run. It doesn't matter whether you're in iTunes or Photoshop or Word. If you can see a menu bar, the Apple menu is there. The Apple menu contains common commands to use no matter where you are in Mountain Lion, such as Restart, Shut Down, and System Preferences.

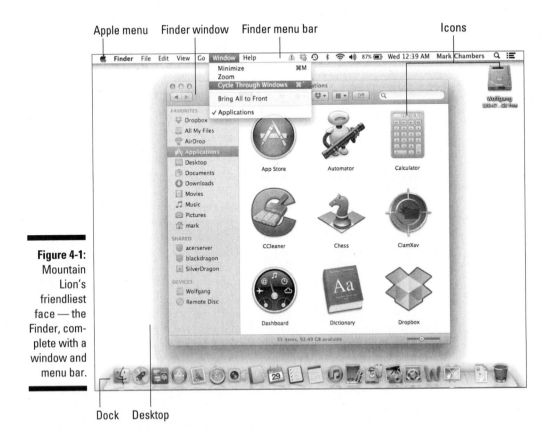

Apple menu   Finder window   Finder menu bar   Icons

Figure 4-1:
Mountain
Lion's
friendliest
face — the
Finder, com-
plete with a
window and
menu bar.

Dock   Desktop

✔ **The Finder menu bar:** Whenever the Finder itself is ready to use (or, in Mac-speak, whenever the Finder is the *active* application, rather than another application), the Finder menu bar appears at the top of your screen. You know the Finder is active and ready when the word *Finder* appears at the left of the menu bar.

For those brand new to computers, a *menu* is simply a list of commands. For example, you click the File menu and then choose Save to save a document. When you click a menu, it extends down so that you can see the commands it includes. While the menu is extended, you can choose any enabled menu item (just click it) to perform that action. You can tell that an item is enabled if its name appears in black. Conversely, a menu command is disabled if it appears grayed out — clicking it does nothing.

When you see a menu path such as File⇨Save, it's just a visual shortcut that tells you to click the File menu and then choose Save from the drop-down menu that appears.

✔ **The desktop:** Your desktop serves the same purpose as your physical desktop: You can store stuff here (files, alias icons, and so on), and it's a solid, stable surface where you can work comfortably. Application windows appear on the desktop, such as your Stickies notes and your DVD player. Just double-click an application there to launch it.

You can easily customize your desktop in many ways. For example, you can use your own images to decorate the desktop, organize it to store new folders and documents, arrange icons how you like, or put the Dock in another location. Don't worry — I cover all these tasks in other areas of the book — I just want you to know that you don't have to settle for what Apple gives you as a default desktop.

✔ **All sorts of icons:** This is a Macintosh computer, after all, replete with tons of make-your-life-easier tools. Check out the plethora of icons on your desktop as well as icons in the Finder window itself. Each icon is a shortcut of sorts to a file, folder, network connection, or device in your system, including applications that you run and documents that you create. Refer to Figure 4-1 to see my MacBook's hard drive icon, labeled Wolfgang. (I'm a huge Mozart fan.) Sometimes you click an icon to watch it do its thing (such as icons in the Dock, which I cover next), but usually you double-click an icon to make something happen.

✔ **The Dock:** The Dock is a launching pad for your favorite applications, documents, folders, network connections, and websites. You can also refer to it to see what applications are running. Click an icon there to open the item. For example, the postage stamp icon represents the Apple Mail application, and clicking the spiffy compass icon launches your Safari web browser.

✔ **The Finder window:** Finally! The basic Finder window in Figure 4-1 displays the contents of my Applications folder. You use Finder windows to launch applications; to perform disk chores, such as copying and moving files; and to navigate your hard drive.

My, what an attractive sidebar . . . and so useful!

Have you noticed the sidebar that typically occupies the left side of a Finder window? It's a pane of links to common locations and devices that you can use to jump like a flash to a specific spot on your hard drive. For example, you can click the Applications link under the Favorites heading, and you're transported to your Applications folder in an instant.

Here's a great example of sidebar magic: I like as few icons on my desktop as possible, so each book I'm working on gets its own folder. All the items for that project that might otherwise end up on my desktop are saved to that folder instead. In fact, I make a point of adding my current book project folder to my Finder window sidebar so that it's available immediately from any Finder window. To do this, just drag the folder into the column at the left side of the Finder window and drop it under the Places heading in the sidebar's list.

You can configure the items that will appear in your sidebar: Click Finder⇨Preferences, and then click the Sidebar tab to display the list. From here, you can select and deselect check boxes to configure your sidebar "just so."

Wait a Second: Where the Heck Are the Mouse Buttons?

Mountain Lion takes a visual approach to everything, and what you see in Figure 4-1 is designed for point-and-click convenience because the *trackpad* is your primary navigational tool while you're using your Mac laptop. You move your finger over the surface of the trackpad, and the cursor follows like an obedient pup. The faster you move your finger, the farther the cursor goes. You click an item, it opens, you do your thing, and life is good.

Never use any object other than your finger on the trackpad! That means no pencils (no, not even the eraser end), pens, or chopsticks; they can damage your trackpad in no time.

If you've grazed on the other side of the fence — one of Those Who Were Once Windows Users — you're probably accustomed to using a mouse with at least two buttons. This brings up the nagging question: "Hey, Mark! Where the heck are the buttons?"

In a nutshell, the buttons simply ain't there if you're using your Mac laptop's trackpad. The entire surface of the trackpad can act as both buttons. To customize how the trackpad operates, click the System Preferences icon in the Dock and then click the Trackpad icon. From the Point & Click pane, for example, you can

- ✔ **Select the Tap to Click check box:** Now, when you tap once anywhere on the trackpad quickly, your Mac laptop counts that as a click. Tap twice quickly, and your MacBook recognizes that as a double-click.

- ✔ **Select the Secondary Click check box:** Suddenly a single tap with two fingers displays the right-click menu (which I cover in more detail in a paragraph or two).

- ✔ **Enable the Look Up check box:** Tap your trackpad with three fingers to look up a selected word in the Dictionary.

- ✔ **Enable the Three Finger Drag check box:** (Sounds like a dance from the '60s, doesn't it?) By using three fingers, you can drag windows around on your desktop to reposition them.

- ✔ **Adjust your tracking speed:** Click and drag the Tracking speed slider to speed up or slow down the rate at which your cursor moves.

Apple has done a great job of illustrating each gesture available from the Trackpad pane in System Preferences — a short video clip shows you both the gesture itself and the effect that gesture will have within OS X.

I'll be honest here: When my laptop is on my desk at home, I plug in a Logitech optical trackball. This neat device has two buttons and a scroll wheel, saving me wear and tear on my trackpad and offering even finer control in my applications. In fact, a new industry is springing up for tiny USB mousing devices especially made for laptops. Some devices are smaller than a business card, but they still carry a full complement of two buttons and a scroll wheel.

In this book I'm going to refer to the *cursor* whether you're using your trackpad or a mouse. So here's a Mark's Maxim that I think you'll appreciate more and more as you use your laptop.

If you can afford a USB or wireless Bluetooth mouse or trackball for your laptop, *buy it*. You can thank me later with an e-mail message, which you can send to mark@mlcbooks.com.™

If you tap the trackpad with two fingertips (or click the right mouse button on a USB mouse), Mountain Lion performs the same default function that a right-click does in Windows. Namely, with a right-click on most items — icons, documents, even your desktop — you get a *shortcut menu* of commands specific to that item.

Doing the Multi-Touch thing

Today's crop of MacBooks has the smartest trackpads on the planet! That's because Apple's mice and trackpads include a feature called *Multi-Touch,* which allows you to control the view of a document by using specific finger motions on the surface of the trackpad or mouse. At the time of this writing, here's the rundown:

✔ **Two-finger zooming:** Pinching your thumb and first fingertip toward each other on the trackpad zooms in on a document or image. The reverse (moving your fingertips away from each other) zooms out.

✔ **Two-finger Smart Zoom:** Tap twice with two fingers to zoom in, and double-tap again with two fingers to zoom back out.

✔ **Two-finger rotating:** Rotate your thumb and first fingertip in a circle on the trackpad to rotate an image or a document in the corresponding direction.

✔ **Two-finger paging:** Swipe your thumb and first fingertip to the left or right across your trackpad to page through a document or move to the next or previous image in a set.

✔ **Three-finger full-screen switching:** Swipe your thumb and first two fingertips to the left or right across your trackpad to move between open applications in full-screen mode.

✔ **Two-finger Notification Center display:** Swipe to the left with two fingers from the right edge of the trackpad, and Mountain Lion displays your Notification Center. To hide the panel, reverse the gesture and swipe from the left edge to the right using two fingers.

✔ **Perform actions in Mission Control, Launchpad, and your desktop:** Using the combination of thumb and fingers you specify, you can configure the display and operation of these features within Mountain Lion.

Unfortunately, not all Multi-Touch gestures work with older MacBook trackpads, and Multi-Touch isn't recognized by every application, but software developers are adding more gesture support all the time.

Figure 4-2 illustrates a typical convenient right-click menu in a Finder window. I have all sorts of cool items at my disposal on this menu because of the applications I've installed that make use of a right-click menu.

If you move two fingers over the surface of the trackpad at once, the Finder window or application *scrolls* the contents of the window in the direction you move. (For example, you can use the scroll function to move up and down through the pages of a document or to move up and down through a long web page.) Who needs scroll bars?

Visit the Mouse pane in System Preferences to configure your mouse as well. (More on the System Preferences window in the next section.)

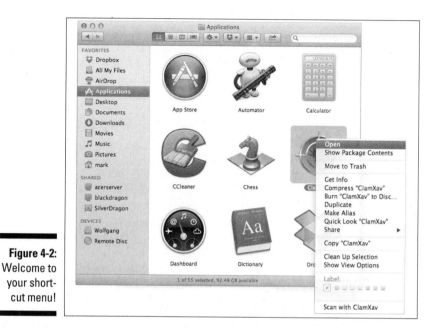

Figure 4-2:
Welcome to
your short-
cut menu!

Launching and Quitting Applications with Aplomb

Now it's time to pair your newly found trackpad acumen with Mountain
Lion's Finder window. Follow along this simple exercise. Move your cursor
over the iTunes icon in the Dock. (This icon looks like an audio CD with a
musical note on it.) Then tap the trackpad once with your fingertip (see the
preceding section for how to set this preference). Whoosh! Mountain Lion
launches (or starts) the iTunes application, and you see a window much like
the one shown in Figure 4-3.

If an application icon is already selected (which I discuss in the next section),
you can simply press ⌘+O to launch it. The same key shortcut works with
documents, too.

Figure 4-3:
Click a Dock
icon to
launch that
application.

Besides the Dock, you have several other ways to launch an application or
open a document in Mountain Lion:

- **From the Apple menu (◉):** A number of different applications can
  always be launched anywhere in Mountain Lion from the Apple menu:

  - *System Preferences:* Change all sorts of settings, such as your
    display background and how icons appear.

  - *Software Update:* Use the Internet to see whether update patches
    are available for your Apple software, as I discuss in Chapter 23.

  - *App Store:* Launch the OS X App Store and display software that you
    can download for your laptop (most are commercial applications
    that you have to pay for, but many great free applications are
    available as well).

- **From Launchpad:** Display all your application icons in a full-screen display. (The Launchpad icon in the Dock is the second one from the left,
  bearing the rocket icon.) If you have more than one screen (or *page*)
  worth of applications, press the arrow keys to move between Launchpad
  pages — using your trackpad, swipe two fingers to the left or right. To
  launch an application, just click the icon. (If you're a proud owner of an
  iPhone, iPad, or iPod touch, the Launchpad will be familiar because it
  corresponds directly to the Home screen on those devices.)

Dig that crazy Launchpad!

You can customize your Launchpad display by dragging icons to display them in the order you prefer. (For example, I have all the applications I use the most on the first Launchpad page.) Drag an application icon to the right or left side of the screen to move it to another page.

Launchpad, like a Finder window, allows you to create folders to help organize your applications. To create a folder in Launchpad, drag one application icon on top of another and then add other icons by dragging them to the folder (or remove them by dragging them out of the folder). To run an application within a folder, click the folder icon to display the icons within it and then click the desired application.

Oh, and there's no need to stick with the boring folder names assigned by Launchpad! To change a folder name, click the folder to open it, click the folder name to display a text-editing box, type the new moniker for the folder, and press Return.

If you want to remove an application from Launchpad — **which also deletes the application from your MacBook entirely** — click the icon and continue pressing on the trackpad until the icons start to wiggle. (Yes, you read that correctly; I wrote _wiggle_. iPhone and iPad owners know what I mean.) Click the tiny delete (x) button that appears next to the icon whose application you want to delete, and the icon — and its application — disappear. Press Esc to stop all that wiggling. (Note that applications supplied with Mountain Lion can't be deleted this way.)

✔ **From the desktop:** If you have a document that you created or an application icon on your desktop, you can launch or open it from the desktop by _double-clicking_ that icon (tapping the trackpad twice with one finger in rapid succession when the cursor is on top of the icon).

Double-clicking a device or network connection on your desktop opens the contents in a Finder window. This method works for CDs and DVDs that you've loaded as well as external drives and USB flash drives. Just double-click 'em to open them and display their contents in a Finder window. Applications and documents typically launch from a CD, a DVD, or an external drive just like they launch from your internal drive (the one that's typically named _Macintosh HD_), so you don't have to copy stuff from the external drive just to use it. Note, however, that running an application directly from your optical or external drive usually results in that application running significantly slower. (Oh, and don't forget that you can't change the contents of most CDs and DVDs; they're read-only, so you can't write to them.)

✔ **From the Recent Items selection:** When you click the Apple menu and hover your cursor over the Recent Items menu item, the Finder displays all the applications and documents that you used over the past few computing sessions. Click an item in this list to launch or open it.

- ✔ **From the login items list:** Login items are applications that Mountain Lion launches automatically each time you log in to your user account. I cover login items in detail in Chapter 11.

- ✔ **From the Finder window:** You can also double-click an icon within the confines of a Finder window to open it (for documents), launch it (for applications), or display the contents (for a folder).

Mountain Lion's Quick Look feature can display the contents of just about any document or file — but without actually opening the corresponding application! *Sweet.* To use Quick Look from a Finder window, click a file to select it and then press the spacebar.

After you finish using an application, you can quit that application to close its window and return to the desktop. Here are a number of different ways to quit an application:

- ✔ **Press ⌘+Q.** This keyboard shortcut quits virtually every Macintosh application on the planet. Just make sure that the application that you want to quit is currently active first!

- ✔ **Choose the Quit command from the application's menu.** To display the Quit command, click the application's name — its menu — from the menu bar. This menu is always to the immediate right of the Apple (⌘) menu. For example, Safari displays a Safari menu, and that same spot in the menu is taken up by Calendar when Calendar is the active application. Refer to Figure 4-3, and look for the iTunes menu, right next to ⌘.

- ✔ **Choose Quit from the Dock.** You can right-click an application's icon in the Dock and then choose Quit from the right-click menu that appears.

  A running application displays a small blue dot under its icon in the Dock.

- ✔ **Click the Close button in the application window (refer to Figure 4-3).** Some applications quit entirely when you close their window, such as the System Preferences window or the Apple DVD Player. Other applications might continue running without any window, such as Safari or iTunes; to close these applications, you have to use another method in this list.

- ✔ **Choose Force Quit from the Apple menu.** *This is a last-resort measure!* Use this method only if an application has frozen and you can't use another method in this list to quit. Force-quitting an application doesn't save any changes to any open documents in that application!

Juggling Folders and Icons

Finder windows aren't just for launching applications and opening the files and documents that you create. You can also use the icons in a Finder window to select one or more specific items or to copy and move items from place to place within your system.

A field observer's guide to icons

Not all icons are created equal. Earlier in this chapter, I introduce you to your MacBook's drive icon on the desktop. Here's a little background on the other types of icons that you might encounter during your mobile Mac travels:

- ✔ **Hardware:** These icons are your storage devices (such as your DVD drive, if you have one) as well as external peripherals (such as your iPod and printer).

- ✔ **Applications:** These icons represent the applications (or programs) that you can launch. Most applications have a custom icon that incorporates the company's logo or the specific application logo, so they're easy to recognize, as you can see in Figure 4-4. Double-clicking an application usually doesn't load a document automatically; you typically get a new blank document or an Open dialog box from which you can choose the existing file you want to open.

Figure 4-4: A collection of some of my favorite application icons.

✔ **Documents:** Many of the files on your hard drive are documents that can be opened in the corresponding application, and the icon usually looks similar to the application's icon. Double-clicking a document automatically launches the associated application (that is, as long as OS X recognizes the file type).

✔ **Files:** Most of the file icons on your system are mundane things (such as preference and settings files, text files, log files, and miscellaneous data files), yet most are identified with at least some type of recognizable icon that lets you guess what purpose the file serves. You'll also come across generic file icons that look like a blank sheet of paper (used when Mountain Lion has no earthly idea about the file type).

✔ **Aliases:** An *alias* acts as a link to another item elsewhere on your system. For example, to launch Adobe Acrobat, you can click an Adobe Acrobat alias icon that you can create on your desktop instead of clicking the actual Acrobat application icon. The alias essentially acts the same way as the original icon, but it doesn't take up the same space — only a few bytes for the icon itself, compared with the size of the actual application. Plus, you don't have to go digging through folders galore to find the original application icon. (Windows switchers know an alias as a *shortcut,* and the idea is the same although Macs had it first. Harrumph.) You can always identify an alias by the small curved arrow at the base of the icon, and the icon might also sport the tag `alias` at the end of its name.

You have two ways to create an alias. Here's one:

  a. *Select the item.*

     The following section has details about selecting icons.

  b. *Choose File⇨Make Alias, or press ⌘+L.*

     Figure 4-5 illustrates aliases for two OS X applications, arranged next to their linked files.

Here's another way to create an alias:

  a. *Hold down ⌘+Option.*

  b. *Drag the original icon to the location where you want the alias.*

     Note that this funky method doesn't add the `alias` tag to the end of the alias icon name, unless you drag the icon to another spot in the same folder!

So why bother to use an alias? Two good reasons:

  ✔ **Launch an application or open a document from anywhere on your drive.** For example, if you occasionally need to use another application while working on a Pages project, you can add an alias and launch the other application directly from the folder where you store those Pages documents. Speed, organization, and convenience . . . life is good.

✔ **Send an alias to the Trash without affecting the original item.** When that school project is finished, you can safely delete the entire folder without worrying about whether Pages will run the next time you double-click the application icon!

Figure 4-5:
No, not the popular girl-spy TV show. These are alias icons in Mountain Lion.

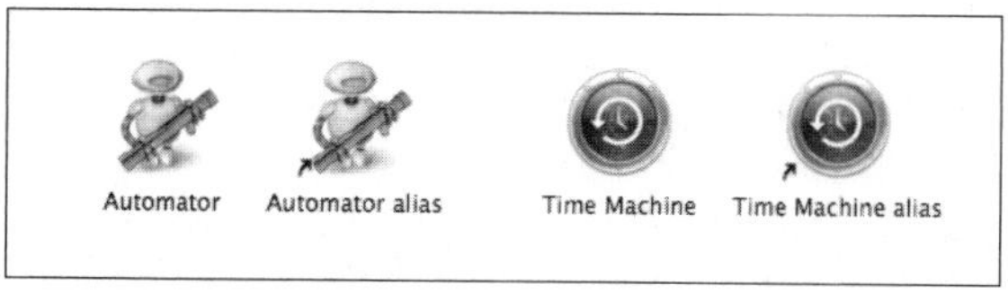

Automator   Automator alias   Time Machine   Time Machine alias

TECHNICAL STUFF

If you move or rename the original file, Mountain Lion is actually smart enough to update the alias, too! However, if the original file is deleted (or if the original is moved to a different volume, such as an external hard drive), the alias no longer works. (Go figure.)

Selecting items

Often, the menu commands or keyboard commands that you perform in the Finder need to be performed on something. Perhaps you're moving an item to the Trash, getting more information on the item, or creating an alias for that item. To identify the target of your action to the Finder, you need to select one or more items on your desktop or in a Finder window. In the following sections, I show you just how to do that.

Selecting one thing

Mountain Lion gives you a couple of options when selecting just one item for an upcoming action:

✔ **Move your cursor over the item and click.** A dark border (or *highlight*) appears around the icon, indicating that it's selected.

✔ **If an icon is already highlighted on your desktop or in a window, move the selection highlight to another icon in the same location by using the arrow keys.** To shift the selection highlight alphabetically, press Tab (to move in order) or press Shift+Tab (to move in reverse order).

Selecting items in the Finder doesn't actually *do* anything to them by itself. You have to perform an action on the selected items to make something happen.

Selecting a whole bunch of things

You can also select multiple items with aplomb by using one of these methods:

✔ **Adjacent items:**

- *Drag a box around them.* If that sounds like ancient Sumerian, here's the explanation: Click a spot above and to the left of the first item; then hold your finger down on the trackpad surface and drag down and to the right. (This is *dragging* in Mac-speak.) A box outline like the one in Figure 4-6 appears, indicating what you're selecting. Any icons that touch or appear within the box outline are selected when you release the button.

- *Click the first item to select it, and then hold down the Shift key while you click the last item.* Mountain Lion selects both items and everything between them.

✔ **Nonadjacent items:** Select these by holding down the ⌘ key while you click each item.

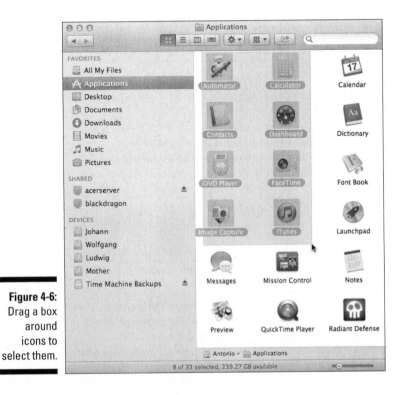

Figure 4-6:
Drag a box around icons to select them.

Check out the status bar (which can appear at the top or the bottom of a Finder window, depending on whether the toolbar is hidden). It tells you how much space is available on the drive you're working in as well as how many items are displayed in the current Finder window. When you select items, it shows you how many you highlighted. (If you don't see a status bar, choose View➪Show Status Bar.)

Copying items

Want to copy items from one Finder window to another, or from one location (like a flash drive) to another (like your desktop)? Très easy. Just use one of these methods:

- ✔ **On the same drive**

    - *To copy one item to another location:* Hold down the Option key (you don't have to select the icon first), and then click and drag the item from its current home to the new location.

        To put a copy of an item in a folder, just drop the item on top of the receiving folder. If you hold the item that you're dragging over the destination folder for a second or two, Mountain Lion opens a new window so that you can see the contents of the target. (This is called a *spring-loaded* folder. Really.) You can turn off this spring-loaded behavior by clicking Finder➪Preferences and clicking the Spring-loaded Folders and Windows check box to disable it.

    - *To copy multiple items to another location:* Select them all first (see the preceding section), hold down the Option key, and then drag-and-drop one of the selected items where you want it. All the items that you selected follow the item you drag. (Rather like lemmings. Nice touch, don't you think?)

    To help indicate your target when you're copying files, Mountain Lion highlights the location to show you where the items will end up. (This works whether the target location is a folder or a drive icon.) If the target location is a window, Mountain Lion adds a highlight to the window border.

- ✔ **On a different drive**

    - *To copy one or multiple items:* Click and drag the icon (or the selected items if you have more than one) from the original window to a window you open on the target drive. (No need to hold down the Option key while copying to a different drive.) You can also drag one item (or a selected group of items) and simply drop the items on top of the drive icon on your desktop.

    The items are copied to the top level, or *root,* of the target drive.

If you try to move or copy something to a location that already has an item with the same name, you will see a dialog that prompts you to decide whether to replace the file or to stop the copy/move procedure and leave the existing file alone. (Heck, you can even keep *both* — OS X performs the copy or move, but also appends the word *copy* to the item being copied.) Good insurance, indeed.

Moving things from place to place

Moving things from one location to another location on the same drive is the easiest action you can take. Just drag the item (or selected items) to the new location. The item disappears from the original spot and reappears in the new spot.

Duplicating in a jiffy

If you need more than one copy of the same item in a folder, use the Mountain Lion Duplicate command. I use Duplicate often when I want to edit a document but want to ensure that the original document stays pristine, no matter what. I just create a duplicate and edit that file instead.

To use Duplicate, you can

- ✔ Click an item to select it and then choose File⇨Duplicate.
- ✔ Right-click the item and choose Duplicate from the menu.
- ✔ Hold down the Option key and drag the original item to another spot in the same window. When you release the trackpad button, the duplicate file appears like magic!

The duplicate item has the word copy appended to its name. A second copy is named copy2, a third is copy3, and so on.

Duplicating a folder also duplicates all the contents of that folder, so creating a duplicate folder can take some time to create if the original folder was stuffed full (or contained files several hundred megabytes or larger in size). The duplicate folder has copy appended to its name, but the contents of the duplicate folder keep their original names.

Keys and Keyboard Shortcuts to Fame and Fortune

Your MacBook's keyboard might not be as glamorous as your trackpad, but any Macintosh power user will tell you that using keyboard shortcuts is usually the fastest method of performing certain tasks in the Finder, such as saving or closing a file. I recommend committing these shortcuts to memory and putting them to work as soon as you begin using your laptop so that they become second nature to you as quickly as possible.

Special keys on the keyboard

The Apple standard keyboard has a number of special keys that you might not recognize — especially if you've made the smart move and decided to migrate from the chaos that is Windows to OS X! Table 4-1 lists the keys that bear strange hieroglyphics on the Apple keyboard as well as what they do.

Table 4-1	Too-Cool Function Keys	
Action	*Symbol*	*Purpose*
Media Eject	⏏	Ejects a CD or DVD from your optical drive (if you have one)
Audio Mute	◀	Mutes (and restores) all sound produced by your MacBook
Keyboard Illumination	☀	Increases, decreases, or turns off the brightness of your keyboard backlighting
Volume Up	◀)))	Increases the sound volume
Volume Down	◀)	Decreases the sound volume
Command	⌘	Primary modifier for menus and keyboard shortcuts

Using Finder and application keyboard shortcuts

The Finder is chock-full of keyboard shortcuts that you can use to take care of common tasks. Some of the handiest shortcuts are shown in Table 4-2.

Table 4-2	Mountain Lion Keyboard Shortcuts of Distinction	
Key Combination	*Location*	*Action*
⌘+A	Edit menu	Selects all (works in the Finder, too)
⌘+C	Edit menu	Copies the highlighted item to the Clipboard
⌘+H	Application menu	Hides the application
⌘+M	Window menu	Minimizes the active window to the Dock (also works in the Finder)
⌘+O	File menu	Opens an existing document, file, or folder (also works in the Finder)
⌘+P	File menu	Prints the current document
⌘+Q	Application menu	Exits the application
⌘+V	Edit menu	Pastes the contents of the Clipboard at the current cursor position
⌘+X	Edit menu	Cuts the highlighted item to the Clipboard
⌘+Z	Edit menu	Reverses the effect of the last action you took
⌘+?	Help menu	Displays the Help system (works in the Finder, too)
⌘+Tab	Finder	Switches between open applications
⌘+Option+M	Finder	Minimizes all Finder windows to the Dock
⌘+Option+W	Finder	Closes all Finder windows

But wait, there's more! Most of your applications also provide their own set of keyboard shortcuts. While you're working with a new application, display the application's Help file and print a copy of the keyboard shortcuts as a handy cheat sheet.

If you've used a PC before, you're certainly familiar with three-key shortcuts — the most infamous being Ctrl+Alt+Delete, the beloved shut-down shortcut nicknamed the *Windows Three-Finger Salute*. Three-key shortcuts work the same way in Mountain Lion (but you'll be thrilled to know you won't need to reboot by using that notorious Windows shortcut!). If you're new to computing, just hold down the first two keys simultaneously and then press the third key.

You're not limited to just the keyboard shortcuts I've listed, either. In System Preferences, visit the Keyboard pane and then click the Keyboard Shortcuts tab to change an existing shortcut or add another!

Performing Tricks with Finder Windows

In the following sections of your introduction to OS X, I describe basic windows management in Mountain Lion: how to move things around, how to close windows, and how to make windows disappear and reappear like magic.

Scrolling in and resizing windows

Can you imagine what life would be like if you couldn't see more than a single window's worth of stuff? Shopping would be curtailed quite a bit — and so would the contents of the folders on your MacBook's drives!

That's why Mountain Lion adds *scroll bars* that you can click and drag to move through the contents of the window. (By default, scroll bars don't appear in Mountain Lion until you move your cursor close to them.) You can

- ✔ Click the scroll box and drag it — for the uninitiated, that means clicking the darker portion of the bar and holding down your finger on the track-pad while you move your finger in the desired direction.

- ✔ Click anywhere in the empty area above or below the scroll box to scroll pages one at a time.

- ✔ Hold down the Option key and click anywhere in the empty area above or below the bar to scroll to that spot in the document.

Of course, you can also drag two fingertips across the trackpad to scroll the contents of a window (both vertically and horizontally). To control trackpad behavior, open System Preferences and click the Trackpad pane. You can read all about configuring trackpad settings in the earlier section, "Wait a Second: Where the Heck Are the Mouse Buttons?"

Figure 4-7 illustrates both vertical and horizontal scroll bars in a typical Finder window.

Close button

Minimize button

Zoom button

Vertical scroll bar

Horizontal scroll bar

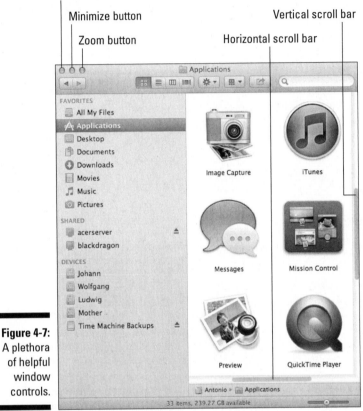

Figure 4-7:
A plethora
of helpful
window
controls.

Often, pressing your Page Up and Page Down keys moves you through a document one page at a time. Also, pressing your arrow keys moves your insertion cursor one line or one character in the four compass directions.

You can also resize most Finder and application windows by enlarging or reducing the window frame itself. Move your cursor over any corner or edge of a window, and then drag the edge in any direction until the window is the precise size you need.

Only one window can be active at once™

Yes, here's a very special Mark's Maxim in the OS X universe:

Only one application window can be active in Mountain Lion at any time.™

You can always tell which window is active:

✔ The active window is on top of other windows.

Tip: You can still use a window's Close, Minimize, and Zoom buttons when the window is inactive.

✔ Any input you make by typing or by moving your finger on the trackpad appears in the active window.

✔ OS X *dims* the title bars of inactive windows that you haven't minimized.

Minimizing and restoring windows

Resizing a window is indeed helpful, but maybe you simply want to banish the doggone thing until you need it again. That's a situation for the Minimize button, which also appears in Figure 4-7. A *minimized* window disappears from the desktop but isn't closed. It simply reappears in the Dock as a miniature icon. Minimizing a window is easy: Move your cursor over the Minimize button at the upper-left corner of the window — a minus sign appears in the button to tell you that you're on target — and then click. Here's a good shortcut: Double-clicking the window's *title bar* (that's the top frame of the window, which usually includes a document or application name) minimizes the window.

Hold down the Shift key while you minimize, and prepare to be amazed when the window shrinks in slow motion like Alice in Wonderland!

To restore the window to its full size again (and its original position on the desktop), just click its window icon in the Dock.

Moving and zooming windows

Perhaps you want to move a window to another location on the desktop so that you can see the contents of multiple windows at the same time. Click the window's title bar and drag the window anywhere you like. Then release the button. (Don't click the icon in the center of the title bar, though. You'll move just the icon itself, not the window.)

Many applications can automatically arrange multiple windows for you. Choose Window⇨Arrange All (if this option appears).

Toggling toolbars the Mountain Lion way

It's time to define a window control that's actually *inside* the window for a change. A *toolbar* is a strip of icons that generally appears under the window's title bar (although toolbars can appear in other locations as well). These icons typically perform the most common actions in an application; the effect is the same as if you use a menu command or press a keyboard shortcut. Toolbars are popular these days. You see 'em in everything from the Finder window to most application windows.

You can usually banish a window's toolbar to make extra room for icons, documents, or whatever the window happens to be holding. Just click View⇨Hide Toolbar. To restore the toolbar to its original position, click View⇨Show Toolbar. *Note:* If you toggle the Finder window toolbar off, you also lose the Finder window sidebar.

To see all that a window can show you, use the Zoom feature to expand any Finder or application window to its maximum practical size. (Zooming a Finder window is different from zooming with the Multi-Touch feature because you're expanding only the Finder window — and not an image or a document.) Note that a zoomed window can fill the entire screen, or (if that extra space isn't applicable for the application) the window might expand only to a larger part of the desktop. To zoom a window, move your cursor over the Zoom button (labeled in Figure 4-7) at the upper-left corner of the window. When the plus sign appears in the Zoom button, click to claim the additional territory on your desktop. (You can click the Zoom button again to automatically return the same window to its previous dimensions.)

Closing windows

When you're finished with an application or no longer need to have a window open, move your cursor over the Close button at the upper-left corner of the window. When the X appears in the button, click it. (And yes, I can get one more reference out of Figure 4-7, which I'm thinking of nominating as Figure of the Year.)

If you have more than one window open in the same application and you want to close 'em all in one swoop, hold down the Option key while you click the Close button in any of the windows.

If you haven't saved a document and you try to close that application's window, the application gets downright surly and prompts you for confirmation. "Hey, human, you don't really want to do this, do you?" If you answer in the affirmative — "Why, yes, machine. Yes, indeed, I do want to throw this away and not save it." — the application discards the document that you were working on. If you decide to keep your document (thereby saving your posterior from harm), you can cancel the action and then save the document within the application.

Chapter 5

Getting to the Heart of Mountain Lion

. . . .

In This Chapter

▶ Making the most of your Home folder

▶ Arranging your desktop for greater efficiency

▶ Adding timesavers to the Dock

▶ Using the Trash (and rescuing precious stuff from it)

▶ Using Mission Control and the Dashboard to perform desktop magic

▶ Printing documents

. . . .

*W*hen you're no longer a novice to Mountain Lion and the basics of the Finder, direct your attention to a number of more advanced topics 'n tricks to turn you into a MacBook power user — which, after all, is the goal of every civilized being on Planet Earth.

Consider this chapter a grab bag of Mountain Lion knowledge. Sure, I jump around a little, but these topics are indeed connected by a common thread: All are surefire problem solvers and speeder-uppers. (I can't believe the latter is really a word, but evidently it is. My editors told me so.)

Home, Sweet Home Folder

Each user account that you create in Mountain Lion is actually a self-contained universe. For example, each user has a number of unique characteristics and folders devoted just to that person, and Mountain Lion keeps track of everything that user changes or creates. (In Chapter 11, I describe the innate loveliness of multiple users living in peace and harmony on your laptop.)

This unique universe includes a different system of folders for each user account on your system. The top-level folder uses the short name that Mountain Lion assigns when that user account is created; don't necessarily look for a folder named Home. Naturally, the actual folder name is different for each person, and Mac techno-types typically refer to this folder as your *Home folder*. (On the sidebar, look for the teeny house icon under the Favorites heading, marked with your account name.)

Each account's Home folder contains a set of subfolders, including

- ✔ Movies
- ✔ Music
- ✔ Pictures
- ✔ Downloads (for files you download by using Safari or through Apple Mail attachments)
- ✔ Public (for files that you want to share with others on your network)
- ✔ Sites (for web pages created by the user)
- ✔ Documents (for files created by the user)

Although you can store your stuff at the *root* (top level) of your drive, that gaggle of files, folders, and aliases can get crowded and confusing quickly. Here's a Mark's Maxim to live by:

Your Home folder is where you hang out and where you store your stuff. Use it to make your computing life *much* easier!™

Create subfolders within your Documents folder to organize your files and folders even further. For example, I always create a subfolder in my Documents folder for every book I write so that I can quickly and easily locate all the documents and files associated with that book project.

I discuss security in your Home folder and what gets stored where in Chapter 12. For now, Figure 5-1 shows how convenient your Home folder is to reach because it appears in the Finder window sidebar. One click of your Home folder, and all your stuff is in easy reach. (If your Home folder doesn't appear in the sidebar, that's easily fixed! Choose Finder➪Preferences, click the Sidebar tab, and then select the check box to display your Home folder.)

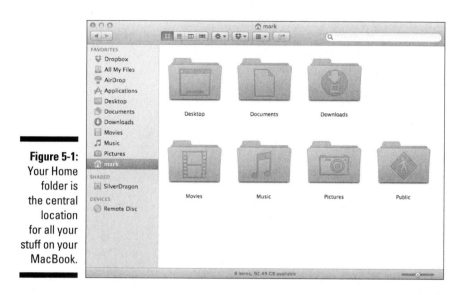

Figure 5-1:
Your Home
folder is
the central
location
for all your
stuff on your
MacBook.

In addition to using the Finder window sidebar, you can reach your Home folder in other convenient ways:

✔ **From the Go menu:** Choose Go➪Home to display your Home folder immediately from the Finder window. Alternatively, you can press ⌘+Shift+H to accomplish the same thing.

✔ **From the Open dialog:** Mountain Lion's standard File Open dialog also includes the same Home folder (and subfolder) icons as the Finder window sidebar.

✔ **In any new Finder window you open:** If you like, you can set every Finder window that you open to automatically display your Home folder:

  a. *Choose Finder➪Preferences and click the General tab to display the dialog that you see in Figure 5-2.*

  b. *Click the arrow button at the right side of the New Finder Windows Show pop-up menu.*

    A menu pops up (hence, the name).

  c. *Click the Home entry in the menu.*

  d. *Click the Close button at the upper-left corner of the dialog.*

    You're set to go. From now on, every Finder window you open displays your Home folder as the starting location!

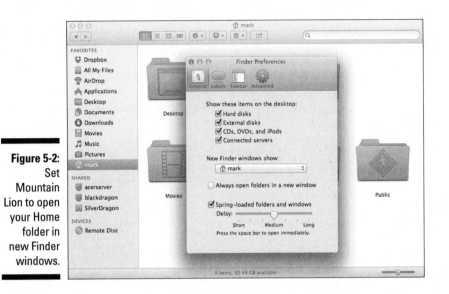

Figure 5-2:
Set
Mountain
Lion to open
your Home
folder in
new Finder
windows.

Here's another reason to use your Home folder to store your stuff: *default locations!* Mountain Lion expects your stuff to be there when you migrate your files from an older Mac to a new Mac, and all iLife and iWork applications look to your Home folder when loading and saving projects.

Personalizing Your Desktop

Most folks put all their documents, pictures, and videos on their Mountain Lion desktop because the file icons are easy to locate! Your computing stuff is right in front of you . . . or *is* it?

Call me a finicky, stubborn techno-oldster — go ahead, I don't mind — but I prefer a clean Mountain Lion desktop without all the iconic clutter. In fact, my desktop usually has just three or four icons even though I use my MacBook several hours every day. It's an organizational thing; I work with literally hundreds of applications, documents, and assorted knickknacks daily. Sooner or later, you'll find that you're using that many, too. When you keep your stuff crammed on your desktop, you end up having to scan your screen for one particular file, an alias, or a particular type of icon, which ends up taking you more time to locate on your desktop than in your Documents folder! And don't forget, open windows hang out on your desktop too — to find anything, you have to close or move those windows!

Plus, you'll likely find yourself looking at old icons that no longer mean anything to you or stuff that's covered in cobwebs that you haven't used in years. Stale icons . . . *yuck.*

I recommend that you arrange your desktop so that you see only a few icons for the files or documents that you use the most. Leave the rest of the desktop for that cool image of your favorite actor or actress.

Besides keeping things clean, I can recommend a number of other favorite tweaks that you can make to your desktop:

✓ **Keep desktop icons arranged as you like.**

   a. From the Finder menu, choose View⇨Show View Options.

   b. Select the Sort By check box.

   c. From the pop-up menu, choose the criteria that Mountain Lion uses to automatically arrange your desktop icons, including the item name, the last modification date, or the size of the items.

   I personally like things organized by name, but many MacBook owners prefer to see things organized by date (putting the most recently modified at the top, for example).

✓ **Choose a favorite background.**

   a. Right-click any open spot on your desktop.

   b. From the right-click menu that appears, choose Change Desktop Background.

   The Desktop & Screen Saver pane appears, as shown in Figure 5-3. Browse through the various folders of background images that Apple provides or use an image from your iPhoto library.

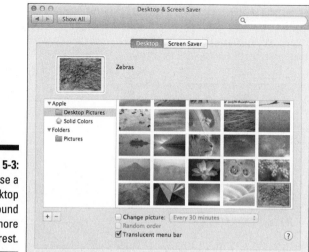

Figure 5-3:
Choose a desktop background of more interest.

✔ **Display all the peripherals and network connections on your system.**

a. Choose Finder➪Preferences.

b. Make sure that all four of the top check boxes (Hard Disks; External Disks; CDs, DVDs, and iPods; and Connected Servers) are selected.

If you're connected to an external network or you've loaded an external hard drive or device, these external storage locations show up on your desktop. You can double-click that Desktop icon to view your external stuff.

Customizing the Dock Just So

If the Dock seems like a nifty contraption to you, you're right again — it's like one of those big control rooms that NASA uses. From the *Dock* — that icon toolbar at the bottom of Mountain Lion's desktop — you can launch an application, monitor what's running, and even use the pop-up menu commands to control the applications that you launch. (Hey, that NASA analogy is even better than I thought!)

By default, the Dock hangs out at the bottom of your screen, but you can move it to another edge, change the size of the icons, or even hide it until you need it. (You can find more details on customizing your Dock in Chapter 6.)

When you launch an application — either by clicking an icon in the Dock, clicking an icon in Launchpad, or by double-clicking an icon in a Finder window or on the desktop — the icon begins to bounce hilariously in the Dock to indicate that the application is loading. (So much for my Mission Control analogy.) After an application is running, the application icon, with a shiny blue below it, appears in the Dock. Thusly, you can easily see what's running at any time just by glancing at the Dock.

You can hide most applications by pressing ⌘+H.

Adding Dock icons

Ah, but we've only scratched the surface: The Dock can offer more than just a set of default icons! You can add your own MIS (or *Most Important Stuff*) to the Dock, making it the most convenient method of taking care of business without cluttering your desktop. You can add

✔ **Applications:** Add any application to your Dock by dragging the application icon into the area to the left of the *separator line* (the vertical line in the Dock that appears between applications and folders or documents).

The existing Dock icons move aside so that you can place the new neighbor in a choice location.

Do not try to add an application anywhere to the right of the separator line. You can't put applications there — and Mountain Lion might even think that you want the application dumped in the Trash! (You can, however, add a stack filled with applications. I discuss stacks in the next bullet.)

✔ **Folders:** Here's where you want to add things to the area to the right of the separator line. A folder or volume icon that you drag to the Dock is called a *stack* in Mountain Lion, and you can display the contents with a single click. (The contents of the folder "fan out" into a half-circle, list or grid arrangement, depending on the number of items in the folder.) To open or launch an item, just click it in the stack display.

Mountain Lion already includes two stacks in the Dock by default: your Documents folder and your Downloads folder.

✔ **Web URLs:** Sure, you can add your favorite website from Safari! Drag it right from the Safari address bar into the area to the right of the separator line. When you click the URL icon, Safari opens the page automatically.

Removing Dock icons

You can remove an icon from the Dock at any time (as long as the application isn't running). In fact, I always recommend that every Mountain Lion user remove the default icons that never get used to make more room available for your favorite icons. The only two icons you can't remove are the Finder and the Trash icons. To remove an icon from the Dock, just click and drag it off the Dock. You're rewarded with a ridiculous puff of smoke straight out of a Warner Brothers cartoon! (One of the OS X developers was in a fun mood, I guess.)

When you delete an icon from the Dock, all you delete is the Dock icon. The original application, folder, or volume is not deleted.

Using Dock icon menus

From the Dock menu, you can open documents, open the location in a Finder window, set an application as a login item, control the features in some applications, and other assorted fun, depending on the item.

To display the Dock shortcut menu for an icon:

1. **Move your cursor over the icon.**

2. **Right-click.**

I cover the Dock settings that you can change in System Preferences in Chapter 6. You can also change the same settings from the Apple menu if you hover your mouse over the Dock menu item, which displays a submenu with the settings.

What's with the Trash?

Another sign of a Mac laptop power user is a well-maintained Trash can. It's a breeze to empty the discarded items you no longer need, and you can even rescue something that you suddenly discover you still need!

The Mountain Lion Trash icon resides in the Dock, and it works just like the Trash has always worked in OS X: Simply drag selected items to the Trash to delete them.

Note one very important exception: If you drag a desktop icon for an external device or a removable media drive to the Trash (such as an iPod, an iPhone, a DVD, or an external hard drive), the Trash icon automatically turns into a giant Eject icon, and the removable device or media is ejected or shut down — not erased. Repeat, *not erased*. (That's why the Trash icon changes to the Eject icon — to remind you that you're not doing anything destructive.)

Here are other methods of chunking items you select to go to the wastebasket:

- ✔ Choose File➪Move to Trash.
- ✔ Click the Action button on the Finder toolbar and choose Move to Trash from the list that appears.
- ✔ Press ⌘+Delete.
- ✔ Right-click the item and choose Move to Trash from the menu that appears.

You can always tell when the Trash contains at least one item because the basket icon is full of crumpled paper! However, you don't have to unfold a wad of paper to see what the Trash holds. Just click the Trash icon in the Dock to display the contents of the Trash. To rescue something from the Trash, drag the item(s) from the Trash folder to the desktop or any other folder in a Finder window. (If you're doing this for someone else who's not familiar with Mountain Lion, remember to act like it was a lot of work, and you'll earn big-time DRP, or *Data Rescue Points*.)

When you're sure that you want to permanently delete the contents of the Trash, use one of these methods to empty the Trash:

✔ Choose Finder⇨Empty Trash.

✔ Choose Finder⇨Secure Empty Trash.

If security is an issue around your laptop and you want to make sure that no one can recover the files you've sent to the Trash, use the Secure Empty Trash command. It takes a little time but helps to ensure that no third-party hard drive repair or recovery program can resuscitate the items you discard.

✔ Press ⌘+Shift+Delete.

✔ Right-click the Trash icon in the Dock and then choose Empty Trash from the menu that appears.

Previewing images and documents the Mountain Lion way

Mountain Lion's Quick Look feature is a favorite of mine. Just select a file and press the space-bar, and Mountain Lion instantly displays the contents of the document or image, *without opening the application.* Heck, I waited for such a magic lamp for two decades!

However, don't forget that OS X has always offered a Swiss Army knife application for viewing image files and documents, namely, Preview. You can use Preview to display digital photos in several popular image formats, including TIFF, GIF, PICT, PNG, JPEG, and Windows Bitmap. You can also display PDF documents without any additional software.

I know, if that were the sum total of Preview's features, it wouldn't deserve coverage here. So, what else can it do? Here's a partial list (just my favorites, mind you):

✔ Use Preview to add a bookmark at the current page in a PDF document by choosing Bookmarks⇨Add Bookmark.

✔ Fill out a form in a PDF document by choosing Tools⇨Text Tool.

Click an area that's marked as an input field, and you can type text into that field.

After you complete the form, you can fax or print it.

✔ Take a *screen snapshot* (saving the contents of your screen as a digital photo) by choosing File⇨Take Screen Shot⇨From Entire Screen.

Preview displays an on-screen timer and then snaps the image for you after ten seconds. (This gives you time to get things just right before saying, "Cheese!")

✔ Convert an image into another format or into a PDF file by choosing File⇨Save.

If a PDF document can be edited, you can delete or insert pages at will.

✔ Resize or rotate an image by using the commands on the Tools menu.

Mountain Lion automatically loads Preview when you double-click an image in a format that it recognizes or when you double-click a PDF file. It also acts as the Print Preview window for some applications, as you can read elsewhere in this chapter. However, if you want to launch Preview manually, click the Launchpad icon in the Dock and then click the Preview icon.

Working Magic with Mission Control and the Dashboard

MacBook power users tend to wax enthusiastic over the convenience features built into Mountain Lion. In fact, we show 'em off to our PC-saddled friends and family. Two of the features that I've demonstrated the most to others are the amazing convenience of Mission Control and Mountain Lion's Dashboard display. In the following sections, I show 'em off to you as well. (Then you can become the Mountain Lion evangelist on *your* block.)

Multitasking with Mission Control

Most MacBook owners are comfortable using the ⌘+Tab keyboard shortcut to switch between open applications. If you've moved to the Mac from a PC running Windows, you might think this simple shortcut is all there is to switching applications. Ah, dear reader, you're in Mountain Lion territory now!

Mission Control sounds complicated, but it's all about convenience. If you typically run a large number of applications at the same time, Mission Control can be a real timesaver, allowing you to quickly switch between a forest of different application windows (or display your desktop instantly without those very same windows in the way). The feature works in three ways:

✔ **Press Control+↑ to show *all* open windows, grouped by application, and then click the one you want.** Move the cursor on top of the window you want to activate — the window turns blue when it's selected — and click once to switch to that window (as shown in Figure 5-4). You can specify which keys you want to use in the Mission Control pane in System Preferences.

✔ **Press Control+↓ to show all open windows from the application that you're currently using; click the one that you want to activate.** This Mission Control function is great for choosing from all the images that you've opened in Photoshop or all the Safari web pages populating your desktop!

Along with the window switch, an astute observer will notice that the application menu bar also changes to match the now-active application.

✔ **Press F11 (or ⌘+F3), and all your open windows scurry to the side of the screen.** (Much like a herd of deer if you dropped a mountain lion in the middle.) Now you can work with drives, files, and aliases on your desktop — and when you're ready to confront those dozen application windows again, just press the keyboard shortcut a second time.

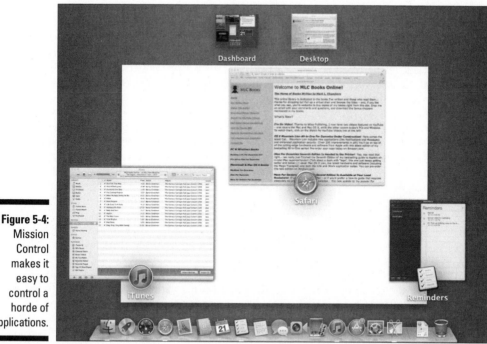

Figure 5-4:
Mission
Control
makes it
easy to
control a
horde of
applications.

Although the Mission Control screen appears automatically when necessary, you can also launch it at any time from your MacBook's Launchpad display, from the Dock icon, or by pressing the Mission Control key on your keyboard. From the trackpad, you can display the Mission Control screen by swiping up with three fingers.

Ah, but what if you want to switch to an entirely different set of applications? For example, suppose that you're slaving away at your pixel-pushing job, designing a magazine cover with Adobe Illustrator. Your page design desktop also includes Photoshop and Aperture, which you switch between often using one of the techniques I just described. Suddenly, however, you realize you need to schedule a meeting with others in your office using Calendar, and you want to check your e-mail in Apple Mail. What to do?

Well, you could certainly open Launchpad and launch those two applications on top of your graphics applications, and then minimize or close them. But with Mission Control's *Spaces* feature, you can press the Control+← or Control+→ sequences to switch to a completely different "communications" desktop, with Calendar and Apple Mail windows already open and in your favorite positions!

After you're done setting up your meeting and answering any important e-mail, simply press Control+← or Control+→ again to switch back to your "graphics" desktop, where all your work is exactly as you left it! (And yes, Virginia, Spaces does indeed work with full-screen applications.)

Now imagine that you've also created a custom "music" desktop for GarageBand and iTunes, or perhaps you paired Photoshop Elements and iPhoto as a "graphics" desktop. See why everyone's so thrilled with Mountain Lion? (Let's see Windows 7 do *that* out of the box.)

To create a new desktop for use in Spaces, click the Mission Control icon in the Dock. Now you can set up new Spaces desktops. Move your pointer to the top right of the Mission Control screen and click the Add (plus sign) button that appears. (If you've relocated your Dock to the right side of the screen, the Add button shows up in the upper-left corner instead.) Spaces creates a new empty desktop thumbnail. Switch to the new desktop by clicking the thumbnail at the top of the Mission Control screen and then open those applications you want to include. (Alternatively, you can drag the applications from Mission Control onto the desired Desktop thumbnail.) That's all there is to it!

To switch an application window between Spaces desktops, drag the window to the edge of the desktop and hold it there. Spaces will automatically move the window to the next desktop. (Applications can also be dragged between desktops within the Mission Control screen.) You can also delete a desktop from the Mission Control screen. Just hover your mouse pointer over the offending Spaces thumbnail and then click the Delete (X) button that appears.

You can jump directly to a specific Spaces desktop by clicking its thumbnail in your Mission Control screen. You can also hold down the Control key and press the number corresponding to a desktop. Finally, you can always use the Control+← and Control+→ shortcuts to move between desktops and full-screen applications.

Using Dashboard

Dashboard allows you to display and use widgets with the press of a button. (Okay, I know that sounds a little wacky, but bear with me.) *Widgets* are small applications — dubbed by some as "applets" — that typically provide only one function. For example, Dashboard comes complete with a calculator, dictionary, clock, weather display, and quick-and-simple calendar. You can display and use these widgets at any time by pressing the Dashboard key; by default, that's F4 on current Apple keyboard models, but you can modify the key on the Mission Control pane in System Preferences. Dashboard appears as a desktop in the Spaces strip on the Mission Control screen, an icon in the Dock, and as an icon in Launchpad. (Personally, I prefer clicking the Dashboard Dock icon to display my widgets. Geez, that sounds kind of racy. Best not to pursue it.)

Figure 5-5 illustrates Dashboard in action. Press the Dashboard key, and the widgets appear, ready for you to use. You can add widgets to your Dashboard by clicking the Add button (which bears a plus sign, naturally) at the lower-left corner of the Dashboard screen. Then, Dashboard displays your entire collection of widgets, and you can click a widget to add it directly to your Dashboard. It's also easy to rearrange the widgets that are already populating Dashboard by dragging them to the desired spot. After you finish customizing your Dashboard display, click the Dashboard background to return to your Dashboard. When it's time to go back to work (or play), press the Dashboard key again to return to your Mountain Lion desktop, or click the right-arrow button at the lower right of the screen.

If you need to use a widget for only a second or two, press and hold down the Dashboard key. When you release the key, you're back to your desktop.

Care to add multiple copies of a widget? Go right ahead! In fact, if you often need to check the time around the world, I highly recommend a bank of World Clock widgets, each displaying the time in your favorite city. (The same goes for the Weather widget.)

Most widgets have an information icon (look for a tiny circle with a lowercase letter *i*). This icon allows you to change things, such as borders, zip codes, and display columns. Click this information icon, and you can tweak whatever options are available for that widget.

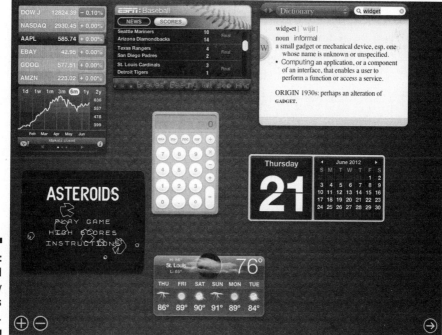

Figure 5-5: Dashboard proudly displays its widgets.

To remove a widget from the Dashboard display, just click the Delete button (which bears a minus sign) and you'll notice a tiny X button appears next to each widget on your Dashboard. Click the X button next to the widget you want to remove, and it vanishes from the display. Note, however, that deleting a widget doesn't remove it from your Mac entirely! You can add that deleted widget back again at any time by clicking the Add button.

While you're adding widgets, you can also click the More Widgets button, which jumps directly to the widget download area on the Apple website.

You can also modify the Dashboard key by turning it into a key sequence, trackpad gesture, or mouse button action, which is A Good Thing if you're already using an application that thrives on F4. Visit the Mission Control pane in System Preferences, and use the Shift, Control, Option, and ⌘ keys with the Dashboard key to specify a modifier, or choose a gesture or mouse button to activate the Dashboard.

Oh, did I mention that Mountain Lion allows you to create your own Dashboard widgets? That's right, this feature is sure to be a winner amongst the In Crowd. Follow these steps to create a new *WebClip* Dashboard widget from your favorite website:

1. **Run Safari and navigate to the site you want to view as a widget.**

2. **Choose File➪Open in Dashboard.**

3. **Select the portion of the page you want to include in your widget and then click Add.**

   Some web pages use frames to organize and separate sections of a page, so this step allows you to choose the frame with the desired content.

4. **Drag the handles at the edges of the selection border to resize your widget frame and then click Add.**

   Bam! Mountain Lion displays your new WebClip widget in Dashboard.

A WebClip widget can include text, graphics, and links, which Dashboard updates every time you display your widgets. Think about that for a second: Dynamic displays, such as weather maps, cartoons, even the Free Music Download image from the iTunes Store, are all good sources of WebClip widgets! (That last one is a real timesaver.)

If you click a link in a WebClip widget, Dashboard loads the full web page in Safari, so you can even use WebClips for surfing the sites you visit often.

Printing in OS X

Mountain Lion makes document printing a breeze. Because virtually all Mac printers use a Universal Serial Bus (USB) port, setting up printing couldn't be easier. Just turn on your printer and connect the USB cable between the printer and your MacBook; Mountain Lion does the rest.

Printer manufacturers supply you with installation software that might add cool extra software or fonts to your system. Even if Mountain Lion recognizes your USB printer immediately, I recommend that you still launch the manu-facturer's OS X installation disc. For example, my Epson printer came with new fonts and a CD/DVD label application, but I wouldn't have 'em if I hadn't installed the Epson software package.

After your printer is connected and installed, you can use the same proce-dure to print from just about every OS X application on the planet! To print with the default page layout settings — standard 8½-x-11-inch paper, portrait mode, no scaling — follow these steps:

1. **In the active application, choose File⇨Print or press the ⌘+P shortcut.**

   OS X displays the Print sheet, as shown in Figure 5-6. Depending on the application, you may see a thumbnail image of the printed document.

Figure 5-6:
Preparing to
print.

2. **Click the Printer pop-up menu and select the printer to which you want to print.**

   In this pop-up menu, Mountain Lion displays all the printers that you can access. You can print from a different printer connected to your laptop or print over a network connection to a shared printer on another computer.

3. **(Optional) If you want to check what the printed document will look like, click Preview.**

   Mountain Lion opens the document in the very same Preview application I discuss earlier in this chapter — note that many applications include a thumbnail preview on the Print sheet instead.

4. **If you have to make changes to the document or you need to change the default print settings, click Cancel to return to your document.**

   (You have to repeat Step 1 to display the Print dialog again.)

5. **If everything looks good at this point and you don't need to change any settings (such as making multiple copies or printing only a portion of the document), click Print — you're done!**

6. **(Optional) For more than one copy, click in the Copies field and type the number of copies that you need.**

   Collation (separating copies) is also available, and it doesn't cost a thing!

7. **(Optional) To print a range of selected pages, select the From radio button and then enter the starting and ending pages.**

   To print the entire document, leave the default Pages option set to All.

8. **(Optional) If the application offers its own print settings, such as collating and grayscale printing, make any necessary changes to those settings.**

   To display these application-specific settings, click the pop-up menu in the Print sheet and choose the settings pane that you need to adjust. (You can blissfully ignore these settings and skip this step if the defaults are fine.)

9. **When you're set to go, click Print.**

You can also save an electronic version of a document in the popular Adobe Acrobat PDF format from the Print dialog — without spending money on Adobe Acrobat. *(Slick.)* Follow these steps:

1. **Click the PDF button to display the destination pop-up menu.**

2. **Click Save as PDF.**

   Mountain Lion prompts you with a Save As dialog, where you can type a name for the PDF document and specify a location on your hard drive where the file should be saved.

Heck, if you like, you can even fax a PDF (with an external USB modem) or send it as an e-mail attachment! Just choose these options from the destination list instead of choosing Save as PDF.

Chapter 6

A Nerd's Guide to System Preferences

In This Chapter

▶ Navigating System Preferences

▶ Searching for specific controls

▶ Customizing Mountain Lion from System Preferences

Remember the old TV series *Voyage to the Bottom of the Sea?* You always knew you were on the bridge of the submarine *Seaview* because it had an entire wall made up of randomly blinking lights, crewmen darting about with clipboards, and all sorts of strange and exotic-looking controls on every available surface. You could fix just about anything by looking into the camera with grim determination and barking out an order. After all, you were On the Bridge. That's why virtually all the dialog and action inside the sub took place on that one (expensive) set: It was the nerve center of the ship, and a truly happenin' place to be.

In the same vein, I devote this entire chapter to the System Preferences window and the most commonly used settings within it. After all, if you want to change how Mountain Lion works or customize the features in our favorite operating system, point yourself immediately toward System Preferences — this one window is the nerve center of OS X, and a truly happenin' place to be. (Sorry, no built-in wall of randomly blinking lights — but you do find exotic controls just about everywhere.)

An Explanation — in English, No Less

The System Preferences window (shown in Figure 6-1) is a self-contained beast, and you can reach it in a number of ways:

✔ Click the Apple menu (■) and choose the System Preferences menu item.

✔ Click the System Preferences icon in the Dock — it's a collection of gears.

✔ Click the Apple menu (■), choose Dock, and then choose the Dock Preferences menu item.

✔ Click the Time and Date display in the menu bar and then choose the Open Date and Time menu item. (In fact, you can also click most of the other menu status icons — including the Bluetooth, Wi-Fi, Display, and Modem icons — and then choose the Open Preferences menu item.)

✔ Right-click any uninhabited area of your desktop and then choose Change Desktop Background.

✔ Last but not least, click the Launchpad icon in the Dock and then click the System Preferences icon.

Figure 6-1:
The pow-
erhouse of
settings and
switches:
System
Preferences.

When the System Preferences window is open, you can click any of the group icons to switch to that group's *pane;* the entire window morphs to display the settings for the selected pane. For example, Figure 6-2 illustrates the Sound pane, which allows you to set a system alert sound, configure your MacBook's built-in microphone, and choose from several different output options.

Many panes also include a number of tabbed buttons at the top — in this case, Sound Effects, Output, and Input. You can click these tabs to switch to another *pane* in the same pane. Many panes in System Preferences have multiple panes. This design allows our friends at Apple to group a large number of related settings in the same pane (without things getting too confusing).

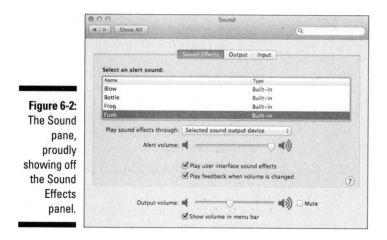

Figure 6-2:
The Sound
pane,
proudly
showing off
the Sound
Effects
panel.

To return to the top-level System Preferences pane from any other pane, just click the Show All button (upper left) or press ⌘+L. You can also click the familiar Previous and Next buttons, respectively, to move backward through the panes you've already visited and then move forward again, in sequence. (Yep, these buttons work just like the browser controls in Safari. Sometimes life is funny that way.)

Although the System Preference panes are arranged by category when you first install Mountain Lion, you can also display the panes in alphabetical order, which makes it easier to choose a pane if you're unsure what group it's in. To do so, choose View➪Organize Alphabetically. Note that you can also select any pane directly from the View menu. Choose View➪Customize, and you can hide specific icons from the System Preferences window. Just deselect the check box next to each icon that you want hidden, and then click Done. You can still reach hidden icons from the System Preferences View menu, so they're not banished forever.

In fact, you can right-click the System Preferences icon in the Dock to jump to any pane from the shortcut menu. *Wowzers!*

You won't find an OK button that you have to click to apply any System Preference changes — Apple's developers do things the right way. Your changes to the settings in a pane are automatically saved when you click Show All or when you click the Close button in the System Preferences window. You can also press ⌘+Q to exit the window and save all your changes automatically . . . a favorite shortcut of mine.

Hey, I got bonus icons in my window!

Some third-party applications and media plug-ins can actually install their own groups in your once-pristine System Preferences window. You'll see them at the bottom of the window, in the Other section. (For example, Adobe's Flash Player adds an icon to the Other section.)

Naturally, I can't document these invited guests in this chapter, but they work the same way as any other group in System Preferences. Click the icon, adjust any settings as necessary, and then close the System Preferences window to save your changes.

If you see an Apply button in a pane, you can click it to immediately apply any changes you made, without exiting the pane. This is perfect for settings that you might want to try first before you accept them, like many of the controls in the Network pane. However, if you're sure about what you changed and how those changes will affect your system, you don't have to click Apply. Just exit the System Preferences window or click Show All as you normally would.

Locating That Certain Special Setting

Hey, wouldn't it be great if you could search through all the different panes in System Preferences — with all those countless radio buttons, check boxes, and slider controls — from one place, even when you're not quite sure exactly what you're looking for?

Figure 6-3 illustrates exactly that kind of activity taking place. Just click in the System Preferences Spotlight Search box (upper right, with the magnifying glass icon) and type just about anything. For example, if you know part of the name of a particular setting you need to change, type that. Mountain Lion highlights the System Preferences panes that might contain matching settings. And if you're a *switcher* from the Windows world, you can even type what you might have called the same setting in Windows XP, Vista, 7, or 8!

The System Preferences window dims, and the group icons that might contain what you're looking for stay highlighted. *Slick.*

You can also search for System Preferences controls by using the Spotlight menu and Spotlight window. Find more on this cool feature in Chapter 7.

If you need to reset the Search box to try again, click the X icon that appears at the right side of the box to clear it.

Figure 6-3:
Searching
for specific
settings is a
breeze with
the Search
box.

Popular Preference Panes Explained

Time to get down to brass tacks. Open the most often-used panes in System Preferences to see what magic you can perform! I won't discuss every pane because I cover many of them in other chapters. (In fact, you might never need to open some System Preferences panes, such as the Language & Text pane.) However, this chapter covers just about all the settings that you're likely to use on a regular basis.

The Displays pane

If you're a heavy-duty game player or you work with applications such as Keynote or Photoshop, you probably find yourself switching the characteristics of your monitor on a regular basis. To easily accomplish switching, visit the Displays pane (see Figure 6-4), which includes two panes:

✔ **Display:** To allow Mountain Lion to choose the best resolution for your display, select the Best for Display radio button. To manually select a resolution, select the Scaled radio button and then click the resolution that you want to use from the Resolutions list on the left. (In most cases, you want to use the highest resolution.) Move the Brightness slider to adjust the brightness level of your MacBook's display.

On the road again? Select the Show Mirroring Options in the Menu Bar When Available check box if you'll be using multiple monitors or a projector with your Mac.

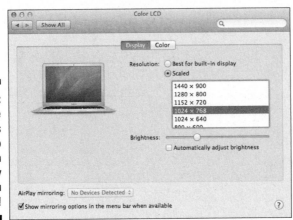

Figure 6-4:
The
Displays
pane also
comes in
a handy
Finder menu
bar size!

Ready to stream content to your TV directly from your MacBook — *without cables*? You can use Mountain Lion's wireless AirPlay Mirroring feature to send the display from your MacBook to your HD-TV. AirPlay Mirroring requires an Apple TV unit that supports this feature. You can also send the audio from your laptop directly to an AirPlay-enabled receiver or speaker system.

✔ **Color:** Click a display color profile to control the colors on your monitor. To load a profile, click the Open Profile button. To create a custom ColorSync profile and calibrate the colors that you see on your monitor, click the Calibrate button to launch the Display Calibrator. This easy-to-use assistant walks you step by step through creating a ColorSync profile matched to your monitor's gamma and white-point values.

The Desktop & Screen Saver pane

Hey, no offense to the awesome Mountain Lion background, but who doesn't want to choose his or her own background? And what about that nifty screen saver you just downloaded from the Apple website? You can change both your background and your screen saver by using these options in the Desktop & Screen Saver pane.

The settings on the Desktop panel (shown in Figure 6-5) are

✔ **Current desktop picture:** You can click a picture in the thumbnail list at the right half of the screen to use it as your desktop background. The desktop is immediately updated, and the thumbnail appears in the *well* (the upper-left square box in Figure 6-5). To display a different image collection or open a folder of your own images, click the Add Folder (plus sign) button at the lower left of the window and browse for your heart's desire; then click Choose to select a folder and display the images it contains.

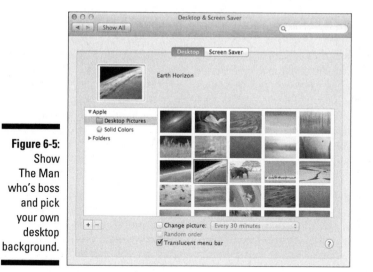

Figure 6-5:
Show
The Man
who's boss
and pick
your own
desktop
background.

✔ **Layout:** You can tile your background image, center it, fill the screen with it, and stretch it to fill the screen. (Note that filling the screen may distort the image.) The layout pop-up menu appears only when you're using your own pictures, so you won't see it if you're using a desktop image supplied by Apple.

✔ **Change Picture:** Change the desktop background automatically after the delay period that you set, including each time you log in and each time your Mac wakes up from sleep mode.

✔ **Random Order:** To display screens randomly, enable the Random Order check box. Otherwise, the backgrounds are displayed in the sequence in which they appear in the thumbnail list.

✔ **Translucent Menu Bar:** When enabled, this feature makes your Finder and application menu bars semi-opaque, allowing them to blend in somewhat with your desktop background. If you'd rather have a solid-color menu bar, deselect this check box.

The settings on the Screen Saver tab are

✔ **Screen Savers:** In the Screen Savers list at the left, click any screen saver to preview (on the right). To try out the screen saver in full-screen mode, click the Test button. (You can end the test by moving your cursor.) If the screen saver module that you select has any configurable settings, click the Screen Saver Options button to display them. (A screen saver is *not* configurable if the Screen Saver Options button isn't enabled.) Choose the Random screen saver to display a different screen saver module each time the screen saver is activated.

✔ **Start After:** Specify the period of inactivity that triggers the screen saver. To disable the screen saver, choose the Never setting at the top of the list.

✔ **Show with Clock:** If you want your selected screen saver to display the time as well, select this check box.

✔ **Hot Corners:** Click any of the four pop-up menus at the four corners of the screen to specify that corner as an *activation hot corner* (immediately activates the screen saver) or as a *disabling hot corner* (prevents the screen saver from activating). As long as the cursor stays in the disabling hot corner, the screen saver doesn't kick in, no matter how long a period of inactivity passes. Note that you can also set the Sleep, Mission Control, Launchpad, Notification Center, and Dashboard activation corners from here. (For the scoop on these features, see the upcoming section, "Mission Control preferences.")

For additional security, check out the Security & Privacy pane in System Preferences, where you find the Require Password After Sleep or Screen Saver Begins check box. Select the check box, and Mountain Lion requires your user account password before allowing anyone to turn off the screen saver (a great idea when traveling, as you can imagine).

Mission Control preferences

Figure 6-6 illustrates the Mission Control, Spaces, and Dashboard settings that you can configure in this group. You can use Mission Control to view all the application windows that you're using at one time so that you can select a new active window. Or you can move all windows aside so that you can see your desktop. Dashboard presents a number of mini-applications (or *widgets*), which you can summon and hide with a single key.

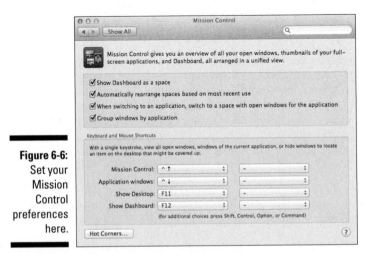

Figure 6-6: Set your Mission Control preferences here.

The settings are

- ✔ **Show Dashboard as a Space:** To display your Dashboard as a space (a virtual desktop) in the Mission Control screen, select the Show Dashboard as a Space check box. If you prefer your Dashboard widgets to appear as an overlay (as in versions of OS X predating OS X 10.7 [Lion]), deselect this check box.

- ✔ **Automatically Rearrange Spaces Based on Most Recent Use:** If this check box is selected, Mission Control presents your most recently used Spaces first in the thumbnails at the top of the screen.

- ✔ **When Switching to an Application:** When selected, this check box allows you to switch applications between spaces desktops by using the ⌘+Tab shortcut. Mountain Lion jumps to the desktop that has an open window for the application you choose, even if that desktop is not currently active.

- ✔ **Group Windows by Application:** When selected, this check box automatically arranges windows in the Mission Control screen by the application that created them.

- ✔ **Keyboard and Mouse Shortcuts:** From each pop-up menu, set the key sequences (and mouse button settings) for Mission Control, Application Windows, Show Desktop, and Show Dashboard.

  You're not limited to just the keyboard and mouse shortcuts in the pop-up menus. Press Shift, Control, Option, and ⌘ keys while a pop-up menu is open, and you see these modifiers appear as menu choices! (Heck, you can even combine modifiers, such as ⌘+Shift+F9 instead of just F9.)

- ✔ **Hot Corners:** Click the button at the lower left to specify your hot corner settings. These four pop-up menus operate just like hot corners and active screen corners in the Desktop & Screen Savers pane, but they control the operation of Mountain Lion's screen management features. Click one to specify that corner as an All Windows corner (displays all windows on your desktop), an Application Windows corner (displays only the windows from the active application), a Desktop corner (moves all windows to the outside of the screen to uncover your Desktop), a Dashboard corner (displays your Dashboard widgets), or a Notification Center corner (displays the Notification Center strip at the right side of your desktop). Choose Launchpad to activate the Launchpad screen. Note that you can also set the Screen Saver Start and Disable corners from here, as well as put your display to sleep.

The General pane

The talented General pane (shown in Figure 6-7) determines the look and operation of the controls that appear in application windows and Finder windows. It looks complex, but I cover each option here.

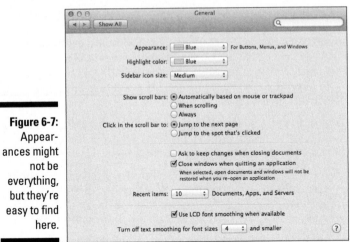

Figure 6-7:
Appear-
ances might
not be
everything,
but they're
easy to find
here.

The settings are

✔ **Appearance:** Choose a color to use for buttons, menus, and windows.

✔ **Highlight Color:** Choose a color to highlight selected text in fields and pop-up menus.

✔ **Sidebar Icon Size:** Select the size of the icons in the Finder window sidebar — that's the strip to the left of the Finder window that displays your devices and favorite locations on your system. If you have a large number of hard drives or you've added several folders to the sidebar, reducing the size of the icons will allow you to display more of them without scrolling.

✔ **Show Scroll Bars:** Specify when Mountain Lion should display scroll bars in a window. By default, they're placed automatically when necessary, but you can choose to display scroll bars always or only when you're actually scrolling through a document. (If you used OS X before Lion, note that the familiar scroll arrows from those past versions of the operating system no longer appear within Mountain Lion.)

✔ **Click in the Scroll Bar To:** By default, OS X jumps to the next or previous page when you click in an empty portion of the scroll bar. Select the Jump to the Spot That's Clicked radio button to scroll the document to the approximate position in relation to where you click.

✔ **Ask To Keep Changes When Closing Documents:** If you select this check box, Mountain Lion prompts you for confirmation if you attempt to close a document with unsaved changes. If the check box is deselected, Mountain Lion will allow the unsaved document to be closed without saving a new version.

- ✔ **Close Windows When Quitting an Application:** If this check box is deselected, Mountain Lion's Resume feature automatically saves the state of an application when you quit. When you launch the application again, Mountain Lion restores all application windows and opens the documents you were working on when you quit. In effect, you can continue using the application just as if you had never quit. If you select the check box, Mountain Lion will not restore your work, and you'll have to load your document again; this is the same action taken by versions of OS X predating 10.7 (Lion).

- ✔ **Recent Items:** The default number of recent applications, documents, and servers (available from the Recent Items item in the Apple menu [🍎]) is 10. To change the default, open the pop-up menus here and choose up to 50. (I like 20 or 30.)

- ✔ **Use LCD Font Smoothing When Available:** By default, this check box is enabled, making the text on your MacBook's display appear more like the printed page. You can turn off this feature to speed up text display slightly.

- ✔ **Turn Off Text Smoothing for Font Sizes:** Below a certain point size, text smoothing isn't much good for most on-screen fonts. By default, any font displayed at 4 point (pt) or smaller isn't smoothed, which is suitable for a high-end video card and monitor. You can speed up the display of text by turning off text smoothing for fonts up to 12 pt.

The Energy Saver pane

I'm an environmentalist — it's surprising how many techno-types are colored green — so these two panels here are pretty doggone important. When you use them correctly, you not only conserve battery power but also invoke the Power of Mountain Lion to automatically start up and shut down your laptop whenever you like!

Move the Computer Sleep slider to specify when OS X should switch to sleep mode (see Figure 6-8). The Never setting here disables sleep mode. To choose a separate delay period for blanking your monitor, drag the Display Sleep delay slider to the desired period. You can also power down the drive to conserve energy and prevent wear and tear (an especially good feature for laptop owners).

If you want to start up or shut down your laptop at a scheduled time, click the Schedule button. Select the desired schedules (the Start Up or Wake check box and the Shut Down/Sleep check box) to enable them; then click the up and down arrows next to the time display to set the trigger time. Click OK to return to the Energy Saver pane.

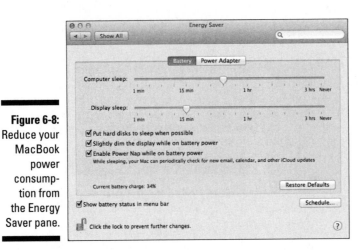

Figure 6-8:
Reduce your
MacBook
power
consump-
tion from
the Energy
Saver pane.

Some of the settings can toggle events that control Mountain Lion's sleep mode, including a network connection by the network administrator (Wake for Ethernet Network Access). You can also set OS X to restart automatically after a power failure, which is a good idea if you're sharing music or files with others. Naturally, MacBook owners will want to click the Show Battery Status in the Menu Bar check box to select it.

Mac laptop owners can set two separate Energy Saver configurations by clicking one of the two tabs at the top of the pane:

✔ **Battery:** Applies when the MacBook is running on battery power

✔ **Power Adapter:** Kicks in when the laptop is connected to an AC outlet

Your MacBook automatically switches to the proper configuration when you plug in or unplug your laptop.

The Dock pane

I'll come clean: I think the Dock is the best thing since sliced bread! (I wonder what people referred to before sliced bread was invented?) You can use the settings, shown in Figure 6-9, to configure the Dock's behavior until it fits your personality like a glove:

✔ **Size:** Pretty self-explanatory. Just drag the slider to change the scale of the Dock.

✔ **Magnification:** When you select this check box, each icon in your Dock swells like a puffer fish when you move your mouse cursor over it. (The Magnification slider determines just how much it magnifies.) I really like this feature because I resize my Dock smaller, and I have a large number of Dock icons.

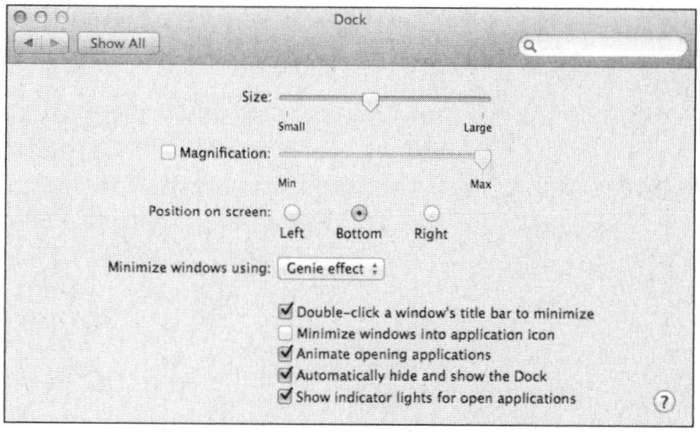

Figure 6-9:
Customize
your Dock
with these
controls.

✔ **Position on Screen:** Select a radio button here to position the Dock on the left, bottom, or right edge of your desktop.

✔ **Minimize Windows Using:** Mountain Lion includes two cool animations that you can choose from when shrinking a window to the Dock (and expanding it back to the desktop). Click the Minimize Using pop-up menu to specify the genie-in-a-bottle effect or a scale-up-or-down-incrementally effect.

✔ **Double-Click a Window's Title Bar to Minimize:** Select this check box to minimize a Finder or an application window by simply double-clicking the window's title bar.

✔ **Minimize Windows into Application Icon:** By default, Mountain Lion minimizes a window as a thumbnail on the right side of the Dock. Select this check box to minimize a window to the icon for the parent application instead. (To restore a window that's been minimized to the application icon, right-click the icon in the Dock and choose Restore from the menu.)

✔ **Animate Opening Applications:** Are you into aerobics? How about punk rock and slam dancing? Active souls who like animation likely get a kick out of the bouncing application icons in the Dock. They indicate that you've launched an application and that it's loading. You can turn off this bouncing behavior by deselecting this check box.

✔ **Automatically Hide and Show the Dock:** Select this check box, and the Dock disappears until you need it. (Depending on the size of your Dock, the desktop that you gain can be significant.) To display a hidden Dock, move your cursor over the corresponding edge of the desktop.

✔ **Show Indicator Lights for Open Applications:** OS X indicates which applications are running in the Dock with a small blue dot in front of the icon. To disable these indicators, deselect this check box.

You can change most of these Dock preference settings also from the Apple menu ().

The Sharing pane

So you're in a neighborly mood, and you want to share your toys with others on your local wired or wireless network. Perhaps you'd like to start your own website or protect yourself against the Bad Guys on the Internet. All these fun diversions are available from the Sharing pane in System Preferences, as shown in Figure 6-10.

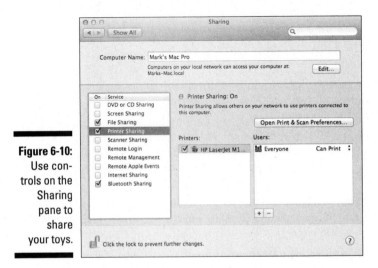

Figure 6-10:
Use controls on the Sharing pane to share your toys.

Click the Edit button to change the default network name assigned to your MacBook during the installation process. Your current network name is listed in the Computer Name text field.

Each entry in the services list controls a specific type of sharing, including DVD or CD Sharing, Screen Sharing, File Sharing (with other Macs and PCs running Windows), Printer Sharing, Scanner Sharing, Remote Login, Remote Management (using Apple Remote Desktop), Remote Apple Events, Internet Sharing, and Bluetooth Sharing. To turn on any of these services, select the On check box for that service. To turn off a service, click the corresponding On check box to deselect it.

From a security standpoint, I highly recommend that you enable only those services that you actually use. Each service you enable automatically opens your Mountain Lion firewall for that service. A Mark's Maxim to remember:

Poking too many holes in your firewall is *not* A Good Thing.™

When you click one of the services in the list, the right side of the Sharing pane changes to display the settings you can specify for that particular service.

The Time Machine pane

Mac users are thrilled with the Time Machine automatic backup feature that's built in to Mountain Lion — I know it's already saved my stuff numerous times — and you can easily configure how Time Machine handles your backups from this pane (as shown in Figure 6-11). Chapter 23 covers how to use Time Machine. Of course, you need an external drive (or a Time Capsule wireless backup device) for the best backup security. Note that Time Machine doesn't work with your CD or DVD rewriteable drive; you must use an external drive or a USB flash drive.

Figure 6-11: Put Time Machine to work, and your data is always backed up.

To enable Time Machine, click the On toggle switch and then select a disk to hold your Time Machine backup data on the sheet that appears; click Use Disk to confirm your choice. (Your external backup drive should be at least twice the capacity of your internal drive, thus ensuring that your backup files have the elbowroom they need.) If you have an external Time Capsule wireless unit, click Set Up instead.

By default, Time Machine backs up all the drives on your system; however, you may not need to back up some folders on your MacBook. To save time and backup drive space, Time Machine allows you to exclude specific folders from the backup process. Click Options and then click the Add button (with the plus sign) to select the drives or folders you want to exclude, and they'll appear in the Exclude These Items list.

To remove an exclusion, select it in the list and click the Delete button (with the minus sign). Note that the Estimated Size of Full Backup figure increases, and Time Machine adds the item you deleted from the list to the next backup.

If you enable the Show Time Machine in Menu Bar check box, you can elect to back up your Mac immediately by clicking the Time Machine icon in the Finder menu bar and then choosing Back Up Now.

By default, Mountain Lion warns you when deleting older backup files, but you can turn this off from the Options sheet as well.

You can elect to back up your MacBook immediately by clicking the Time Machine icon in the Finder menu bar and choosing Back Up Now.

iCloud preferences

From Mountain Lion's iCloud Preference pane, you can specify which types of data will be automatically pushed to your MacBook and iOS devices. If you haven't created an iCloud account yet — or if you signed out of an existing account earlier — System Preferences will prompt you to enter your Apple ID and password. Click Sign In to display the contents of the iCloud pane, shown in Figure 6-12.

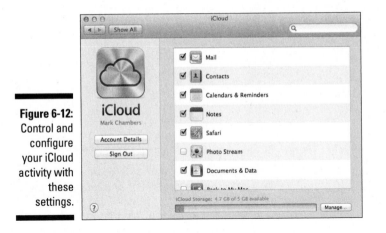

Figure 6-12: Control and configure your iCloud activity with these settings.

The check boxes for each category are

- **Mail:** Synchronize your Mail account settings between devices.
- **Contacts:** Push your Contact cards between devices.
- **Calendars & Reminders:** Push your calendar and reminders to and from your iOS devices.
- **Notes:** Synchronize your Notes between devices.
- **Safari:** Synchronize your Safari bookmarks.
- **Photo Stream:** Push the latest photos and video clips you've added in iPhoto to other devices, and update your iPhoto library with photos and video clips pushed from your iOS devices.
- **Documents & Data:** Automatically synchronize the documents you create and your personal settings between your MacBook and other iOS devices.

- **Back to My Mac:** Control file and screen sharing across all the Macs sharing this iCloud account. Back to My Mac must be enabled on all computers that will use this feature.

- **Find My Mac:** Locate your MacBook from a web browser or your iOS device, and you can also choose to remotely lock your computer — or even *wipe your laptop's hard drive completely* to prevent someone from stealing your data!

Locking or wiping your MacBook remotely will prevent it from being located in the future. These are drastic steps, indeed!

To display the storage currently being used by your mail, backups, documents, and application data, click the Manage button at the lower right of the pane. Apple provides each iCloud account 5GB of space for free, but you can also elect to buy additional storage from this sheet.

Notifications preferences

Mountain Lion's Notifications group is shown in Figure 6-13. Each application that can display notifications appears in the list at the left of the pane. Click an application and then choose from these settings at the right:

- **Alert Style:** These three buttons specify which type of alert should appear under the Notification Center icon in the menu bar. You do not need to display the Notification Center to see alerts, which appear on your desktop. Choose None to disable alerts for this application. Choose Banners to display alert messages that will automatically disappear after a delay. Choose Alerts to display alert messages that remain onscreen until you click the confirmation button in the Alert dialog.

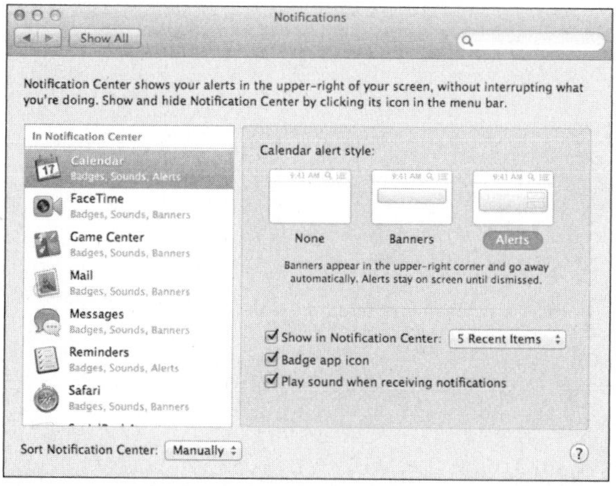

Figure 6-13: Each application that uses notifications can be individually configured.

![Screenshot of the Notifications System Preferences pane showing the list of applications including Calendar, FaceTime, Game Center, Mail, Messages, Reminders, and Safari on the left, with Calendar alert style options None, Banners, and Alerts on the right.]

✔ **Show in Notification Center:** To display notification messages from this application in the Notification Center, select this check box. You can also specify how many recent messages from this application will be displayed.

✔ **Badge App Icon:** This check box toggles on and off the display of this application's icon in alert boxes and in the Notification Center, as well as activates the numeric display of pending items on the icon itself (for example, unread mail and messages).

✔ **Play Sound When Receiving Notifications:** To play a sound when alerts appear, enable this check box.

Chapter 7

Sifting through Your Stuff

*W*hat would you say if I told you that you could search your entire system for all the data connected with a person — and in only the short time it takes to type that person's name? And I'm not just talking about files and folders that might include that person's name. I mean *every* e-mail message and *every* Calendar event that references that person — and even that person's Contacts card to boot? Heck, how about if that search could dig up every occurrence of the person's name inside your electronic PDF documents?

You'd probably say, "That makes for good future tech — I'll bet I can do that in five or ten years. It'll take Apple at least that long to do it . . . and just in time for me to buy a new MacBook! (Harrumph.)"

Don't be so hasty. You can do all this, right now (in fact, it's been part of OS X for a number of years). The technology is the OS X feature named *Spotlight,* built right into Mountain Lion. In this chapter, I show you how to use it like a Mac power guru. I also show you how to take advantage of Internet search widgets you can display within Dashboard. (From what I hear, there's good stuff on the Internet, too.)

A Not-So-Confusing Introduction to Spotlight

Invoking the magic of Spotlight is a snap. As you can see in Figure 7-1, the Spotlight search field always hangs out on the right side of the Finder menu

bar. You can either click once on the magnifying glass icon or just press
⌘+spacebar. Either way, Mountain Lion displays the Spotlight search box.

Spotlight works by *indexing* — in other words, searching for and keeping
track of keywords in your files. (In case you've never heard the term before,
a *keyword* is a word in the title or innards of a document that describes the
contents, such as *Mountain Lion, music,* or *soda.* That last one turns up a lot
in my documents.)

In fact, Mountain Lion indexes virtually all the contents of your MacBook's
drives, maintaining that humongous index continuously while you create new
files and modify existing files. Mountain Lion can search this index file in a
fraction of a second after you enter your search criteria. Your index file contains all sorts of data, including quite a bit of information from various documents, hence Spotlight's capability to present matching data from your files
and application records.

Spotlight search box

Figure 7-1:
The
Spotlight
search box.

When you first boot Mountain Lion, it spends anywhere from a few minutes to an hour or two creating the initial Spotlight index file. A blue dot appears in the middle of the magnifying glass icon while indexing is underway. Creating this full index happens only once, so it's no great burden to bear.

You can search for any string of text characters in Spotlight, and you'll be surprised at everything this plucky feature can search. For example, Spotlight searches through your Contacts database, Mail messages, Calendar events, Notes, Reminders, temporary web page cache, and even System Preferences! Yep, you can even use it to find specific settings in all those System Preferences panes, such as *printer sharing* or *Dashboard.* Of course, Spotlight includes matching files and folders — like that other operating system that runs on PCs — but it does so in the blink of an eye.

Spotlight matches all the items that include all your search text. Therefore, if you enter just the word *horse,* you're likely to get far more matches than if you enter a more restrictive word string, such as *horse show ticket.*

If you add *metadata* to your documents — such as a Comment field in a Word document (which you can display in the Get Info dialog box) — Spotlight matches that information as well. Other recognized file formats include iWork documents, Excel spreadsheets, and third-party applications that offer a Spotlight plug-in. (Speaking of the Get Info dialog box, you'll notice that you can add a Spotlight Comment to any file or folder.)

Searching with Spotlight

To begin a Spotlight topic search, click within the Spotlight box and start typing. As soon as your finger presses the first key, matching items start to appear. Check out Figure 7-2, in which I typed only a single character (*L*). You don't need to press Return to start the process, by the way. When you type more characters, Spotlight's results are updated in real time to reflect those more restrictive qualifiers. For example, if I had typed three characters — say, *Lio* — my results would be far more specific: everything from *Mountain Lion* to *Lionel Trains.*

Spotlight displays what it considers the top 20 matching items in the Spotlight menu itself. These most relevant hits are arranged into categories, such as Documents, Images, and Folders. You can change the order in which categories appear (by using the Spotlight pane in System Preferences, which I cover a bit later in this chapter).

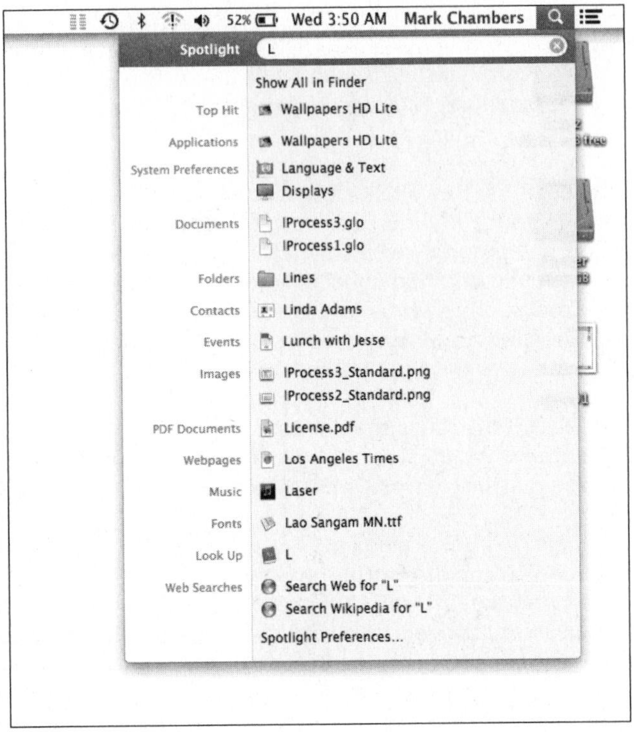

Figure 7-2:
A Spotlight
menu
search
takes as
little as one
character.

Spotlight	L
	Show All in Finder
Top Hit	Wallpapers HD Lite
Applications	Wallpapers HD Lite
System Preferences	Language & Text
	Displays
Documents	IProcess3.glo
	IProcess1.glo
Folders	Lines
Contacts	Linda Adams
Events	Lunch with Jesse
Images	IProcess3_Standard.png
	IProcess2_Standard.png
PDF Documents	License.pdf
Webpages	Los Angeles Times
Music	Laser
Fonts	Lao Sangam MN.ttf
Look Up	L
Web Searches	Search Web for "L"
	Search Wikipedia for "L"
	Spotlight Preferences...

With its internal magic, Spotlight presents the category Top Hit (with what it considers the single, most relevant match) at the top of the search results (refer to Figure 7-2). You'll find that the Top Hit is often just what you're look-ing for. To open or launch the Top Hit item from the keyboard, just press Return.

Hover your cursor over an item in the Spotlight menu and — *shazam!* — Spotlight uses the Quick Look technology built into Mountain Lion to display information on the item! If the item is a song, you can even move your cursor on top of the thumbnail in the Quick Look display and click to play it — all without leaving the Spotlight menu.

Didn't find what you were after? Click the X button that appears at the right side of the Spotlight box to reset the search box, and then start over.

If all you know about the item you're searching for is its file type, you can dis-play all the files of a particular type on your system by using the file type as the keyword. For example, to provide a list of all images on your system, just use *images* as your keyword — the same goes for *movies, contacts, applica-tions* and *audio,* too.

How secure is Spotlight?

Say you're sharing your MacBook as a multiuser computer, or accessing other Macs remotely. What about all those files, folders, contacts, and events that you *don't* want to appear in Spotlight? Can other folks search for and access your personal information through Spotlight?

Definitely not! The results displayed by Spotlight, just like the applications that create and display your personal data, are controlled by file and folder permissions as well as your account login. For example, you can't access other users' private calendars by using Calendar, and they can't see your Mail messages. Only *you* have access to *your* data, and

only after you log in with your username and password. Spotlight works the same way. If a user doesn't normally have access to an item, it simply doesn't appear when that user performs a Spotlight search. (In other words, only you get to see your stuff.)

However, you can hide certain folders and disks from your own Spotlight searches if necessary. Perhaps you'd prefer keeping your tax and financial records away from Spotlight's all-searching eye. Check out the section of this chapter titled "Marking stuff off-limits" for details on setting private locations in your system.

Here's another trick that's built into Spotlight: You can type a date that a file was created or received, such as **modified:=>10/01/12**, to match all items modified on or after October 1, 2012. Heck, you can even combine criteria, such as **audio created:07/18/12**. *Note:* Be sure to include a space between the criteria. Spotlight then matches every audio file that was created on that date. One hundred percent *sassy!*

To allow even greater flexibility in your searches, Apple uses those helpful Boolean search friends that you might be familiar with: AND, OR, and NOT (separated by spaces). For example, in Mountain Lion, you can perform Spotlight searches such as

- ✔ Horse AND cow: Collects all references to both barnyard animals into one search

- ✔ Batman OR Robin: Returns all references to either Batman or Robin

- ✔ Apple NOT PC: Displays all references to Apple that don't include any information on dastardly PCs

Working with matching stuff

After you run a fruitful search and Spotlight finds the proverbial needle in your system's haystack, what's next?

Just click the item — that's all it takes. Depending on the type of item, Mountain Lion does one of four things:

- ✔ Launches an application
- ✔ Opens a specific pane in System Preferences (if the match is the name of a setting or is contained in the text on a Preferences pane)
- ✔ Opens a document or data item, such as a Contacts card
- ✔ Displays a folder in a Finder window

To see all sorts of useful info about each Spotlight menu item — otherwise known as *filtering* — click the Show All item (above the Top Hit listing; refer to Figure 7-2) to expand your Spotlight menu into the Results window, as shown in Figure 7-3. From the keyboard, you can press the Results window shortcut key, which you can set from System Preferences (more on this in a page or two).

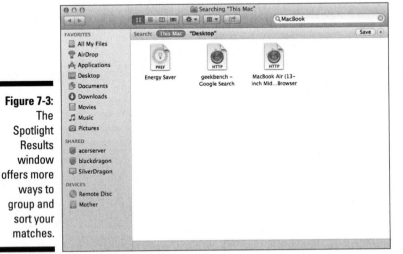

Figure 7-3: The Spotlight Results window offers more ways to group and sort your matches.

To further filter the search, click one of the buttons on the Spotlight Results window toolbar or create your own custom filter. Click the button with the plus sign to display the search criteria bar, and then click the pop-up menus to choose from criteria, such as the type of file, the text content, or the location on your system (such as your drive, your Home folder, or a network server). You can also filter your results listing by the date when the items were created or last saved. To add or delete criteria, click the plus button or minus button, respectively, at the right side of the search criteria bar. To save a custom filter that you created, click Save.

After you locate the item you want, click it to open, launch, or display it, just like you would on the Spotlight menu.

Tweaking Spotlight in System Preferences

The System Preferences window boasts a Spotlight pane, which you can use to customize what search matches you see and how they are presented. To adjust these settings, click the System Preferences icon in the Dock (look for the Three Gears of Justice) and then click the Spotlight icon (under Personal).

Configuring the Search Results settings

Figure 7-4 illustrates the Search Results tab of the Spotlight Preferences pane. From here, you can

- **Choose your categories.** To disable a category (typically because you don't use those types of files), select the check box next to the unnecessary category to clear it — thereby making more room for other categories that you will use.

- **Specify the order in which categories appear in Spotlight.** Drag the categories into the order in which you want them to appear on the Spotlight menu and in the Results window.

- **Select new Spotlight menu and Spotlight Results window keyboard shortcuts.** In fact, you can enable or disable either keyboard shortcut, as you like. Click the pop-up menu to choose a key combination. (This setting is good news for applications such as Photoshop that demand to use the ⌘+Space shortcut for themselves!)

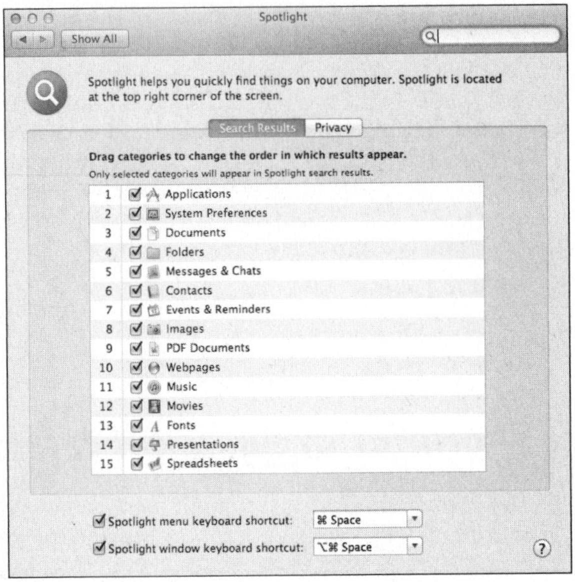

Spotlight

Show All

Spotlight helps you quickly find things on your computer. Spotlight is located at the top right corner of the screen.

Search Results | Privacy

Drag categories to change the order in which results appear.
Only selected categories will appear in Spotlight search results.

1 ☑ Applications
2 ☑ System Preferences
3 ☑ Documents
4 ☑ Folders
5 ☑ Messages & Chats
6 ☑ Contacts
7 ☑ Events & Reminders
8 ☑ Images
9 ☑ PDF Documents
10 ☑ Webpages
11 ☑ Music
12 ☑ Movies
13 ☑ Fonts
14 ☑ Presentations
15 ☑ Spreadsheets

☑ Spotlight menu keyboard shortcut: ⌘ Space
☑ Spotlight window keyboard shortcut: ⌥⌘ Space

Figure 7-4:
These settings control how your matches are presented in Spotlight.

Marking stuff off-limits

Click the Privacy tab (shown in Figure 7-5) to add disks and folders that should never be listed as results in a Spotlight search. The disks and folders that you add to this list won't appear even if they match your search string, no matter what type of search you use. This safeguard can come in handy for organizations (such as hospitals) that are required by law to protect their patient or client data.

To add a private location, click the Add button (which bears a plus sign) and navigate to the desired location. Then click the location to select it, and click Choose.

If you already have the location open in a Finder window, you can drag folders or disks directly from the window and drop them into the list.

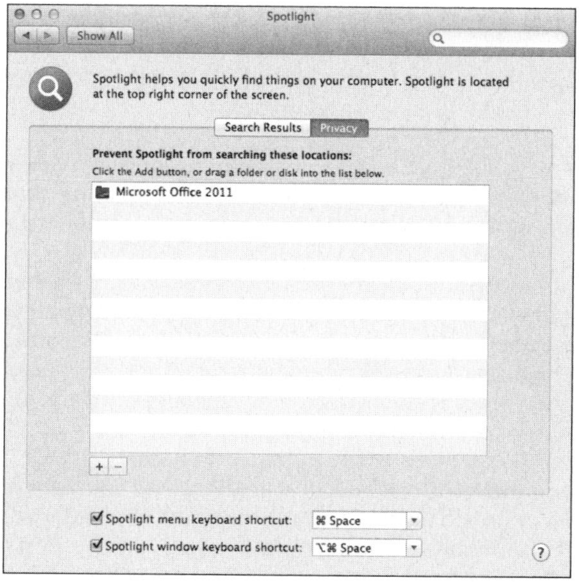

Figure 7-5:
You can
specify
that things
that should
never be
seen.

Other Search Tools Are Available, Too

The Finder window toolbar has featured a search box for a few years now (and Mountain Lion includes a Find dialog), but even the older Search features in Mountain Lion have been updated to take advantage of Spotlight technology. Now you can even use relative time periods (such as *yesterday* and *last week*) in the Finder window search box and Find displays!

Typically, I use the Finder window search box if I need to do a simple file or folder name search (or when I want to collect a group of items for a move or copy operation). The process is the same as using the Spotlight search field. Just begin typing. To reset the field and start anew, click the X button in the search box. To choose a specific location for your search — say, your Home folder or a drive — click the desired button along the top of the Search Results display. The Finder window automatically turns into a Results display.

Mountain Lion also includes the oldest Search method in the book: the Find display. (The Find display used to be a dialog all by itself, but now it's more of an extension to the Finder window because Find controls are displayed in the Finder window.) Choose File⇨Find or press ⌘+F to display the Find controls. From here, you can click pop-up menus to choose a specific filename or portion of a filename. Other modifiers include the file type, the content, the file size, and the most recent date when the file was opened. Again, click the location buttons at the top of the window to choose where to search.

For a truly mind-blowing list of modifiers, click the Other item in the modifier menu. You'll find you can search for all photos where a certain shutter speed was used or all files that are read-only. Heck, I sometimes use this expanded list to search for documents that use a certain font!

You can click the plus (+) button next to a search criterion field in the Find display to add another field, allowing matches based on more than one condition. Click the minus (–) button next to a search criterion field to remove it.

After you find a match, both older Search methods work the same: Click the item once to display its location, or double-click it to launch or open it. Files can also be moved or copied, respectively, from the Results and Find displays with the standard drag or Option+drag methods. You can return to the more mundane Finder window display by clicking the Back button on the toolbar to erase the contents of the Spotlight box.

These older Search methods can also do one thing that Spotlight doesn't offer: You can use them to create a new *smart folder,* which is a folder with contents that Mountain Lion automatically updates according to the criteria you set — the same modifiers I discuss earlier.

Click the Save button in either the Finder window Search Results or Find display. You're prompted to specify the name and location for the new smart folder and whether it should appear in the Finder window sidebar.

After you create the folder, Mountain Lion automatically updates the contents of the smart folder with whatever items match the criteria you saved. You never have to search by using the same text or criteria again because the search is saved as part of the smart folder! (Each icon in a smart folder is a link to the file or folder — just like an alias — so nothing gets moved, and no extra space is wasted with multiple copies of the same items.) In other words, you can work with the files and folders inside a smart folder as if they were the items themselves.

With Widgets, the Internet Is Your Resource

No chapter on searching within OS X would be complete without a discussion about the Internet resources available through your Mountain Lion Dashboard. (I describe widgets in illuminating detail in Chapter 5.) Figure 7-6 illustrates many of these widgets:

✔ **Dictionary:** This multipurpose widget can display the Oxford American dictionary or thesaurus entry for the word you enter.

✔ **Flight Tracker:** Keep tabs on the arrival and destination time for the flight you specify.

✔ **Movies:** This widget displays a number of movie poster thumbnails. Click a thumbnail to view the trailer or buy tickets through Fandango.

✔ **Weather:** Check out the six-day forecast for a specific zip code or city-and-state combination at a glance.

To enter the location data, click the tiny *i* button that appears when you mouse-over the bottom-right corner of the widget. This trick works with just about every widget, allowing you to set any options it offers.

Okay, I know you're going to roll your eyes, but I have to remind you that you need an Internet connection to use most of these widgets. Otherwise, widgets such as Movies and Flight Tracker are about as useful as a pair of swim fins in the Sahara Desert.

Naturally, you can find countless other Internet-enabled widgets on the Apple website, in the Download area. For all the details on adding built-in widgets to your Dashboard, visit Chapter 5.

Figure 7-6: These widgets use the Internet to help you search for answers to life's persistent questions.

Chapter 8

Using Reminders, Notes, and Notifications

In This Chapter

▶ Setting reminders

▶ Making notes

▶ Using the Notification Center

*A*s I've said many times before in my books, "If it works in one place, it's likely to show up in another." In this case, three popular time-saving (and headache-preventing) apps have crossed over from the world of iOS devices — the iPhone, iPad, and iPod touch — and have securely landed on your Mountain Lion desktop! Those apps are Reminders, Notes, and Notification Center, all taken from iOS 5.

That's not the only good news, though: These three Mac applications work seamlessly with an iCloud account, so if you also use an iOS device (with the same Apple ID), the notes you take and the reminders you make are automatically synchronized between all your Apple computers and devices! (If you didn't create an Apple ID when you installed Mountain Lion, visit Chapter 2 for the details.)

Because all three of these new applications have a similar goal — namely, to keep you in touch with the information, daily tasks, and digital events that matter to you — I decided to cover them in one shiny chapter. Consider this chapter a guide that demonstrates how you can note, remind, and notify like a mobile power user!

Remind Me to Use Reminders

You don't need to look far to find the new Reminders application on your MacBook. Just click the Reminders icon in the Dock to display the main window, as shown in Figure 8-1.

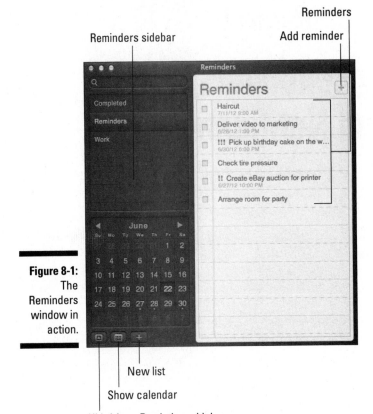

Reminders sidebar

Reminders

Add reminder

Figure 8-1:
The
Reminders
window in
action.

Hide/show Reminders sidebar

Show calendar

New list

The highlights of the Reminders window include the following:

✔ **Search box:** Click here and type a phrase or name to search for it among your reminders.

✔ **Reminders sidebar**: You can add as many separate reminder lists as you like in the application (one for work, for example, and another for your Mac user group). In the sidebar, you can switch quickly between your lists. (Note that two lists, Reminders and Completed, already appear.)

✔ **Hide/Show Reminders Sidebar:** Click this button to hide or show the Reminders sidebar. You save a significant amount of screen real estate when the sidebar is hidden.

✔ **Calendar:** This handy calendar indicates which days of the current month already have pending reminders, which are displayed with a dot under the date. You can jump to any date by clicking it. To move forward and backward through the months, click the Previous and Next buttons next to the month name. (Note that this calendar does not sync or exchange reminder dates with your MacBook's Calendar application.)

✓ **New List button:** Click this button to add a new reminder list to the sidebar; from the keyboard, press ⌘+L. The list name is highlighted in a text box, so you can simply type the new name and then press Return.

✓ **Reminders:** These entries are the actual reminders themselves. Each is prefaced by a check box so you can select the check box when the reminder is complete, thereby moving that reminder automatically to the Completed list. And yes, if you select the Completed list in the sidebar and deselect the check box for a reminder, it returns (like a bad penny) to the original list.

✓ **Add Reminder button:** Click this button to add a new reminder to the currently selected list; from the keyboard, press ⌘+N. In its simplest form, a reminder is just a short phrase or sentence. Press Return afterward to save the reminder to your list.

Adding a reminder is pretty straightforward. First, click a date in the calendar display to jump to that date, and then click the Add Reminder button. Type a few words and press Return to create a basic reminder. However, if you hover the cursor over the reminder you just created, an Info button (a lowercase *i* in a circle button) appears next to the text. The game is afoot! Click the Info button to display the settings shown in Figure 8-2.

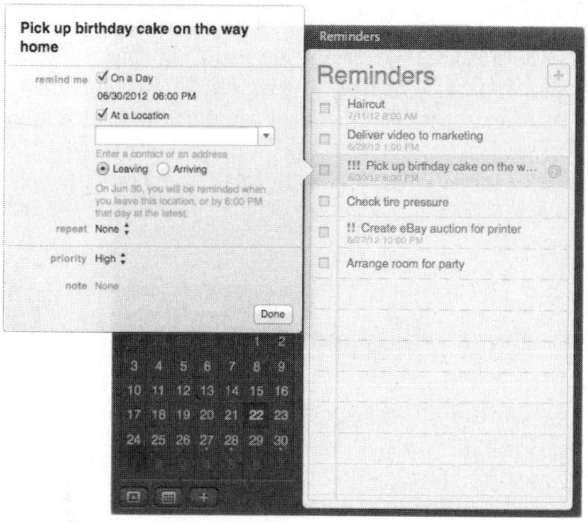

Figure 8-2:
Editing a
reminder.

The fields on the Edit sheet are

- ✔ **Reminder text:** Click this text to edit the reminder text itself.

- ✔ **On a Day:** Select this check box if the reminder should appear in the Notification Center on a particular day. By default, the date is the one selected when you created the reminder. You can click the Date and Time fields to change them.

- ✔ **At a Location:** Here's a powerful feature. Select this check box, and you can choose a card from your Contacts application that includes an address (or simply type an address in the box). Now reminders will monitor your current location on your 3G/4G iOS device, and notify you when you're leaving or arriving at that location (and optionally, on the date and time you specify in the On a Day field). For example, you could create a reminder that notifies you on your iPhone when you're arriving at the mall on September 15 to pick up the watch that's being repaired. *Shazam!*

- ✔ **Repeat:** Set this reminder to automatically repeat every day, week, two weeks, month, or year at the same time.

- ✔ **Priority:** You can assign one of four priorities to the reminder: Low, Medium, High, or None. Assigning a priority prefaces the reminder text with one (Low), two (Medium), or three (High) red exclamation points so that the reminder stands out from the crowd.

- ✔ **Note:** Click next to the Note field to enter a free-form text note along with the reminder.

Click Done on the Edit sheet when you've finished making changes. You can edit a reminder as often as you like. For example, I sometimes have to change the date on a reminder multiple times as my schedule changes.

To delete a reminder from a list, right-click it and choose Delete from the menu that appears.

Taking Notes the Mountain Lion Way

Imagine a notepad of unlimited pages that's always available whenever you're around your MacBook, iPhone, iPod touch, or iPad — that's the idea behind Notes, and it's superbly simple! To open the application, click the Notes icon in the Dock. The window shown in Figure 8-3 appears.

Search box

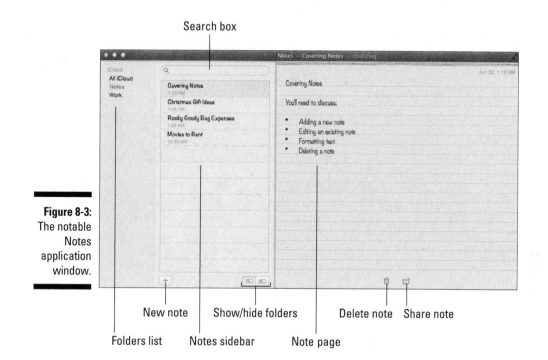

Figure 8-3:
The notable
Notes
application
window.

New note   Show/hide folders   Delete note   Share note

Folders list   Notes sidebar   Note page

You'll find the following salient stuff in the Notes window:

- ✔ **Search box:** To hunt for a specific note, click in this box and type a search phrase or name.

- ✔ **Folders list:** You can create new folders to hold specific kinds of notes. In Figure 8-3, for example, I added a Work folder. To add a new folder, choose File⇨New Folder or press ⌘+Shift+N, and then type the new folder name. To switch between folders, display the Folders list and click the desired folder.

- ✔ **Notes sidebar:** Each note you create appears as a separate entry in the sidebar. You can click a note to switch to it immediately.

- ✔ **New Note icon:** Click this icon to add a new note. You can also right-click the sidebar and choose New Note from the shortcut menu. Notes uses the first line of text that you type as the title of the note, which appears in the sidebar.

- ✔ **Show and Hide Folders List icons:** You can click these two icons to display or hide the Folders list.

- ✔ **Note page:** This free-form pane is where you type the body of your note. You can also drag images from a Finder window and include them in the body of the note, and even attach files by dragging them from a Finder window as well.

✔ **Delete Note icon:** Click the Trash icon at the bottom of the Note page to delete the current note. The application will prompt you for confirmation before the deed is done.

✔ **Share Note icon:** Open this pop-up menu to share the contents of the current note, just like the Share icon that appears on the Finder window toolbar. Sharing options can include a new e-mail message, a new message in the Messages application, and new postings to Twitter and Facebook.

To edit a note, click it to select it in the sidebar, and then simply make your changes or additions in the Note page. Use the Format menu to format the text — everything from different fonts and colors to inserting bulleted and numbered lists.

Staying Current with Notification Center

Of the iOS newcomers to OS X, the Notification Center is unique — it's not actually an application you launch! Instead, the Notification Center is always running.

Find the Notification Center icon at the far right side of the Finder menu bar. Click the icon (or, if you prefer using gestures on your trackpad, swipe from the right edge to the left) to display your notifications, as shown in Figure 8-4. These notifications can be generated by a host of Mountain Lion applications, including Calendar, Mail, FaceTime, Reminders, Game Center, Messages, Safari, and even the Apple App Store.

I love how the Notification Center doesn't interfere with open applications. Instead, it simply moves the entire desktop to the left so that you can see your notifications. You can close the Center at any time by clicking anywhere on the desktop to the left, by clicking the Notification Center icon on the Finder menu bar again, or by swiping in the opposite direction.

Notification entries that appear in the Center are grouped under the application that created them. Many entries can be deleted from the Center by clicking the Delete button that appears next to the application heading (it bears an X symbol). Other entries, such as Calendar alerts, remain in the Notification Center until a certain time has elapsed.

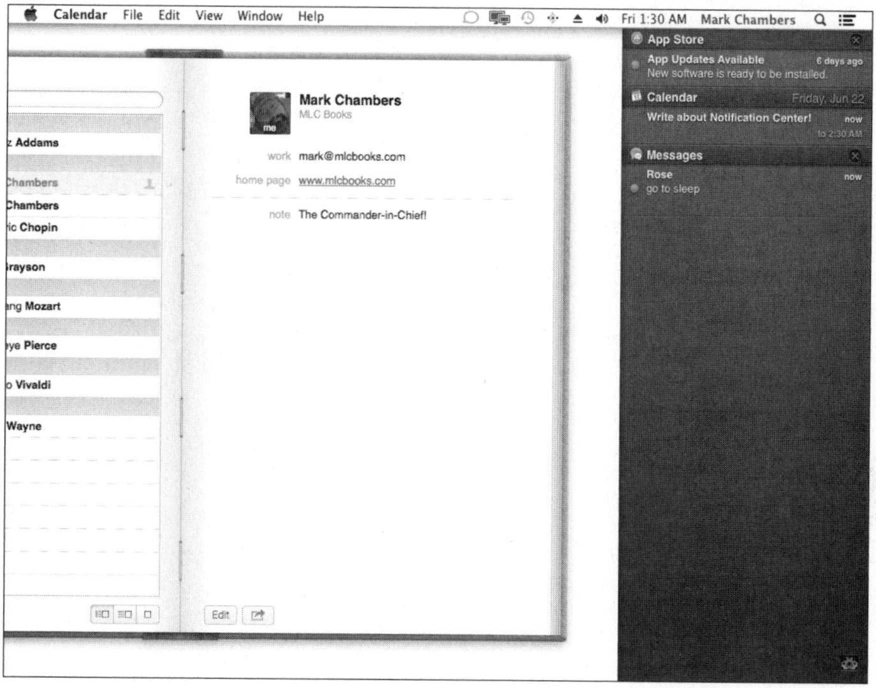

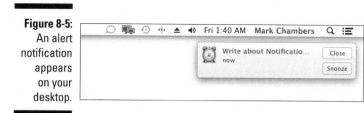

Figure 8-4:
The Notification Center muscles your desktop to the side.

But wait, the Notification Center is more than just a strip of happenings! Depending on the settings you choose, notifications can also appear without the Notification Center being open. These notifications are displayed as pop-up *banners* (which disappear in a few seconds) and *alerts* (which must be dismissed by clicking a button). Figure 8-5 illustrates a typical alert notification.

Figure 8-5:
An alert notification appears on your desktop.

You can configure the notifications for all your applications from the Notifications pane in System Preferences, which you can reach easily if the Notification Center is open. Just click the icon at the lower right of the Center (which looks just like the System Preferences icon in the Dock). I discuss the settings on the Notifications pane in Chapter 6.

Part III
Connecting and Communicating

In this part . . .

You want to do the Internet thing, don't you? Sure, you do! In this part, I describe and demonstrate your Safari web browser. You also find out about Apple's iCloud service, which allows you to synchronize all your personal data between your Mac laptop and iOS devices such as the iPhone, iPad, and iPod touch.

Ready to share your Mac laptop among all the members of your family? If you decided to build a home network (wired or wireless), you've come to the right place. In this part, I show you how to provide others with access to your documents and data — securely, mind you, and with the least amount of hassle.

Finally, this part fills you in on connecting important stuff, such as printers and scanners, as well as how you can use your laptop's built-in FaceTime HD webcam with applications such as Messages and Photo Booth.

Chapter 9

Let's Go on Safari!

1 proudly surf the web via a lean, mean — and *very* fast — browser application. That's Safari, of course, and it just keeps getting better with each new version of OS X. (Heck, if you like, you can even enlist your friends using PCs on this expedition — you can find a version of Safari for Windows as well.)

If you need a guide to Safari, this is your chapter. Sure, you can start using it immediately, but wouldn't you rather read a few pages so you can surf like a power user?

Pretend You've Never Used This Thing

Figure 9-1 illustrates the Safari window. You can launch Safari directly from the Dock, or you can click the Safari icon in Launchpad. Major sections of the Safari window include

> ✔ **The toolbar:** You find the most-often-used commands on this toolbar — for tasks such as navigating, adding bookmarks, and searching Google (or Yahoo! or Bing). Plus, here you can type or paste the address for websites that you'd like to visit. The toolbar can be hidden to provide you with more real estate in your browser window for web content. To

toggle hidden mode on and off, press ⌘+| (the vertical bar right above the backslash) or choose View➪Hide/Show Toolbar.

✔ **The Bookmarks bar:** Consider this a toolbar that allows you to jump directly to your favorite websites with a single click or two. I show you later, in the section "Adding and Using Bookmarks," how to add and remove sites from your Bookmarks bar. For now, remember that you can toggle the display of the Bookmarks bar by choosing View➪Hide/Show Bookmarks Bar or by pressing ⌘+Shift+B.

✔ **The Content pane:** Congratulations! At last, you've waded through all the pregame show and you've reached the area where web pages are actually displayed. The Content window can be scrolled; when you minimize Safari to the Dock, you get a *thumbnail* (minimized) image of the Content window.

The Content window often contains underlined (or highlighted) text and graphs that transport you to other pages when you click them. These underlined words and icons are *links,* and they make it easy to move from one area of a site to another or to a completely different site. You can tell when your cursor is resting on a link because the cursor changes to that reassuring pointing-finger hand. Handy!

Toolbar   Bookmarks bar

Figure 9-1:
Safari at a glance.

Status bar   Content window

✔ **The status bar:** The status bar displays information about what the cursor is currently resting upon, such as the address for a link or the name of an image; it also updates you on what's happening while a page is loading. To hide or display the status bar, press ⌘+/ (forward slash) or choose View⟿Hide/Show Status Bar.

Visiting Websites

Here's the stuff that virtually everyone over the age of 5 knows how to do . . . but I get paid by the word, and some folks might not be aware of the myriad ways of visiting a site. You can load a web page by using any of the following methods:

✔ **Type (or paste) a website address into the Address box on the toolbar, and then press Return.**

If you're typing in an address and Safari recognizes the site as one that you've visited in the past, it helps by autocompleting the address for you. Press Return if you want to accept the suggested site. If this is a new site, just keep typing.

The Safari Address box also acts as a *smart address* field, displaying a new pop-up menu of sites that match the text you've entered. Safari does this by using sites taken from your History file and your bookmarks, as well as sites returned from Google, Yahoo!, or Bing. If the site you want to visit appears in the list, click it to jump there immediately.

✔ **Click a Bookmarks entry in Safari.**

✔ **Click the iCloud Tabs button on the toolbar.**

This button (which bears a cloud icon) displays the tabs you've opened in Safari among all Macs and iOS devices that use the same Apple ID — simply click a site name in the list to load that page. (To use iCloud tabs, all Macs must be running Mountain Lion and using Safari 6 or later. On the iOS side, your iPhone, iPad, or iPod touch must be running iOS 6 or later.) You discover more about tabs later in this chapter.

✔ **If the Home button appears on your toolbar, click it to return to the home page that you specify.**

You find more on this in the section "Setting Up Your Home Page," later in this chapter.

✔ **Click the Show Top Sites button on the toolbar.**

Safari displays a wall of preview thumbnail pages from your most frequently visited sites, and you can jump to a site just by clicking the preview. You can "anchor" a thumbnail to keep it on the screen permanently by clicking the pin icon next to the desired thumbnail. Click the Edit button on the Top Sites screen to delete a preview thumbnail (click the X). You can also choose the size of the preview thumbnails in Edit mode.

Because each thumbnail is updated with the most current content, the Top Sites wall makes a great timesaver — you can quickly make a visual check of all your favorite haunts from one screen!

✔ **In the Reading list, click an item you saved earlier.**

✔ **Click a page link in Apple Mail or another Internet-savvy application.**

Some Mac applications require you to hold down ⌘ while clicking to open a web page. (Note that if the link is in plain text, you can often select the text, right-click, and choose Open URL from the menu that appears.)

✔ **Select a web address in a document, click the Services menu, and choose Open Page in Safari.**

✔ **Click a page link in another web page.**

✔ **Type a search term in the Address box on the toolbar.**

By default, Safari uses Google as a search engine, but you can also use Yahoo! or Bing if you prefer. To set the default search engine, choose Safari➪Preferences; then, on the General tab, open the Default Search Engine drop-down menu. (You can immediately switch to another search engine from the bottom of the menu that appears as you're typing in the Address box.)

Click in the Address box, type the contents that you want to find, and then press Return. Safari presents you with the search results page on Google for the text that you entered. (In case you've been living under the Internet equivalent of a rock for the last couple of years, *Google.com* is the preeminent search site on the web — people use Google to find everything from used auto parts to ex-spouses.)

✔ **Click a Safari page icon in the Dock or a Finder window.**

Drag a site from your Bookmarks bar (or drag the icon from the left side of the Address box) and drop it on the right side of the Dock. Clicking the icon that you add launches Safari and automatically loads that site.

This trick works only on the side of the Dock to the right of the vertical line. More on this important divider in a bit.

If you minimize Safari to the Dock, you can see a thumbnail of the page with the Safari logo superimposed on it. Click this thumbnail in the Dock to restore the page to its full glory.

Speaking of full glory, Safari supports the same full-screen mode as other Mountain Lion applications. Click the Full Screen icon at the top-right corner of the Safari window to switch to full-screen mode, or press the Control+⌘+F shortcut (a good shortcut to memorize because it works with virtually all Mountain Lion–compatible applications). To make things convenient for you, the Address box remains, as do the iCloud Tabs, Share, Back, and Forward icons. To exit full-screen mode, press Esc or the Control+⌘+F shortcut again.

Navigating the Web

A typical web-surfing session is a linear experience — you bop from one page to the next, absorbing the information that you want and discarding the rest. However, after you visit a few sites, you might find that you need to return to where you've been or head to the familiar ground of your home page. Safari offers these default navigational controls on the toolbar:

- ✔ **Back:** Click the Back button (the left-facing arrow) on the toolbar to return to the last page you visited. Additional clicks take you to previous pages, in reverse order. The Back button is disabled if you haven't visited at least two sites. If you click and hold down the Back button, Safari displays a pop-up menu with all the pages to which you can return — just click the desired page to jump right to it.

- ✔ **Forward:** If you've clicked the Back button at least once, clicking the Forward button (the right-facing arrow) takes you to the next page (or through the pages) where you originally were, in forward order. The Forward button is disabled if you haven't used the Back button and haven't navigated to another page. As with the Back button, you can click and hold down the Forward button to display a pop-up menu of pages, allowing you to jump forward to a desired page.

Safari supports a number of trackpad gestures that make life easier with your MacBook. For example, you can swipe in either direction with two fingers to move backward and forward, just as you would move with the Forward and Back buttons. To zoom in and out in the Content pane, you can either double-tap the trackpad or pinch with two fingers — yes, just like an iPhone. (Ever get the notion that someday we'll just have a single box called "The Device" that does it all?)

- ✔ **Home:** Click the Home button, which looks like a little house, to immediately return to your home page. (More on setting your home page in the next section.)

Not all these buttons and controls must appear on your toolbar. In fact, you may never see many of these toolbar controls unless you add them. To display or hide toolbar controls, choose View⇨Customize Toolbar. The sheet that appears works just like the Customize Toolbar sheet in a Finder window: Drag the control you want from the sheet to your Safari toolbar, or drag a control that you don't want from the toolbar to the sheet.

- ✔ **New Tab:** Click this button (it looks like a little tab with a plus sign) to open a new tab in the Content pane. I get knee-deep into tabbed browsing later in the chapter.

- ✔ **AutoFill:** If you fill out a lot of forms online — when you're shopping on websites, for example — you can click the AutoFill button (which looks like a little text box and a pen) and have the forms completed for you. You can set what information is used for AutoFill by choosing Safari⊅Preferences and clicking the AutoFill toolbar button.

To be honest, I'm not a big fan of releasing *any* of my personal information to *any* website, so I don't use AutoFill often. If you do decide to use this feature, make sure that the connection is secure (look for the padlock icon in the Address box) and read the site's Privacy Agreement page first to see how your identity data will be treated.

✔ **Top Sites:** Click this button to display the Top Sites screen I discuss earlier. If you're having trouble finding it, the button bears a tiny, fashionable grid of squares.

✔ **Reading List:** Click the snazzy eyeglasses icon to display or hide the Reading list pane, where you can save entire pages for later perusal. From the keyboard, press ⌘+Shift+L. When the Reading list pane is visible, click the Add Page button to add the current page to the list; you can quickly add a link to the list by holding down the Shift key and clicking the link. Click the Reading List button again to banish the Reading list pane.

Ah, but when you click one of those entries in the Reading list, you may see a blue Reader button at the right side of the Address box. Click the Reader button, and the real magic begins! The Reader panel appears to display text articles free of advertisements and silly pop-ups. And if an article is continued over multiple web pages, the Reader panel automatically "stitches" them together to form a continuous block of text. (Think of an e-book shown on your iPad or iPhone, and you get the idea.) You can also print or e-mail the article from the Reader panel.

If the Reader button is blue in Safari's Address box — and you're *not* using the Reading list — don't panic! Because the page you're reading contains text articles, Safari is offering to display it in the Reader panel. (If a page has nothing to display in the Reader panel, the button remains gray.) To display the page in the Reader panel, click the blue Reader button in the Address box. To return to your mundane browsing experience, click the Reader icon again.

✔ **Zoom:** Use this button to shrink or expand the size of text on the page, offering smaller, space-saving characters (for the shrinking crowd) or larger, easier-to-read text (for the expanding crowd). Hence the button, which is labeled with a small and large letter *A*. From the keyboard, you can press ⌘+plus sign to expand and ⌘+minus sign to shrink.

✔ **Bookmarks Bar:** Click this button (which carries the Bookmarks symbol sandwiched between two horizontal lines) to display or hide the Bookmarks bar.

✔ **Stop/Reload:** Click Reload at the right side of the Address box (look for the circular arrow) to *refresh* (reload) the contents of the current page. Although most pages remain static, some pages change their content at regular intervals or after you fill out a form or click a button. Reload allows you to see what's changed on these pages. (I use Reload every hour or so with CNN.com, for example.) While a page is loading, the

Reload button turns into the Stop button — with a little X — and you can click it to stop the loading of the content from the current page. This feature is a real boon when a download takes *foorrevverr,* which can happen when you're trying to visit a popular or slow website (especially if you're using a dial-up modem connection to the Internet). Using Stop is also handy if a page has a number of very large graphics that are likely to take a long time to load.

✔ **Bookmarks:** Click this toolbar button (which carries an open book icon) to hide or display the Bookmarks pane. You can find the complete description of the Bookmarks pane in an upcoming section.

✔ **History:** Click this button (which bears a clock symbol) to display or hide the History list, which I discuss later in the chapter.

✔ **Downloads:** Click this toolbar button to display the files you've downloaded recently. Click the Clear button to clear the contents of the Download list. Note that clearing the list does not delete the files you've downloaded; it simply cleans things up. You can also double-click a completed download in the list to open it immediately. (More on downloading in a page or two.)

When you're downloading a file, a tiny progress bar appears in the Downloads button on the toolbar to show you how much you've received. Now that, good reader, is *progress!* (Let's see whether my editor allows such a horrible pun to remain.)

✔ **Open in Dashboard:** Click this button to create a Dashboard widget by using the contents of the currently displayed web page. Safari prompts you to choose which clickable section of the page to include within the widget's borders (such as the local radar map on your favorite weather website). Click Add, and Dashboard loads automatically with your new widget. (More on widgets in Chapter 5.)

✔ **Mail:** Click this button (bearing an envelope icon) to send an e-mail message with a link to the current page, just as if you chose File➪Mail Link to This Page. Safari automatically opens your default mail application (typically Apple Mail) and creates a new message with the link already in the body. *Shazam!*

✔ **Add Bookmark:** Click this toolbar button (which carries a plus sign) to add a page to your Bookmarks bar or Bookmarks menu. (More on this button in a minute.)

✔ **Print:** Click this convenient button to print the contents of the Safari window. (Dig that crazy printer icon!)

✔ **Share:** If you have an iPhone, iPod touch, or iPad, you're probably already familiar with this button, which carries a symbol of a rectangle and curved arrow. Click the Share button to send the current page (or a link to it) to a number of different destinations, including your Reading list, an e-mail message, your Messages application, Facebook, or Twitter. You can also add a bookmark to the current page using the Share button. Figure 9-2 illustrates the Share button in action.

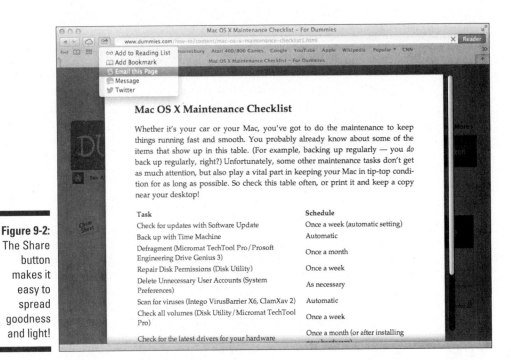

Figure 9-2:
The Share
button
makes it
easy to
spread
goodness
and light!

Setting Up Your Home Page

Choosing a home page is one of the easiest methods of speeding up your web surfing, especially if you're using a dial-up modem. However, a large percentage of the Mac owners whom I've talked with have never set their own home page; instead, they simply use the default home page provided by their browser! With Safari running, take a moment to follow these steps to declare your own freedom to choose your own home page:

1. **In Safari, display the web page that you want as your new home page.**

   I recommend selecting a page with few graphics or a fast-loading popular site.

2. **Choose Safari➪Preferences or press ⌘+, (comma).**

3. **Click the General button.**

   You see the settings shown in Figure 9-3.

4. **Click the Set to Current Page button.**

   Choose Top Sites from the New Windows Open With pop-up menu to display the Top Sites screen (described earlier) each time you open a new window. Alternatively, choose Empty Page if you want Safari to open a new window with a blank page. (A blank page is the fastest choice of all for a home page.)

5. **Click the Close button to exit the Preferences dialog.**

TIP

Visit your home page at any time by clicking the Home button on the toolbar. If the Home button doesn't appear on your toolbar, you can add it by choosing View⇨Customize Toolbar.

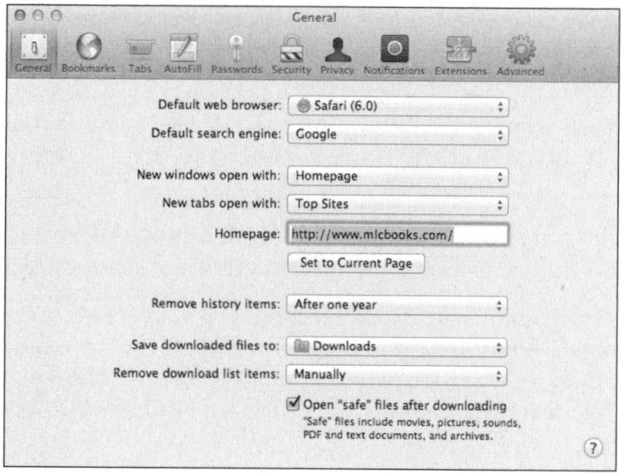
General
General
Bookmarks
Tabs
AutoFill
Passwords
Security
Privacy
Notifications
Extensions
Advanced
Default web browser:
Safari (6.0)
Default search engine:
Google
New windows open with:
Homepage
New tabs open with:
Top Sites
Homepage:
http://www.mlcbooks.com/
Set to Current Page
Remove history items:
After one year
Save downloaded files to:
Downloads
Remove download list items:
Manually
Open "safe" files after downloading
"Safe" files include movies, pictures, sounds, PDF and text documents, and archives.

Figure 9-3: Adding your own home page is easy.

Adding and Using Bookmarks

No doubt about it: Bookmarks make the web a friendly place. As you collect bookmarks in Safari, you can immediately jump from one site to another with a single click of the Bookmarks menu or the buttons on the Bookmarks bar.

To add a bookmark, first navigate to the desired page and then do any of the following:

- **Choose Bookmarks⇨Add Bookmark.**
- **Press ⌘+D.**

  Safari displays a sheet where you can enter the name for the bookmark and also select where it appears (on the Bookmarks bar, Top Sites display, or Bookmarks menu).

- **Drag the icon next to the web address from the Address field to the Bookmarks bar.**

  This trick works also with other applications besides Safari, including in a Mail message or a Messages conversation. Drag the icon from the Safari Address field to the other application window, and the web page link is added to your document.

You can also drag a link on the current page to the Bookmarks bar, but note that doing this adds a bookmark only for the page that corresponds to the link — not the current page.

To jump to a bookmark, use any of the following methods:

✔ **Choose it from the Bookmarks menu.**

If the bookmark is contained in a folder, which I discuss later in this section, move your cursor over the folder name to show its contents and then click the bookmark.

✔ **Click the bookmark on the Bookmarks bar.**

If you've added a large number of items to the Bookmarks bar, click the More icon on the edge of the Bookmarks bar to display the rest of the buttons.

✔ **Click the Show All Bookmarks button (which looks like a small, opened book) on the Bookmarks bar, and then click the desired bookmark.**

The Bookmarks pane that you see in Figure 9-4 appears — complete with a swanky Cover Flow display — so you can review each collection of bookmarks at your leisure. As you might expect, Safari's Cover Flow works just like the Cover Flow view does in a Finder window.

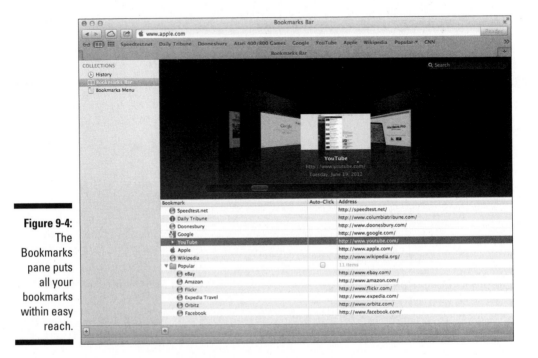

Figure 9-4: The Bookmarks pane puts all your bookmarks within easy reach.

The more bookmarks you add, the more unwieldy the Bookmarks menu and the Bookmarks pane become. To keep things organized, choose Bookmarks⇨Add Bookmark Folder and then type a name for the new folder. With folders, you can organize your bookmarks into *collections,* which appear in the column at the left of the Bookmarks pane (or as separate submenus in the Bookmarks menu). You can drag bookmarks into the new folder to help reduce the clutter.

To delete a bookmark or a folder from the Bookmarks window, click it and then press Delete.

Downloading Files

A huge chunk of the fun that you'll find on the web is the ability to download images and other files. If you've visited a site that offers files for downloading, typically you just click the Download button or the download file link, and Safari takes care of the rest. While the file is downloading, feel free to continue browsing or even download additional files; the Downloads status list helps you keep track of what's going on and when everything will be finished transferring. To display the Download status list from the keyboard, press ⌘+Option+L. You can also click the Download button at the upper-right corner of the window to display the Download list.

By default, Safari saves any downloaded files to the Downloads folder that appears in your Dock, which I like and use. To change the specified location where downloaded files are stored — for example, if you'd like to save them directly to the desktop or scan them automatically with an antivirus application — follow these steps:

1. **Choose Safari⇨Preferences or press ⌘+, (comma).**

2. **Click the General tab (refer to Figure 9-3), and then click the Save Downloaded Files To pop-up menu.**

3. **Choose Other.**

4. **Navigate to the location where you want the files to be stored.**

5. **Click the Select button.**

6. **Click the Close button to exit Preferences.**

To download a specific image that appears on a web page, move your pointer over the image, right-click, and choose Save Image As from the pop-up menu that appears. Safari prompts you for the location where you want to store the file.

You can choose to automatically open files that Safari considers safe — things such as movies, text files, and PDF files that are *very* unlikely to store a virus or a damaging macro. By default, the Open "Safe" Files after Downloading check box is selected in the General pane. However, if you're interested in preventing *anything* you download from running until you've manually checked it with your antivirus application, you can deselect the check box and breathe easy.

Luckily, Safari has matured to the point where it can seamlessly handle most multimedia file types that it encounters. However, if you've downloaded a multimedia file and Safari doesn't seem to be able to play or display it, try loading the file in QuickTime Player. QuickTime Player can recognize a huge number of audio, video, and image formats. (I also recommend the freeware *Perian QuickTime plug-in*, available for downloading from `http://perian.org`. Installing Perian adds support to QuickTime Player for a wide range of additional audio and video formats.)

Using History

To keep track of where you've been, you can display the History list by clicking the History menu. To return to a page in the list, just choose it from the History menu. Note that Safari also arranges older history items by the date you visited the site, so you can easily jump back a couple of days to that page you forgot to bookmark!

In fact, Safari also searches the History list automatically when it fills in an address that you're typing — that's the feature I mention in the earlier section, "Visiting Websites."

To view your Top Sites thumbnail screen, press ⌘+Shift+1 or choose Show Top Sites from the History menu. You can also click the Top Sites button on the toolbar.

If you're worried about security and would rather not keep track of where you've been online, I show you how to clear the contents of the History file in the "Handling ancient history" section, later in this chapter.

Tabs Are Your Browsing Friends

Safari also offers *tabbed browsing,* which many folks use to display (and organize) multiple web pages at the same time. For example, if you're doing a bit of comparison shopping for a new piece of hardware among different online stores, tabs are ideal.

When you hold down the ⌘ key and click a link or bookmark by using tabs, a tab that represents the new page appears at the top of the Safari window (as shown in Figure 9-5). Just click the tab to switch to that page. (If you don't hold down ⌘, things revert to business as usual, and Safari replaces the contents of the window with the new page.) If you hold down *both* Shift and ⌘ while you click, Safari opens a new tab and automatically switches to the new tab.

You can also open a new tab by clicking the plus sign that appears at the upper-right corner of the Safari window (or by pressing ⌘+T).

MacBook owners, don't forget Safari's two new gestures that control tabs! With multiple tabs active, you can

✔ Pinch to display them all in a new *tab view* (as shown in Figure 9-5).

✔ Swipe to switch between tabs.

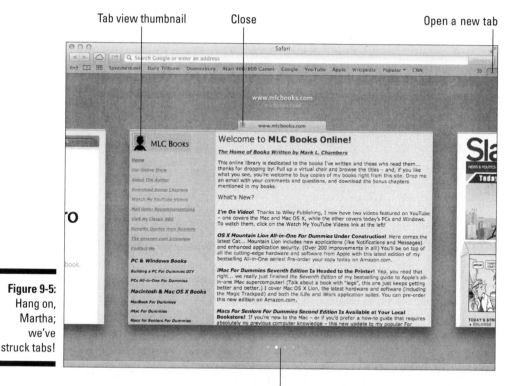

Figure 9-5: Hang on, Martha; we've struck tabs!

Tab view thumbnail   Close   Open a new tab

Tab navigation

To display your tabs in tab view without a trackpad — if you're using an external pointing device instead — click the Show All Tabs button that appears at the right side of the Safari window (next to the Open a New Tab button). From tab view, you can click the white dots that appear below the thumbnails to view your tabs, and click any tab thumbnail to switch immediately to that tab. To close a tab in tab view, click the Close button at the top of the thumbnail.

To fine-tune your tabbed browsing experience, choose Safari⇨Preferences to display the Preferences dialog; then click Tabs. From here, you can specify whether a new tab or window automatically becomes the active window within Safari.

Done with a page? You can remove a tabbed page by clicking the X button next to the tab's title.

Saving Web Pages

If you've encountered a page that you'd like to load later, you can save it to disk in its entirety. (Just the text, mind you, not the images.) Follow these steps:

1. **Display the desired page.**

2. **Choose File⇨Save As or press ⌘+S.**

3. **In the Save As text field, type a name for the saved page.**

4. **From the Where pop-up menu, navigate to the location where you want to store the file in your system.**

   To expand the sheet to allow navigation to any location in your system, click the button with the downward arrow.

5. **Click the Format pop-up menu to choose the format for the saved page.**

   Usually, you'll want to choose Web Archive, which saves the entire page and can be displayed just as you see it. (Note that some pages that use plug-ins or offer dynamic content may require an Internet connection to display properly as a web archive.) However, if you want to save just the HTML source code, choose Page Source.

6. **Click Save to begin the download process.**

   After the saved file has been created, double-click it to load it in Safari.

A quick word about printing a page in Safari: Some combinations of background and text colors might conspire to render your printed copy practically worthless. In a case like that, use your printer's grayscale setting (if it has one) or deselect the Print Backgrounds check box in the Print dialog (doing so can save you quite a bit of ink or toner). Alternatively, you can simply click and drag to select the text on the page, press ⌘+C to copy it, and then paste the text into TextEdit, Word, or Pages, where you can print the page on a less-offensive background (while still keeping the text formatting largely untouched). You can also save the contents of a page as plain text, as I just demonstrated.

If you'd rather e-mail the contents of a web page to a friend — or just send the friend a link to the page, which is faster — choose either File➪Mail Contents of This Page or File➪Mail Link to This Page. (From the keyboard, press ⌘+I to send the contents in an e-mail message or press ⌘+Shift+I to send a link in e-mail. If you've added the Mail button to your Safari toolbar, one click does the job.) Mail loads automatically, complete with a prepared e-mail message. Just address it to the recipients and then click Send!

Protecting Your Privacy

No chapter on Safari would be complete without a discussion of security, against both outside intrusion from the Internet and prying eyes around your MacBook. Hence this last section, which covers protecting your privacy.

Although diminutive, the padlock icon that appears at the left side of the Address box when you're connected to a secure website means a great deal! A *secure site* encrypts the information that you send and receive, making it much harder for those of unscrupulous ideals to obtain private data, such as credit card numbers and personal information. You can click the padlock icon (next to the site name) to display the security certificate in use on that particular site. A secure website address begins with the protocol prefix `https:` instead of `http:`. (The extra *s* stands for *secure.* A Good Thing.)

Yes, there are such things as bad cookies

First, here's a definition of this ridiculous term: A *cookie,* a small file that a website automatically saves on your hard drive, contains information that the site can use on your future visits. For example, a site might save a cookie to preserve your site preferences for the next time or — in the case of a shopping site such as Amazon.com — to identify you automatically and help customize the offerings that you see.

In and of themselves, cookies aren't bad things. Unlike a virus, a cookie file isn't going to replicate itself or wreak havoc on your system, and only the original site can read the cookie that it creates. However, many folks don't appreciate acting as a gracious host for a slew of little snippets of personal information. (Not to mention that some cookies have highly suggestive names, which could lead to all sorts of conclusions. End of story.)

You can choose to accept all cookies or you can opt to disable cookies altogether. You can also set Safari to accept cookies only from the sites you choose to visit. To change your *Cookie Acceptance Plan* (or CAP, for those who absolutely crave acronyms), follow these steps:

1. **Choose Safari➪Preferences.**

2. **Click the Privacy toolbar button.**

   Safari displays the preference settings shown in Figure 9-6.

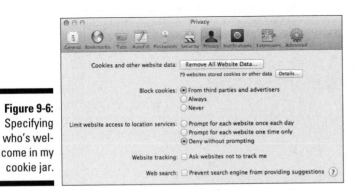

Figure 9-6: Specifying who's welcome in my cookie jar.

3. **Choose how to block cookies via these radio button choices:**

   • *From Third Parties and Advertisers:* I use this option, which allows sites such as Amazon.com to work correctly without allowing a barrage of superfluous cookies.

   • *Always:* Block cookies entirely.

   • *Never:* Accept all cookies.

4. **To view the cookies currently on your system, click the Details button.**

   If a site's cookies are blocked, you might have to take care of things manually, such as by providing a password that used to be read automatically from the cookie.

5. **Click the Close button to save your changes.**

Feeling nervous about the data stored by the websites you visit? You can delete *all* that stored information with a single click. From the Privacy pane in the Safari Preferences window, click the Remove All Website Data button. You'll be asked to confirm your draconian decision.

The Privacy pane also includes the Ask Websites Not to Track Me check box, which works . . . *sometimes.* Unfortunately, each website decides whether to honor Safari's request for privacy. (Also, some sites — such as Amazon.com — use tracking legitimately, to keep track of your likes and purchases each time you return.) If you're especially worried about leaving a trail of breadcrumbs behind you on the web, however, I recommend selecting this check box.

Cleaning your cache

Safari speeds up the loading of websites by storing often-used images and multimedia files in a temporary storage, or *cache,* folder. Naturally, the files in your cache folder can be displayed (hint), which could lead to assumptions (hint, hint) about the sites you've been visiting (hint, hint, hint). (Tactful, ain't I?)

Luckily, Safari makes it easy to dump the contents of your cache file. Just close all tabs and open windows, choose Safari⇨Empty Cache, and then click Empty to confirm that you want to clean up your cache.

Handling ancient history

As you might imagine, your History file leaves a very clear set of footprints indicating where you've been on the web. To delete the contents of the History menu, close all open Safari tabs and windows, and then choose History⇨Clear History (at the very bottom of the History menu).

Safari also allows you to specify an amount of time to retain entries in your History file. Open the Safari Preferences dialog, click the General tab, and then click the Remove History Items pop-up menu and specify the desired amount of time. Items can be rolled off daily, weekly, biweekly, monthly, or yearly.

Avoiding those @*!^%$ pop-up ads

I hate pop-up ads, and I'm sure you do, too. To block most of those pop-up windows with advertisements for everything from low-rate mortgages to "sure-thing" Internet casinos, click the Safari menu and verify that Block Pop-Up Windows is selected. (If it's not selected, click the menu item to toggle it on.)

From time to time, you might run across a website that actually does something *constructive* with pop-up windows, such as present a download or login prompt. If you need to temporarily deactivate pop-up blocking, press ⌘+Shift+K to toggle it off. Then press ⌘+Shift+K again to turn pop-up blocking back on after you've finished with the site.

Chapter 10

iCloud Is Made for MacBooks

*R*eaders often ask me to name my favorite reasons why they should switch — that is, why should a Windows user who *thinks* all is well move to the Apple universe? Of course, I always mention the superior hardware and how much better of a job Mountain Lion does as an operating system. My favorite selling point is *innovation.* Apple comes up with the best ideas first, and everyone else plays catch-up.

Here's the perfect example: The folks at Apple got tired of constantly synchronizing their iOS devices with their computers over a USB cable. Remember those archaic days? When you took a photo with your iPhone or created a new document with your iPad, your new additions just *sat* there (in their original location) until you had a chance to sync your device with your MacBook. Ah, but with Apple's iCloud functionality, your stuff gets *automatically* synchronized and backed up across the Internet!

In this chapter, I save you the trouble of researching all the benefits of iCloud. Heck, that's one of the reasons why you bought this book, right?

So How Does iCloud Work, Anyway?

Today's Apple iOS devices can display or play the same media: photos, music, books, TV shows, and such. (Heck, some iOS devices, such as your iPhone and iPod touch, can even share applications that you install.) Therefore, it makes sense to effortlessly share all your digital media across these devices, and that's what iCloud is all about. Apple calls this synchronization *pushing.*

Here's a look at how the pushing process works. Imagine that you just completed a Pages document (an invitation for your son's birthday party) on your MacBook, but you're at the office, and you need to get the document to your family so that they can edit and print it using your son's iPad.

Before iCloud, you had to attach the document to an e-mail message, or upload it to some type of online storage such as Microsoft's SkyDrive, and then a family member had to download and save the document to the iPad before working with it. With iCloud, you simply save the document on your MacBook, and OS X automatically pushes the document to the iPad! Your document appears on the iPad, ready to be opened, edited, and printed — and it appears on any other iOS 5 (or later) devices as well. Figure 10-1 gives you an idea of what's happening in the background when one of your devices pushes data using iCloud.

iCloud isn't limited to just digital media, though. Your MacBook can also automatically synchronize your e-mail, Calendar calendars, and Contacts entries with other iOS5 (or later) devices across the Internet, so staying in touch is much easier (no matter where you are or which device you're using at the moment).

Apple also throws in 5GB of free online storage that you can use for all sorts of things: not only digital media files but also documents that you'd like to save online for safekeeping. In fact, items you buy through the iTunes Store — music, video, and applications — do not count against your 5GB limit. (More on how you can expand that 5GB limit later in the chapter.)

Figure 10-1:
iCloud works by pushing data between all your iOS devices.

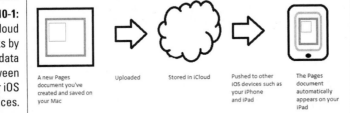

A new Pages document you've created and saved on your Mac   Uploaded   Stored in iCloud   Pushed to other iOS devices such as your iPhone and iPad   The Pages document automatically appears on your iPad

To join the iCloud revolution, you need an Apple ID. If you didn't create an Apple ID during the initial Mountain Lion setup, you can create one from within the App Store. To see how, read Chapter 2.

Configuring iCloud

You control all the settings for iCloud from Mountain Lion's iCloud pane in System Preferences (shown in Figure 10-2). Click the System Preferences icon in the Dock and then click the iCloud icon. At the sign-in prompt, enter your Apple ID and your password. System Preferences will then guide you through basic iCloud configuration with a number of questions.

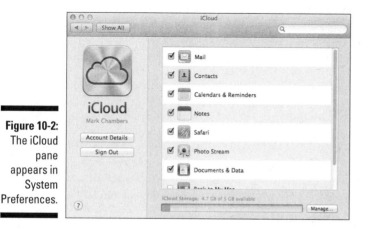

Figure 10-2: The iCloud pane appears in System Preferences.

Most of the check boxes on the iCloud Preferences pane control whether a particular type of data is pushed among all your Macs, iOS devices, and even Windows PCs — data like Contacts entries, Mail messages, and calendars in Calendar. However, you can enable three other unique features from this pane as well:

- ✔ **Photo Stream:** Turning on Photo Stream allows your laptop to automatically receive photos from your iOS devices. Take a photo with your iPhone, for example, and that image is immediately pushed to your MacBook, iPad, and iPod touch. On the MacBook, however, Photo Stream goes one step further: The photos appear automatically in iPhoto or Aperture within a special album titled *Photo Stream*.

  To turn on Photo Stream in iPhoto, choose iPhoto⇨Preferences, click the Photo Stream button, and then select all three check boxes. Photo Stream must also be turned on in the iCloud Preferences pane.

✔ **Back to My Mac:** If you enable Back to My Mac, you can remotely control your MacBook from another Mac computer (or vice versa) using Mountain Lion's Screen Sharing feature. (Read about that feature in Chapter 13.) You can also transfer files between the two computers. Back to My Mac works over both a broadband Internet connection and a local network. Available Mac computers show up in the Shared section of the Finder window sidebar. Note that you must manually turn on Screen Sharing in the System Preferences Sharing pane before you can remotely control another Mac.

✔ **Find My Mac:** Talk about Buck Rogers, this feature is wonderful for MacBook owners! Imagine locating a lost or stolen MacBook from your iPhone or iPad — the laptop's current location appears on a map, just as if you were using your iOS Map app. (You can also use Find My Mac from the iCloud website, at www.icloud.com.) Now think about this: With Find My Mac, you can even lock or completely wipe your laptop's drive *remotely*, preventing unauthorized use and erasing your private data! After you access your MacBook from another Mac or an iOS device, you can play a sound on the laptop's speakers, send a message to be displayed on-screen, remotely lock the machine, or remotely wipe the drive.

After you lock or wipe the drive, though, you can't locate your MacBook on the map again. *These data protection measures should be taken only if you have no other recourse!*

Managing Your iCloud Storage

Naturally, Apple knows that you're curious about how much space you've taken up in your own personal iCloud. To monitor your iCloud storage, click the Manage button at the bottom-right corner of the iCloud Preferences pane. From the sheet that appears, you can see how much space you're using for document and data storage, as shown in Figure 10-3.

Click the data type in the left column, and iCloud displays the amount of storage space that's being used for that data. For instance, in Figure 10-3, I'm checking the amount taken by my iPad and iPhone backups. (I set both my iPad and iPhone to back up wirelessly to my iCloud storage.) Other items that might appear in this sheet include Mail and selected iPad and iPhone apps that support iCloud.

If you find yourself running out of iCloud storage space, delete any stored item by selecting it in the list at the right side of the sheet and then clicking Delete.

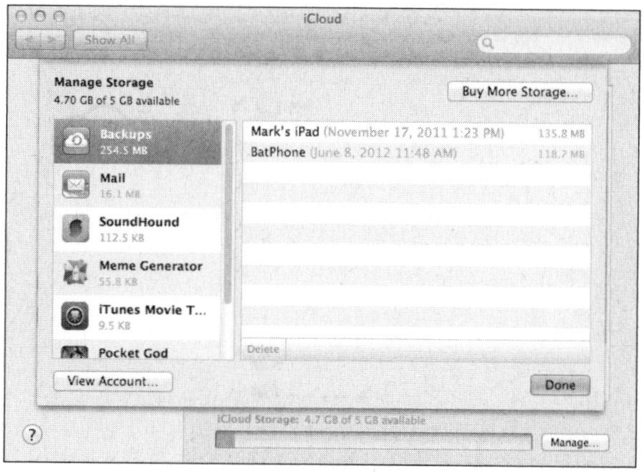

Figure 10-3:
Checking on
your iCloud
storage.

And if you need more elbow room than 5GB, Apple is happy to provide 10, 20, or even 50GB of additional storage for an annual subscription fee of $20, $40, or $100 per year, respectively. Click the Manage button on the iCloud pane in System Preferences, and then click the Buy More Storage button.

Chapter 11

Your Laptop Goes Multiuser

*E*verybody wants a piece — of your laptop, that is.

Perhaps you live in a busy household with kids, significant others, grandparents, and a wide selection of friends — all of them clamoring for a chance to spend time on the Internet, take care of homework, or enjoy a good game.

On the other hand, your MacBook might occupy a college classroom or boardroom at your office — and suddenly your classmate or coworker wants his own Private iDaho on-the-road warrior, complete with a reserved spot on the drive and his own hand-picked attractive desktop background. (Even flying at 30,000 feet, your coworker will be eyeing your MacBook.)

Before you throw your hands up in the air in defeat, read this chapter and take heart! Here you find all the step-by-step procedures, explanations, and tips to help you build a *safe* multiuser MacBook that's accessible to everyone with clean hands.

Oh, and you still get to use it, too. And, no, that's not being selfish.

Once Upon a Time (an Access Fairy Tale)

Okay, so you don't have Cinderella, Snow White, or that porridge-loving kid with the trespassing problem. Instead, you have your brother Bob.

Every time Bob visits your place, it seems he needs to do "something" on the Internet, or he needs a moment with your MacBook Air to bang out a quick message, using his web-based e-mail application. Unfortunately, Bob's forays onto your laptop always end up changing stuff, such as your desktop settings, Contacts database, and Safari bookmarks.

What you need, good reader, is a visit from the Account Fairy. Your problem is that you have but a single user account on your system, and Mountain Lion thinks that Bob is *you*. By turning your MacBook into a multiuser system and giving Bob his own account, Mountain Lion can tell the difference between the two of you, keeping your druthers separate!

With a unique user account, Mountain Lion can track all sorts of things for Bob, leaving your computing environment blissfully pristine. A user account keeps track of stuff such as

- Contacts cards
- Safari bookmarks and settings
- Desktop settings (including background images, screen resolutions, and Finder tweaks)
- iTunes Libraries, just in case Bob brings his own music (resigned "sigh")

Plus, Bob gets his own reserved Home folder on your laptop's hard drive, so he'll quit complaining about how he can't find his files. Oh, and did I mention how user accounts keep others from accessing *your* stuff? And how you can lock Bob out of where-he-should-not-be, such as certain applications, Messages, Mail, and websites (including that offshore Internet casino site that he's hooked on)?

User accounts affect just about everything you can do in Mountain Lion and on your laptop. The moral of my little tale? A Mark's Maxim to the rescue:

Assign others their own user accounts, and let Mountain Lion keep track of everything. Then you can share your MacBook with others and still live happily ever after!™

Big-Shot Administrator Stuff

Get one thing straight right off the bat: *You* are the administrator of your MacBook. In network-speak, an *administrator* (or *admin* for short) is the one with the power to Do Unto Others — creating new accounts, deciding who gets access to what, and generally running the multiuser show. In other words, think of yourself as the Monarch of OS X. (The ruler, not the butterfly.)

I always recommend that you have only one (or perhaps two) accounts with administrator-level access on any computer. In this way, you can be assured that no one can monkey with your laptop while you're away from the keyboard. So why might you want a second admin account? Well, if you're away from your laptop — think "daughter takes it with her on trip to Europe" — you might need to assign a second administrator account to a *trusted* individual who knows as much about your road warrior as you do. (Tell 'em to buy a copy of this book.) That way, if something breaks or an account needs to be tweaked in some way, the other person can take care of it while you're absent (but without giving that person access to your personal data).

In the following sections, I explain the typical duties of a first-class MacBook administrator.

Deciding who needs what access

The three most common user account levels are

- ✔ **Admin (administrator):** See the beginning of this section.
- ✔ **Standard level:** Perfect for most users, these accounts allow access to just about everything but don't let the user make drastic changes to Mountain Lion or create new accounts.
- ✔ **Managed with parental controls level:** These accounts are standard accounts with specific limits assigned by you or another admin account.

Assign other folks standard-level accounts, and then decide whether each new account needs to be modified to restrict access as a managed account. Another Mark's Maxim is in order:

Never **assign an account admin-level access unless you deem it truly necessary.™**

Standard accounts are quick and easy to set up, and I think they provide the perfect compromise between access and security. You'll find that standard access allows your users to do just about anything they need to do, with a minimum of hassle.

Managed accounts (with parental controls) are highly configurable so you can make sure that your kids don't end up trashing the hard drive, sending junk mail, or engaging in unmonitored chatting. (*Note:* Attention, all parents, teachers, and those folks designing a single public access account for a library or organization — this means *you.*)

Adding users

All right, Mark, enough pregame jabbering — show this good reader how to set up new accounts! Your laptop already has one admin-level account set up for you (created during the initial Mountain Lion setup process), and you need to be logged in with that account to add a user. To add a new account, follow these steps:

1. **In the Users & Groups pane (from System Preferences), click the New User button (plus sign) at the bottom of the accounts list to display the empty user record sheet that you see in Figure 11-1.**

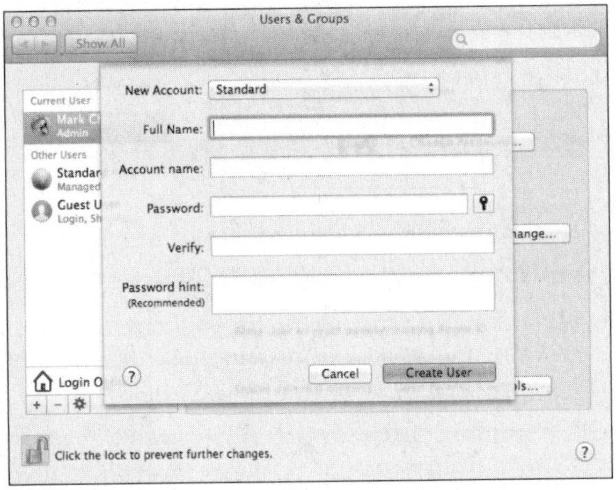

Figure 11-1:
Fill out those fields, and you have a new user.

If the New User button is disabled and you can't click it, click the padlock at the bottom left of the System Preferences pane and provide your password to unlock the Users & Groups pane.

2. **Select the access level for this user from the New Account pop-up menu.**

By default, the user receives a standard level account. You can also choose an administrator account, a managed standard account with parental controls already enabled, or a sharing-only account.

The sharing-only account allows the user to copy or open shared files from your MacBook remotely (from another computer), but that user can't directly log in to your laptop.

3. **In the Full Name text box, type the name that you want to display for this account (both in the Current User list and on the Login screen) and then press Tab to move to the next field.**

OS X automatically generates a *short name* in the Account Name field for use as your screen and buddy name in Messages and various network applications. The short name is also the name of the folder that OS X creates on the computer's hard drive for this user. You can keep the default short name or type a new one, but it cannot contain any spaces.

4. **Press Tab again.**

5. **In the Password text box, type the password for the new account.**

Click the button with the key icon next to the Password field, and Mountain Lion is happy to display Password Assistant, complete with a suggestion. Click the Suggestion pop-up menu to see additional suggestions. You can choose the length of the password and select among several types: letters and numbers, numbers only, memorable, completely random, or even government-quality. Password Assistant automatically copies the current password you're considering in the Password text box.

As always, when you enter a password or its verification, OS X displays bullet characters for security.

6. **Press Tab, type the password in the Verify text box, and press Tab again.**

7. **(Optional) If you decide to use the password hint feature, you can enter a short sentence or question in the Password Hint text box.**

The hint is displayed after three unsuccessful attempts at entering the account password.

From a security standpoint, password hints are taboo. (Personally, I *never* use 'em. If someone is having a problem logging in to a computer I administer, you better believe I want to know *why*.) Therefore, despite the recommendation that Mountain Lion shows here, I strongly recommend that you skip this field. If you decide to offer a hint, *keep it vague!* Avoid hints like, "Your password is the name of the Wookie in Star Wars." *Geez.*

8. **Click the Create User button to finish and create the account.**

The new account shows up in the Current User list and in the Login screen.

Each user's Home folder has the same default subfolders, including Movies, Music, Pictures, and Sites. A user can create new subfolders within his or her Home folder at any time.

Here's one more neat fact about a user's Home folder: No matter what the account level, most of the contents of a Home folder can't be viewed by other users. (Yes, that includes admin-level users. This way, everyone using your MacBook Pro gets his or her own little area of privacy.) In the Home folder, only the Sites and Public folders can be accessed by other users — and only in a limited fashion. More on these folders later in this chapter. (And read all about Home folders in Chapter 5.)

Modifying user accounts

Next, consider the basic modifications that you can make to a user account, such as changing existing information or selecting a new picture to represent that user's unique personality.

To edit an existing account, log in with your admin account, display the System Preferences window, and click Users & Groups to display the account list. Then follow these steps:

1. **In the list to the left of the window, click the account that you want to change.**

   If the accounts in the list are disabled and you can't select one, you must unlock the Users & Groups pane. Click the lock at the bottom left of the System Preferences pane (and type your password, if prompted).

2. **Edit the settings that you need to change.**

   Examples include enabling administrator rights for an account temporarily (by selecting the Allow User to Administer This Computer check box) and changing the account password (by clicking the Change Password button).

3. **Click the square picture well (the square that displays the image) to specify the thumbnail image that appears in the Login list next to the account name.**

   Apple provides a number of good images in the preview collection. Just click a thumbnail to select it.

4. **To replace your account image, drag a new image from a Finder window or the iPhoto window and drop it into the picture well.**

   - *To choose an image from the default set of Mountain Lion icons:* Click the picture well, click the Defaults tab, click the desired image, and then click Done (see Figure 11-2).

   - *To choose an icon image from those you've recently used:* Click the Recents tab, click the desired image, and then click Done.

Alternatively, you can click the picture well and click the Camera tab to grab a picture from your MacBook's built-in FaceTime HD camera. When you're set to take the photo, click the camera icon and then click Done to accept it. *Most* cool.

5. **After you make your changes, press ⌘+Q to save them and close the System Preferences window.**

Figure 11-2: Choose the image that best represents a user.

Standard-level users have some control over their accounts — they're not helpless, after all. Standard users can log in, open System Preferences, and click Users & Groups to change the account password or picture as well as the My Card assigned to them in the Mountain Lion Contacts application. All standard users can also set up login items, which I cover later in this chapter. Note, however, that managed users might not have access to System Preferences, so they can't make changes. (Read about this in the upcoming section, "Managing access settings for an account.")

I banish thee, mischievous user!

Not all user accounts last forever. Students graduate, coworkers quit, kids move out of the house (at last!), and Bob might even find a significant other who has a faster cable modem. We can only hope.

Anyway, no matter what the reason, you can delete a user account at any time. Log in with your admin account, display the Users & Groups pane in System Preferences, and then follow these steps to eradicate an account:

1. **In the user list to the left of the window, click the account that you want to delete.**

2. **Click the Delete User button (which bears the Minus Sign of Doom).**

   OS X displays the confirmation sheet that you see in Figure 11-3.

Figure 11-3:
This is your last chance to save the stuff from a deleted user account.

Note that the contents of the user's Home folder can be saved in a disk image in the Deleted Users folder (just in case you need to retrieve something). Alternatively, you can choose to leave the deleted user's Home folder as is, without removing it.

If you're absolutely sure you won't be dating that person again, select the Delete the Home Folder radio button (which doesn't save anything in the Deleted Users folder). You regain all the drive space that was being occupied by the contents of the deleted user's Home folder. As an extra measure of protection, you can also choose to securely erase the contents of the deleted user's Home folder.

3. **To delete the account, click Delete User. If you're not sure, click the Cancel button to abort and return to the Accounts list.**

Time once again for a Mark's Maxim:

Always **delete unnecessary user accounts. Otherwise, you're leaving holes in your laptop's security.™**

Working with the Guest account

The *Guest* account is a convenient method of granting someone temporary access to your MacBook. In fact, your guest doesn't even need a password to log in! Your Guest account has all the attributes of a standard account, so the visitor has little chance of accidentally (or purposefully) damaging your system. However, after the guest user logs out, the Guest account is "flushed," and all the data and files that person created using the account are deleted automatically. (This allows the next guest to start with a clean slate.)

By default, the Guest account is disabled. To turn on this feature, open System Preferences, click Users & Groups, and then click the Guest User entry in the list. (You may have to click the Lock icon in the lower-left corner of the Users & Groups pane and provide your admin password before you can continue.) Click the Allow Guests to Log In to This Computer check box to enable it.

Oh, and don't forget that you can enable specific parental controls for the Guest account, just as you can for any other standard-level account. This feature should come in handy if your child has a slumber party coming up this weekend.

Setting up login items and parental controls

Every account on your MacBook can be customized. Understandably, some settings are accessible only to admin-level accounts, and others can be adjusted by standard-level accounts. In the following sections, I introduce you to the things that can be enabled (or disabled) in a user account.

Automating with login items

Login items are applications or documents that can be set to launch or load automatically as soon as a specific user logs in — for example, Apple Mail or Contacts. In fact, a user must be logged in to add or remove login items. Even an admin-level account can't change the login items for another user.

A user must have access to the Users & Groups pane in the System Preferences window to use login items. As you can read in the following section, a user can be locked out of System Preferences, which makes it more difficult for login items to be deleted for that account. (Go figure.) Therefore, if the account is managed and access to System Preferences has been turned off, an administrator will have to enable the account's access to System Preferences, allowing the managed user to delete login items.

To set login items for your account, follow these steps:

1. **Click the System Preferences icon in the Dock, and then click the Users & Groups icon.**

2. **Click the Login Items tab to display the settings that you see in Figure 11-4.**

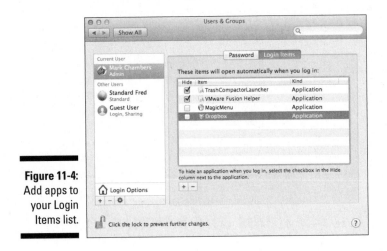

Figure 11-4:
Add apps to your Login Items list.

3. **Click the Add button (with the plus sign) to display a file selection sheet.**

4. **Navigate to the application you want to launch each time you log in, click it to select it, and then click Add.**

   If you're in the mood to drag and drop, just drag the applications you want to add from a Finder window and drop them directly into the list.

5. **Press ⌘+Q to quit System Preferences and save your changes.**

If the application is running at the moment, you can take an easy shortcut and avoid these steps: Simply right-click the application icon in the Dock and choose Open at Login from the pop-up menu that appears.

Login items are launched in the order in which they appear in the list, so feel free to drag the items into any order you like.

Managing access settings for an account

A standard-level account with restrictions is a *managed* account. (You can read about these accounts earlier in this chapter.) With these accounts, you can restrict access to many different places in Mountain Lion and your laptop's applications by using *parental controls*. (Naturally, admin-level accounts don't have parental controls because an admin account has no restrictions.)

In short, parental controls come in handy in preventing users — family members, students, coworkers, friends, or the public at large — from damaging your files, your software, or Mountain Lion itself. If an account has been restricted with parental controls, the account description changes from Standard to Managed in the Accounts list.

To display the parental controls for a standard account, start here:

1. **Log in with an admin-level account.**

2. **Open System Preferences and then click Users & Groups.**

3. **Click the desired Standard account in the list and then select the Enable Parental Controls check box.**

   If necessary, click the Lock icon in the lower-left corner to confirm your access.

Now click the Open Parental Controls button to display the five categories (tabs) that you see in Figure 11-5:

✔ **Apps:** These settings (which I discuss in more detail in a second) affect what the user can do in Mountain Lion as well as what the Finder itself looks like to that user.

✔ **Web:** Mountain Lion offers three levels of control for websites:

   • *Allow Unrestricted Access:* Select this radio button to allow unfettered access for this user.

   • *Try to Limit Access:* You can allow Safari to automatically block websites it deems adult. To specify particular sites that the automatic "adult filter" should allow or deny, click the Customize button.

   • *Allow Access to Only These Websites:* Choose this radio button to specify which websites the user can view. To add a website, click the Add (plus sign) button, and respond to the Mountain Lion prompt for a title and the website address.

✔ **People:** You can specify whether the user can join in Game Center multiplayer games, as well as allow or prevent the user from adding friends in Game Center.

   Select the Limit Mail and Limit Messages check boxes to specify the e-mail and instant messaging addresses that this user can communicate with. (Note that these options affect only Apple Mail and Messages; other mail clients, web-based mail, instant messaging applications, and audio/video chat applications aren't controlled.) To add an address to which the user can e-mail or chat, click the Add button, which bears the familiar plus sign.

   If you want a notification if the user is attempting to send an e-mail to someone not in the list, select the Send Permission Requests To check box and then type your e-mail address in the text box.

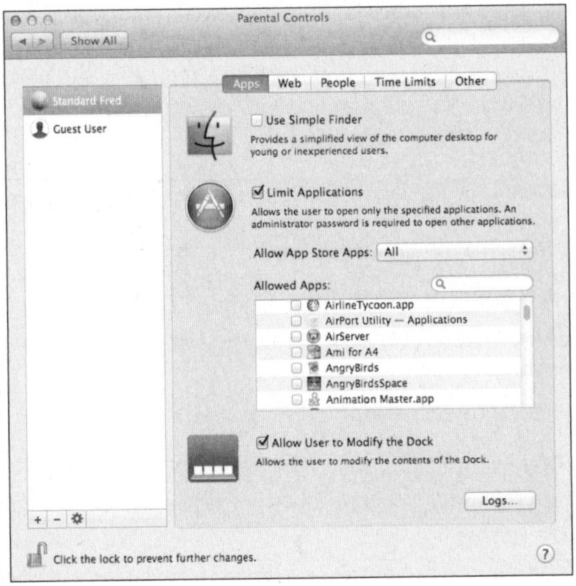

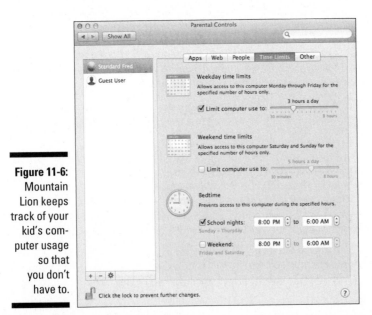

Figure 11-5:
You can restrict access to many functions in a Standard account.

Figure 11-5:
You can restrict access to many functions in a Standard account.

✔ **Time Limits:** Parents, click the Time Limits button, and you'll shout with pure joy! Check out the options on this pane in Figure 11-6. You can limit an account to a certain number of hours of usage per weekday (Weekday Time Limits) and per weekend day (Weekend Time Limits), and set a bedtime computer curfew time for both weekdays (called "School Nights" here) and weekend days.

Figure 11-6:
Mountain Lion keeps track of your kid's computer usage so that you don't have to.

✔ **Other:** These settings control the Dictionary and hardware devices such as your printer and DVD burner. They include

- *Hide Profanity in Dictionary:* With this check box selected, profane terms are hidden in the Dictionary for this user.

- *Limit Printer Administration:* With this check box selected, the user cannot modify the printers and printer queues in the Print & Scan pane in System Preferences. If this option is enabled, the user can still print to the default printer and switch to other assigned printers but can't add or delete printers or manage the OS X print queue. (If the print job encounters a problem, that user has to bug you to fix things. Go figure.)

- *Limit CD and DVD Burning:* Select this check box to prevent the user from recording CDs or DVDs via the built-in disc-recording features in OS X. (Note, however, that if you load a third-party recording program, such as Toast, the user can still record discs with it — unless you also disable access to that program in the Apps section.)

- *Disable Changing the Password:* Select this check box to prevent the user from changing the account password.

If you're creating a single standard-level account for an entire group of people to use — for example, if you want to leave the laptop in kiosk mode in one corner of the office or if everyone in a classroom will use the same account on the MacBook — I recommend disabling the ability to change the account password. (Oh, and please do me a favor . . . *don't* create a system with just one admin-level account that everyone is supposed to use! Instead, keep your one admin-level account close to your bosom and create a standard-level account for the Unwashed Horde.)

Mountain Lion keeps a number of different types of *text log files* (which track where the user goes on the Internet, the applications launched by the account, and the contents of any Messages conversations in which the user was a participant). Click the Logs button on any Parental Controls screen to monitor all the logs for a particular account.

You can always tell whether an account has been assigned parental controls because the account description changes from Standard to Managed in the User list.

Of particular importance are the Finder and the applications controls. Click the Apps tab (refer to Figure 11-5) to modify these settings:

✔ **Use Simple Finder:** I discuss the Simple Finder later in this section; it's a great idea for families and classrooms with smaller children.

✔ **Limit Applications:** When this option is selected, you can select the specific applications that appear to the user. These restrictions are in effect whether the user has access to the full Finder or just the Simple Finder.

From the Allow App Store Apps pop-up menu, you can choose to block the account from launching any applications purchased from the Apple App Store or limit the user to installed App Store apps rated for specific ages.

To allow access to all the applications of a specific type — App Store, Other Apps (such as the iLife and iWork suites), Widgets, and Utilities — select the check box next to the desired group heading. To restrict access to all applications within a group, select the check box next to any heading to deselect it. You can also toggle the restriction on and off for specific applications in these groups by clicking the triangle icon next to each group heading to expand the list and then selecting or deselecting the check box next to the desired applications. To locate a specific application, click in the Search box and type the application name.

To add a new application to the Allowed Apps list, drag its icon from the Finder and drop it in the list in the Other Apps group. After you add an application, it appears in the Other Apps group, and you can toggle access to it just like the applications in the named groups.

These settings can work hand-in-hand with Mountain Lion's new *Gatekeeper* feature, which prevents anyone from launching applications that were not downloaded from the App Store (or are not Apple-approved).

✔ **Allow User to Modify the Dock:** Select this check box, and the user can remove applications, documents, and folders from the Dock in the full Finder. (If you don't want the contents of the Dock changing according to the whims of other users, go ahead and deselect this check box.)

You can restrict your standard-level users even further by assigning them the Simple Finder set of limitations. The Simple Finder is a highly simplified version of the regular OS X Finder, complete with a simplified Dock that contains only the following: the Finder icon, the Trash icon, and the folders for the user's approved applications, documents, and shared files.

The Simple Finder is the network administrator's idea of a foolproof interface for OS X: A user can access only those system files and resources needed to do a job, with no room for tinkering or goofing off.

A Simple Finder user can still make the jump to the full version of the Finder by clicking the Finder menu, choosing Run Full Finder, and entering an admin-level username and password.

Would you like to set up a public access MacBook? You can also change the Automatic Login account from the Users & Groups pane. Click the Login Options button under the User list and then click the Automatic Login pop-up menu to choose the account that automatically logs in when OS X starts. On the confirmation sheet that appears, enter the account password and click

OK. Although I've made it clear elsewhere that Automatic Login is not a good security feature in many cases (such as with a laptop on the road), it can be a good feature for those preparing a Mac for public use because if you set the Automatic Login to your public standard-access account, OS X automatically uses the correct account if the Mac is rebooted or restarted.

You can always choose Log Out from the Apple menu (🍎) to log in under your own account, or use the fast user switching feature I describe in the next section.

Mundane Chores for the Multiuser Laptop

After you're hip on user accounts and the changes you can make to them, turn to a number of topics that affect all users of your MacBook — things such as how they log in, how a user can share information with everyone else on the computer, and how each user account can be protected from unscrupulous outsiders with state-of-the-art encryption. (Suddenly you're James Bond! I told you Mountain Lion would open new doors for you.)

Logging in and out in Mountain Lion For Dummies

Hey, how about the login screen itself? How do your users identify themselves? Time for another of my "Shortest books in the *For Dummies* series" special editions. (The title is practically longer than the entire book.)

Mountain Lion offers four methods of logging folks in to your multiuser laptop:

- ✔ **The username and password login:** This screen is the most secure type of login screen you'll see in Mountain Lion because you have to type your account username and your password. (A typical hacker isn't going to know all the usernames on your MacBook.) Press Return to complete the process.

  When you enter your password, you see bullets rather than your password because Mountain Lion displays bullet characters to ensure security. Otherwise, someone could simply look over your shoulder and see your password.

  Keep your laptop secure: Use a username and password login, and always choose a password that's tough to guess.™

✔ **The list login:** This login screen offers a good middle of the road between security and convenience. Click your account image in the list and type your password when the login screen displays the password prompt. Press Return to continue.

✔ **Fast user switching:** This feature allows another user to sit down and log in while the previous user's applications are still running in the background. This is perfect for a fast e-mail check or a scan of your eBay bids without forcing someone else completely off the MacBook. When you turn on Fast User Switching, Mountain Lion displays the currently active user's name at the right side of the Finder menu bar.

To switch to another account:

    a. Click the current user's name in the Finder menu (see Figure 11-7).

    b. Click the name of the user who wants to log in.

        Mountain Lion displays the login window, just as if the laptop had been rebooted.

        The previous user's stuff is still running, so you definitely shouldn't reboot or shut down the computer!

To switch back to the previous user:

    a. Click the username again on the Finder menu.

    b. Click the previous user's name.

        For security, Mountain Lion prompts you for that account's login password.

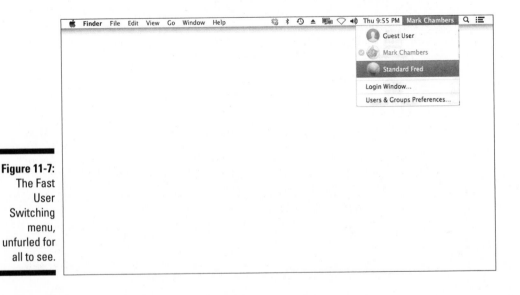

Figure 11-7:
The Fast
User
Switching
menu,
unfurled for
all to see.

✔ **Auto login:** This option is the most convenient method of logging in but offers *no* security whatsoever. Mountain Lion automatically logs in the specified account when you start or reboot your MacBook.

I *strongly recommend* that you use auto login only if

- Your laptop is in a secure location — say, your home or a locked office. If you're on the road, you and your data need the protection of a username and password login!

- You're the only one using your laptop.

- You're setting up a public-access laptop kiosk, in which case you want your MacBook to immediately log in with the public account.

Working in a public environment? *Never* set an admin-level account as the auto login account. This is the very definition of a SDI, or *Supremely Dumb Idea.*

To set up a username/password or list login, open System Preferences, click the Users & Groups icon, and then display the Login Options settings, as shown in Figure 11-8. (If necessary, click the Lock icon in the lower-left corner to confirm your access.) Select the List of Users radio button for a list login screen, or select the Name and Password radio button to require your users to type their full username and password.

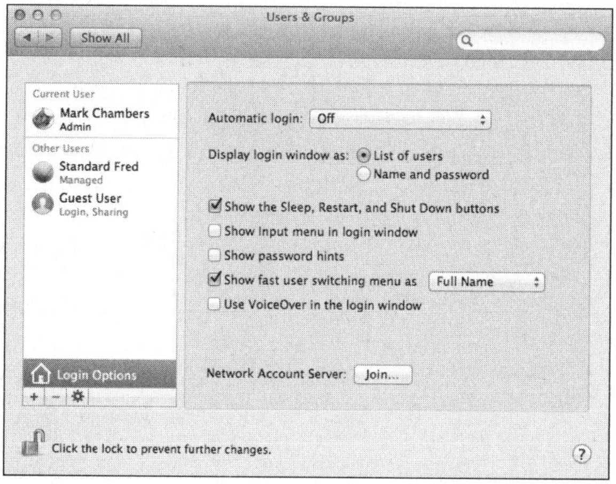

Figure 11-8:
Configure
your login
settings
from the
Login
Options
pane.

To enable fast user switching, select the Show Fast User Switching Menu As check box (also shown in Figure 11-8), and click the pop-up menu to specify how accounts should appear in the Finder menu (as full names, short names, or account icons).

To set Auto Login, click the Automatic Login pop-up menu and choose the account that Mountain Lion should use (shown also by the now-legendary Figure 11-8).

Logging out of Mountain Lion all the way (without fast user switching) is a cinch. Just click the Apple menu (⌘) and then choose Log Out. (From the keyboard, press ⌘+Shift+Q.) A confirmation dialog appears that automatically logs you off in one minute. And that one minute is important because if someone walks up and clicks Cancel, he'll be using your laptop with your account! Your MacBook returns to the login screen, ready for its next victim. Heed this Mark's Maxim:

Always **click the Log Out button in the logout confirmation dialog before you leave your MacBook.™**

Interesting stuff about sharing stuff

You might wonder where shared documents and files reside on your MacBook. That's a good question. Like just about everything in Mountain Lion, the answer is simple. The Users folder on your laptop has a *Shared* folder within it. To share a file or folder, it should be placed in the Shared folder.

You don't have to turn on file sharing in the Sharing pane of System Preferences to use Shared folders on your laptop. File sharing affects only network access to your machine by users of other computers.

Each user account on your MacBook also has a *Public* folder in that user's Home folder. The Public folder is a read-only folder that other users on your laptop (and across the network) can access. They can only open and copy the files that it contains. (Sorry, no new documents or changes to existing documents from other users.) Every user's Public folder contains a *Drop Box* folder, where other users can copy or save files but can't view the contents. Think of the Drop Box as a mailbox where you drop off stuff for the other user.

Encrypting your Home folder can be fun

Allowing others to use your Mac laptop always incurs a risk — especially if you store sensitive information and documents on your computer. Although your login password should ensure that your Home folder is off-limits to everyone else, consider an extra level of security to prevent even a dedicated hacker from accessing your stuff. All it takes is a forgetful moment in an airport or classroom, and your personal and business data is suddenly within someone else's reach. Adequate security is a Supremely Good Thing!

To this end, Mountain Lion includes *FileVault,* which automatically encrypts the contents of your MacBook's drive. Without the proper key (in this case, either your login password or the FileVault recovery key), the data stored on your drive is impossible for just about anyone to read. (I guess the FBI or NSA would be able to decrypt it, but they're not likely a worry at your place!)

The nice thing about FileVault is that it's completely transparent to you and your users. In other words, when you log in, Mountain Lion automatically takes care of decrypting your files and folders for you. You literally won't know that FileVault is on the job for you (which is how computers are *supposed* to work).

To turn on FileVault protection for a specific account, follow these steps:

1. **Click the System Preferences icon in the Dock, and then click the Security & Privacy icon.**

2. **Click the FileVault tab, and then click the Turn On FileVault button.**

3. **If necessary, click Enable User, provide the login password for each user on your account, and then click Continue.**

   Each user on your MacBook has to be enabled to use your laptop after FileVault has been turned on. If you don't know the login passwords for the other user accounts on your system, you'll have to ask each person to provide his or her password to continue.

4. **Write down the FileVault recovery key displayed by Mountain Lion and store that key in a safe place.**

   To avoid mistakes, you can capture an image of your screen using ⌘+Shift+3. The screenshot appears on your desktop — from there, you can open it and print a paper copy, or even copy the image file to a USB flash drive or another computer on your network for safekeeping.

5. **Decide whether or not to allow Apple to store your FileVault recovery key.**

   If you want this extra safeguard, click the Store the Recovery Key with Apple radio button and click Continue, then provide three security questions and the answers to each. Note that your answers must be entered *exactly* as you provide them to retrieve your key! If you're satisfied with the copy (or copies) of your key that you've made yourself and you'd rather not bring Apple into the picture, click Do Not Store the Recovery Key with Apple and click Continue.

6. **Click the Restart button on the confirmation screen.**

   Your MacBook automatically reboots and begins the encryption process — you can continue to use your laptop normally during the encryption.

   You're done!

Personally, I love the FileVault feature, and I use it on all my Macs running Mountain Lion. Yet a risk is involved (insert ominous chord here). To wit: **Do not forget your login password, and make *DOGGONE* sure that you (or your Admin user) has access to a copy of that all-important FileVault recovery key!** OS X displays a dire warning for anyone who's considering using FileVault: If you forget these safeguards, you can't retrieve any data from your MacBook's drive — even the smartest Apple support technician will tell you that nothing can be done. As Jerry Reed used to say, "It's a gone pecan" (with *pecan* pronounced Southern style, "puh-KAHN").

Chapter 12

Working Well with Networks

*I*n my book, network access ranks right up there with air conditioning and the microwave oven. Like other "I can't imagine life without them" kinds of technologies, it's hard to imagine sharing data from your laptop with others around you without a network. Sure, I've used a *sneakernet* (the old-fashioned term for running back and forth between computers with a floppy disk), but for a long time now, Apple computers don't even come with floppy drives. (I guess sneakernets have been updated with USB flash drives.)

Nope, networking is here to stay. Whether you use it to share an Internet connection, challenge your friends to a nice relaxing game of WWII battlefield action, or stream your MP3 collection to other computers that use iTunes, you'll wonder how you ever got along without one. In this chapter, I fill you in on all the details you need to know to get your road warrior hooked up to a new (or an existing) network.

What Exactly Is the Network Advantage?

If you have other family members with computers or if your MacBook is in an office with other computers (*including* those rascally PCs), here's just a sample of what you can do with a network connection:

✔ **Share an Internet connection:** This is *the* major reason why many families and most small businesses install a network. Everyone can simultaneously use the same digital subscriber line (DSL) or cable Internet connection on every computer on the network.

✔ **Share a printer:** You say your fellow employee — or even worse, your big sister — has a great printer connected to his or her computer? Luckily, that printer can be shared with anyone across your network.

✔ **Copy and move files of all sizes:** Need to get a Keynote presentation from one Mac to another? With a network connection, you can accomplish this task in just seconds. Otherwise, you'd have to copy that file to a USB flash drive, burn it to a DVD-R, or use an external hard drive. A network connection makes copying as simple as dragging the project folder from one Finder window to another.

✔ **Share documents across your network:** Talk about a wonderful collaboration tool! For example, you can drop a Word document or Keynote presentation file in your Public folder and ask for comments and edits from others in your office (or around the planet).

✔ **Stream music and video:** With iTunes, you can share your audio and video media collection on your MacBook Pro with other Macs and PCs (and even devices such as an Apple TV or an AirPlay speaker system) on your network. Your eyes and ears can't tell the difference!

✔ **Play multiplayer games:** Invite your friends over and tell 'em that you're hosting a *LAN party* (the techno-nerd term for a large gathering of game players, connected through the same network, all playing the same multiplayer game). Suddenly you'll see firsthand just how devious a human opponent can be. Each participant needs to buy a copy of the same game, naturally, but the fun you'll have is worth every cent you spend. Don't forget the chips!

If your laptop isn't within shouting distance of an existing network or you don't plan on buying any additional computers, stop right here because a lone MacBook hanging out in your home with no other computers around probably won't need a network.

If you have just your Mac laptop and an Internet connection (either through a dial-up modem or a high-speed DSL/cable modem) and you have no plans to add another computer, wireless equipment, a network printer or a mobile device, a network isn't necessary.

Should You Go Wired or Wireless?

After you decide that you indeed need a network for your home or office, you have another decision to make: Should you install a *wired* network (running cables between your computers) or a *wireless* network? Heck, should you throw caution completely to the wind and build a combination network with both wireless and wired hardware?

Your first instinct is probably to choose a wireless network for convenience. After all, this option allows you to eliminate running cables behind furniture, in the walls, or in your office ceiling. Ah, but I must show you the advantages to a wired network as well. Table 12-1 shows the lowdown to help you make up your mind.

Table 12-1	Wireless versus Wired Networks	
Factor	*Wireless Networks*	*Wired Networks*
Speed	Moderate	Much faster
Security	Moderate	Better
Convenience	Better	Worse
Compatibility	Confusing standards	Easier to understand
Cables	Few (or none)	Required

As I call it, here are the advantages of choosing a wired versus a wireless network setup:

✔ **Wired:** Using a wired network offers two significant perks over a wireless network:

- *Faster speeds:* In general, wired networks that are compatible with your MacBook are many, many times faster than the fastest 802.11n wireless connections.

  The performance of a wireless connection can be compromised by interference (from impeding structures, such as concrete walls, and from household appliances, such as some wireless phones and microwave ovens) and by distance. Wired networks have no such problems (as long as you keep your cables to lengths of 25 feet or less).

- *Better security:* A wired network doesn't broadcast a signal that can be picked up outside your home or office, so it's more secure.

  Hackers can attack through your Internet connection, though, even if you're using a wired network. Hence the section "USE YOUR FIREWALL!," later in this chapter.

✔ **Wireless:** A wireless connection really has only one advantage, but it's a big one: *convenience* (which, in this case, is another word for *mobility* for all your networked devices). Laptop owners crave this independence — a freedom that desktop computer owners can only dream about.

Accessing your network anywhere within your home or office — without cables — is so easy. Connecting a wireless printer is a breeze. And when using an AirPort Express mobile Base Station, even your home stereo can get connected to your MP3 collection on your MacBook. Read more about base stations later on.

Be a Pal — Share Your Internet!

Time to see what's necessary to share an Internet connection. In the following sections, I cover two methods of connecting your network to the Internet. (And before you open your wallet, keep in mind that you might be able to use your laptop to share your broadband connection across your network!)

Using your MacBook as a sharing device

You can use your MacBook to provide a shared Internet connection across a simple wireless network, using either

- A broadband DSL or cable connection
- An external USB dial-up modem

I recommend sharing a dial-up modem Internet connection *only* if you have no other option. A dial-up modem connection really can't handle the data transfer speeds for more than one computer to access the Internet comfortably at one time. (In plain English, an external USB modem that you add to your MacBook isn't fast enough for both you and your significant other to surf the web at the same time.) Sharing a dial-up connection just isn't practical.

Because your MacBook has built-in AirPort Extreme wireless hardware, it's easy to share your broadband connection wirelessly with other computers in your home or office.

When your laptop is working as an Internet-sharing device, your MacBook uses the OS X Mountain Lion built-in Internet-connection-sharing feature to get the job done, *but your MacBook must remain turned on to allow Internet sharing.* I show you how to do this in the upcoming section, "Network Internet connections."

Grafting wireless access to a wired network

Maybe you're caught in the middle, choosing between wired and wireless networking? Or perhaps you're already using a wired network but would be absolutely thrilled by the idea of sitting on your deck in the sunshine while checking your e-mail on your laptop, untethered. By combining both technologies, you can get the faster transfers of a wired network between all the computers in your office and the freedom you crave.

In my home office, I use a wireless base station that also includes a built-in wired switch, a common feature in today's wireless routers and base stations. My family gets all the convenience a wireless network offers, and everyone can connect to the Internet from anywhere in our house. On the other hand, my office computers have the faster performance and tighter security of a wired network. *Sassy* indeed!

Using a dedicated Internet-sharing device

You can also choose to use a dedicated Internet-sharing device (often called an *Internet router*) to connect to your cable or DSL modem. You do have to buy this additional hardware, but here's the advantage: Your MacBook doesn't have to remain turned on just so everyone can get on the Internet.

As I mentioned, Internet routers usually include either wired or wireless network connections, and many include both.

Setting up an Internet router is usually a simple matter, but the configuration depends on the device manufacturer and usually involves a number of different settings in System Preferences that vary according to the router model. Grab a diet cola, sit down with the router's manual, and follow the installation instructions you find there. (In many cases, you must set up your cable or DSL modem as a *bridge* between your ISP and your router, which should be covered in your modem and router manuals as well.)

Most Internet routers offer a DHCP server, which automatically assigns Internet protocol (IP) addresses, and I *strongly* recommend that you turn on this feature! (You can read more on DHCP later in this chapter, in the sidebar "The little abbreviation that *definitely* could.")

What Do I Need to Connect?

Most *normal* folks — whom I define as those who have never met a network system administrator, and couldn't care less — think that connecting to a network probably involves all sorts of arcane chants and a mystical symbol or two. In the following sections, I provide you with the shopping list that you need to set up a network — or connect to a network that's already running.

Wireless connections

Today's Mac laptops come complete with a built-in AirPort Extreme wireless card, so if you already have an AirPort Extreme or Express Base Station, you're set to go. Otherwise, hold on tight while I lead you through the hardware requirements for wireless networking.

 The maximum signal range — and effectiveness — of any wireless network can be impeded by intervening walls or by electrical devices, such as microwave ovens and some wireless phones, all of which can generate interference.

Connecting a MacBook to an existing wireless network

Connecting a MacBook to an existing wireless network requires no extra hardware because your hardware is already built in. (Whew. That was easy!)

Using a base station to go wireless

If you decide that you want to build your own wireless network, you eschew cables, or you want to add wireless support to your existing wired network, you need a *base station*. (If you do have an existing wired network, the base station can act as a bridge between computers using wireless hardware and your wired network, allowing both types of computers to talk to each other.) Such a wireless base station will have either

- ✔ A port that can connect to your existing wired network's switch
- ✔ A full built-in switch for wired connectivity (which means you can sell your old wired Ethernet switch to your sister in Tucson)

And, of course, a base station can simply act as a central switch for your wireless network (with no support for a wired network).

You can use either a cool Apple Base Station or a boring 802.11n generic wireless base station; however, the Apple hardware requires less configuration and tweaking. (Sounds like a Mark's Maxim!)

If you don't want the hassle of tweaking PC hardware to accommodate your MacBook, buy Apple hardware and software.™

Apple Base Station models

As listed in the upcoming Table 12-2, your MacBook can work with four Apple Base Station models for wireless networking:

✔ **AirPort Extreme:** I recommend using AirPort Extreme if your network needs an enhanced antenna, which provides greater range. You can read about connectivity ranges in the upcoming Table 12-2.

✔ **Time Capsule:** Apple's *Time Capsule* unit (an external wireless backup unit) isn't just a wireless remote hard drive. It can also act as a full AirPort Extreme Base Station. In fact, the wireless specifications for a Time Capsule unit and an AirPort Extreme Base Station are almost identical.

✔ **AirPort Express:** I recommend using AirPort Express if you want to

- *Carry your wireless base station with you.* Express is much smaller than the other Apple Base Station models. (Think "party on the patio" or a LAN gaming get-together at a friend's house.)

- *Extend the range of your existing wireless network.* If your network signal fades by the pool or the potting shed, consider adding an AirPort Express at the edge of your current range to extend the reach of your wireless network.

- *Connect your home stereo or speakers for wireless music streaming using AirPlay.* You can connect a pair of speakers to your AirPort Express and use AirPlay to play music from your MacBook's iTunes library. (Heck, you're not just limited to playing the music on your laptop — you can also stream music from your iPhone, iPad, or iPod touch!)

✔ **AirPort (discontinued):** You might find an original 802.11b or 802.11g AirPort Base Station on eBay or at a garage sale. Go ahead and pick it up if you want to save cash, unless you're considering multiplayer gaming or using high-speed file transfers over your wireless network.

The 802.11n standard used by the AirPort Extreme, Time Capsule, and AirPort Express Base Stations delivers a connection that's several times faster than the old AirPort Base Station's 802.11b/802.11g standards. 802.11n is also compatible with *all* the older standards — 802.11b/a/g — so I highly recommend that you stick with 802.11n in the future. It plays well with others, and at warp speed to boot!

Table 12-2	Apple Wireless Network Base Stations		
Feature	*AirPort Extreme/ Time Capsule*	*AirPort Express*	*AirPort*
Price	$180/$299	$99	$30 (used)
Users (maximum)	50	50	50
802.11n support	Yes	Yes	No
802.11g support	Yes	Yes	Depends on the model
802.11b support	Yes	Yes	Yes
LAN Ethernet jack (high-speed Internet connection)	Yes	Yes	Yes
WAN Ethernet jack (wired computer network)	Yes	Yes	No
Stereo mini-jack for AirPlay	No	Yes	No
USB printer port	Yes	Yes	No
Maximum signal range (approximate)	150 feet (standard); 250 feet (with add-on antenna)	150 feet	100 feet
AC adapter	Separate on AirPort Extreme/built in on Time Capsule	Built in	Separate

The names of the Apple Base Stations are irritatingly similar; Apple usually does a better job of differentiating its product names. Jot down the name of your model on a Post-it note on your laptop's desktop just so that you don't get confused.

Installing an Apple Base Station is simple. Follow these steps:

1. **If you have a DSL or cable modem, connect it to the WAN (wide-area network) port on the base station with an Ethernet cable.**

2. **If you have an existing wired Ethernet computer network with a switch or router, connect it to the Ethernet LAN port on the base station with an Ethernet cable.**

3. **If you have a USB printer, connect it to the USB port on the base station.**

As I note in Table 12-2, older AirPort Base Stations didn't have USB ports.

I cover the steps to share a printer in the upcoming section, "Sharing a network printer."

4. **Connect the power cable from the AC power adapter.**

    The AirPort Express and Time Capsule units have a built-in AC adapter, so if you're using one of these models, just plug the cord from the device itself into the wall.

5. **Switch on your base station.**

6. **Run the installation software provided by Apple on your laptop.**

Using non-Apple base stations

If any company other than Apple manufactured your wireless base station, the installation procedure is almost certainly the same. (Naturally, you should take a gander at the manufacturer's installation guide just to make sure, but I have added many brands of these devices and used the same steps for each one.)

However, I should note that Apple wireless hardware uses a slightly different security encryption standard than most PC wireless hardware, which results in an extra hurdle to connecting to a non-Apple base station or access point with your laptop. (More on this in the next section. For now, just remember that I recommend using Apple wireless hardware with your MacBook whenever possible because the installation process is easier!)

Joining a wireless network

As far as I'm concerned, the only two types of base stations on the planet are Apple and non-Apple (which includes all 802.11n and 802.11g base stations and access points). In the following two sections, I relate what you need to know to get on-board with either type of hardware.

Apple AirPort Base Stations

To join a wireless network that's served by any flavor of Apple Base Station, follow these steps on each Mac with wireless support:

1. **Click the System Preferences icon in the Dock.**

2. **Click the Network icon.**

3. **From the Connection list on the left, click Wi-Fi.**

4. **Select the Show Wi-Fi Status in Menu Bar check box.**

5. **Click the Apply button.**

6. **Press ⌘+Q to quit System Preferences and save your settings.**

7. **Click the Wi-Fi status icon (which looks like a fan) on the Finder menu bar and choose an existing network connection that you'd like to join.**

    The network name is the same as the network name you chose when you set up your AirPort Base Station.

8. **If you set up a secure network, enter the password you assigned to the network during setup.**

Transferring files the easy AirDrop way

AirDrop is the local Mac-to-Mac file transfer feature built in to OS X Mountain Lion, and it couldn't be much easier to use. No setup and no passwords involved! However, here are three caveats:

✔ AirDrop works only with Macs running Lion and Mountain Lion, and only with specific models: MacBook Pro (late 2008 or newer), MacBook Air (late 2010 or newer), and MacBook (late 2010 and newer). The 17" MacBook Pro (late 2008) doesn't support AirDrop.

✔ AirDrop uses the Wi-Fi hardware built in to today's Mac laptops and desktops, so don't forget to turn on Wi-Fi first. (If you're displaying the Wi-Fi status icon on your Finder menu bar, click the icon and choose Turn Wi-Fi On.)

✔ You have to be within Wi-Fi signal range of another Mac to use AirDrop. Note, however, that the two computers *don't* have to be using the same Wi-Fi network. (For example, my iMac uses a wired connection to my network, but because the iMac has internal Wi-Fi hardware, I can use AirDrop to send files to my MacBook Air.) Because AirDrop uses a Wi-Fi connection, file transfers are significantly slower (and less secure) than they would be over a wired Ethernet network.

To use AirDrop to transfer files to another Mac, both users should click the AirDrop icon in any Finder window sidebar to join the AirDrop group. After a short delay, you'll see the account pictures for all Macs within signal range and with AirDrop open. Just drag the files you want to transfer to the person's picture. Both you and the recipient are prompted for confirmation before the transfer begins. After the transfer is complete, the files you sent are saved in the recipient's Downloads folder.

When you're done using AirDrop, just close the Finder window displaying the account pictures (or click another location in the Finder window sidebar) to exit from the AirDrop group. (Don't forget that you have to open AirDrop again if someone wants to send you files; I leave my AirDrop Finder window open and minimized to the Dock.)

By the way, security is always A Good Thing, and I strongly recommend that you enable the password encryption features of your Apple Base Station while installing it! (Luckily, the Apple Base Station setup application leads you through this very process.) In the words of an important Mark's Maxim:

Keep uninvited guests out of your network! Use your base station's security features and encrypt your data by using WPA2 encryption!™

Some wireless networks might not appear in your Wi-Fi menu list. These are *closed networks,* which can be specified when you set up your AirPort Base Station. You can't join a closed network unless you know the exact network name (which is far more secure than simply broadcasting the network name). To join a closed network, follow these steps:

1. **Choose Join Other Network from the Wi-Fi menu.**

   To open the menu, click the Wi-Fi status icon (which looks like a fan) on the Finder menu bar.

2. **Type the name of the network.**

3. **If the network is secured with WPA, WPA2, WEP, or LEAP encryption — the security standards for protecting your data through encryption — click the Security pop-up menu and choose which type of encryption is being used.**

   I recommend avoiding WEP encryption whenever possible — your best bet is WPA2 encryption, which is the current standard for home wireless networks.

4. **Enter the network password, if required.**

To disconnect from a Wi-Fi network, click the Wi-Fi menu and either choose Turn Wi-Fi Off or connect to another wireless network. In other words, if you choose another available wireless network from the Wi-Fi menu, your MacBook will automatically drop the previous connection. (You can be connected to only one wireless network at a time, which makes Good Sense.)

Using non-Apple Base Stations

If you're using your MacBook to connect to a non-Apple base station at your office, you might need to follow a specific procedure that takes care of the slightly different password functionality used by standard 802.11b/g/n hardware.

Mountain Lion can take care of many potential wireless "language barriers" caused by security encryption — the two most common forms are WPA2 and WEP — so whether you need to massage your password to connect to your non-Apple base station depends on the specific hardware and encryption system that it uses.

To read or print the latest version of this procedure, fire up Safari, visit `http://kbase.info.apple.com/index.html`, and search for HT1126. This search term is the Apple Knowledge Base article number, which you can type in the first search field. The article (*AirPort: Joining an encrypted WEP or WPA Wi-Fi network*) provides the details on how to convert a standard wireless encrypted password to a format that your AirPort Extreme hardware can understand.

Wired connections

If you're installing a wired network, your MacBook Pro (standard display) already comes with most of what you need for joining your new cabled world. You just connect the hardware and configure the connection. Don't forget that you also need cables and an inexpensive Ethernet switch. (If you're using an Internet router or other hardware sharing device, it almost certainly has a built-in 4- or 8-port switch.)

Owners of MacBook Air and MacBook Pro Retina laptops: Your machine doesn't come from Apple with a wired Ethernet port onboard, but you can add a Thunderbolt-to-Ethernet connector that allows you to use a wired network. After you add the connector to your system, you can follow along without any problem.

Connecting a MacBook Pro to a wired network

Your Ethernet 10/100/1000 port (which looks like a slightly oversized telephone jack) is located on one of the sides of your MacBook Pro, ready to accept a standard Ethernet Cat5/Cat5E/Cat6 cable with RJ-45 connectors. (If you've connected a Thunderbolt-to Gigabit-Ethernet adapter to your MacBook Pro Retina or MacBook Air, you're also in business.)

If you're connecting to an existing wired network, you need a standard Cat5/Cat5E/Cat6 Ethernet cable of the necessary length. I recommend a length of no more than 25 feet because longer cables are often subject to line interference (which can slow or even cripple your connection). You also need a live Ethernet port from the network near your laptop. Plug the cable into your MacBook, and then plug the other end into the network port.

Wired network hardware

If you don't know your switch from your NIC, don't worry. Here, I provide you with a description of the hardware that you need for your wired network.

Wired network components

If you're building your own wired network, you need

- ✔ **A switch:** This gizmo's job is to provide more network ports for the other computers in your network. Switches typically come in 4- and 8-port configurations.

  As I mention earlier in this chapter, most Internet routers (sometimes called *Internet-sharing devices*) include a built-in switch, so if you've already invested in an Internet router, make doggone sure that it doesn't come equipped with the ports you need before you go shopping for a switch!

- ✔ **A number of Ethernet cables:** Exactly how many cables you need is determined by how many computers and other devices (such as a network printer) you're connecting. If you're working with a Gigabit Ethernet system, you need Cat5E or Cat6 cables. Cat6 cables provide better performance, but they are more expensive.

Naturally, if you're using a broadband Internet connection, you also have a DSL or cable modem. These boxes always include a port for connecting to your wired Ethernet network. (If you have one of the new breed of *wireless* modems — which acts as a wireless base station — don't panic because it should also have a wired port for connecting to your existing switch.)

Wired network connections

After you assemble your cables and your router or switch, connect the Ethernet cables from each of your computers to the router or switch and then turn on the device. (Most need AC power to work.) Check the manual that comes with your device to make sure that the lights you're seeing on the front indicate normal operation. (Colors vary by manufacturer, but green is usually good.)

Next, connect your cable or DSL modem's Ethernet port to the WAN port on your switch with an Ethernet cable. If your modem isn't already on, turn it on now and check for normal operation.

When your router or switch is powered on and operating normally, you're ready to configure OS X for network operation. Just hop to the upcoming section, "Connecting to the Network." (How about that? Now you can add network technician to your rapidly growing computer résumé!)

Joining a wired Ethernet network

After all the cables are connected and your central connection gizmo is plugged in and turned on, you've essentially created the hardware portion of your network. Congratulations! (Now you need a beard and suspenders.)

With the hardware in place, it's time to configure Mountain Lion. In this section, I assume that you're connecting to a network with an Internet router or switch that includes a DHCP server. (Jump to the sidebar "The little abbreviation that *definitely* could," later in this chapter, for more on DHCP.)

Follow these steps on each Mac running OS X that you want to connect to the network:

1. **Click the System Preferences icon in the Dock.**
2. **Click the Network icon (under Internet & Network).**
3. **From the Connection list on the left, click Ethernet.**
4. **Click the Configure IPv4 pop-up menu (see Figure 12-1) and choose Using DHCP.**
5. **Click the Apply button.**

   Enjoy the automatic goodness as OS X connects to the DHCP server to obtain an IP address, a subnet mask, a gateway router IP address, and a Domain Name System (DNS) address. (Without a DHCP server, you'd have to add all this stuff manually. Ugh.)

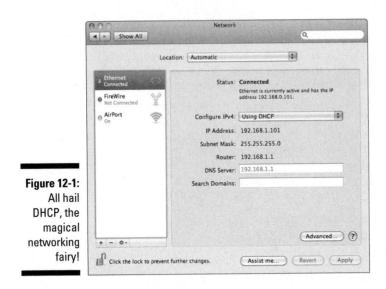

Figure 12-1:
All hail
DHCP, the
magical
networking
fairy!

A few seconds after clicking the Apply button, you should see the information. You might also notice that the DNS Server field is empty, but fear not because OS X is really using DNS server information provided by the DHCP server.

6. **Press ⌘+Q to quit System Preferences and save your settings.**

You're on!

Connecting to the Network

All right! The hardware is powered up, the cables (if any) are installed and connected, and you have configured Mountain Lion. You're ready to start (or join) the party. In the following sections, I show you how to verify that you're connected as well as how to share data and devices with others on your network.

Verifying that the contraption works

After you have at least two computers on a wired or wireless network, test whether they're talking to each other over the network by *pinging* them. (No, I didn't make up the term, honest.) Essentially, pinging another computer is like yelling, "Are you there?" across a crevasse.

The little abbreviation that *definitely* could

You know, some technologies are just *peachy*. (So much for my über-tech image.) Anyway, these well-designed technologies work instantly, you don't have to fling settings around like wrapping paper on Christmas day, and every computer on the planet can use them: Mac, Windows, Linux, and even the laptops used by funny looking folks from Roswell, New Mexico.

Dynamic Host Configuration Protocol, or *DHCP* for short, is about as peachy as it gets. This protocol enables a computer to automatically get all the technical information necessary to join a network. Let me hear you say, *"Oh yeah!"* Virtually all network devices can use DHCP these days, including Internet routers, switches, and (go figure) OS X. Today's networking hardware and operating systems provide a *DHCP server,* which flings the proper settings at every computer on the network all by itself. Your MacBook just accepts the settings and relaxes in a placid networking nirvana.

In this book, you can bet the farm that I assume that you want to use DHCP and that your network hardware supports it as well. That way, I won't spend 30 pages leading you through the twisting alleyways of manual network settings. (If you're really into such things, I spend those 30 pages and explain every single techno-wizard detail in my book *OS X Mountain Lion All-in-One For Dummies* [published by Wiley]. It's about 800 pages long — hence the comprehensive angle.)

If you're connecting to an existing network, tell the network administrator that you're taking the easy route and using DHCP. A warning, however: Adding more than one DHCP server on a single network causes a civil war, and your system *will* lock up tight. Therefore, before adding hardware with a DHCP server to an existing network, ask your network administrator to make sure that you aren't making a mistake.

To ping another computer on the same network from any Mac running Mountain Lion, follow these steps:

1. **Click the Launchpad icon in the Dock, and then click the Utilities folder.**

2. **Click the Network Utility icon to launch the application.**

3. **Click the Ping tab; see Figure 12-2.**

Figure 12-2:
Look, Ma,
I'm pinging!

```
         ⊖ ⊖ ⊖                    Network Utility
              Info   Netstat   Ping   Lookup   Traceroute   Whois   Finger   Port Scan

         Enter the network address to ping.

                       192.168.0.102           (ex. 10.0.2.1 or www.example.com)

          ◯ Send an unlimited number of pings
          ⦿ Send only 5        pings                                    Ping

          Ping has started...

          PING 192.168.0.102 (192.168.0.102): 56 data bytes
          64 bytes from 192.168.0.102: icmp_seq=0 ttl=128 time=0.464 ms
          64 bytes from 192.168.0.102: icmp_seq=1 ttl=128 time=0.543 ms
          64 bytes from 192.168.0.102: icmp_seq=2 ttl=128 time=0.363 ms
          64 bytes from 192.168.0.102: icmp_seq=3 ttl=128 time=0.413 ms
          64 bytes from 192.168.0.102: icmp_seq=4 ttl=128 time=0.528 ms

          --- 192.168.0.102 ping statistics ---
          5 packets transmitted, 5 packets received, 0.0% packet loss
          round-trip min/avg/max/stddev = 0.363/0.462/0.543/0.068 ms
```

4. **In the Enter the Network Address to Ping text field, enter the IP address of the computer that you want to ping.**

   • *If you're pinging another Mac running OS X,* you can get the IP address of that machine by simply displaying its Network pane in System Preferences, which always displays the IP address.

   • *If you're trying to ping a PC running Windows* and you don't know the IP address of that machine, follow these steps:

   a. Click Start, right-click My Network Places (XP)/Network (Vista, Windows 7 and Windows 8), and then choose Properties.

   b. From the Network Connections window, right-click your Local Area Network connection icon and then choose Status from the menu that appears.

   c. Click the Support tab.

   The IP address of that PC is proudly displayed.

5. **Select the Send Only x Pings radio button and enter** 5 **in the text field.**

6. **Click the Ping button.**

   • *Yay!:* If everything is working, you should see results similar to those shown in Figure 12-2, in which I'm pinging my Windows server at IP address 192.168.1.102, across my wired Ethernet network.

   The address 192.168.1.*xxx* is a common series of local network IP addresses provided by Internet routers, hubs, and switches with DHCP servers, so don't freak if you have the same local IP address. Similarly, Apple tends to use the form 10.0.1.*xxx* for local networks.

   • *Nay:* If you *don't* get a successful ping, check your cable connections, power cords, and OS X settings. Folks using a wireless connection might have to move closer to the network base station to connect successfully, especially through walls.

Sharing stuff nicely with others

It works . . . by golly, it works! Okay, now what do you *do* with your all-new shining chrome network connection? Ah, my friend, let me be the first to congratulate you and the first to show you around! In the following sections, I cover the most popular network perks. (And the good news is that these perks work with both wired and wireless connections.)

Network Internet connections

If your DSL or cable modem plugs directly into your MacBook (rather than into a dedicated Internet-sharing device or Internet router), you might ponder just how the other computers on your network can share that spiffy high-speed broadband connection. If you're running a wireless network, it comes to the rescue!

Follow these steps to share your connection wirelessly:

1. **Click the System Preferences icon in the Dock.**
2. **Click the Sharing icon (under Internet & Wireless).**
3. **Click the Internet Sharing entry in the Services list to the left of the pane.**
4. **From the Share Your Connection From pop-up menu, choose Ethernet.**
5. **Select the Wi-Fi check box (in the To Computers Using list).**

    Mountain Lion displays a warning dialog stating that connection sharing could affect your Internet service provider (ISP) or violate your agreement with your ISP. I've never heard of this actually happening, but if you want to be sure, contact your ISP and ask the good folks there.

6. **Click Start in the warning dialog to continue.**
7. **Select the On check box next to the Internet Sharing entry in the Services list.**
8. **Click the Close button to exit System Preferences.**

Sharing an Internet connection (without an Internet router or dedicated hardware device) through OS X requires your computer to remain on continuously. Remind others in your office or your home that the svelte laptop must remain on, or they'll lose their Internet connection! Naturally, when you take off on your next trip with your road warrior, the folks left at your home or office will be without an Internet connection until you return.

If your MacBook has an external USB modem, you can indeed share a dial-up modem Internet connection. Just don't be too surprised if you quickly decide to shelve the idea. Those dinosaurs are s-l-o-w beyond belief.

Don't forget, you won't need to configure Internet sharing if your DSL or cable modem connects to a dedicated sharing device or router. That snazzy equipment automatically connects your entire network to the Internet.

Network file sharing

You can swap all sorts of interesting files with other Macintosh computers on your network. When you turn on file sharing, Mountain Lion lets all Macs on the network connect to your MacBook and share the files in your Public folder. (Note that sharing across a network is different from sharing a single computer betwixt several people. I cover that environment in Chapter 11.)

Follow these steps to start sharing files and folders with others across your network:

1. **Click the System Preferences icon in the Dock.**

2. **Click the Sharing icon.**

3. **Select the On check box next to the File Sharing service entry to enable the connections for Mac and Windows sharing.**

   Other Mac users can connect to your computer by clicking Go in the Finder menu and choosing the Network menu item. The Network window appears, and your laptop is among the choices. If the other Macs are running Mountain Lion, your MacBook's shared files and folders appear in a Finder window, and they're listed under the Shared heading in the sidebar.

   Windows XP users should be able to connect to your Mac from their My Network Places window, and Vista, Windows 7, and Windows 8 users can use the Network window. (Users of pre-XP versions of Windows, head to Network Neighborhood.) Those lucky Windows folks also get to print to any shared printers you've set up. (The following section covers shared printers.)

4. **Click the Close button to exit System Preferences.**

Mountain Lion conveniently reminds you of the network name for your MacBook at the top of the Sharing pane.

Sharing a network printer

Boy, howdy, do I love describing easy procedures, and sharing a printer on a Mac network ranks high on the list! You can share a printer that's connected to your laptop (or your AirPort Extreme, Time Capsule, or AirPort Express Base Station) by following these simple steps:

1. **Click the System Preferences icon in the Dock.**

2. **Click the Sharing icon.**

3. **Select the On check box next to the Printer Sharing service entry.**

4. **Select the check box next to the printer you want to share from the list at the right of the System Preferences window.**

5. **Click the Close button to exit System Preferences.**

A printer that you share automatically appears in the Print dialog on other computers connected to your network.

USE YOUR FIREWALL!

Yep. That's the only heading in this *entire book* that's all uppercase. It's that important.

The following Mark's Maxim, good reader, isn't a request, a strong recommendation, or even a regular Maxim. Consider it an **absolute commandment** (right up there with *Pay your taxes*).

Turn on your firewall *now*.™

When you connect a network to the Internet, you open a door to the outside world. As a consultant to several businesses and organizations in my hometown, I can tell you that the outside world is chock-full of malicious individuals who would *dearly love* to inflict damage on your data or take control of your MacBook for their own purposes. Call 'em hackers, call 'em delinquents, or call 'em something I can't repeat, but *don't let them in!*

Mountain Lion comes to the rescue again with the built-in firewall in OS X. When you use the firewall, you essentially build a virtual brick wall between you and the hackers out there (both on the Internet and within your local network). Follow these steps:

1. **Click the System Preferences icon in the Dock.**
2. **Click the Security & Privacy icon.**
3. **Click the Firewall tab.**
4. **Click the Turn On Firewall button to activate your firewall.**
5. **Click the Firewall Options button.**
6. **Select the Enable Stealth Mode check box.**

    This important feature prevents hackers from trolling for your MacBook on the Internet — or, in normal-speak, searching for an unprotected computer — so it's much harder for them to attack you. (Stealth mode also prevents other computers from pinging you, so don't be surprised if your MacBook suddenly clams up if you try to ping it.)

7. **Click OK.**
8. **Click the Close button to exit System Preferences.**

Mountain Lion even keeps track of the Internet traffic that you *do* want to reach your laptop, such as web page requests and file sharing. When you activate one of the network features that I demonstrate in the preceding section, Mountain Lion automatically opens a tiny hole (called a *port* by net-types) in your firewall to allow just that type of communication to your Mac.

For example, if you decide to turn on printer sharing (as I demonstrate earlier), Mountain Lion automatically allows incoming print jobs from other computers.

You can also add ports for applications that aren't on the firewall's Allow list, such as third-party instant messaging clients and multiplayer game servers. Depending on the type of connection, Mountain Lion will often automatically display a dialog prompting you for confirmation before allowing certain traffic, so most folks won't need to do anything manually.

However, you *can* manually add a program to your list of allowed (or blocked) firewall ports. Follow these steps:

1. **Click the System Preferences icon in the Dock.**

2. **Click the Security & Privacy icon.**

3. **Click the Firewall tab, and then click the Firewall Options button.**

4. **Click the Add button (which carries a plus sign).**

   Mountain Lion displays a standard file-browsing sheet.

5. **Browse to the application that requires access to the outside world — or the application that you want to block from outside communication — and click it to select it.**

6. **Click the Add button in the File sheet.**

   The application appears in the Firewall list. By default, it's set to Allow Incoming Connections.

7. **If you want to block any incoming communication to the application, click the Allow Incoming Connections pop-up menu and choose Block Incoming Connections instead.**

8. **Click the Close button to exit System Preferences.**

Chapter 13

Spreading the Word with Messages and FaceTime

Throughout humankind's history, our drive has been toward communication: from the earliest cave paintings, through written language, to the telegraph, telephone, and now the ultimate in human interaction — the text message. Ah, technological rapture! Of course, the very same text messages that your family craves can also send your mobile phone bill through the roof. (The classic Catch-22 quandary.)

Luckily, Apple and Mountain Lion come to the rescue — forget that silly mobile phone and your complicated calling plan! As long as you have OS X and an Internet connection, you can instantly chat with your friends and family whether they're in another bedroom, across the aisle in another cube, or halfway around the world. In fact, you can text anyone with a Mac or an iOS 5 or later device (such as an iPhone, iPad, or iPod touch) absolutely free. And, by golly, if the two of you have a FaceTime HD camera, Mac-compatible web camera, or digital video (DV) camcorder connected to your computers, you'll *see* each other in glorious, full-color video!

These modern marvels are *Messages* and *FaceTime,* and they fulfill the decades-old promise of the video telephone quite well, thank you. (Don't forget the legalese: Sending and receiving iMessages requires iOS 5 or later, and FaceTime requires iOS 4.1 or later.) If you've used previous versions of OS X, you'll recognize Messages as an update to the older iChat application.

In this chapter, I show you how to gab with all your instant-messaging and texting friends, including anyone who uses AIM (AOL Instant Messaging), Jabber, Yahoo!, or Google Talk, and anyone who participates in an AOL chat room.

Let's get connected!

Configuring Messages

The first time you run Messages (click the Messages icon in the Dock or in Launchpad), you're prompted to create an iMessage account by entering your Apple ID (which you created while setting up Mountain Lion, or through the App Store as I discuss in Chapter 2). You use your iMessage account to send and receive free messages to others using either a Mac or an iOS 5 device (such as an iPhone, iPod touch, or iPad).

An *instant message* (IM, like those exchanged on AIM and Google Talk) is different from an *iMessage* (which can be exchanged only with others using Macs or Apple iOS 5 devices). Messages can send and receive both types. If you used iChat in an earlier version of OS X, you were limited to just instant messages, audio chatting, and video chatting.

If you're already using AIM, Jabber, Yahoo!, or Google Talk and you want to use your existing IM account, open the Account Type pop-up menu and choose the correct type; then enter your existing account name and password instead.

Alternatively, select the type of account you want and click the Get an Account button. Messages launches Safari and whisks you to the web page where you can sign up for that type of account.

You can also choose to set up Bonjour messaging. Think of *Bonjour* as plug-and-play IM for your local network. In Messages, Bonjour allows you to see (and yak with) anyone on your local network without having to know his or her account information because Bonjour automatically announces all the Messages and iChat users who are available on your network. If you have others using Messages, Jabber, Yahoo!, or AIM on your local network, go for this option; if you're not connected to a local network, however, Bonjour messaging isn't necessary. Also, if you're on a public Wi-Fi network or if you're connecting to the Internet with an external modem through dial-up, I recommend disabling Bonjour messaging. (I cover how you can network like a pro in Chapter 12.) To turn on Bonjour messaging, choose Messages⇨Preferences, click the Accounts tab, click the Bonjour account to select it, and then select the Enable Bonjour Instant Messaging check box.

Working with Messages

After you finish these configuration necessities, Messages displays the window that you see in Figure 13-1. Time for introductions all around!

Conversation list

Search box   Compose new message   FaceTime

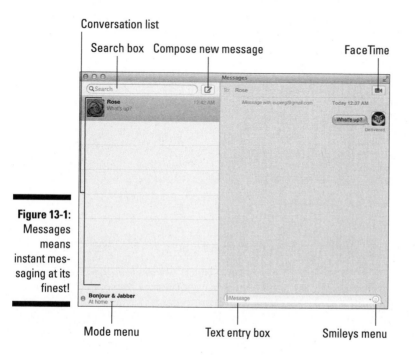

Figure 13-1:
Messages
means
instant mes-
saging at its
finest!

Mode menu   Text entry box   Smileys menu

If you want to send an iMessage to other Mac owners (or owners of iOS 5 devices), use the Messages window. In fact, if you already have an iPhone, iPod touch, or iPad running iOS 5 or later, you'll probably immediately recognize the Conversation list on the left, which displays each individual with whom you've recently exchanged iMessages. Click an individual in the list to review past conversations (and optionally continue them). The right side of the Messages window contains the actual iMessages sent back and forth, which I cover later in the chapter.

Only folks using either a Mac running Mountain Lion or an iOS 5 device can send and receive iMessages.

If you've used iChat in previous versions of OS X, you may be lamenting the demise of your old friend, the buddies list; but don't despair — it's still around! You can display the familiar Buddies window (shown in Figure 13-2) at any time by pressing ⌘+1 or by choosing Window➪Buddies from the Messages menu bar. Use the Buddies window to invite others to chat using instant messaging (such as AIM, Google Talk, or Jabber).

Buddy list

Mode menu   Video chat indicator

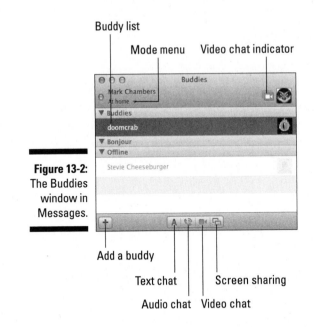

Figure 13-2:
The Buddies
window in
Messages.

Add a buddy

Text chat   Screen sharing

Audio chat   Video chat

A few things to note here about these two windows in Messages:

- ✔ **If you don't like your picture, don't panic.** By default, Messages uses your user account thumbnail image as your visual persona. However, you can add a picture to Messages by dragging an image to the well next to your name at the top of the Buddies window. If necessary, Messages asks you to position and size the image so that it fits in the (admittedly limited) space. This picture is then sent along with your words when you chat. In the figures for this chapter, I borrow the somewhat dour expression of a screech owl.

  Click your image to display your recent thumbnails. This way, you can use a different thumbnail image for each of your many moods. (Geez.) Also, you can click Camera from the pop-up menu and capture a new thumbnail with your MacBook's FaceTime HD camera.

- ✔ **Check out the buttons along the bottom of the Buddies window.** In order, these buttons are

  - *Add a New Buddy:* Covered in the following section

  - *Start a Text Chat:* Plain, old-fashioned chatting using the keyboard

  - *Start an Audio Chat:* Chatting with your voice, using microphones

  - *Start a Video Chat:* The ultimate chat, where the parties can both see and hear each other

  - *Start Screen Sharing:* Where you can view — or even remotely control — a buddy's computer

These buttons handle about 90 percent of the commands that you need to give while using Messages, so use 'em!

✔ **Hey, look, there's a Messages menu bar icon!** When you're running Messages, you can add a balloon menu bar icon in the upper-right corner of your screen. Click it to display the options that you see in Figure 13-3. You can change your online/offline status, immediately invite a buddy for a chat, or display the buddy list (which I discuss later in the section, "Will You Be My Buddy?"). The menu bar icon appears only if you select the Show Status in Menu Bar check box. To find that check box, click Messages in the menu and choose Preferences; then click the General button in the Preference dialog.

The Messages menu bar icon can even launch the application! Click the Messages icon in the Finder menu bar and select New Message at the bottom of the menu, and Mountain Lion launches Messages automatically.

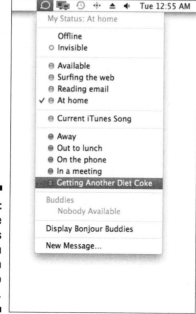

Figure 13-3:
The
Messages
Finder menu
bar icon
leaps into
action.

Changing Modes in Messages

Here's an important note: Just because Messages is running doesn't mean you're ready to converse! If you're not already familiar with the terms *online* and *offline*, here's the scoop: When you're *online*, folks can invite you to chat and communicate with you. When you're *offline*, you're disconnected:

Messages isn't active, you can't be paged, you can't chat, and that is that. Your status applies only to IM and IM chat although not to iMessages, which can be sent or received at any time.

Switching modes is easy, and you can do it in several ways:

- ✔ Choose Available or Offline from the friendly Messages Finder menu bar icon (which looks like a speech bubble from a comic book).
- ✔ If the Messages window is visible, open the Mode pop-up menu at the lower left of the window.
- ✔ If the Buddies window is visible, open the Mode pop-up menu under your name at the upper left of the window.
- ✔ If the Buddies window is visible, you can also click a buddy name directly, which automatically switches Messages to online mode and starts a conversation with that buddy.

You can use Away mode whenever Messages is running and you're still online but not available. For example, if I'm away from my MacBook Air for a few minutes, I leave Messages running, but I switch myself to Away mode. My buddies get a message saying that I'm away, so they won't bother trying to contact me. When I return to my computer, I simply move my cursor, and Messages intelligently inquires as to whether I'd like to return to Available mode. You can also use the Messages menu bar icon to switch from Away to Available (or my other favorite mode, Twiddling My Thumbs).

Messages can even display which iTunes song you're listening to. Choose Current iTunes Song from the menu and impress your friends with your digital audio techno-powers.

Speaking of modes, you, too, can create a custom mode — like *Bored stiff!* or *Listening to the Pointy-Haired Boss* — and use it instead of the somewhat mundane choices of Available and Away. You can create a mode from either the Messages or the Buddies window: Open the Mode pop-up menu in either window, and then click Custom Available or Custom Away to create your new mode. An edit box appears, in which you can type the new mode; press Return to automatically add the newcomer to your mode list.

To choose an existing mode, click it; modes with a green bullet are online modes, and red bullet modes are offline modes. (Apple provides you with some starting choices, such as *Surfing the Web* for *Available* and *In a Meeting* for *Away*.) Notice in Figure 13-3 that I created a custom mode called *Getting Another Diet Coke . . .* cAfFeInE fills my life.

If you decide your status list is getting a bit too lengthy with all those custom messages, open the Mode pop-up menu in either window and choose Edit Status Menu. Both the Available and Away list boxes have a Delete button (a minus sign). Just click the offending status message to select it and then click the Delete button to take care of business.

Will You Be My Buddy?

I know that "Will you be my buddy?" sounds a little personal, but in Messages, a *buddy* is anyone with whom you want to chat using instant messaging, whether the topic is work-related or your personal life. Messages keeps track of your buddies in the buddy list. You can also add them to your Contacts database or use the AIM entry in a Contacts card to generate a new buddy identity.

To add a buddy, display the Buddies window by pressing ⌘+1 and follow these steps:

1. **With the Buddies window visible, choose Buddies⇨Add Buddy (or click the Add a New Buddy button at the bottom of the Buddies window and choose Add Buddy from the pop-up menu, or press ⌘+Shift+A).**

   Messages displays a sheet where you can enter the instant messaging account information for your new buddy.

2. **Do one of the following:**

   • **To create a buddy entry from a Contacts card that has an IM username:** Click the down-arrow button next to the Last Name box to display the Contacts list. Click the entry to select it.

   As a shortcut, you can also click in the First Name box and then type the person's first name or click in the Account Name box and type the person's IM account name.

   • **To add a new person who's not already in your Contacts database:** Type the person's IM account name.

3. **Click Add to save the buddy information.**

Even when you add a new buddy and that name appears in the buddy list, don't be surprised if the name actually fades out after a few seconds. That action indicates that the person is offline and unavailable. You can tell when a person is available if his or her name appears with a green bullet in the buddy list.

You can also specify a number of actions that Messages should take if a buddy logs in or out of instant messaging, or if a buddy changes status to Available. To display these actions, click the desired buddy's entry in your buddy list and then press ⌘+Shift+I. (From the menu, choose Buddies⇨Show Info.) Click the Alerts button and then, from the Event pop-up menu, choose the event that should trigger the action. Select the desired check box to specify whether Messages should play the sound that you select, run an AppleScript, speak an announcement, or animate the Messages icon by "bouncing" it in the Dock.

Click the Address Card button on the Info dialog to enter or edit the person's

- ✔ Real first and last names
- ✔ Nickname
- ✔ E-mail address
- ✔ Phone number
- ✔ Instant messaging address
- ✔ Buddy picture

The View menu offers a number of neat options to help you organize and customize your buddy list. You can sort your buddy list by first name, last name, or availability, and you can choose to display full names, short names or handles (nicknames). You can also toggle the display of offline buddies.

Chat! Chat, I Say!

Turn your attention to getting the attention of others — by inviting others to chat. Good chatting etiquette implies inviting someone to a conversation rather than barging in unannounced. Note that you don't have to invite someone to start an iMessage conversation in the Messages window. Here, I'm talking about either an IM chat or an existing IM chat room.

If you want to join a chat already in progress, choose File⇨Go to Chat Room (or press ⌘+Control+G). Depending on the service being used, you might have to specify both the type of chat and the specific chat room name.

At this point, it's time to draw your attention to the green phone and video camera icons that may appear next to each person in your buddy list (as well as next to your own name at the top of the list). If the green phone icon appears next to your buddy's name, you can enjoy a two-way audio (voice) chat. If your buddy is lucky enough to have a FaceTime HD camera, USB webcam, or DV camera connected to his or her computer, you can jump into a real-time, two-way video chat room, complete with audio. Time for an important Mark's Maxim that's violated a surprising number of times:

Always wear a shirt while chatting with video, no matter your impressive physique. _Always._™

Because your MacBook has a microphone and FaceTime HD camera built in, you should *always* see both the video camera and phone icons next to your thumbnail at the top of the Buddies window. If you don't see these icons, click the Video menu and make sure that the Audio Chat Enabled and Video Chat Enabled menu items are selected.

To invite someone to a simple text-only IM chat, click the desired buddy in the buddy list, click Buddies, and then choose Start New Chat. (Using the trackpad, right-click the buddy in the list and choose Send Instant Message.)

To invite someone to an IM audio chat, choose Buddies⇨Invite to Audio Chat. To invite a buddy to an IM video chat, choose Buddies⇨Invite to Video Chat. You can also click directly on the phone or video camera icon next to the person's name in your buddy list.

If you're ready to video chat with a FaceTime-compatible Mac, iPhone, iPad, or iPod touch owner, read the discussion of FaceTime at the end of this chapter. Unlike an IM video chat, you start a FaceTime conversation by clicking the FaceTime icon in the Dock, or by clicking the FaceTime icon at the top right of the Messages window. Both methods will launch the FaceTime application.

The recipient of your IM audio or video chat invitation can decline or accept your chat invitation. You're notified (as delicately as possible) if the chat has been declined. After you invite someone to chat (or you opt to simply send an IM), the action switches to the Messages window (for text chats) or to a separate window (for audio and video chats). For text chats, simply type in the text box at the bottom of the Messages window and then press Return to send the message.

Messages displays what type of conversation you're having in two spots — at the top of the window and in the text box — making it easier to differentiate between IM and iMessage conversations. For example, in Figure 13-4, you can see the word iMessage displayed at the top of the conversation and in the text box.

If you'd like to add a *smiley* (often called an emoticon) to your message, click the Smileys drop-down menu at the right of the text box (as shown in Figure 13-4) and choose just the right symbol. (You can also choose Edit⇨Insert Smiley.)

While text chatting, you don't have to alternate sending messages back and forth between participants because everyone in a chat can compose and send messages at the same time. Me, I like to alternate when I'm chatting one-on-one.

If someone invites you to an audio or a video chat, you get the opposite side of the coin: A prompt dialog appears, and you can choose to accept or decline the invitation. (If it's a video chat, you even get a video preview of the person inviting you.)

You can also change fonts and colors while composing a line of text. Simply select the text and then choose Format⇨Show Fonts or Format⇨Show Colors. (Press ⌘+T or ⌘+Shift+C to display the Font panel and Color Picker, respectively.) These windows can be resized and moved wherever you like, as shown previously in Figure 13-4.

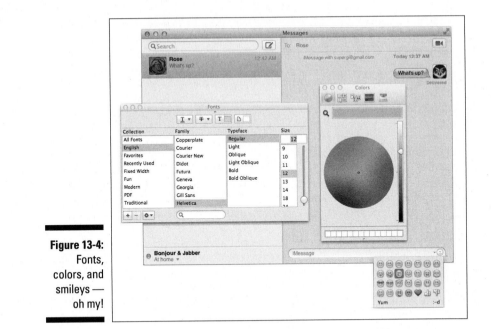

Messages doesn't limit you to just a chat between computers! You can also choose to ship off an e-mail message from Messages. Click a person in the buddy list, click the Buddies menu, and then click Send Email to automatically launch Apple Mail (or your default mail application).

When the Messages window is active, a number of display choices can be made from the View menu. Click the Messages item in the View menu to display options such as the following:

✔ **Show as Text:** Each line that you write and receive in a chat can be displayed in *balloons* (just like your favorite comic) or as simple text. You can also choose to display text lines in the more traditional boxes or as compact text (allowing more room for more characters in the Messages window).

✔ **Show Names and Pictures:** Each line can be displayed with the individual's picture, just the name, or both the name and picture.

If you're tired of the default background for the chat window — or you want to select a default font and text color for either your messages or those from others — click Messages and choose Preferences from the menu, and then click the Messages toolbar button. Use the Background Color, Font Color, and Set Font controls to fine-tune things as you like.

Curious about the capabilities of your MacBook's hardware in Messages? Choose Video➪Connection Doctor, where you can view statistics and information about your current chat, display the features of Messages that are supported by your laptop and your connection, and view any error messages generated by Messages during this session.

If you're holding multiple conversations in the Messages window, you can switch between windows by clicking the desired conversation in the Conversation list to make it active. To close an IM chat or an iMessage conversation, click a conversation in the list to select it and then click the Close button that appears (it bears an X symbol).

Conversing with iMessages

So you'd like to send and receive those free iMessages I mentioned earlier with your sister in Poughkeepsie? As long as she has a Mac of her own (or a snazzy iOS 5 or later device) and a Wi-Fi, 3G, or 4G connection, you're ready to go.

Click the Compose New Message icon at the top of the Messages window to start a new conversation. The cursor appears in the To field, and you can

- **Do things manually.** Type the person's name, e-mail address, or telephone number directly in the To field. The information you enter depends on the recipient's device — for example, sending an iMessage to an iPhone requires a telephone number, and an iPad or iPod touch needs an e-mail address — and whether that person has a card in your Contacts database that already has the required information.

- **Choose a contact or buddy.** Click the blue plus sign to display a pop-up menu, where you can select a buddy from your list or a person from your Contacts database. To search for a specific person, click in the Search box and type a portion of the name.

From this point on, an iMessage conversation is similar to an IM chat; Figure 13-5 illustrates an iMessage conversation in progress. Type the desired text in the box at the bottom of the window and then press Return to send your iMessage. To close a conversation, right-click it in the list and choose Close Conversation. (You can also select the conversation and click the Close button that appears, which carries an X.)

Sharing things with Theater

But wait. . . . What if you don't *want* to control Aunt Mildred's Mac? Perhaps you just want to share a document during an IM chat with her instead? For example, you could show off some photos or a movie you've just finished, or visit your family web page. Now you're talking the *Theater* feature, where you can share a document, web page, or video during a video chat and hold a conversation while viewing the content. Theater falls between Screen Sharing and a simple file download, which I cover in the next section.

After you've started an IM video chat, you can click the Invite button (a plus sign) and choose Share iPhoto with Theater (to share images from your iPhoto library), Share Webpage with Theater (to share a web page in Safari), or Share a File with Theater (to share movies and other documents). Messages displays a standard Open dialog, in which you can select one or more items. Or, if you're showing a web page, you're prompted for the page's address (URL) to share. When you're ready to begin your Theater presentation, click Share. If you're using a video camera, your video appears as a thumbnail, while your content gets center stage. To stop sharing, click the Close button (which bears an X).

Theater works with anything that can be displayed in Quick Look or located with Spotlight, including slideshows from iPhoto, a Keynote presentation, or a QuickTime movie.

Figure 13-5: An iMessage conversation between a Mac and an iPod touch.

Sharing Screens with Aplomb

How often have you wanted to show someone a neat new application, or lead your Aunt Mildred through the paces of setting up an Apple TV connection on her system? That's the idea behind the ultimate collaboration tool, *Sharing Screens*, where you can watch (or even remotely control) the display on another person's Mac, across any broadband Internet or local network connection.

Screen Sharing must be turned on for you to send or receive sharing invites. Choose Video➪Screen Sharing Enabled. A check mark appears next to the menu item when the feature is enabled.

If a buddy invites you to share a screen, you receive a prompt that you accept or decline. (You can also request to share a buddy's screen by choosing Buddies➪Ask to Share Screen.) If you accept the sharing invitation, Messages automatically initiates an audio chat (so that you can gab away to each other while things are happening on-screen). Suddenly, you're seeing the desktop and applications that your buddy is running, and you can both control the cursor and left- or right-click.

Throughout the screen-sharing session, Messages maintains a semi-opaque panel on your screen that has three buttons:

✔ **End the Shared Screen Session:** Click this button to exit shared screen mode.

✔ **Switch Desktops:** Click this button to swap between your Mac's screen and the remote Mac's screen. (Those Mac owners who have enabled Fast User Switching will recognize the cool screen swap animation.)

✔ **Mute Audio:** Click this button to mute the audio during the screen-sharing session.

To invite a buddy to share your screen, choose Buddies➪Share My Screen.

Okay, if sharing a screen with someone you don't absolutely know and trust doesn't set off alarm bells in your cranium, it **should.** Remember, anyone with shared screen access to you computer can perform most of the same actions on your Mac as you can, just as if that person were sitting in front of your Mac. Granted, most of the truly devastating things would require you to type your admin password, but a malicious individual could still delete files or wreak havoc any number of ways on your system. **Be careful with whom you share your screen!**

Sending Files with Messages

To send a file to a buddy through instant messaging, click the desired entry in the buddy list and then choose Buddies➪Send File. Alternatively, you can

✔ Use the ⌘+Option+F keyboard shortcut.

✔ Right-click the buddy in the list and choose Send a File.

✔ Drag the file from a Finder window to the person's entry in the buddy list.

✔ Drag the file into the text-typing window.

How's that for convenience? No matter how you start the transfer, a dialog appears to indicate that the recipient is being offered a file transfer request. If the file transfer request is accepted by your buddy, the transfer begins and is saved where the recipient specifies on his or her system.

If a buddy sends you a file, the Incoming File Request pane appears. You can then either click the Decline button (to decline the file transfer) or the Save File button (to save the incoming file to any spot on your system).

To send a file during an iMessage conversation, choose Buddies⇨Send File, use the ⌘+Option+F keyboard shortcut, or drag the file from a Finder window and drop it into the text box in the Messages window.

WARNING!

Always check any files that you receive from Messages with your antivirus-scanning software before you run them!

TIP

If you're looking for another easy method of sending files between Mac computers running Mountain Lion, don't forget to check out AirDrop. I discuss this new feature in Chapter 12. Messages does, however, have two important advantages over AirDrop: The two computers don't have to be within Wi-Fi range of each other, and Messages can transfer files with a wider range of computers (PCs running Windows, Macs running older versions of OS X, and PCs running Linux).

Eliminating the Riffraff

Here I need to explain something that I hope you won't have to use — what I like to call the *Turkey Filter*. Messages is a little more subtle. You just "ignore" people.

To ignore someone in a chat group, click the person's name in the list and choose Buddies⇨Ignore *<person>*. When someone is ignored in a chat group, you don't see anything that she or he types or have to respond to any file transfer requests from that person.

If only it were that easy to ignore someone when the person is standing close to you.

Anyway, if the person becomes a royal pain, you can also choose to *block* that person entirely. That way, the offensive cur doesn't even know that you're online, and he or she can't reach you at all using that name. Click the person in the list and choose Buddies⇨Block *<person>*. The deed is done.

Adding Visual Effects

Our esteemed Apple software developers decided to bring a little Hollywood special effects flash to Messages with video backdrops. You can also use many of the special effects filters provided by Photo Booth to keep your video chat room laughing!

To add a video backdrop to your video feed, choose Video⇨Video Preview to display your stunning self in a live video feed; then choose Video⇨Show Video Effects. Use the scroll buttons to move to the backdrop thumbnails toward the end of the Effects library. When you click one, Messages prompts you to leave the frame for a few seconds so that the plain background behind you can be correctly masked (just like those blockbuster special effects used in today's films). When your background has been captured and masked, Messages prompts you to return to your spot, and you'll see that your new static or animated backdrop is in place. *Just plain cool!*

The plainer the background behind you, the better Messages can process and mask your background. A plain wall painted a single color (blue or green are preferred) works best.

"But, Mark, I want my *own* movies and photos for backgrounds!" No problem. Messages provides eight user-defined backdrop slots for your own selections at the end of the Video Effects collection. (Click the right scroll arrow in the Video Effects window until you reach the last couple of pages.) To add your own visuals, you can

- ✔ Drag a video from iMovie (or a photo from iPhoto) to an empty User Backdrop well in the Video Effects window.

- ✔ Drag a video (or photo) from a Finder window to an empty User Backdrop well in the Video Effects window.

As long as an item can be displayed in Quick Look, it can be used as a video background. Think of the possibilities!

To try out a Photo Booth effect in Messages, choose Video⇨Video Preview to display your live video feed; then choose Video⇨Show Video Effects (or press ⌘+Shift+E). Figure 13-6 illustrates the Video Preview and Video Effects windows; click a video effect thumbnail to see how it looks on you in the Preview window! Effects range from simple Black & White to a Thermal Camera look, an Andy Warhol–style Pop Art display, and a number of really cool optical distortions (such as Twirl and Light Tunnel).

After you find just the right video effect, close the two windows and start chatting. If you decide you'd rather return your video persona to something more conventional, display the Video Effects window again and click the Original thumbnail (which appears in the center of each screen of thumbnails).

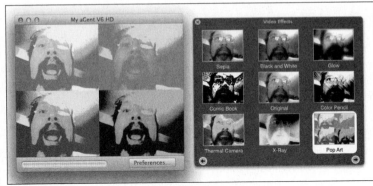

Figure 13-6:
Andy
Warhol
would be
impressed
by my
Messages
video effect!

Conversing with FaceTime

Although Messages' standard video chat is downright nifty, it has limits: You're confined to your IM buddies, and those folks may not have the necessary video hardware. With Apple's FaceTime technology, however, you can video chat with owners of iOS devices and Macs without the constraints of instant messaging accounts — and if they can run FaceTime, they're guaranteed to have the right video hardware.

At the time of this writing, FaceTime-compatible devices are

✔ **Macs running Lion and Mountain Lion**

Mac owners running Snow Leopard 10.6.6 or later can also buy the FaceTime application from the App Store.

✔ **An iPhone 4 or 4s running iOS 4.1 or higher**

✔ **A second- or third-generation iPad running iOS 4.1 or higher**

✔ **A fourth generation or later iPod touch running iOS 4.1 or higher**

If you're running a device under iOS 6 or later, you can use FaceTime over Wi-Fi, 3G, and 4G connections. If you're using a device running iOS 5 or earlier, however, you'll need a Wi-Fi connection to use FaceTime with a mobile device. A 3G or 4G cellular connection will not work. A Mac requires either a wired or Wi-Fi connection to the Internet to use FaceTime.

To launch FaceTime, click the jaunty- looking video camera icon in the Dock. The first time you use the application, you have to enter your Apple ID and your e-mail address. The folks you chat with on the other end use that same e-mail address to call you via FaceTime. (iPhone 4 or later owners can be called using their telephone numbers.)

To change the e-mail address that other FaceTime users use to call you, choose FaceTime⇨Preferences and then click the E-mail link under the heading You Can Be Reached for Calls At.

After you sign in, FaceTime displays your Contacts database by default. To initiate a call with any contact, click the name in the list, and FaceTime displays the e-mail and telephone numbers for the contact (once again, taken from your Contacts). Click the e-mail or telephone number that FaceTime should use, and the connection process begins. To return to the Contacts list and choose another person, click the All Contacts button at the top of the window.

Apple isn't satisfied with a mere Contacts list, however. You can use a number of other methods of selecting someone to call:

✔ **Recent Calls:** Click the Recents button to choose a contact that you've called (or attempted to call) in the recent past. Click the All or Missed buttons at the top of the window to further filter the Recents list.

✔ **Groups:** If you've set up one or more groups in your Contacts database, you can display them by clicking the Groups button. For example, if you've created a Contacts group containing all fellow employees in your company, you can easily locate and call a specific person without wading through all your friends and family as well.

✔ **FaceTime Search:** Click in the familiar Search box and begin typing the contact's first or last name, and FaceTime displays the matching entries.

✔ **Favorites:** Sure, you have folks you like to chat with all the time, and it's easy to add them to the Favorites list. (Those who don't make the Favorites list don't have to know, right?) Click the desired contact, and then click the Add to Favorites button. To display your favorite contacts at any time, click the Favorites button in the FaceTime window.

When the call is accepted, you'll see a large video window with a smaller picture-in-picture display (you can drag the smaller display to any desired spot in the window). The video from the other person fills the large window, and the video that you're sending to them appears in the small display, as shown in Figure 13-7.

FaceTime with Mark Chambers

Figure 13-7:
The
FaceTime
window in
action.

Move your cursor into the FaceTime window, and you'll see the window controls appear, as well as three icons at the bottom of the window:

✓ **Mute:** Click the mute icon to turn off the sound coming from your MacBook. FaceTime displays a reminder that mute is enabled. (You'll continue to hear the audio from the other person.) To restore your audio feed, click the mute icon again.

✓ **End:** Click this icon to end the FaceTime call.

✓ **Full-screen:** Click the full-screen icon (or press ⌘+Shift+F) to switch FaceTime into full-screen display mode. To return to windowed mode, press ⌘+Shift+F again, or move your cursor and click the full-screen icon again.

To switch FaceTime to landscape mode and take advantage of your MacBook's widescreen display, choose Video➪Use Landscape, or press ⌘+R. (Why let the iPhone, iPod touch, and iPad owners have all the landscape fun?)

Part IV
Living the iLife

"Awww, cool — a web cam! You should point it at something interesting to watch. The fish bowl! The fish bowl!"

In this part . . .

Here they are, the applications that everyone craves. This part covers iTunes, iPhoto, iMovie, and GarageBand like your grandma's best quilt. You discover how to share your images, music, and video clips among the iLife applications on your Mac laptop and how to create everything from your own music to a truly awesome hardcover photo album!

Chapter 14

The Multimedia Joy of iTunes

Sometimes, words just aren't enough. iTunes is that kind of perfection.

To envision how iTunes changes your MacBook, you have to paint the picture with *music* — music that's easy to play, easy to search, and easy to transfer from device to device. Whether you prefer classical, alternative, jazz, rock, hip-hop, or folk, I can guarantee that you won't find a better application than iTunes to fill your life with music. And podcasts. And video. And TV shows. And Internet radio. And college lectures. (See how hard it is to pin down this wonderful application? Along with your MacBook, iTunes really does form the hub of your digital lifestyle — including that snazzy new iPhone, iPod, or iPad.)

In this chapter, I lead you through all the features of my absolute favorite member of the iLife suite . . . and how much I appreciate this one piece of software will be pretty doggone obvious.

What Can I Play on iTunes?

Simply put, iTunes is a media player; it plays audio and video files. These files can be in many different formats. Some of the more common audio formats that iTunes supports are

✔ **MP3:** The small size of MP3 files has made them popular for file trading on the Internet. You can reduce MP3 files to a ridiculously small size (albeit at the expense of audio fidelity), but a typical CD-quality, three-minute pop song in MP3 format has a size of 3–5MB.

✔ **AAC:** *AAC* (short for Advanced Audio Coding) is an audio format that's similar to MP3; in fact, AAC files typically offer better recording quality at the same file sizes. However, this format is less compatible with non-Apple MP3 players and software. (Luckily, you can still burn AAC tracks to an audio CD, just as you can MP3 tracks.) The tracks that you download from the iTunes Store are in AAC format.

The iTunes Store's *iTunes Plus* tracks are also in AAC format, and they're encoded at a higher-quality 256-Kbps rate — hence their higher price.

✔ **Apple Lossless:** Another format direct from Apple, *Apple Lossless* format provides the best compromise between file size and sound quality: These tracks are encoded without loss of quality, although Apple Lossless tracks are somewhat larger than AAC. This format is generally the favorite of discerning audiophiles.

✔ **AIFF:** The standard Macintosh audio format produces sound of the absolute highest quality. This high quality, however, also means that the files are pretty darn huge. AIFF recordings typically require about 10MB per minute of audio.

✔ **WAV:** Not to be outdone, Microsoft created its own audio file format (WAV) that works much like AIFF. It can reproduce sound at a higher quality than MP3, but the file sizes are very large, virtually identical in size to AIFF files. (Again, think 10MB per minute of audio.)

✔ **CD audio:** iTunes can play audio CDs. Because you don't usually store CD audio anywhere but on an audio CD, file size is no big whoop — but once again, 10MB of space per minute of music is a good approximation.

✔ **MP2:** A close cousin of the far more popular MP3 format, MP2 is the preferred format in radio broadcasting and is a standard audio format for HDV camcorders. MP2 produces file sizes similar to MP3 format.

✔ **Movies and video:** You can buy and download full-length movies, TV shows, music videos, and movie trailers from the iTunes Store. And with an Apple TV unit connected to your home theater system, you can watch those movies and videos from the comfort of your sofa on the other side of your living room (or even from your bedroom on the other side of your house).

✔ **Podcasts:** These audio downloads are like radio programs for your iPod — but iTunes can play and organize them, too. Some podcasts include video and photos to boot.

✔ **iTunes U:** iTunes offers educational materials (think slideshows, presentations, and class recordings) from a wide variety of colleges and technical institutions — and virtually all free for the download.

✔ **Ringtones:** iPhone owners, rejoice! iTunes automatically offers to create ringtones for your iPhone (and iPad and iPod touch) from the tracks you bought from the iTunes Store. (You can also create ringtones with GarageBand, using songs you added to your iTunes Library or recorded yourself.) You can even use these ringtones on your Mac, with Mountain Lion's FaceTime and Messages applications!

✔ **Audiobooks:** No longer do you need cassettes or audio CDs to enjoy your spoken books — iTunes can play them for you, or you can send them to your iPod for listening on the go.

✔ **Streaming Internet radio:** You can listen to a continuous broadcast of songs from one of tens of thousands of Internet radio stations, with quality levels ranging from what you'd expect from FM radio to the full quality of an audio CD. You can't save the music in iTunes, but listening to Internet radio is still great fun. (In fact, I run my own station . . . more on MLC Radio later in the chapter.)

Playing an Audio CD

If your MacBook has an internal or external DVD drive, it's easy to play an audio CD in iTunes. Just insert the CD in your MacBook's disc slot, start iTunes by clicking its icon in the Dock, and click the Play button. (Note that your MacBook might be set to automatically launch iTunes when you insert an audio CD.) The iTunes interface resembles that of a traditional cassette or CD player. The main playback controls in iTunes are Play/Pause, Previous Song, Next Song, and the volume slider, as shown in Figure 14-1.

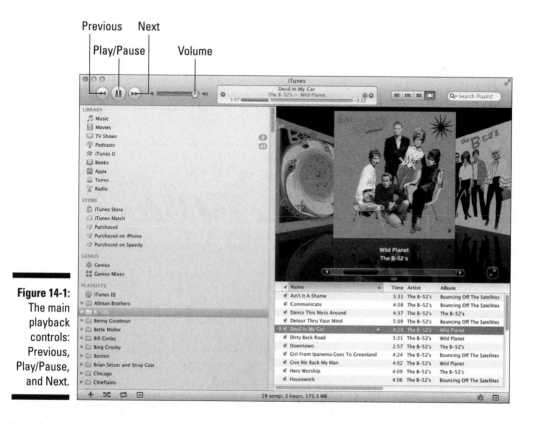

Figure 14-1: The main playback controls: Previous, Play/Pause, and Next.

Click the Play button to begin listening to a song. While a song is playing, the Play button toggles to a Pause button. Clicking that button again pauses the music. If you don't feel like messing around with the trackpad, you can always use the keyboard. The spacebar acts as the Play and Pause buttons. Press the spacebar to begin playback; press it again to stop.

Click the Next Song button to advance to the next song on the CD. The Previous Song button works like the Next Song button but with a slight twist: If a song is currently playing and you click the Previous Song button, iTunes first returns to the beginning of the current song (just like a CD player). To advance to the previous song, double-click the Previous Song button. To change the volume of your music, click and drag the volume slider.

As with other Macintosh applications, you can control much of iTunes with the keyboard. Table 14-1 lists some of the more common iTunes keyboard shortcuts.

Table 14-1	Common iTunes Keyboard Shortcuts
Press This Key Combination	**To Do This**
Spacebar	Play the currently selected song if iTunes is idle.
Spacebar	Pause the music if a song is playing.
→	Advance to the next song.
←	Go back to the beginning of a song. Press a second time to return to the previous song.
⌘+↑	Increase the volume of the music.
⌘+↓	Decrease the volume of the music.
⌘+Option+↓	Mute the audio if any is playing. Press again to play the audio.

Playing Digital Audio and Video

In addition to playing audio CDs, iTunes can play the digital audio files that you download from the Internet or obtain from other sources in the WAV, AAC, Apple Lossless, AIFF, MP2, and MP3 file formats.

Enjoying a digital audio file is just slightly more complicated than playing a CD. After downloading or saving your audio files to your MacBook, open the Finder and navigate to the stored files. Then simply drag the music files (or an entire folder of music) from the Finder to the Music entry in the iTunes Source list. The added files appear in the Music section of your iTunes Library. Think of the Library as a master list of your digital media. To view the Music Library, select the Music entry in the left column of the iTunes player, as shown in Figure 14-2. Heck, you can also drag a song file from a Finder window and drop it on the iTunes icon on the Dock, which adds the song to your Music Library as well.

TIP

If you drop the file on top of a playlist name in the Source list, iTunes adds it to that particular *playlist* as well as the main Library. (More about playlists in a bit.) If you drop a folder of songs on top of the playlists header, iTunes creates a new playlist using the name of the folder and adds all the songs in the folder to the new playlist.

To play a song, just double-click it in the Music list. Alternatively, you can use the playback controls (Play, Previous Song, and Next Song) that I discuss earlier in this chapter (refer to Figure 14-1).

The iTunes Source list can list up to eight possible sources for music:

- ✔ **Library:** This section includes Music, Movies, TV Shows, Podcasts, Books, iTunes U, Apps (for iPhone, iPod touch, and iPad), Ringtones, iPod Games, and Radio. (Think *Internet radio,* which I discuss further in the section "iTunes Radio," later in this chapter.)

- ✔ **Devices:** If an iPod, iPhone, or iPad is connected, it appears in the list. (And yes, Virginia, other models of MP3 players from other companies also appear in the list if they're supported in iTunes.)

- ✔ **Audio CD:** A standard audio CD . . . anything from the Bee Gees to Katy Perry.

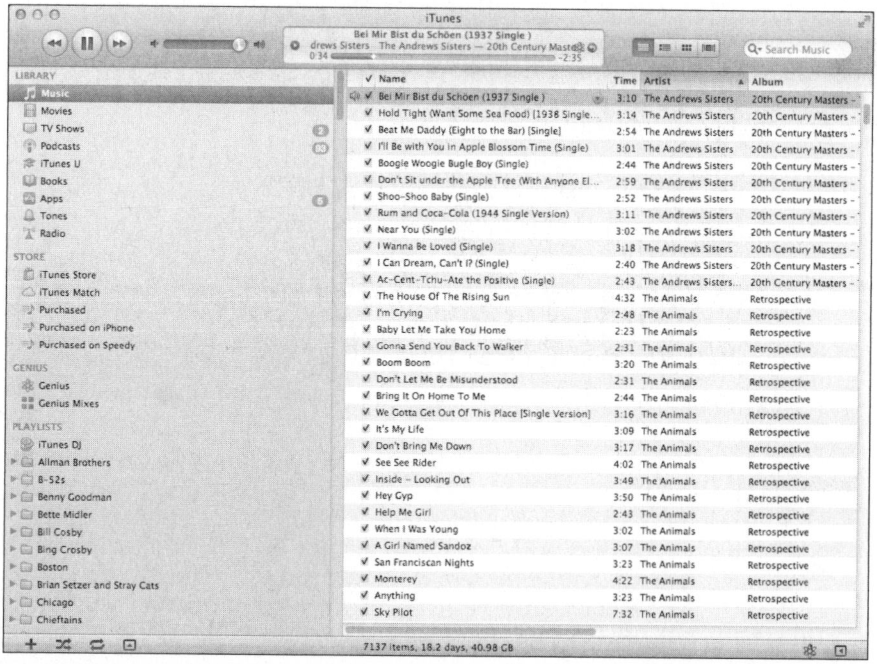

Figure 14-2:
The Music Library keeps track of all your audio files.

- ✔ **Store:** I discuss the iTunes Store in the section "Buying Digital Media the Apple Way," later in this chapter.

- ✔ **Genius:** Why not let iTunes match new music to your tastes? Click the Genius heading and then click the Turn On Genius button to allow iTunes to automatically create playlists from songs in your iTunes Music Library. You can also allow Genius to recommend music, movies, and TV shows to purchase based on the titles you already have in your iTunes Library. You'll find out more about the Genius feature later in this chapter in the section "Keeping Slim Whitman and Slim Shady Apart: Organizing with Playlists."

- ✔ **Shared:** If another Mac or PC on your local network is running iTunes and is set to share part or all of its Library, you can connect to the other computer for your music. (Shared music on another Mac appears as a separate named folder in the Source list.)

- ✔ **Home Sharing:** You can turn on Home Sharing to share your Mac's media library across your wireless network with up to five other computers (both Macs and PCs), as well as iPhone, iPad and iPhone touch devices. (More on Home Sharing later in the chapter.)

- ✔ **Playlists:** Think of playlists as folders you use to organize your music. (More on playlists later in this chapter.)

If you have a first-generation Apple TV, it will appear in the list as well, allowing iTunes to share media with your Apple TV, which in turn sends it to your ED (enhanced definition) or HD (high definition) TV.

Notice also that the Library lists information for each song that you add to it, such as

- ✔ **Name:** The title of the song

- ✔ **Time:** The length of the song

- ✔ **Artist:** The artist who performs the song

- ✔ **Album:** The album on which the song appears

If some of the songs that you're adding don't display anything for the title, album, or artist information, don't panic; most MP3 files have embedded data that iTunes can read. If a song doesn't include any data, you can always add the information to these fields manually. I show you how later, in the section "Setting or changing the song information manually."

Clicking any of the column headings in the Library causes iTunes to reorder the Library according to that category. For example, clicking the Song Name column heading alphabetizes your Library by song title. I click the Time heading often to sort my Library according to the length of the songs. Oh, and you can drag column titles to reorder them any way you like (as long as the Name column remains at the far left of the named columns).

Will I trash my Count Basie?

Novice iTunes users, take note: iTunes watches your back when you trash tracks. To illustrate: Suppose you delete a song from the Library located only in the iTunes music folder (which you didn't copy into iTunes from another location on your drive). That means you're about to delete the song entirely, and there'll be no copy remaining on your laptop. Rest assured, though, that iTunes prompts you to make sure that you really want to move the file to the Trash. (I get fearful e-mail messages all the time from readers who are loath to delete *anything* from iTunes because they're afraid they'll trash their digital music files completely.)

Remember: If you delete a song from the Library that *also* exists elsewhere on your drive (outside the reach of the iTunes music folder), it isn't deleted from your MacBook. In fact, if you mistakenly remove a song that you meant to keep, just drag it back into iTunes from the Finder or even from the Trash. 'Nuff said.

iTunes can display your Music Library in four ways: By default, the application uses the *list view* you see in Figure 14-1, where each song is one entry. A click on the second View button (at the top of the iTunes window) sorts your library into tracks by *album*. Click the third View button to group tracks together by album artwork in *grid view*. Click the fourth View button, and you're browsing by album cover in *Cover Flow view,* complete with reflective surface!

Browsing the Library

After you add a few dozen songs to iTunes, viewing the Library can become a task. Although a master list is nice for some purposes, it becomes as cumbersome as an elephant in a subway tunnel if the list is very long. To help out, iTunes can display your Library in another format, too: namely, browsing mode. To view the Library in browsing mode, click the View menu and click the Show Browser item, or press the ⌘+B keyboard shortcut.

The browsing mode of iTunes displays your Library in a compact fashion, organizing your tunes into four sections:

- ✔ Genre
- ✔ Artist
- ✔ Album
- ✔ Song Name

Selecting an artist from the Artist list causes iTunes to display that artist's albums in the Album list. Select an album from the Album list, and iTunes displays that album's songs in the bottom section of the Browse window. (Those

Apple software designers . . . always thinking of you and me.) You can also switch between sort fields for the Browse window from the View⇨Column Browser menu item.

Finding songs in your Music Library

After your collection of audio files grows large, you might have trouble locating that Swedish remix version of "I'm Your Boogie Man." To help you out, iTunes has a built-in Search function. To find a song, type some text in the search field of the main iTunes window. While you type, iTunes tries to find a selection that matches your search text. The search is quite thorough, showing any matching text from the artist, album, song title, and genre fields in the results. For example, if you type **electronic** in the field, iTunes might return results for the band named *Electronic* or other tunes that you classified as *electronic* in the Genre field. (The section "Know Your Songs," later in this chapter, tells you how to classify your songs by genre, among other options.) Click the magnifying glass at the left side of the search field to restrict the search to Artists, Albums, Composers, and Songs.

Removing old music from the Library

After you spend some time playing songs with iTunes, you might decide that you didn't *really* want to add 40 different versions of "Louie Louie" to your Library. (Personally, I prefer either the original or the cast recording from the movie *Animal House*.) To remove a song from the Library, click the song to select it and then press Delete.

You can also remove a song from the Library by dragging it to the Trash in your Dock.

Watching video

Watching video in iTunes is similar to listening to music. To view your video collection, click one of these entries in the Source list:

- ✔ Movies
- ✔ TV Shows

iTunes displays your videos as thumbnails, as a list, or in Cover Flow view. Music videos appear as a smart playlist. (Read more about these in the sidebar, "Some playlists are smarter than others.")

From your collection, you can

> ✔ **Double-click a video thumbnail or an entry in the list.**

> ✔ **Drag a QuickTime–compatible video clip from the Finder window to the iTunes window.** Video files that can be viewed by using QuickTime typically have file extensions of `.mov`, `.mv4`, or `.mp4`.

iTunes plays video in the box below the Source list, in the iTunes window, in a separate window, or in full-screen mode, depending on the settings you choose from the View➪Video Playback menu item. In full-screen mode, move your cursor to display a control strip at the bottom of the screen. The control strip sports a slider bar that you can drag to move through the video, a volume control, and Play/Pause and Fast Forward/Reverse buttons.

Keeping Slim Whitman and Slim Shady Apart: Organizing with Playlists

Your iTunes Music Library can contain thousands upon thousands of songs: If your Library grows anywhere near that large, finding all the songs in your lifelong collection of Paul Simon albums is *not* a fun task. Furthermore, with the Library, you're stuck playing songs in the order that iTunes lists them.

To help you organize your music into groups, use the iTunes playlist feature. A *playlist* is a collection of songs from the Library you want to group. You can create as many playlists as you want, and each playlist can contain any number of songs. Whereas the Library lists all available songs, a playlist displays only the songs that you add to it. Further, any changes that you make to a playlist affect only that playlist, leaving the Library intact.

To create a playlist, you can do any of the following:

> ✔ **Choose File➪New Playlist.**

> ✔ **Press ⌘+N.**

> ✔ **Choose File➪New Playlist from Selection.** This creates a new playlist and automatically adds any tracks that are currently selected.

> ✔ **Drag a folder containing audio files from a Finder window to the Playlists heading.**

> ✔ **Click a song to select it; then click the Genius button at the lower-right corner of the window.** (The Genius button bears a striking atomic symbol.) iTunes builds a playlist of songs that are similar in some way (typically by matching the genre of the selection or the beats per minute, but also based on recommendations from other iTunes members). Your MacBook needs an Internet connection to create a Genius

playlist, and the larger your Music Library, the longer it will take iTunes to build the playlist.

✔ **Click the iTunes DJ entry in the Playlist section on the left side of the window.** iTunes delivers a random selection of songs taken from your iTunes Music Library — perfect for your next spontaneous party! You can change the order of the songs in the iTunes DJ playlist (known as Party Shuffle in older versions of iTunes), add songs from your Library, or delete songs that don't fit the scintillating ambience of your gathering. Enjoy!

✔ **Click the New Playlist (plus sign) button in the lower-left corner of the iTunes window.** You get a newly created empty playlist (the toe-tappin' *untitled playlist*).

All playlists appear in the Source list. To help organize your playlists, it's a good idea to . . . well, *name* them. (Aren't you glad that you have this book?) For example, suppose that you want to plan a party for your polka-loving friends. Instead of running to your computer after each song to change the music, you could create a polka-only playlist. Select and start the playlist at the beginning of the party, and you won't have to worry about changing the music the whole night. (You can concentrate on the accordion.) To load a playlist, select it in the Source list; iTunes displays the songs for that playlist.

The same song can appear in any number of playlists because the songs in a playlist are simply pointers to songs in your Music Library — not the songs themselves. Add them to or and remove them from any playlist at will, secure in the knowledge that the songs remain safe in the Library. Removing a playlist is simple: Select the playlist in the Source list and then press Delete.

Removing a playlist doesn't delete any songs from your Library.

Know Your Songs

Besides organizing your music into Elvis and non-Elvis playlists, iTunes gives you the option to track your music at the song level. Each song that you add to the Music Library has a complete set of information associated with it. iTunes displays this information on the Info tab:

✔ **Name:** The name of the song

✔ **Artist:** The name of the artist who performed the song

✔ **Composer:** The name of the astute individual who actually *wrote* the song

✔ **Album Artist:** The name of the artist responsible for a compilation or tribute album

  ✔ **Album:** The album where the song appears

  ✔ **Grouping:** A group type that you assign

  ✔ **Year:** The year the artist recorded the song

  ✔ **BPM:** The beats per minute (which indicates the song's tempo)

  ✔ **Track Number:** The position of the song on the original album

  ✔ **Disc Number:** The original disc number in a multi-CD set

  ✔ **Comments:** A text field that can contain any comments on the song

  ✔ **Genre:** The classification of the song (such as rock, jazz, or pop)

You can display this information by clicking a song name and pressing ⌘+I. The fields appear on the Info tab.

Some playlists are smarter than others

Click the File menu, and you see the New Smart Playlist menu command. (You can create a new smart playlist also by holding down the Option key while you click the Add button, which carries a plus sign, at the bottom of the Source list.) The contents of a *smart playlist* are automatically created from a specific condition or set of conditions that you set via the Smart Playlist dialog: You can limit the track selection by mundane things, such as album, genre, or artist; or you can get funky and specify songs that were played last, by the date you added tracks, or even by the sampling rate or total length of the song. For example, iTunes can create a playlist packed with songs that are shorter than three minutes, so you can fill your iPod Shuffle with more stuff! Ah, but wait, you're not limited to a single criterion. If you want to add another criterion, click the plus sign at the right side of the dialog and you get another condition field to refine your selection even further.

You can choose the maximum number of songs to add to the smart playlist, or limit the size of the playlist by the minutes or hours of play or the number of megabytes or gigabytes the playlist will occupy. (Again, this is great for automatically

gathering as much from your KISS collection as will fit into a specific amount of space on a CD or your iPod.) Select the Live Updating check box for the ultimate in convenience. iTunes automatically maintains the contents of the smart playlist to keep it current with your conditions at all times in the future. (If you remove tracks manually from a smart playlist, iTunes adds other tracks that match your conditions, if there are any to be found.)

Now think about what all these settings mean when combined . . . *whoa*. Here's an example yanked directly from my own iTunes Library. I created a smart playlist that selects only those songs in the Rock genre. It's limited to 25 songs, selected by least often played, and live updating is turned on. The playlist is named Tracks I've Gotta Hear because it finds the 25 rock songs (from my collection of more than 7,000 songs) that I've heard least often! After I listen to a song from this smart playlist, iTunes automatically "freshens" it with another song, allowing me to catch up on the tracks I've been ignoring. Completely, unbelievably *sweet* — and another reason that iTunes is the best music player on Planet Earth!

Setting song information automatically

Each song that you add to the iTunes Music Library might have song information included with it. If you add music from a commercial audio CD, iTunes
connects to a server on the Internet and attempts to find the information for
each song on the CD. If you download a song from the Internet, it often comes
with some information embedded in the file; the amount of included information
depends on what the creator supplied. (And believe me, it's often misspelled as
well — think *Leenard Skeenard*.) If you don't have an Internet connection, iTunes
can't access the information and displays generic titles instead.

Setting or changing the song information manually

If iTunes can't find your CD in the online database or someone gives you an
MP3 with incomplete or inaccurate information, you can change the information yourself — believe me, you want at least the artist and song name, as
well as the genre! To view and change the information for a song, perform the
following steps:

1. **Select the song in either the Library's Music category or a playlist.**

2. **Press ⌘+I or choose File⇨Get Info.**

3. **Edit the song's information under the Info tab, as shown in Figure 14-3.**

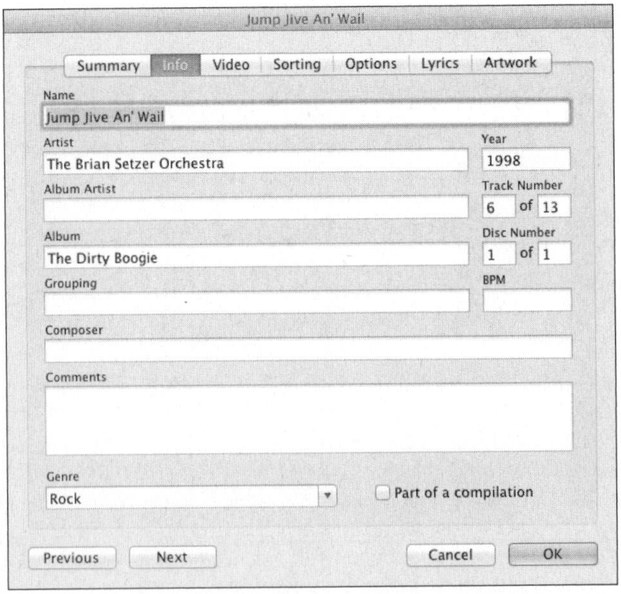

Figure 14-3:
View and
edit song
information
here.

Keep in mind that the more work you put into setting the information of the songs in your Library, the easier it is to browse and use iTunes. Incomplete song information can make it more difficult to find your songs in a hurry. If you prefer, you don't have to set all the information about a song. (Life is just easier later if you do.) Normally, you can get away with setting only a song's title, artist, and genre. The more information you put in, however, the faster you can locate songs and the easier they are to arrange. iTunes tries to help by automatically retrieving known song information, but sometimes you have to roll up your sleeves and do a little work. (Sorry, but some things just can't be automated.)

"What about cover art, Mark?" Well, I'm overjoyed that you asked! iTunes can try to locate artwork automatically for the tracks you select. (Note that adding large images can significantly increase the size of the song file.) Follow these steps to locate cover art:

1. **Select the desired songs from the track list.**

2. **Choose Advanced⇨Get Album Artwork.**

You can set iTunes to automatically attempt the addition of album artwork every time you rip tracks from an audio CD or when you add songs without artwork to your Music Library. Click iTunes and choose Preferences; then click the Store button and select the Automatically Download Missing Album Artwork check box to enable it.

Want to manually add album covers to your song info? If you select just one song in the track list, you can display the Info dialog and then click the Artwork tab. If you select multiple songs from the same album, first display the Info dialog. Now launch Safari, visit Amazon.com, and do a search on the same album (or search an online artwork library, such as AllCDCovers.com). Drag the cover image from the web page right into the Info dialog, and drop it on top of the "sunken square" artwork image well. When you click OK, the image appears in the Summary pane, and you can display it while your music is playing by pressing ⌘+G or by clicking the Show or Hide Song Artwork button at the lower left of the iTunes window.

By the way, if you buy tracks or an album from the iTunes Store, Apple always automatically includes album covers.

Ripping Audio Files

You don't have to rely on Internet downloads to get audio files. You can create your own MP3, AAC, Apple Lossless, AIFF, and WAV files from your audio CDs with iTunes. (If you have a MacBook Air or MacBook Pro Retina, you need an external drive to read audio CDs. Go figure.) The process of converting audio files to different formats is called *ripping*. (Audiophiles with technical teeth also call this process *digital extraction,* but the popular crowd usually ignores them at parties.) Depending on what hardware or software you use, each has its own unique format preferences. For example, most iPod owners prefer MP3 or AAC files, but your audio CDs aren't in that format. Being able to convert files from one format to another is like having a personal translator in the digital world. You don't need to worry about whether you have the wrong format; you can simply convert it to the format that you need.

The most common type of ripping is to convert CD audio to the AAC or MP3 format. To rip MP3s from an audio CD, follow these simple steps:

1. **Launch iTunes by clicking its icon in the Dock.**

   Alternatively, you can locate iTunes in Launchpad.

2. **Choose iTunes⇨Preferences.**

3. **In the Preferences window that appears, click the General toolbar button.**

4. **Click the Import Settings button, which appears at the bottom of the iTunes window.**

5. **On the Import Using pop-up menu, choose MP3 Encoder.**

6. **On the Setting pop-up menu, choose High Quality (160 Kbps) and then click OK.**

   This bit rate setting provides the best compromise between quality (it gives you better than CD quality, which is 128 Kbps) and file size (tracks you rip will be significantly smaller than audiophile bit rates such as 192 Kbps or higher).

7. **Load an audio CD into your MacBook's drive.**

   The CD title shows up in the iTunes Source list (under the Devices heading), which is on the left side of the iTunes window. The CD track listing appears on the right side of the window.

   If iTunes asks you whether you want to import the contents of the CD to your Music Library, you can click Yes and skip the rest of the steps. If you've disabled this prompt, however, continue with the remaining two steps.

8. **Clear the check box of any song that you don't want to import from the CD.**

   All songs on the CD have a check box next to their title by default. Unmarked songs aren't imported.

   The Browse button changes to Import CD.

9. **Click the Import CD button.**

TIP

Another form of ripping is available: If you have a USB turntable or cassette deck connected to your MacBook, you can digitize your old analog recordings on albums and cassettes into shiny digital audio files using the application that comes with the device. Often it's simpler to just buy the same music from the iTunes Store, but if your treasured music isn't available from the iTunes Store or on audio CD, digitizing is the next best thing!

Tweaking the Audio for Your Ears

Besides the standard volume controls that I mention earlier in this chapter, iTunes offers a full equalizer. An *equalizer* permits you to alter the volume of various frequencies in your music, allowing you to boost low sounds, lower high sounds, or change anything in between. Now you can customize the way your music sounds and adjust it to your liking.

To open the Equalizer (shown in Figure 14-4), do one of the following:

- ✔ Choose Window⇨Equalizer.
- ✔ Press ⌘+Option+2.

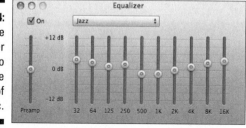

Figure 14-4: Use the Equalizer sliders to tweak the sound of your music.

The Equalizer window has an impressive array of 11 sliders. Use the leftmost slider (Preamp) to set the overall level of the Equalizer. The remaining sliders represent various frequencies that the human ear can perceive. Setting a slider to a position in the middle of its travel causes that frequency to play back with no change. Move the slider above the midpoint to boost that frequency; conversely, move the slider below the midpoint to reduce the volume of that frequency.

Continue adjusting the Equalizer sliders until your music sounds the way you like it. When you close the Equalizer window, iTunes remembers your settings until you change them again. In case you prefer to leave frequencies to the experts, the iTunes Equalizer has several predefined settings to match most musical styles. Click the pop-up menu at the top of the Equalizer window to select a genre.

What's with the numbers next to the station names?

When choosing an Internet radio station, keep your Internet connection speed in mind. If you're using a broadband DSL or cable connection — or if you're listening at work over your company's high-speed network — you can listen to stations broadcasting at 128 Kbps (or even higher). The higher the bit rate, the better the music sounds. At 128 Kbps, for example, you're listening to sound that's almost as good as an audio CD.

However, if you're listening over a dial-up modem connection, iTunes can't keep up with audio streaming at higher bit rates, so you're limited to stations broadcasting at 56 Kbps or lower.

After you adjust the sound to your satisfaction, close the Equalizer window to return to the iTunes interface and relax with those funky custom notes from James Brown.

A New Kind of Radio Station

In addition to playing back your favorite audio files, iTunes can also tune in to Internet radio stations from around the globe. You can listen to any of a large number of preset stations, seek out lesser-known stations not recognized by iTunes, or even add your favorite stations to your playlists. The following sections show you how to do it all.

iTunes Radio

Although it's not a radio tuner in the strictest sense, iTunes Radio can locate virtual radio stations all over the world that send audio over the Internet — a process usually dubbed *streaming*. iTunes can track down hundreds of Internet radio stations in a variety of styles with only a few clicks.

To begin listening to Internet radio with iTunes, click the Radio icon located beneath the Library icon in the Source list. The result is a list of more than 20 types of radio stations, organized by genre.

When you expand a Radio category by clicking its disclosure triangle, iTunes queries a tuning server and locates the name and address of dozens of radio stations for that category. Whether you like Elvis or not-Elvis (those passing fads, like new wave, classical, or alternative), something's here for everyone. The Radio also offers news, sports, and talk radio.

After iTunes fetches the names and descriptions of radio stations, double-click one that you want to hear. iTunes immediately jumps into action, loads the station, and begins to play it.

Tuning in your own stations

Although iTunes offers you a large list of popular radio stations on the web, it's by no means comprehensive. Eventually, you might run across a radio station that you'd like to hear, but it's not listed in iTunes. Luckily, iTunes permits you to listen to other stations, too. To listen to a radio station that iTunes doesn't list, you need the station's web address.

In iTunes, choose Advanced⇨Open Stream (or press ⌘+U). In the Open Stream dialog that appears (see Figure 14-5), enter the URL of your desired radio station and then click OK. Within seconds, iTunes tunes in your station.

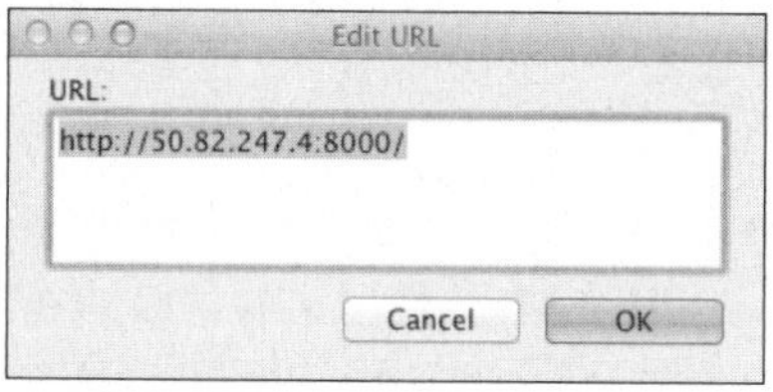

Figure 14-5:
Tuning into
MLC Radio,
my Internet
radio station.

Edit URL

URL:

http://50.82.247.4:8000/

Cancel   OK

Radio stations in your playlists

If you find yourself visiting an online radio station more than once, you'll be glad to know that iTunes supports radio stations in its playlists. To add a radio station to a playlist from the Radio list, do the following:

1. **Open the category that contains the station you want to add to your playlist.**

2. **Locate the station that you want to add to your playlist and drag it from the Radio list to the desired playlist on the left.**

   If you haven't created any playlists yet, see the section "Keeping Slim Whitman and Slim Shady Apart: Organizing with Playlists," earlier in this chapter, to find out how.

"I have an itch to hear 'Kung Fu Fighting'!"

This particular technology author has a preference for a certain hot jam spot: *MLC Radio,* the Internet radio station I've been running for several years now. I call my station a '70s Time Machine because it includes hundreds of classic hits from 1970 to 1979, inclusive. You hear everything from "Rock and Roll Hoochie Koo" by Rick Derringer to "Moonlight Feels Right" by Starbuck. (Hey, I'm summing up a decade here, so be prepared for both Rush and the Captain and Tennille.) The station broadcasts at 128 Kbps (near audio CD quality), so you need a broadband connection to listen. For the radio's Internet address or help connecting to MLC Radio, visit my website at www.mlcbooks.com — and then follow the steps in the next section to add MLC Radio to your playlists!

Adding a radio station that doesn't appear in the Radio list is a bit trickier but possible nonetheless. Even though iTunes allows you to load a radio station URL manually by using the Open Stream command on the Advanced menu, it doesn't give you an easy way to add it to the playlist. Follow these steps to add a specific radio station to a playlist:

1. **Add any radio station from the Radio list to your desired playlist.**

   Any station in the list will do, as you'll immediately change both the station's URL and name to create your new station entry in the playlist.

2. **Press ⌘+I or choose File➪Get Info to open the information dialog for that station.**

3. **Click the Summary section.**

4. **Change the URL by clicking the Edit URL button, entering the desired URL, and clicking OK.**

5. **Click the Info tab, type the new station name, and then click OK.**

iSending iStuff to iPod

If you own an iPod, you'll be happy to know that iTunes has features for your personal audio and video jukebox as well. *iPods,* Apple's multimedia players, comprise an entire family of portable devices (ranging from $49 to about $249) that can hold anywhere from several hundred to literally thousands of songs, as well as podcasts, photos, and video. These great gadgets and those like them have become known worldwide as *the* preferred portable digital media players. (Heck, even the iPhone and iPad can act as an iPod!)

If you own an iPod touch, iPhone, or iPad, you can also buy all sorts of applications for these devices on the iTunes Store. iTunes even keeps track of these applications as part of your iTunes Library.

You connect your iPod with its included cable to any Macintosh or Windows PC with USB 2.0 ports. (The iPod touch can even connect to your MacBook or PC over your wireless network.) After the iPod is connected, it automatically synchronizes to the playlists in iTunes. The iPod and the iTunes software communicate with each other and figure out what items are in your iTunes Library (as compared with the iPod Library). If they discover songs, podcasts, and video in your iTunes Library that are missing from your iPod, the items automatically transfer to the iPod. Conversely, if the iPod contains stuff that's no longer in iTunes, the iPod automatically removes those files from its drive.

Go back and reread that last sentence about the iPod *automatically removing* files from its drive. (I'll wait here.) Apple added this feature in an effort to be attentive to copyright concerns. The reasoning is that if you connect your iPod to your friend's computer, you can't transfer songs from the iPod to that computer. Of course, you could always look at it from the marketing perspective as a feature that makes sure that your MacBook and iPod are always in total sync. Whatever the case, pay close attention and read all warning dialogs when connecting to an iTunes library other than your own (or when you connect to your MacBook using another account), or you might wipe out your iPod's library.

The best thing I can say about the iPod and iTunes combination is . . . well . . . that there *isn't* anything else to say about them. The autosync feature is so easy to use, you forget about it almost immediately.

This chapter — even as long as it is — just can't explain all the ins and outs of the iTunes/iPod relationship! For a complete look at both iTunes and the iPod, I can heartily recommend a fellow *For Dummies* book, *iPod & iTunes For Dummies*, 10th Edition, by Tony Bove (Wiley).

Sharing Media across a Network

Ready to share music, podcasts, and video — *legally,* mind you — with other folks on your local network? You can offer your digital media to other iTunes users across your home or office. Follow these steps:

1. **Choose iTunes⇨Preferences to open the Preferences dialog.**
2. **Click Sharing.**
3. **Select the Share My Library on My Local Network check box.**
4. **Specify whether you want to share your entire library or only selected playlists and files.**

Sharing selected playlists is a good idea for those Meatmen and Sex Pistols fans who work at a cubicle farm in a big corporation.

5. **If you want to restrict access to just a few people, select the Require Password check box; then type a password in the text box.**

6. **Click OK.**

Your shared folder appears within the Source list for all iTunes users who selected the Look for Shared Libraries check box on the same pane of their iTunes Preferences dialog. Note that the music you share with others can't be imported or copied, so everything stays legal.

Want to change that frumpy default name for your shared Media Library to something more exotic, like "Dan's Techno Beat Palace"? No problem — display the Preferences dialog again, but this time click the General button and click in the Library Name text box. Edit your network entertainment persona to your heart's content.

You can also share your media library using *Home Sharing*, which allows up to five devices — including Macs, PCs, second- and third-generation Apple TVs, and iOS devices (your iPad, iPhone and iPod touch, running iOS 4.3 or later) — to join in the fun. Home Sharing requires a network connection for all your devices, and you'll have to enter the same Apple ID information on each device. To turn on Home Sharing in iTunes, click Advanced on the iTunes menu and choose Turn On Home Sharing. (Don't forget to repeat this setup on each computer.) After Home Sharing is enabled, shared libraries will appear in the Source list under the Shared heading.

Burning Music to Shiny Plastic Discs

Besides being a great audio player, iTunes is adept at creating CDs, too. iTunes makes the process of recording songs to a CD as simple as a few clicks. Making the modern version of a compilation (or *mix*) tape is easier than getting a kid to eat ice cream. If your MacBook sports an internal or external optical drive, iTunes lets you burn CDs in one of three formats:

✓ **Audio CD:** This CD is the typical kind of commercial music CD that you buy at a store. Most typical music audio CDs store up to 800MB of data, which translates into about 80 minutes of music.

✓ **Data CD or DVD:** A standard CD-ROM or DVD-ROM is recorded with the audio files. This disc can't be played in any standard audio CD player (even if it supports MP3 CDs, which I discuss next). Therefore, you can listen to these songs only by using iTunes (or another media player) on a Mac or a PC.

✔ **MP3 CD:** As does the ordinary computer CD-ROM that I describe, an MP3 CD holds MP3 files in data format. However, the files are arranged in such a way that they can be recognized by audio CD players that support the MP3 CD format (especially boom boxes, DVD players, personal CD players, and car stereos). Because MP3 files are so much smaller than the digital audio tracks found on traditional audio CDs, you can fit as many as 160 typical 4-minute songs on one disc. These discs can also be played on your MacBook via iTunes.

Keep in mind that MP3 CDs aren't the same as the standard audio CDs that you buy at the store, and you can't play them in older audio CD players that don't support the MP3 CD format. Rather, this is the kind of archival disc that you burn at home for your own collection.

To begin the process, select an existing playlist that you want to record or create a new playlist and add to it whatever songs you would like to have on the CD. (See the earlier section, "Keeping Slim Whitman and Slim Shady Apart: Organizing with Playlists," if you need a refresher.) With the songs in the correct order, right-click the playlist and choose Burn Playlist to Disc to commence the disc-burning process. Click the desired recording format (again, usually Audio CD) in the Burn Settings dialog that appears.

To save yourself from sonic shock, I always recommend that you select the Sound Check check box before you burn. iTunes will adjust the volume on all the songs on your audio CD so that they'll play at the same volume level.

Ready to go? Click Burn and load the blank disc, and iTunes lets you know when the recording is complete.

Sending music elsewhere with AirPlay

If your Mac has an AirPort Extreme wireless card and you're using an AirPort Express portable wireless Base Station, you can ship your songs from iTunes right to your Base Station, and from there to your home stereo, speakers, or boom box! Pick up an AirPlay-enabled sound system, and you can eliminate the stereo, speakers, or boom box and the AirPort Express device entirely. (I get into some serious discussion of AirPort Express in Chapter 12.)

After your AirPort Express Base Station is plugged in and you connect your home stereo (or a boombox or a pair of powered stereo speakers) to the stereo minijack on the Base Station, you see a Speakers pop-up list button at the bottom of the iTunes window. (If the Speakers button doesn't appear, choose iTunes➪Preferences to open the Preferences dialog and then click the Devices button on the toolbar. Make sure that you've selected the Allow iTunes Audio Control from Remote Speakers check box.)

Click the Speakers button, and you can choose to broadcast the music you're playing in iTunes across your wireless network. Ain't technology truly *grand?*

Feasting on iTunes Visuals

By now, you know that iTunes is a feast for the ears, but did you know that it can provide you with eye candy as well? With just a click or two, you can view mind-bending graphics that stretch, move, and pulse with your music, as shown in Figure 14-6.

To begin viewing iTunes visuals, choose View⇨Show Visualizer (or press ⌘+T). Immediately, most of your iTunes interface disappears and begins displaying groovy lava lamp–style animations (like, *sassy,* man). To stop the visuals, choose View⇨Hide Visualizer (or press ⌘+T again). The usual sunny aluminum face of iTunes returns.

You can also change the viewing size of the iTunes visuals. From the View menu item, choose Full Screen (or press ⌘+F). To escape from the Full Screen mode, move your finger on the trackpad or press Esc.

You can still control iTunes with the keyboard while the visuals are zooming around your screen. See Table 14-1, earlier in this chapter, for a rundown on common keyboard shortcuts.

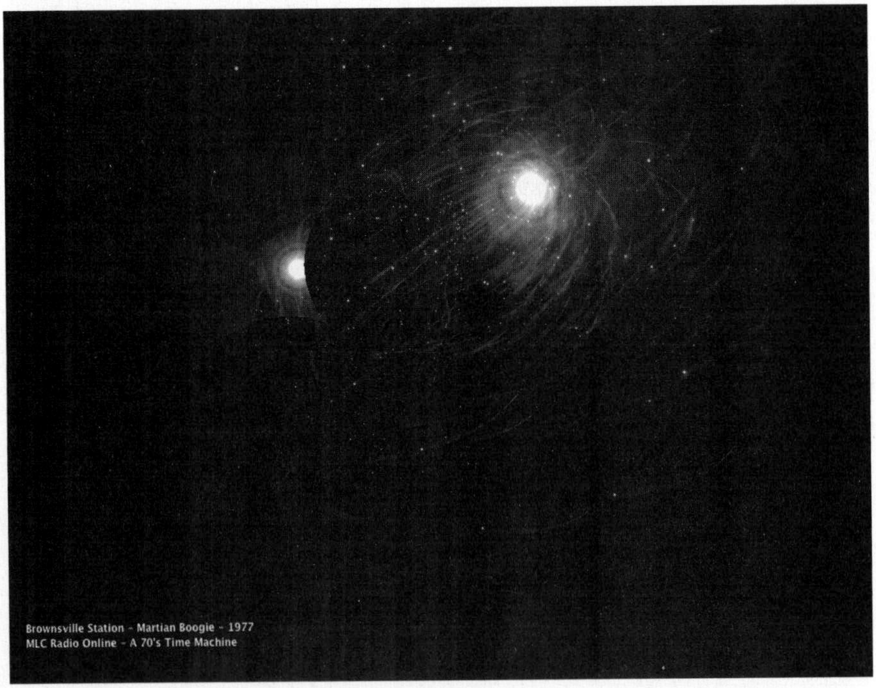

Figure 14-6:
iTunes can display some awesome patterns!

Brownsville Station - Martian Boogie - 1977
MLC Radio Online - A 70's Time Machine

Backing up in iTunes

If your laptop can burn discs, iTunes offers a built-in backup feature for your media library. See? I told you this was the best media player ever designed!

You can choose to back up your entire iTunes Library and all your playlists (which I recommend) or just the content you've purchased from the iTunes Store. Personally, if I lost everything in my collection except for what I've bought from the iTunes Store, I'd be just as crushed. Back it all up, and you won't be sorry. If you're already backing up your Mac's hard drive using Time Machine, there's no reason to back up your library separately to disc unless you crave the heightened peace of mind, or you

want to transport your iTunes Library to another computer.

Choose File⇨Library⇨Back Up to Disc to start the process. Click Back Up, and iTunes will prompt you for blank CDs or DVDs. If you need to restore from your completed backup, just launch iTunes and load the first backup disc into your drive.

How often is often enough when it comes to backing up your content? That depends completely on how often your media library changes. The idea is to back up often enough so that you always have a recent copy of your media files close by.

The iTunes Visualizer has many hidden features. While viewing the Visualizer, press ? to see a list of hidden Visualizer settings.

But wait, more Easter eggs are to be found! Again, while viewing the Visualizer, press one of following keys:

- **M:** Changes the Visualizer pattern
- **P:** Changes the Visualizer color scheme

Press either of these keys repeatedly to cycle through the various patterns and color schemes lurking deep within the Visualizer. (Personally, I'm a random Visualizer guy . . . so many patterns and schemes are available that I just let my MacBook do all the work.)

Additionally, you'll find third-party Visualizer plug-ins available for downloading on Apple's website and other Mac-related download sites — heck, some even display lyrics, karaoke-style! Choose a different Visualizer plug-in from the View⇨Visualizer menu item. (Call me old-fashioned, but I like the default iTunes Visualizer.)

Exercising Parental Authority

Do young children use your laptop? I'll be honest here: A large amount of content in the iTunes Store, including audio, movies, and even apps, is stuff that I don't consider suitable for kids. And what about the media that others in the family may decide to share? Such is the world we live in today, and the good folks at Apple recognize that you may not want to inadvertently allow your kids to have access to explicit content.

Luckily, you can use the Parental settings in iTunes to build a secure fence around content that's for grown-ups only. Heck, you can even banish items from the Source list entirely. Figure 14-7 illustrates the Parental Preferences pane in the iTunes Preferences dialog.

You must log in with an Administrator account to change these settings, just like with the Parental Controls in Mountain Lion's System Preferences dialog. If the settings are *locked* — the padlock icon at the bottom of the dialog is closed — click the icon and supply your administrator password to unlock the settings.

To enable parental control, follow these steps:

1. **Choose iTunes⇨Preferences.**

2. **Click the Parental tab.**

3. **Select any of the Disable check boxes to prevent access to those features.**

You'll notice that any features you disable disappear completely from the Source list at the left side of the iTunes window after you click OK at the end of these steps.

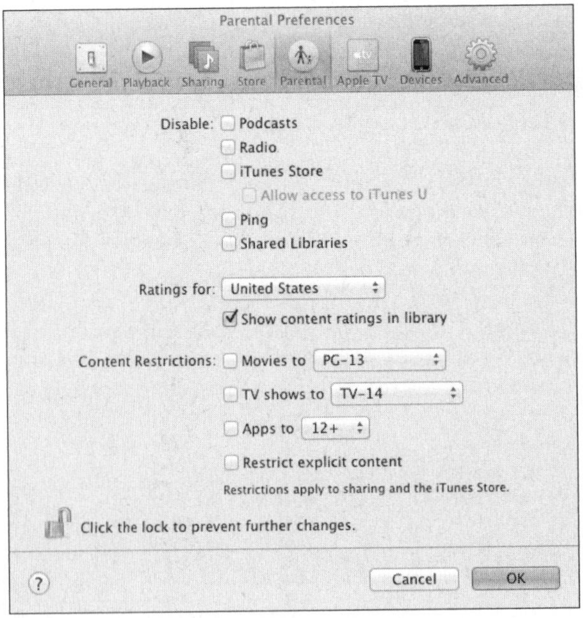

Figure 14-7:
Protect your
kids from
explicit
content.

4. **Click the Ratings For pop-up menu and choose your country.**

   Because Apple maintains separate iTunes Stores for different nations, you can choose which country's iTunes Store to monitor. If you like, you can disable the display of content ratings in your iTunes library by deselecting the Show Content Ratings in Library check box.

5. **To restrict specific content in the iTunes Store, select the check box next to the source, and then make choices from the corresponding pop-up menu to choose the restriction level.**

   Note that these restrictions apply only to content in the iTunes Store and media shared with your MacBook. Content in your iTunes Library is never restricted.

6. **Click the padlock icon at the bottom of the dialog to close it and prevent any changes.**

7. **Click OK.**

Buying Digital Media the Apple Way

Before we wave good-bye to the happy residents of iTunes iSland, I won't forget to mention the hottest spot on the Internet for buying music and video: the iTunes Store, which you can reach from the cozy confines of iTunes. (That is, as long as you have an Internet connection. If you don't, it's time to turn the page to a different chapter.)

Click the iTunes Store item in the Source list, and after a few moments, you're presented with the latest offerings. Click a link in the store list to browse according to media type, or click the Power Search link to search by song title, artist, album, or composer. The Back and Forward buttons at the top of the iTunes Store window operate much the same as those in Safari, moving you backward or forward in sequence through pages you've already seen. Clicking the Home button (which, through no great coincidence, looks like a miniature house) takes you back to the Store's main page.

To display the details on a specific album, track, video, podcast, or audiobook (whew), just click it. If you're interested in buying just certain tracks (for that perfect road warrior mix), you get to listen to 90 seconds of any track — for free and at full sound quality. To add an item to your iTunes Store shopping cart, click the Add Song/Movie/Album/Video/Podcast/Audiobook button (sheesh!). When you're ready to buy, click the Shopping Cart item in the Source list and then click the Buy Now button. (At the time of this writing, tracks are usually 99 cents a pop, and an entire album is typically $9.99 . . . what a bargain!)

The iTunes Store creates an account for you based on your Apple ID, and it keeps secure track of your payment information for future purchases. After you use the iTunes Store once, you rarely have to log in or retype your credit card information again.

The tracks and files that you download are saved to a separate playlist called Purchased. After the download is finished, you can play them, move them to other playlists, burn them to a CD or DVD, share 'em over your network, or ship them to your iOS devices using iCloud, just as you can any other item in your iTunes Library.

You can also put the Genius button to work for you, in league with the iTunes Store. Click the Show Genius Sidebar button at the lower-right corner of the iTunes window — it looks like an arrow inside a square — and iTunes displays the Genius sidebar, where iTunes recommends music you can buy in the iTunes Store that's similar to the albums in your Music Library. Click the button again to banish the sidebar.

With Apple's iCloud sync feature, iTunes can automatically download the media you purchase on another iCloud device (including another Mac, a PC running Vista, Windows 7, or Windows 8, and an iPhone, iPad, or iPod touch). To set up automatic downloading, choose iTunes⇨Preferences to open the Preferences dialog, and then click the Store tab. After you're signed in at the iTunes Store, you can choose to download music, app, or book purchases, and you have the option to check for new downloads automatically. Click OK to save your changes.

Remember all those skeptics who claimed that buying digital audio and video could never work over the Internet because of piracy issues and high costs? Well, bunkie, hats off to Apple: Once again, our favorite technology leader has done something the *right* way!

Chapter 15

The Masterpiece That Is iPhoto

In This Chapter

▶ Importing pictures from your hard drive or digital camera

▶ Organizing images with iPhoto

▶ Tweaking the appearance of photographs

▶ Creating a photo book

▶ Sharing photos with your friends

*V*irtually every MacBook owner is likely to have a digital camera or a scanner. Digital video (DV) camcorders have certainly grown more plentiful over the past fifteen years or so, and the iPod is still the hottest piece of music hardware on the planet at the time of this writing. The digital camera, however, has reached what those funny (strange) marketing people refer to as *saturation,* and iPhoto was written to address the needs of the vast majority of MacBook owners!

With iPhoto, you organize, edit, and even publish your photographs. (It sports more features than a handful of Swiss Army knives.) After you shoot your photos with a digital camera (or with your laptop's built-in FaceTime HD camera), you can import them into iPhoto, edit them, and publish them. You're not limited to photos that you take yourself, either; you can edit, publish, and organize all kinds of digital image files. You can even create a photo album and use the iPhoto interface to order a handsome hard-bound copy shipped to you.

To sum it all up, I'm willing to bet that iPhoto is either the first or the second iLife application that you fall in love with (running neck and neck with iTunes). In this chapter, I show you how you can work digital image magic with true Apple panache!

Delving into iPhoto

In Figure 15-1, you can see most of the major controls offered in iPhoto. (Other controls automatically appear in the window when you enter different modes; I cover them in upcoming sections of this chapter.)

Source list

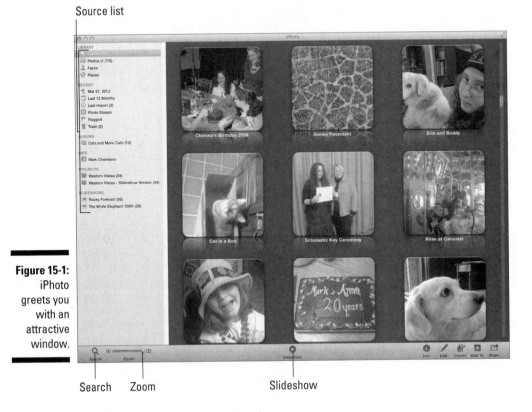

Figure 15-1:
iPhoto
greets you
with an
attractive
window.

Search   Zoom   Slideshow

Although these controls and sections of the window are covered in more detail in the following sections, here's a quick rundown of what you're looking at when you launch iPhoto:

- ✔ **Source list:** This list of image locations determines which photos iPhoto displays.

  - You can choose to display either your entire image library or just the last set of digital images that you downloaded from your camera.

  - You can create new *albums* of your own that appear in the Source list; albums make it much easier to organize your photos. (Albums are the traditional method of grouping photos, which you may be familiar with from older versions of iPhoto.)

  - Photos can be grouped by *event* (when they were taken), *faces* (who appears in the photos), and *places* (where photos were taken).

  - Photos synced with your iOS devices (such as your iPhone and iPad) appear in *Photo Stream*. You can also create your own Shared Photo Streams from devices running iOS 6 or later (and using iCloud). You specify who can see the photos in a Shared Photo Stream, and the contents are synced automatically with your MacBook and other iOS devices.

- You can create books, calendars, cards, and slideshows.

✔ **Viewer:** This pane displays the images from the currently selected photo source.

You can drag or click to select photos in the Viewer for further tricks, such as assigning keywords and image editing.

✔ **Create:** Click this button to add a new blank album, Smart Album, book, calendar, card, or slideshow to your Source list (or the item selected in the Source list).

✔ **Info:** Click this button to display information on the currently selected photos.

✔ **Edit:** Click this button to edit the selected photos. (I cover editing in depth later in the chapter.)

✔ **Full Screen:** Click this button, in the upper-right corner of the iPhoto window, to switch to a full-screen display of your photos. In full-screen mode, the Source list disappears, and both images and events appear as thumbnails. You can double-click a thumbnail to view the image (or the contents, if it's an event), using your Mac's entire screen real estate. You can also use the same controls that I discuss later in this chapter for sharing and editing images; the toolbar is still available at the bottom of the screen.

✔ **Play Slideshow:** Select an event, an album, a book, or a slideshow in the Source list (or multiple images you've selected in the Viewer) and click this button to start a full-screen slideshow using those images.

✔ **Search:** Click the Search button to display the Search text box. Click in the box and start typing to locate photos by specific criteria, or by description and title.

✔ **Add To:** Click this button to add the currently selected photos to an existing album, slideshow, book, card, or calendar.

✔ **Share:** Click this button to share the currently selected photos on Flickr or Facebook (and those from your other iOS devices via Photo Stream, if you're using Apple's iCloud feature) — you can also order prints or e-mail the photos.

✔ **Zoom:** Drag this slider to the left to reduce the size of the thumbnails in the Viewer. This allows you to see more thumbnails at one time, which is a great boon for quick visual searches. Drag the slider to the right to expand the size of the thumbnails, which makes it easier to differentiate details between similar photos in the Viewer.

Importing stored images from your drive

If you have a folder of images that you've already collected on your drive, a CD, a DVD, an external drive, or a USB flash drive, adding them to your library is easy. If the images are in a folder, just drag that folder from a Finder window and drop it into the Albums header (within the Source list in the iPhoto window). iPhoto automatically creates a new album using the folder name, and you can sit back while the images are imported into that new album. iPhoto recognizes images in these formats: JPEG, GIF, RAW, PNG, PICT, PSD, PDF, and TIFF.

If you have individual images, you can drag and drop them as well. Select the images in a Finder window and drag them into the desired album in the Source list. To add them to the album displayed in the Viewer, drag the selected photos and drop them in the Viewer instead.

If you'd rather import images using a standard Mac Open dialog, choose File➪Import to Library. Simplicity strikes again!

Working with Images in iPhoto

Even a superbly designed image display and editing application such as iPhoto would look overwhelming if everything were jammed into one window. Thus, Apple's developers provide different operational modes (such as editing and book creation) that you can use in the one iPhoto window. Each mode allows you to perform different tasks, and you can switch modes at just about any time by clicking the corresponding toolbar button.

In the following sections, I discuss three of these modes — import, organize, and edit — and what you can do when you're in them. Then I conclude the chapter with sections on publishing and sharing your images.

Import Images 101

In *import* mode, you're ready to download images directly from your digital camera — as long as your specific camera model is supported in iPhoto. You can find out which cameras are known to be supported by visiting the Apple iPhoto support page at www.apple.com/support/iphoto. And you're not limited to cameras, of course: You can also import photos from a memory card reader (such as the SD or SDXC card slots sported by most current MacBooks), or even a Kodak PhotoCD. Depending on the camera, iPhoto may also import video clips.

Follow these steps to import images:

1. **Connect your digital camera to your MacBook.**

Plug one end of the USB cable into your camera and the other end into your laptop's USB port, and prepare your camera to download images.

2. **Launch iPhoto.**

   Your MacBook will probably launch iPhoto automatically when your camera is detected, but you can always launch iPhoto manually by clicking its icon in the Dock (or from Launchpad).

3. **Type an event name for the imported photos, such as** Birthday Party **or** Godzilla Ravages Tokyo **(depending on your birthday parties, this could be the same event).**

4. **To have iPhoto automatically separate images into separate events based on the date they were taken, select the Split Events check box.**

5. **Click the Import All button to import your photographs from the camera.**

   The images are added to your Photo Library, where you can organize them as you want.

   To select specific images to import, hold down the ⌘ key and click each desired photo; then click Import Selected rather than Import All.

6. **Specify whether the images you're importing should be deleted from the camera afterward.**

   If you don't expect to download these images again to another computer or another device, you can choose to delete the photos from your camera automatically. This saves you a step, frees space for new photos, and helps eliminate the guilt that can crop up when you nix your pix. (Sorry, I couldn't resist.)

"What's that about an event, Mark?" After you download the contents of your digital camera, those contents count as a virtual *event* in iPhoto — based on either the date that you imported them or the date they were taken. (Yet another reason to set your camera's internal clock!) For example, you can always display the last images you imported by clicking Last Import. If you want to see photos from your son's graduation, they appear as a separate event. (Both of these organizational tools appear in the Source list.) Think about that . . . it's pretty tough to arrange old-fashioned film prints by the moment in time that they document, but iPhoto makes it easy for you to see which photos are part of the same group! I explain more about events in the next section.

Organize mode: Organizing and sorting your images

In the days of film prints, you could always stuff another shoebox with your latest photos or buy another sticky album to expand your library. Your digital camera, though, stores images as files instead, and many folks don't print their digital photographs. Instead, you can keep your entire collection of digital photographs and scanned images well ordered and easily retrieved by using iPhoto's *Organize* mode. Then you can display them in a slideshow, e-mail them, order prints online, print them to your printer, use them as desktop backgrounds, or burn them to an archive disc.

A new kind of photo album

The most familiar method of organizing images in iPhoto is the *album*. Each album can represent any designation you like, be it a year, a vacation, your daughter, or your daughter's ex-boyfriends. Follow these steps to organize your images:

1. **Create a new album.**

   You can either choose File➪New Album (as shown in Figure 15-2) or press ⌘+N. iPhoto creates a new entry under the Albums heading in the Source list.

2. **Type the name for your new photo album.**

3. **Press Return.**

Figure 15-2:
Add a new album in iPhoto.

iPhoto also offers a special type of album called a *smart album,* which you can create from the File menu (or from the keyboard by pressing Option+⌘+N). A smart album contains only photos that match certain criteria that you choose, including the keywords and rating that you assign your images. Other criteria include text in the photo filenames, dates the images were added to iPhoto, and any comments you might have added (as well as camera-specific data such as ISO and shutter speed). Now here's the really nifty angle: iPhoto *automatically* builds and maintains smart albums for you, adding new photos that match the criteria and deleting those that you remove from your Photo Library (as well as removing the photos that no longer match the smart album's criteria)! Smart albums' icons carry a gear symbol in the Source list.

You can display information about the currently selected item in the information pane at the far right of the window. Just click the Info button at the bottom of the iPhoto window, which sports the familiar *i*-in-a-circle logo. You can also type a short note or description in the Description box that appears in the Info pane, or add keywords to help you organize your photos.

You can also change information on an image by selecting it in the Viewer and clicking the Info button. For example, click the Title heading in the pane, and you can simply click in the box to type a new name.

You can drag images from the Viewer into any album you choose. For example, you can copy an image to another album by dragging it from the Viewer to the desired album in the Source list.

To remove a photo that has fallen out of favor, follow these steps:

1. **In the Source list, select the desired album.**

2. **In the Viewer, select the photo (click it) that you want to remove.**

3. **Press Delete.**

When you remove a photo from an album, you *don't* remove the photo from your collection (which is represented by the Photos entry under the Library heading in the Source list). That's because an album is just a group of links to the images in your collection. If you want to completely remove an offending photo from iPhoto, click the Photos entry under the Library heading to display your entire collection of images and delete the picture there. The photo disappears from all albums and projects with which it is associated.

To remove an entire album from the Source list, just click it in the Source list to select it — in the Viewer, you can see the images that it contains — and then press Delete. (Alternatively, right-click the offending album and choose Delete Album from the shortcut menu.)

To rename an album, click the entry under the Albums heading in the Source list to select it and then click again to display a text box. Type the new album name and press Return.

Change your mind? iPhoto comes complete with a handy-dandy Undo feature. Just press ⌘+Z, and it's as though your last action never happened (a great trick for those moments when you realize you just deleted your only image of your first car from your library). Because Undo works on only the last few actions you took, make sure you back up your MacBook's drive using Time Machine!

Arranging stuff by events

As I mention earlier, an event is a group of images that you shot or downloaded at the same time — iPhoto figures that those images belong together (which is usually a pretty safe assumption). Figure 15-3 illustrates some of the events I've created in my iPhoto collection.

As can an album, an event can be renamed — you just use a different procedure. Click the Events entry under the Library heading in the Source list to display your events in the Viewer; then click the existing event name in the caption underneath the thumbnail. A text box appears in which you can type a new name; click Return to update the event.

Although a photo can appear in multiple albums, it can appear in only one event.

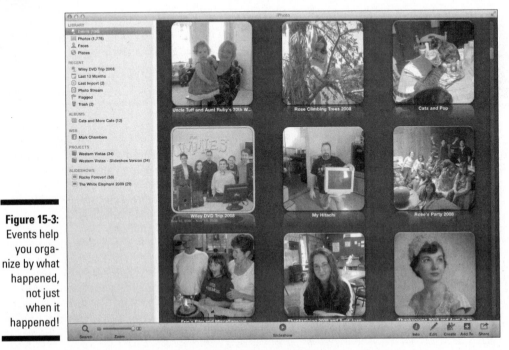

Figure 15-3:
Events help you orga-nize by what happened, not just when it happened!

Try moving your cursor over an event thumbnail in the Viewer and you see that iPhoto displays the date range when the images were taken, as well as the total number of images in the event. Ah, but things get *really* cool when you move your cursor back and forth over an event with many images: The thumbnail animates and displays all the images in the event! (Why can't I think of this stuff? The future is now, dear readers.)

To display the contents of an event in the Viewer, just double-click the Event thumbnail. To return to the events thumbnails, click the All Events button at the top of the Viewer.

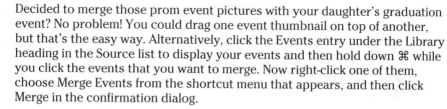

Decided to merge those prom event pictures with your daughter's graduation event? No problem! You could drag one event thumbnail on top of another, but that's the easy way. Alternatively, click the Events entry under the Library heading in the Source list to display your events and then hold down ⌘ while you click the events that you want to merge. Now right-click one of them, choose Merge Events from the shortcut menu that appears, and then click Merge in the confirmation dialog.

While organizing, you can create a brand-new empty event by choosing Events⇨Create Event. Feel free to drag photos from albums, other events, or your Photo Library into your new event.

Working with Faces and Places

iPhoto has two organizational tools called Faces and Places. These two categories appear in the Library section of the Source list.

First, let's tackle Faces. This feature is a sophisticated recognition system that automatically recognizes human faces in the photos that you add to your library. (I don't know whether it works well with pets — but you can try, anyway.) Naturally, you have to identify faces first before iPhoto can recognize them, which it does through a process called *tagging*.

To tag a face, follow these steps:

1. **In the Source list, click the Photos item to display your image library.**

2. **In the Viewer, click the photo containing a person you want to tag.**

   The photo is selected, as indicated by the yellow border.

3. **Click the Info button in the iPhoto toolbar at the bottom of the window.**

   iPhoto displays the Info pane you see in Figure 15-4.

4. **In the Faces section of the Info pane, click the Add a Face link.**

   Note that iPhoto has indicated each person's face in the photo with a label. If a face has already been tagged, the label will match the person's face.

Figure 15-4:
Adding
another
mug to my
collection of
Faces. (That
just doesn't
sound right.)

5. If the face is unrecognized (labeled as Click to Name), click the label to open a text box and type the person's name.

If iPhoto recognizes the face correctly and the name matches the person, click the check mark to confirm the tag. If the face is incorrectly identified, click the X at the right of the text box and enter a new name.

If the name appears on a Contacts contact card — or is recognized as one of your Facebook friends — you can click the matching entry that appears to confirm the identity. Wowzers!

To delete a face recognition box that isn't necessary, hover your mouse cursor over the box and click the X button that appears at the top-left corner of the box.

If iPhoto doesn't recognize a face in the photo (which can happen if the person's face is turned at an angle to the camera or is in a darker area of the photo), click the box border and drag the box over the person's face. If necessary, you can resize the box using its four corner handles. Now you can click the label and type the person's name.

6. After you've identified all the faces in the photo, click the Info button to hide the Info pane.

After you tag an image, it appears in your Faces collection, which you can view by clicking the Faces entry in the Source list. You can double-click a portrait in your Faces collection to see all the images that contain that person. As you might expect, the more tags you add for a specific person, the better iPhoto gets at recognizing that person!

Notice the Confirm Additional Faces button that appears next to the person's name? Click it, and iPhoto displays other photos that may contain this person's face, allowing you to tag the person there as well. If a face is a match, click the thumbnail to confirm it.

The Places feature makes it easy to track the location where photos were taken, but it requires a digital camera that includes GPS tracking information in the image metadata for iPhoto to do so without your help. (This feature is relatively new for digital cameras, so older models aren't likely to support GPS tracking. Owners of current iPhone and iPad models will be happy to hear that GPS tracking is supported by these devices.) Places also requires an Internet connection, because it uses Google Maps.

Click the Places entry in the Source list to display a global map, with pushpins indicating where your photos were taken. You can switch the Places map between terrain and satellite modes, or choose a hybrid display. If you're familiar with Google Maps, these settings are old friends of yours.

If you click a specific photo (that includes location information) to select it and then click the Info button, you'll see a close-up map of the location where the photo was taken.

Alternatively, click the Location buttons at the top of the map to display a browser where you can click country, state, and city names.

No matter which view mode you choose, clicking a pushpin or location displays the images taken in that area.

Organizing with keywords

"Okay, Mark, albums, events, Faces, and Places are great ideas, but there has to be a way to search my collection by category!" Never fear, good road warrior. You can also assign descriptive *keywords* to images to help you organize your collection and locate certain pictures fast. iPhoto comes with a number of standard keywords, and you can create your own as well.

To illustrate, suppose you'd like to identify your images according to special events in your family. Birthday photos should have their own keyword, and anniversaries deserve another. By assigning keywords, you can search for Elsie's sixth birthday or your silver wedding anniversary (no matter what event or album they're in), and all related photos with those keywords appear like magic! (Well, *almost* like magic. You need to choose View⇨Keywords, which toggles on and off the keyword display in the Viewer.)

iPhoto includes a number of keywords that are already available:

- ✔ Favorite
- ✔ Family
- ✔ Kids
- ✔ Vacation
- ✔ Birthday
- ✔ RAW
- ✔ Photo Booth
- ✔ Movie
- ✔ Checkmark

What's the Checkmark keyword all about, you ask? It's a special case: Adding this keyword displays a tiny check mark icon in the lower-right corner of the image. The Checkmark keyword comes in handy for temporarily identifying specific images because you can search for just your checkmarked photos.

To assign keywords to images (or remove keywords that have already been assigned), select one or more photos in the Viewer. Choose Window⇨Manage My Keywords or press ⌘+K to display the Keywords window, as shown in Figure 15-5.

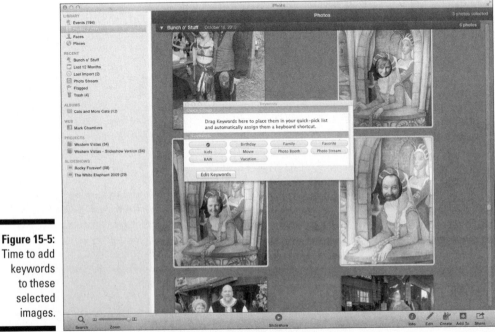

Figure 15-5:
Time to add keywords to these selected images.

You're gonna need your own keywords

I'll bet you take photos of other things besides just kids and vacations — and that's why iPhoto allows you to create your own keywords. Display the iPhoto Keywords window by pressing ⌘+K, click the Edit Keywords button, and then click Add (the button with the plus sign). iPhoto adds a new unnamed keyword to the list as an edit box, ready for you to type its name.

You can rename an existing keyword from this same window, too. Click a keyword to select it and then click Rename. Remember, however, that renaming a keyword affects *all the images*

that were tagged with that keyword. That might be confusing when, for example, photos originally tagged as Family suddenly appear with the keyword Foodstuffs. (I recommend applying a new keyword and deleting the old one if this problem crops up.)

To change the keyboard shortcut assigned to a keyword, click the Shortcut button. To remove an existing keyword from the list, click the keyword to select it and then click the Delete button, which bears a minus sign.

Click the keyword buttons that you want to attach to the selected images to mark them. Or click the highlighted keyword buttons that you want to remove from the selected images to disable them.

Drag the keyword buttons that you use the most to the Quick Group section of the Keywords window, and iPhoto automatically creates a keyboard shortcut for each keyword in the Quick Group. Now you don't even need to display the Keywords window to get business done!

Digging through your library with keywords

Behold the power of keywords! To sift through your entire collection of images by using keywords, click the Search button on the toolbar, and then click the magnifying glass icon next to the Search box and choose Keyword from the pop-up menu. iPhoto displays a pop-up Keywords panel, and you can click one or more keyword buttons to display just the photos that carry those keywords.

The images that remain in the Viewer after a search must have *all* the keywords that you specified. If an image is identified, for example, by only three of four keywords you chose, it isn't a match and it doesn't appear in the Viewer. (You can create a Smart Album with specific keywords to get around this limitation — use *any* instead of *all* as the argument.)

To search for a photo by words in its description, just click in the Search box and start typing. You can also click that same magnifying glass by the Search box to search through your images by date and rating as well.

Speaking of ratings . . .

Playing favorites by assigning ratings

Be your own critic! iPhoto allows you to assign any photo a rating of anywhere from zero to five stars. I use this system to help me keep track of the images that I feel are the best in my library. Select one (or more) image and then assign a rating by using one of the following methods:

- ✔ Choose Photos⇨My Rating and then choose the desired rating from the pop-up submenu.

- ✔ Hover your cursor over the photo and click the More button that appears in the lower-right corner of the thumbnail, and then click the desired star rating on the menu that appears.

- ✔ Use the ⌘+0 through ⌘+5 shortcuts.

Sorting your images just so

The View menu provides an easy way to arrange your images in the Viewer by a number of different criteria. Choose View⇨Sort Photos and then click the desired sort criteria from the pop-up submenu. You can arrange the display by date, keyword, title, or rating. If you select an album in the Source list, you can also choose to arrange photos manually, which means that you can drag and drop thumbnails in the Viewer to place them in the precise order you want them.

Edit mode: Removing and fixing stuff the right way

Not every digital image is perfect — just look at my collection if you need proof. For those shots that need a pixel massage, iPhoto includes a number of editing tools that you can use to correct common problems.

The first step in any editing job is to select the image you want to fix in the Viewer. Then click the Edit button on the iPhoto toolbar to display the edit mode controls at the right side of the window, as shown in Figure 15-6. Now you're ready to fix problems, using the tools that I discuss in the following sections. (If you're editing a photo that's part of an event, an album, Faces, or Places, note the spiffy scrolling photo strip at the bottom, which allows you to switch to another image from the same grouping to edit.)

If you'd prefer to edit images with more of your screen real estate, click the Full Screen button in the upper-right corner of the iPhoto window (refer to Figure 15-1). To switch back to the standard window arrangement, press Esc.

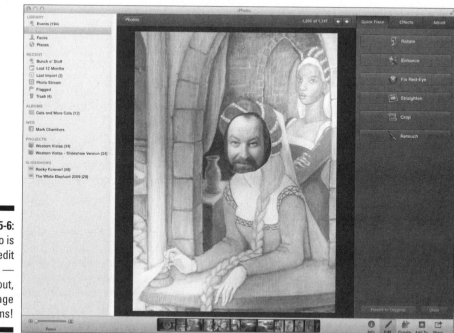

Figure 15-6:
iPhoto is now in edit mode — watch out, image problems!

Need more features than iPhoto provides when editing a prized photograph? iPhoto allows you to specify another image-editing application such as Photoshop Elements (in addition to the built-in editing controls that I cover in this chapter). First, choose iPhoto⇨Preferences⇨Advanced. From the Edit Photos pop-up menu, opt for Choose App. Navigate to the image editor you want to use, select it, and click Open. Close the Preferences dialog, and iPhoto automatically opens the application you selected when you click the Edit button. If you decide to return to iPhoto's built-in editing controls, just open the Advanced pane again, click the Edit Photos pop-up menu again, and choose In iPhoto.

When you're done with edit mode, click the Edit button again to return to the Viewer.

While you're editing, you can use the Next and Previous buttons at the left of the Quick Fix tab button to move to the next image in the current group (or back to the previous image).

When you first enter edit mode, the Quick Fixes tab is selected, providing you with the tools I've already covered. (You use these tools for the changes you'll make most often, so having Quick Fixes as the default selection makes sense.)

However, you can also choose to apply an effect from the Effects tab, or make specific changes to the appearance of an image from the Adjust tab.

Rotating tipped-over shots

If an image is in the wrong orientation and needs to be turned to be displayed correctly, click the Rotate button to turn it once in a counterclockwise direction. Hold down the Option key while you click the Rotate button to rotate in a clockwise direction.

Find yourself using that Option key often while rotating images? Consider reversing the default direction. Choose iPhoto➪Preferences, click the General tab, and then select the Rotate radio button to change the default direction.

Crop 'til you drop

Does that photo have an intruder hovering around the edges of the subject? You can remove some of the border by *cropping* an image, just as folks once did with film prints and a pair of scissors. (We've come a long way.) With iPhoto, you can remove unwanted portions of an image; cropping is a great way to get Uncle Milton's stray head (complete with toupee) out of an otherwise perfect holiday snapshot.

Follow these steps to crop an image:

1. **Click the Crop button on the Editing toolbar.**

2. **Select the portion of the image that you want to keep.**

   In the Viewer, click and drag the handles on the rectangle to outline the part of the image that you want. Remember, whatever's outside this rectangle disappears after the crop is completed.

   When you drag a corner or edge of the outline, a semi-opaque grid (familiar to amateur and professional photographers as the nine squares from the Rule of Thirds) appears to help you visualize what you're claiming. (Check out the grid in Figure 15-7.)

   You can expand the outline to the full dimensions of the image at any time — just click the Reset button.

3. **(Optional) Choose a preset aspect ratio.**

   If you want to force your cropped selection to a specific aspect ratio — such as 4 x 3 or 16 x 9 for an iMovie project — select the Constrain check box and choose that ratio from the Constrain pop-up menu.

4. **Click the Done button.**

   Oh, and don't forget that you can use iPhoto's Undo feature if you mess up and need to try again. Just press ⌘+Z.

Figure 15-7:
Select the
stuff that
you want to
keep in your
photo.

iPhoto features multiple Undo levels, so you can press ⌘+Z several times to travel back through your last several changes. Alternatively, you can always return the image to its original form (before you did any editing) by clicking the Revert to Original button.

Straightening what's crooked

Was your camera slightly tilted when you took the perfect shot? Never fear! Click the Straighten button and then drag the slider to tilt the image in the desired direction — iPhoto also slightly crops the image to return it to a rectangular shape. Click the Done button to return to edit mode.

Enhancing images to add pizzazz

If a photo looks washed out, click the Enhance button to increase (or decrease) the color saturation and improve the contrast. Enhance is automatic, so you don't have to set anything — but be prepared to use Undo if you're not satisfied with the changes.

Removing rampant red-eye

Unfortunately, today's digital cameras can still produce the same "zombies with red eyeballs" as traditional film cameras. *Red-eye* is caused by a camera's flash reflecting off the retinas of a subject's eyes, and it can occur with both humans and animals. (I'm told that pets get *blue-eye* or *green-eye,* but iPhoto can handle that, too!)

E-mailing photos to Aunt Mildred

iPhoto can help you e-mail your images by automating the process. The application can prepare your image and embed it automatically in a new message.

To send an image through e-mail, select it, click the Share button on the toolbar, and then click the Email menu item. Choose a theme for your message (complete with a background image and matching font selection). You can also specify the size of the image from the Photo Size pop-up menu, which can save considerable downloading time for those recipients who still use a dial-up connection. To add the image as an attachment to the message, select the Attach Photos to Message check box.

Most ISP (Internet service provider) e-mail servers don't accept an e-mail message larger than 3MB to 5MB, so watch that Size display at the bottom of the window. (In fact, the encoding necessary to send images as attachments can *double* the size of each image!) If you're trying to send a number of images and the size goes over 3MB, try clicking the Photo Size pop-up menu and choosing a smaller size (reducing the image resolution) to get them all to fit in a single message.

When you are satisfied with the total file size, click the Send button. iPhoto automatically creates a new message containing the images, ready for you to add a personal note (if desired). When the message is ready, click Send!

iPhoto can turn frightening zombies back into your family and friends! Click the Red-Eye button and then select a demonized eyeball by clicking in the center of it. (If the circular cursor is too small or too large, drag the Size slider to adjust the dimensions.) To complete the process, click the Done button.

Retouching like the stars

The iPhoto Retouch feature is perfect for removing minor flecks or lines in an image (especially those you scanned from prints). When Retouch is active, the cursor turns into a circle. (Drag the Size slider to change the size of the Retouch cursor.) Simply drag the cursor across the imperfection and click Done when you're finished touching up. Don't forget to take a moment and marvel at your editing skill!

Switching to black-and-white or sepia

Ever wonder whether a particular photo in your library would look better as a black-and-white (or *grayscale*) print? Or perhaps an old-fashioned *sepia* tone in shades of copper and brown? Trying out iPhoto's effects on your photos is fun! Just click the Effects tab, which offers nine effects you can apply to the photo, including black-and-white and sepia. You can also make one-click photo changes from the Effects tab, including lightening and darkening an image or enhancing the contrast.

Adjusting photo properties manually

Click the Adjust tab to perform manual adjustments to brightness and contrast (the light levels in your image), as well as attributes such as the sharpness, shadow, and highlight levels. To adjust a value, make sure that nothing's selected in the image and then drag the corresponding slider until the image looks the way you want. Click the Close button to return to edit mode.

Producing Your Own Coffee-Table Masterpiece

Book mode unleashes what I think is probably the coolest feature of iPhoto: the chance to design and print a high-quality bound photo book! After you complete an album — all the images have been edited just the way you want, and the album contains all the photos you want to include in your book — iPhoto can send your images as data over the Internet to a company that prints and binds your finished book for you. (No, they don't publish *For Dummies* titles, but then again, I don't get high-resolution color plates in most of my books, either.)

At the time of this writing, you can order many different sizes and bindings. The largest size is a 13" x 10" hardcover book with 20 double-sided pages for about $50 (extra pages cost $1.50 each). Smaller sizes include an 8.5" x 11" softcover book with 20 double-sided pages for about $20 and a hardcover 8.5" x 11" album with 20 double-sided pages for about $30 (shipping included for both). Extra pages can be added at $0.70 and $1.00 a pop, respectively.

iPhoto can also produce and automatically order calendars and cards, using a process similar to the one I describe in this section for producing a book. Who needs that stationery store in the mall anymore? (You can even order old-fashioned prints from the Share toolbar menu.)

If you're going to create a photo book, make sure that the images have the highest quality and highest resolution. The higher the resolution, the better the photos look in the finished book. I personally always try to use images of more than 1,200 pixels in the shortest dimension. (Full-page prints should be at least 2,000 pixels in both dimensions.)

To create a photo book, follow these steps:

1. **In the Source list, click the desired album to select it.**

   Make sure that no individual photos are selected in the Viewer. This way, iPhoto uses all the images in the chosen album.

2. **Click the Create toolbar button, and then choose Book from the pop-up menu.**

3. **Select the type of book using the Binding buttons (Hardcover, Softcover, or Wire-bound) at the top of the window and the Size buttons (Small,**

Medium, Large and Extra-Large, depending on the binding) at the left side of the window.

Your choices determine the number of pages and the size of the book. iPhoto displays the approximate cost of your book as you browse the options.

4. **Choose a theme.**

Use the left- and right-arrow keys to cycle through the theme selections. The theme you choose determines both the layout scheme and the background graphics for each page. To change the color scheme for a theme, click one of the color swatches at the right side of the window.

5. **Click Create.**

iPhoto adds your new book project under the Projects heading in the Source list, and you see the controls shown in Figure 15-8.

In book mode, the Viewer displays a collection of thumbnail images, each of which represents a portion of your book — the front cover, internal pages, or the back cover. To display the photos you selected, click the Photos button on the toolbar. You can drag any image thumbnail into one of the photo placeholders to add it to the page.

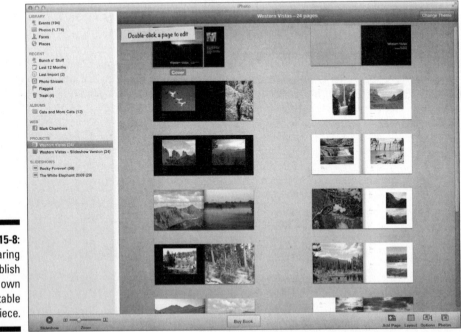

Figure 15-8:
Preparing
to publish
my own
coffee-table
masterpiece.

I really need a slideshow

You can use iPhoto to create slideshows! In the Source list, click the album or event you want to display, and then click the Create button and choose Slideshow. Note that iPhoto adds a Slideshows item in the Source list. A scrolling thumbnail strip appears at the top of the Viewer, displaying the images in the album or event. Click and drag the thumbnails so that they appear in the desired order.

Click the Themes button on the Slideshow toolbar to choose the theme for your slideshow. The theme you choose controls the animation, transition type, and screen layout that iPhoto will use — everything from the classic Ken Burns moving-photo animation to a really nifty Sliding Panels layout.

To choose background music for your slideshow, click the Music button on the Slideshow toolbar to display Apple's theme music, as well as the tracks from your iTunes Library. To choose a standard theme, click the Source pop-up menu and choose Theme Music; select that perfect song and click Choose. To choose an iTunes song or playlist, click the Source pop-up menu and choose a playlist (or throw caution completely to the wind and choose one of your GarageBand compositions). (Read all about GarageBand in Chapter 17.) You can also create a custom playlist by selecting the Custom Playlist for Slideshow check box. Then drag the individual songs you want to the song list at the bottom of the sheet. (You can drag them to rearrange their order in the list as well.) Click Choose to accept your song list.

To configure your slideshow, click the Settings button on the Slideshow toolbar and click the All Slides tab. In the dialog that appears, you can specify the amount of time that each slide remains on the screen, as well as an optional title slide. Widescreen Mac owners appreciate the Aspect Ratio pop-up menu, which allows you to choose a 16:9 widescreen display for your slideshow.

Click the This Slide tab to set the selected photo to display in black and white, sepia, or antique coloring.

To display a quick preview of your slideshow without leaving the iPhoto window, click Preview; this option is a handy way of determining whether the theme and music you've selected are really what you want. When you're ready to play your slideshow, click the Play button, and iPhoto switches to full-screen mode. To create a movie file from your completed slideshow, click Export on the Slideshow toolbar.

Switch to another theme at any time by clicking the Change Theme button at the top of the window.

6. **Rearrange the page order to suit you by dragging the thumbnail of any page from one location to another.**

   If you prefer a book without page numbers, right-click any page and choose Show Page Numbers to toggle it off. The check mark next to the menu item disappears.

7. **Need to change the look of a single page? Click either cover or a page to select it, and then click the Design button on the toolbar to change the color and design layout for that element.**

   Clicking a design thumbnail automatically updates the page display.

8. **Double-click a page to edit captions and short descriptions.**

   Click any one of the text boxes in the page display and begin typing to add text to that page. Some themes don't have caption or description text boxes, but you can add them by displaying the Design pane, clicking the desired photo placeholder, and then clicking one of the Border thumbnails that includes a text box.

   After you're done editing, click the All Pages button at the top of the window to return to your full spread.

9. **To add pages to your book, click the Add Page button on the toolbar.**

   As I mention earlier, the price for additional pages varies according to the size and type of binding you choose.

10. **To view the book at any time, right-click any page and choose Preview Book.**

    After a short wait, Mountain Lion's Preview application opens, and you can then scroll through the contents of your book (or even print a quick copy). To close the Preview window, choose Preview➪Quit Preview.

    Why limit yourself to just paper copies of your publishing success? You can also right-click any page and choose Save Book as PDF to create a snazzy electronic version of your book.

11. **When you're ready to publish your book, click the Buy Book button.**

12. **In a series of dialogs that appears, iPhoto guides you through the final steps to order a bound book.**

    You'll be asked for credit card information, so have that plastic ready.

Do I spy Facebook and Flickr?

Wondering whether you are seeing Facebook and Flickr in iPhoto? Indeed you are! iPhoto introduced a direct connection to both your Facebook social networking account (at www.facebook.com) and your Flickr online gallery account (at www.flickr.com), allowing you to simply select one or more photos and send them automatically to either service! Click the Share button on the toolbar to select either type of account.

The first time you select photos in the Viewer (or an album or event in the Source list) and choose either option, iPhoto prompts you for permission to set up your connection. (Of course, connecting to these accounts requires you to enter your Facebook and Flickr account information — hence the confirmation request.) Click Set Up and provide the data that each site requires.

After you set up your accounts, simply select your photos, albums, or events, click the Share toolbar button, and then choose the menu item for the desired service. Apple, you absolutely *rock!*

Putting Photo Stream to Work

iPhoto includes a feature called *Photo Stream* that automatically shares the photos you take between your Mac, your PC, and any Apple device running iOS 5.0 or later (which includes iPhone 4 and 4S, second- and third-generation iPads, and iPod touch). Click Share and choose Photo Stream, and iPhoto automatically sends the selected images to all compatible devices over your Wi-Fi connection. (Note that all devices using Photo Stream must be configured with the same iCloud account, using the same Apple ID.)

To turn on Photo Stream, choose iPhoto⇨Preferences and click the Photo Stream toolbar button. Select the Enable Photo Stream check box.

Optionally, you can also specify whether iPhoto should automatically import Photo Stream photos to your library, and whether iPhoto should automatically upload the most recent 1,000 photos to Photo Stream for sharing with your other devices.

Chapter 16

Making Film History with iMovie

*R*emember those home movies that you used to make in high school? They were entertaining and fun to create, and your friends were impressed. In fact, some kids are so downright inspired that you're not surprised when you discover at your high school reunion that they turned out to be graphic artists or got involved in video or TV production.

iMovie, part of the iLife suite, makes moviemaking as easy as those home-made movies. Apple has simplified all the technical stuff, such as importing video and adding audio, leaving you free to concentrate on your creative ideas. In fact, you won't find techy terms such as *codecs* or *keyframes* in this chapter at all. I guarantee that you'll understand what's going on at all times. (How often do you get a promise like that with video-editing software?)

With iMovie, your digital video (DV) camcorder, and the other parts of the iLife suite, you can soon produce and share professional-looking movies, with some of the same creative transitions and titles used by Those Hollywood Types every single day — all on your MacBook, all by yourself.

If you turn out to be a world-famous Hollywood Type Director in a decade or so, don't forget the little people along the way!

Shaking Hands with the iMovie Window

If you've ever tried a professional-level video-editing application, you probably felt as though you were suddenly dropped in the cockpit of a jumbo jet. In iMovie, though, all the controls you need are easy to use and logically placed.

To launch iMovie, click the iMovie icon in the Dock. (It looks like a star from the Hollywood Walk of Fame.) You can also run Launchpad and click the iMovie icon there.

Follow these strenuous steps to create a new movie project:

1. **Choose File⇨New Project (or press ⌘+N).**

   iMovie displays the sheet you see in Figure 16-1.

Figure 16-1:
Creating a new movie project in iMovie.

2. **Type a name for your project.**

3. **Select the aspect ratio (or screen dimensions) for your movie.**

   You can select a widescreen display (16:9), a standard display (4:3), or a display especially suited for an iPhone (3:2). If compatibility with the familiar SDTV (standard definition TV) format is important, I recommend that you choose the standard (4:3) ratio. If you're shooting in 16:9 format, choosing 16:9 for an SDTV set will result in those familiar black *letterbox* bars at the top and bottom of the screen, but you won't lose any content from the sides of the frame if you use 16:9. On the flip side, choosing 4:3 results in *pillarboxing* (black bars on the left and right) when shown on an HD set.

4. **Choose the frame rate.**

   The default frame rate is 30 frames per second (fps), which is normal for the North American NTSC video standard. However, you can choose a slower frame rate if necessary, such as the 25 fps setting for the international PAL and SECAM video standards.

5. **Click a Project Theme thumbnail to select a theme to apply to your finished movie.**

   If you choose a theme, iMovie automatically adds the transitions and titles that correspond to that theme. (Typically, this is what you want to do. However, if you want to add transitions and titles manually, click the Automatically Add Transitions and Titles check box to deselect it.)

   If you decide not to use a theme (by selecting the None thumbnail), iMovie can still add an automatic effect between clips. Select the Automatically Add check box and click the pop-up menu to choose the desired effect.

   You can also create movie trailers in iMovie, which I demonstrate later in this chapter. Generally, however, I recommend that you create your trailer project *after* your movie project is complete (unless, of course, you're specifically creating just a trailer project). Why? For the same reason that studios create trailers when the filming is finished: After you complete your movie, all the clips will be imported already, and you'll have a better idea of what you want to include while "teasing" your audience!

6. **Click Create.**

   You're on your way! Check out Figure 16-2: This is the whole enchilada, in one window.

Project Library/Project/Trailer pane

Playhead   Editing toolbar   Monitor

Media Browser toolbar

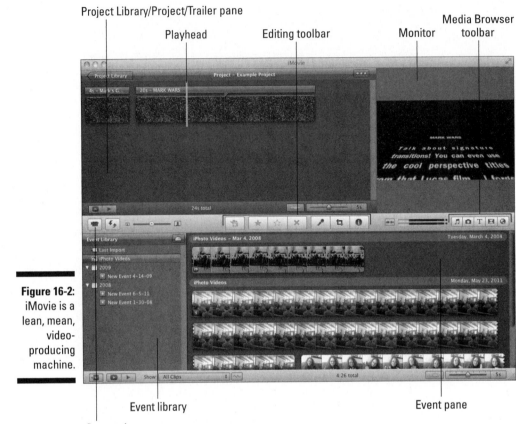

Figure 16-2:
iMovie is a
lean, mean,
video-
producing
machine.

Event library

Camera import

Event pane

The controls and displays that you'll use most often follow:

- ✔ **Monitor:** Think of the monitor as being just like your TV or computer monitor. Your video clips, still images, and finished movie play here.

- ✔ **Media Browser toolbar:** This row of buttons allows you to switch between your media clips (video clips, photos, and audio) and the various tools that you use to make your film. The selected items fill the right side of the browser pane below the monitor.

- ✔ **Event Library:** This list (lower left) displays all the video clips you can add to your project, including video clips you've created in iPhoto. These clips are organized as *events,* which I'll discuss later in the chapter.

- ✔ **Event pane:** If you select a video clip in the Event Library list, iMovie displays a thumbnail of the content in the Event pane. If you decide to include the clip, you can add it to your project. I show you what each of the panes in the iMovie workspace looks like when you tackle different tasks in this chapter.

✓ **Project Library/Project/Trailer pane:** iMovie displays the movie projects that you create in the *Project Library* pane. Note that when you double-click a project in the Project Library pane, it turns into the *Project* pane, which displays the elements you added to that specific project (such as video clips, still photos, and audio clips). If you drag an element into the Project Library pane, it turns into the Project pane for the selected project; if you're working on a movie trailer, the Project Library pane turns into the Trailer pane.

The Project Library pane displays different content, depending on the action you've taken.

✓ **Playhead:** The red vertical line that you see in the Event and Project Library panes is the *playhead,* which indicates the current editing point while you're browsing clips or creating your movie. When you're playing your movie, the playhead moves to follow your progress through the movie.

✓ **Editing toolbar:** This strip of buttons allows you to control editing functions such as cropping; audio and video adjustments; voiceovers; and selecting items.

✓ **Camera Import window:** Click this switch to import DV clips from your DV camcorder or your MacBook's built-in FaceTime HD camera.

Those elements are the major highlights of the iMovie window. A director's chair and megaphone are optional, of course, but they do add to the mood.

A Bird's-Eye View of Moviemaking

I don't want to box in your creative skills here — after all, you can attack the moviemaking process from a number of angles. (Pun, unfortunately, intended.) However, I've found that my movies turn out the best when I follow a linear process, so before I dive into specifics, allow me to provide you with an overview of moviemaking with iMovie.

Here's my take on the process, reduced to seven steps:

1. **Import your video clips directly from your DV camcorder, FaceTime HD camera, iPhoto, or your hard drive.**

2. **Drag your new selection of clips from the Event pane to the Project pane and arrange them in the desired order.**

3. **Import or record audio clips (from iTunes, GarageBand, or external sources, such as audio CDs or audio files that you've recorded yourself) and add them to your movie.**

4. **Import your photos (directly from iPhoto or from your hard drive) and place them where needed in your movie.**

5. **Add professional niceties, such as voiceovers, transitions, effects, and text to the project.**

6. **Preview your film and edit it further if necessary.**

7. **Share your finished film with others through the web, e-mail, your Apple TV, or an iOS device (an iPhone, iPad, or iPod touch).**

As you might imagine, this chapter simply can't hold a full description of every setting and every procedure in iMovie — but luckily, Tony Bove has done exactly that in his book *iLife '11 For Dummies* (Wiley). Tony will take you from the basics to all the in-depth features of each iLife application!

Importing the Building Blocks

Sure, you need video clips to create a movie of your own, but don't panic if you have but a short supply. You can certainly turn to the other iLife applications for additional raw material. (See, I told you that integration thing would come in handy.)

Along with video clips you import from your DV camcorder, built-in FaceTime HD camera, and hard drive, you can also call on iPhoto for still images (think credits) and iTunes for background audio and effects. In the following sections, I show you how.

Pulling in video clips

Your MacBook is already equipped with the large drive you need for editing digital video. In fact, because your MacBook has a FaceTime HD camera on-board, you're a self-contained movie studio! Of course, you can also use clips filmed with a camcorder — depending on the MacBook model and camcorder you're using, you may be using either a FireWire or a USB connection. (Fear not, the instructions I give in this section are easily modified for your particular device! Only a few steps are different, and I cover them shortly.) Note that MacBook Pro Retina and MacBook Air models do not have a FireWire port, and the FireWire 800 port on the MacBook Pro requires a special cable to connect to older FireWire 400 camcorders.

Here's the drill if your clips are on your FireWire mini-DV camcorder or a mass-storage USB camcorder:

1. **Plug the proper cable into your laptop.**

2. **Set the camcorder to VTR (or VCR) mode.**

   Some camcorders call this Play mode.

3. **Click the Camera Import button (labeled in Figure 16-2).**

   iMovie opens a new window.

4. **Click the Camera pop-up menu (at the bottom of the Import window) and select your DV camcorder, iSight camera (on older MacBooks), or FaceTime camera.**

   If you're using a tape-based camcorder, playback controls appear under the Camera Import window, mirroring the controls on your DV camcorder. This setup allows you to control the unit from iMovie. *Keen!* If you're using a mass-storage camcorder connected by USB, you instead get Import All and Import Checked buttons below the thumbnails of available clips.

   To capture video from your iSight or FaceTime HD camera, open the Video Size pop-up menu to choose the dimensions of the clip; then click Capture. On the sheet that appears, choose the location where the video will be saved and also whether to add this video to an existing event or create a new event. Click Capture to start recording, and click Stop when your video is complete. (You can skip the rest of the steps in this section, which deal only with FireWire external camcorders.)

   iMovie can analyze your incoming video for one of three post-recording procedures. Select the After Import Analyze For check box, and then choose Stabilization (which helps smooth shaky camera work), People (which marks a clip as including people, making it easier to locate) or Stabilization and People (which, predictably, does both). The Stabilization option is especially good if your camcorder doesn't have a built-in stabilization function (and you weren't shooting with a tripod), but beware: Any of these settings will add significant time to the import process!

5. **To import selected clips from your DV camcorder, set the Automatic/ Manual switch to Manual and advance the video to a couple of seconds before the point where you want to start your capture, and then click Import.**

   To import all clips, set the Automatic/Manual switch to Automatic and then click Import.

6. **(Optional) If you're using a mass-storage USB camcorder, clear the check boxes next to the clips that you don't want to import (to deselect them) and then click the Import Checked button.**

7. **From the Save To pop-up menu, choose the drive that should store your clips.**

   You can choose to add the new clips to an existing event or create a new event. Heck, if the event spanned more than one day, you can create a new event for each day. (How do they think up these things?)

8. **Click OK and admire your handiwork.**

   iMovie begins transferring the footage to your MacBook and automatically adds the imported clips to your Event Library.

If your clips are already on your drive, rest assured that iMovie can import them, including those in *high-definition video* (HDV) format. iMovie also recognizes a number of other video formats, as shown in Table 16-1.

Table 16-1	Video Formats Supported by iMovie
File Type	**Description**
DV	Standard 4:3 digital video
DV Widescreen	Widescreen 16:9 digital video
MOV	QuickTime movies
HDV & AVCHD	High-definition (popularly called widescreen) digital video, in 720p and 1080i
MPEG-2	Digital video format used for DVD movies and digital TV
MPEG-4	A popular format for streaming Internet and wireless digital video, as well as handheld iOS devices such as iPad, iPhone, and iPod touch

It's easy to get lost in the morass of video formats and assorted standards in use today. Although I can't cover them all in a single chapter, I can recommend the wonderful website www.videohelp.com, which offers comprehensive information on video recording, optical hardware, and format-conversion software.

To import a movie file, follow this bouncing ball:

1. **Choose File⇨Import and then choose Movies from the submenu.**

2. **Open the Optimize Video pop-up menu. If you're importing 1080i video clips, choose the Full quality setting. Otherwise, use the default Large setting.**

   The Large setting saves you a significant amount of drive space, but the Full setting preserves the original resolution and detail. (The Full setting demands a significant chunk of the CPU and RAM resources your MacBook can offer, so expect slower multitasking while importing.)

3. **Click OK.**

4. **Click the drive that should store your clips in the File Open sheet sidebar, and then navigate to the desired location.**

5. **Specify whether you want to add the imported video to an existing event or create a new event.**

   If you choose to add the video to an existing event, click the pop-up menu and select an event.

6. **Specify whether you want to copy the video (leaving the original movie intact) or whether the original movie should be moved (the original deleted after a successful import).**

7. **Click Import.**

   Alternatively, you can also drag a video clip from a Finder window and drop it in the Project pane.

Making use of still images

Still images come in handy as impressive-looking titles or as ending credits to your movie. (Make sure that you list a gaffer and a best boy to be truly professional.) However, you can use still images also to introduce scenes or to separate clips according to your whim. For example, I use stills when delineating the days of a vacation within a movie or different Christmas celebrations over time.

Here are two methods of adding stills to your movie:

✔ **Adding images from iPhoto:** Click the Photo Browser button on the Browser toolbar (or press ⌘+2), and you'll experience the thrill that is your iPhoto Library, right from iMovie (as shown in Figure 16-3). You can elect to display your entire iPhoto Library or more selective picks such as specific albums or events. When you find the image you want to add, just drag it to the correct spot in the Project pane. Videos from your iPhoto Library are automatically added to your iMovie Event Library — it doesn't get much easier than that.

✔ **Importing images from your hard drive:** If you're a member of the International Drag-and-Drop Society, you can drag TIFF, JPEG, GIF, PICT, PNG, and PSD images directly from a Finder window and drop them into the Project pane as well.

Transitions

Titles

Photo Browser

Music and sound effects

Play project full screen

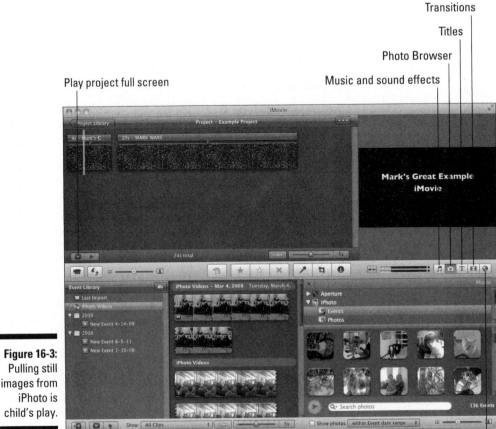

Figure 16-3:
Pulling still
images from
iPhoto is
child's play.

Play event full screen

Map and background

Importing and adding audio from all sorts of places

You can pull in everything from Wagner to Weezer as both background music and sound effects for your movie. In this section, I focus on how to get those notes into iMovie and then how to add them to your movie by dragging them to the Project pane.

You can add audio from a number of sources:

✔ **Adding songs from iTunes:** Click the Show Music and Sound Effects button on the Media Browser toolbar (or press ⌘+1) to display the contents of your iTunes Library. Click the desired playlist in the scrolling list box, such as the ABBA playlist I selected in Figure 16-4. (If you exported any original music you composed in GarageBand to your iTunes Library, you can use those songs in your own movie!) You can add a track to your movie by dragging the song entry from the Music and Sound Effects list to the desired spot in the Project pane.

Adding sound effects: Yep, if you need the sound of a horse galloping for your Rocky Mountain vacation clips, click either iMovie Sound Effects or iLife Sound Effects in the scrolling list box. iMovie includes a number of top-shelf audio effects that you can use in the second audio track on the timeline viewer. This way, you can add sound effects even when you've already added a background song. Again, to add a sound effect, drag it to the perfect spot in the Project pane.

If you have several gigabytes of music in your iTunes Library, locating Janis Joplin's rendition of "Me and Bobby McGee" might be more of a challenge, especially if the song is included in a compilation. Let your MacBook do the digging for you! Click in the Search box below the track list and begin typing a song name. iMovie narrows the song titles displayed to those that match the characters you type. To reset the search box and display all your songs in the Library or selected playlist, click the X icon that appears to the right of the box.

- **Ripping songs from an audio CD:** Load an audio CD and then choose Audio CD from the scrolling list box. iMovie displays the tracks from the CD, and you can add them at the current playhead position the same way as you would iTunes songs.

- **Recording directly from a microphone:** Yep, if you're thinking voiceover narration, you've hit the nail on the head. Check out the nearby sidebar, "Narration the easy way," for the scoop.

Narration the easy way

Ready to create that award-winning nature documentary? You can add voiceover narration to your iMovie project that would make Jacques Cousteau proud. In fact, you can record your voice while you watch your movie play, allowing perfect synchronization with the action! To add narration, follow these steps:

1. **Click the Voiceover button on the Editing toolbar — it sports a microphone icon — to open the Voiceover window.**

2. **Click the Record From pop-up menu and select the input device.**

   All MacBook models sport a decent internal microphone, but you can always add a USB microphone to your system.

3. **Drag the input volume slider to a comfortable level.**

   You can monitor the volume level of your voice with the left and right input meters — try to keep the meters at 50 percent or so for the proper volume level.

4. **To block out ambient noise levels, drag the Noise Reduction slider to the right if necessary.**

   If you'd like iMovie to enhance your voice electronically for a more professional sound, click the Voice Enhancement check box to select it. If you need to hear the audio from your movie project while you speak, click the Play Project Audio While Recording check box to select it. Note, however, that you need to listen to the audio while using a set of headphones (plugged in to your laptop's headphone jack) to avoid feedback problems.

5. **Click in the desired spot within a clip in the Project pane where the narration should begin.**

6. **Begin speaking when prompted by iMovie.**

7. **Watch the video while you narrate so that you can coordinate your narration track with the action.**

8. **Click anywhere in the iMovie window to stop recording (or wait until the clip ends).**

   iMovie adds a tiny microphone icon to the Project pane underneath the video with the voiceover.

9. **Click the Close button in the Voiceover window.**

You can fine-tune both the audio within a video clip or the audio clips that you add to your project. With the desired clip selected, click the Inspector button on the Editing toolbar (it bears a proud letter *i*) to display the Inspector window and then click the Audio tab. The Audio Adjustments window that appears includes an array of audio controls that allow you to change the volume of the selected clip or to give that audio priority over other audio playing simultaneously (such as a sound effect that needs to be clearly heard over background music and the video clip).

If the volume of one of your clips is dramatically higher or lower, select the clip that you want to set to optimum volume and then click Normalize Clip Volume. You can also set an automatic or manual Fade-in/Fade-out for the audio. When you're done tweaking, click Done. (Oh, and don't forget that you can always return the clip to its original volume; just open this window again and click Revert to Original.)

On the Video tab in the Inspector window, you can vary the exposure, brightness, contrast, and saturation of your clip. Click the Auto button, and iMovie will perform what it considers the best job of improving your video.

Building the Cinematic Basics

Time to dive in and add the building blocks you imported to create your movie. Along with video clips, audio tracks, and still images, you can add Hollywood-quality transitions, optical effects, and animated text titles. In the following sections, I demonstrate how to elevate your collection of video clips into a real-life gen-u-wine *movie*.

Adding clips to your movie

You can add clips to your movie by using the Project pane and the Event pane. The Dynamic Duo work like this:

- **Project pane:** This pane displays the media you've added to your project so far, allowing you to rearrange the clips, titles, transitions, and still images in your movie. (If the pane is titled `Project Library`, remember that you have to double-click the desired project to select it. After you select a project, the Project Library pane turns into the Project pane.)

✔ **Event pane:** This pane displays your video clips arranged by event (the date they were shot or the date they were imported), acting as the source repository for all your clips. Movies pulled into iMovie, imported into iPhoto, or added manually from the Finder appear here.

To add a clip to your movie, follow these steps:

1. **Move your cursor across clips in the Event pane to watch a preview of the video.**

2. **After you decide what to add to your project, you can add the entire clip or a selection:**

   • To select an entire clip, right-click the clip's thumbnail and choose Select Entire Clip from the menu that appears.

   • To select a portion of a clip, drag your cursor across the thumbnail. A yellow frame appears around your selection. To change the length of the selected video, drag the handles that appear on either side. If you make a mistake while selecting video, just click any empty space in the Event pane to remove the selection frame and try again.

3. **Drag the selection from the Event pane to the spot where it belongs in the Project pane.**

   Alternatively, you can press E or click the Add to Project button (the first button on the Editing toolbar) to add the selection to the end of the current project.

Do these steps several times, and you have a movie, which you created just like the editors of old used to by working with actual film clips. This is a good point to mention a moviemaking Mark's Maxim:

Preview your work — and do it often.™

iMovie offers two Play Full Screen buttons: one under the Event Library and one under the Project Library. Select the project or event you want to play and then click the corresponding button (or press ⌘+G). You can also choose View➪Play Full Screen to watch the selection. Press the spacebar to pause, and press Esc to return to iMovie. You can also move your cursor to display a filmstrip that you can click to skip forward or backward in the project or event.

To play a selection from the beginning, press \ (backslash). (If you've ever watched directors at work on today's movie sets, you may have noticed that they're constantly watching a monitor to see what things will look like for the audience. You have the same option in iMovie!)

While you're watching video in the Event pane, you may decide that a certain clip has a favorite scene or that another clip has material you don't want, such as Uncle Ed's shadow puppets. (Shudder.) iMovie features *Favorite* and *Rejected* frames, allowing you to view and use your best camera work (and ignore the worst stuff). To mark video, select a range of frames or an entire clip and then click the Mark as Favorite button on the Editing toolbar. Click the Reject button to hide the selected video or frames from view. (You can always unmark a Favorite or Rejected scene by using the Unmark button on the Editing toolbar — click the Show pop-up menu, at the bottom of the window, and choose Rejected to display hidden material.)

Removing clips from your movie

Don't like a clip? Bah. To banish a clip from your movie, follow these steps:

1. **Click the offending clip in the Project pane to select it.**

2. **Press Delete.**

   Alternatively, you can right-click the clip (or a selection you made by dragging) and choose either Delete Entire Clip or Delete Selection from the menu that appears. (Note that this action deletes the clip from the Project, but the clip still remains in the Event library.)

If you remove the wrong clip, don't panic. Instead, use iMovie's Undo feature (press ⌘+Z) to restore it.

Reordering clips in your movie

If Day One of your vacation appears after Day Two, you can easily reorder your clips and stills by dragging them to the proper space in the Project pane. When you take your finger off the trackpad, iMovie automatically moves the rest of your movie aside with a minimum of fuss and bother.

iMovie allows you to switch to the familiar timeline view, which many users of previous versions of the application will recognize (and prefer, including this particular moviemaker). Click the Swap Events and Projects button — it's next to the Camera Import button, and it bears two arrows — to move the Project pane to the bottom of the window and the Event Library to the top, which switches you to timeline view.

Editing clips in iMovie

If a clip has extra seconds of footage at the beginning or end (as it should to ensure you get all the action), you don't want that superfluous stuff in your masterpiece. Our favorite video editor gives you the following functions:

- ✔ **Crop:** Removes unwanted material from a video clip or still image
- ✔ **Rotate:** Rotates a clip or image on its center axis
- ✔ **Trim:** Trims frames from a video clip

Before you can edit, however, you have to select a section of a clip:

1. **Click a clip or image in either the Project pane (where changes you make are specific to this project) or the Event pane (where edits you make are reflected in any project using that footage).**

   iMovie displays the clip or image in the monitor.

2. **To select the entire clip or image, simply click it.**

3. **Drag your cursor across the thumbnail to select the section of the media you want to edit.**

   Note that some editing functions, such as Crop and Rotate, automatically apply to the entire clip.

   A yellow frame surrounds the selected region. You're ready to edit that selected part of the clip.

Note the handles that appear at the beginning or ending of the selection. You can make fine changes to the selected section by dragging them or by pressing the arrow keys.

- ✔ **To crop:** Click the Crop button on the Editing toolbar to display the frame in the Monitor pane and then click Crop at the top of the Monitor pane. Drag the edges of the frame and the handles to select the section you want to keep. To preview your selection, click the Play button at the top of the monitor. When you're ready, click Done, and everything but the selected region is removed.

- ✔ **To rotate:** Click the Crop button on the Editing toolbar and then click one of the two rotation buttons (which carry a curved arrow icon). Each click rotates the media 90 degrees in that direction. Click Done when the clip or image is properly oriented.

- ✔ **To trim:** Right-click the selection (or choose Edit on the iMovie menu bar), and then choose Trim to Selection. iMovie removes the frames from around the selected video.

Edits that you make to one clip or still image can actually be copied to multiple items! Select the edited clip and choose Edit⇨Copy. Now you can select one or more clips and choose Edit⇨Paste Adjustments to apply video, audio, or crop edits. (To apply all three types of edits, just choose All.)

Transitions for the masses

Many iMovie owners approach transitions as *visual bookends:* They merely act as placeholders that appear between video clips. Nothing could be further from the truth, because judicious use of transitions can make or break a scene. For example, which would you prefer after a wedding ceremony — an abrupt, jarring cut to the reception or a gradual fadeout to the reception?

Today's audiences are sensitive to transitions between scenes. Try not to overuse the same transition — pick two or three that match the mood of your film. Also, weigh the visual impact of a transition carefully. You might even decide that no transition is most effective; directors call this deliberate lack of a transition a *jump cut.*

iMovie includes a surprising array of transitions, including old favorites (such as Fade In and Dissolve) and some nifty stuff you might not be familiar with (such as Cube and Page Curl). To display your transition collection (see Figure 16-5), click the Show Transitions button on the Media Browser toolbar (or press ⌘+4).

Figure 16-5: Add transitions for flow between clips in iMovie.

To see what a particular transition looks like, move your cursor over the thumbnail to display the transition in miniature.

Adding a transition couldn't be easier: Drag the transition from the list in the Transitions Browser pane and drop it between clips or between a clip and a still image in the Project pane. In iMovie, transitions are applied in real time.

Even Gone with the Wind had titles

The next stop on our iMovie Hollywood Features Tour is the Titles Browser, as shown in Figure 16-6. You can find it by clicking the Title button on the Media Browser toolbar (which bears a big capital *T*) or by pressing ⌘+3. You can add a title with a still image, but iMovie also includes everything you need to add basic animated text to your movie.

Figure 16-6: Add titles for your next silent film.

Most of the controls you can adjust are the same for each animation style. You can change the font, the size of the text, and the color of the text. To add a title manually, follow these steps:

1. **Select an animation thumbnail from the Title Browser pane and drag it to the desired spot in the Project pane.**

2. **Click a background thumbnail to select a background for your title.**

   You'll see the same backgrounds in the Map, Background, and Animatic Browser, which I discuss in the next section.

3. **In the monitor window, click the Show Fonts button to make any changes to the fonts or text attributes.**

4. **Click in a text box to type your own line of text.**

5. **Click the Play button to preview your title.**

   iMovie displays a preview of the effect in the monitor with the settings that you choose.

6. **Click Done.**

   The title appears in the Project pane.

Adding maps and backgrounds

iMovie includes easy-to-use animated maps — think Indiana Jones traveling by airplane from place to place — and static backgrounds that can be used with your titles. To display them, click the Map, Background, and Animatic Browser button on the Media Browser toolbar or press ⌘+5.

To use an animated map, drag one of the globe or map thumbnails to the Project pane. After the globe or map is created, click it to display the Inspector window. Now you can click the Start Location and End Location buttons, respectively, to enter the start and stop points for the animation. Type a city or place name to see your choices. (Heck, you can even type an airport code or decimal coordinates to specify the spot.) After you're finished, click OK, and then click Done in the Inspector window. Now play the clip, and watch as iMovie animates your location (or your trip) in seconds!

To add a static background from the browser, drag it to the desired spot in the Project pane.

Creating an Honest-to-Goodness Movie Trailer

Yes, friends, you read that correctly! As I mention at the beginning of the chapter, iMovie includes a Movie Trailer feature that can turn your film clips into a Hollywood-class preview, complete with genre transitions and background music.

To create a trailer project, follow these steps:

1. **Choose File⇨New Project or press ⌘+N.**

2. **Type a name for your project.**

3. **Select the aspect ratio for your movie.**

   See the earlier section "Shaking Hands with the iMovie Window" for a discussion of standard (4:3) and widescreen (16:9) aspect ratios.

4. **Choose the frame rate.**

5. **Click a Movie Trailer thumbnail to select it.**

   iMovie displays a nifty preview of the selected trailer style. Click the thumbnails to preview their look before you make your decision. Naturally, you'll want to choose a trailer style that most closely matches the mood you want to project with your movie.

   Each trailer has a suggested number of cast members; this number reflects the number of people that will appear in the clip placeholders during the editing process. (More on this in a page or two.)

6. **Click Create.**

iMovie replaces the Project Library pane with the Trailer pane, as shown in Figure 16-7. On the Outline tab, you can edit the titles used in the trailer. The pop-up lists allow you to add information such as the gender of the star(s) and the logo style you want for your "studio" at the beginning of the trailer. To change a text field, click in it and type the new text. You'll see the changes you make in the Trailer display appear in the monitor in real time.

After you complete your edits to the titles, click the Storyboard tab. There, you can edit the text for each transition; simply click the text to display the edit box and type. You can also drag clips from your Event Library (or from a Finder window) to fill the storyboard's placeholders for video clips. To delete a clip from the storyboard, click it to select it and then press Delete.

To preserve the look and feel of the trailer storyboard, try to match your clips with the description and suggested activity indicated by the placeholder. (In other words, don't stick a wide-angle video clip of the family dog cavorting in the yard in a placeholder marked Closeup — you get the idea.)

The Storyboard tab might not look like an editing timeline, but you can move the cursor anywhere within the storyboard to preview your trailer. The playhead indicator appears wherever the cursor appears, allowing you to watch the clip or transition that it's resting on. You'll soon be sweeping your mouse to the left or right to move through each section of your trailer.

For an overall listing of each clip required for the full trailer, click the Shot List tab. On this tab, clips are organized by type. For example, all the action clips appear in one section, and all the landscape and close-up clips are grouped together as well. If necessary, you can also add, delete, or swap video clips from the Shot List.

Figure 16-7:
Build your
movie trailer
from the
Trailer pane.

To preview your trailer in its entirety, click the Play Full-Screen button at the top-right corner of the Trailer pane. (Any storyboard placeholder that you haven't filled with a clip will display just the placeholder.)

After you're satisfied with your finished trailer — or if you'd like to work on another project — click the Project Library button at the top of the Trailer pane, and you'll see that iMovie has added your trailer as a new project in the Library list.

I bet all those hard-working Hollywood video editors are fuming at how easy it is to create a trailer in iMovie!

Sharing Your Finished Classic with Others

Your movie is complete, you've saved it to your hard drive, and now you're wondering where to go from here. Click Share on the application menu bar, and you see that iMovie can unleash your movie upon your unsuspecting family and friends (and even the entire world) in a number of ways:

- ✔ **iTunes:** Send your movie to your iTunes Library as a movie.

- ✔ **Media Browser:** Make your iMovie project available in other iLife applications, in five different sizes suited to different display devices. Note that the Media Browser is also available for other Apple applications such as Final Cut Pro X, and to third-party applications such as Toast Titanium.

- ✔ **Podcast Producer:** You can send your movie to Apple's Podcast Producer application for incorporation into your newest podcasting epic.

- ✔ **YouTube/Facebook/Vimeo/CNN iReport:** Yep, you read right, you can send your iMovie directly to any of these websites! Can it get more convenient than that? (I think not.)

- ✔ **Export Movie:** Create a copy of your movie on your hard drive in one of five different sizes.

- ✔ **Export using QuickTime:** Create a QuickTime movie with your project, using the QuickTime encoding engine (allowing greater control over the export process and the attributes of the finished movie file).

    If you use this option, any computer with an installed copy of QuickTime can display your movies, and you can use QuickTime movies in Keynote presentations as well.

- ✔ **Export to Final Cut XML:** If you'd like to transfer your iMovie project to Final Cut Pro X, use this option to create a compatible XML file.

When you choose a sharing option, iMovie displays the video quality for the option and makes automatic changes to the movie attributes. (For example, choosing Tiny reduces the finished movie as far as possible in file size, and the audio is reduced to mono instead of stereo.)

Need to take a movie offline or stop sharing it? You can remove a project from iTunes, your iLife Media Browser, or the YouTube website by using the Sharing menu. Just click the corresponding Remove From menu item. (Of course, you can share the project again at any time.)

If you're worried about permanently reducing the quality of your project by sharing it in a smaller size, fear not! When you choose a sharing option to export your movie, your original project remains on your hard drive, unchanged, so you can share a better-quality version at any time in the future!

After you adjust any settings specific to the desired sharing option, click Publish (or Save) to start the ball rolling.

Chapter 17

Recording Your Hits with GarageBand

Do you dream of making music? I've always wanted to join a band, but I never devoted the time nor learned to play the guitar. You know the drill: Those rock stars struggled for years to gain the upper hand over an instrument, practicing for untold hours, memorizing chords, and . . . wait a second. I almost forgot. You don't need to do *any* of that now!

Apple's GarageBand lets a musical wanna-be (like yours truly) make music with a MacBook — complete with a driving bass line, funky horns, and perfect drums that never miss a beat. In fact, the thousands of prerecorded loops on tap in this awesome application allow you to design your music to match that melody running through your head, from techno to jazz to alternative rock.

Oh, and did I mention that you can also use GarageBand to produce podcasts? That's right! You can record your voice and easily create your own show, and then share it with others from your website! Heck, add photos if you like. You'll be the talk of your family and friends and maybe even your Mac user group.

This chapter explains everything you need to know to create your first song. I also show you how to import your hit record into iTunes so that you can listen to it on your iPod with a big silly grin on your face (like I do) or add it to your next iMovie project as a royalty-free soundtrack. Heck, you can even turn that hit into your own personal ringtone and use it on your MacBook, iPhone, iPad, or iPod touch!

Don't be too smug when you think of all that practicing and hard work you missed out on. What a shame you missed out on all that preparatory stuff!

Shaking Hands with Your Band

As you can see in Figure 17-1, the GarageBand window isn't complex at all, and that's good design. In this section, I list the most important controls so that you know your Play button from your Loop Browser button.

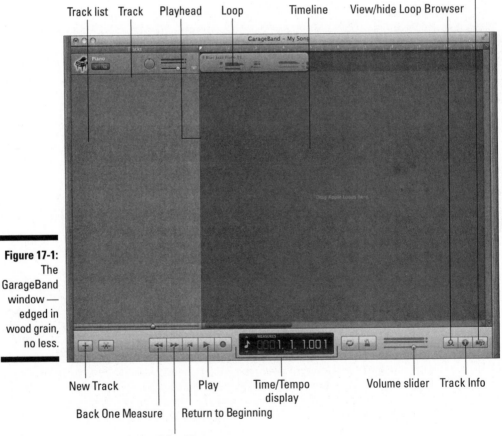

Track list Track Playhead Loop   Timeline View/hide Loop Browser View/hide Media Browser

Figure 17-1:
The GarageBand window — edged in wood grain, no less.

New Track   Play   Time/Tempo display   Volume slider Track Info

Back One Measure   Return to Beginning

Forward One Measure

Your music-making machine includes

- **Track list:** In GarageBand, a *track* is a discrete instrument that you set up to play one part of your song. For example, a classical piece for string quartet would have four component tracks — one each for violin, viola, cello, and bass. The Track list contains all the tracks in your song arranged so that you can easily see and modify them, like the rows in a spreadsheet. A track begins in the list, stretching out to the right all the way to the end of the song. As you can see in the upper left of Figure 17-1, I already have one track defined — a Piano.

  If you're creating a podcast, a *Podcast artwork track* can also appear. Video podcasts can include a movie track as well.

- **Timeline:** This scrolling area holds the loops (see the following bullet) that you add, compose, or record, allowing you to move and edit them easily. When a song plays, the timeline scrolls to give you a visual look at your music. (Bear with me; you'll understand that cryptic statement in a page or two.)

- **Loop:** A *loop* is a prerecorded short clip of an instrument being played in a specific style and tempo. *Loops* — the building blocks of your song — are a maximum of five seconds, and others are even shorter. You can drag loops from the Loop Browser to a track and literally build a bass line or a guitar solo. (The process is a little like adding video clips in iMovie to build a film.) Loops can also be repeated within a track, which I'll discuss further in a page or two.

- **Playhead:** This vertical line is a moving indicator that shows you the current position in your song while it scrolls by in the timeline. You can drag the playhead to a new location at any time. The playhead also acts like the insertion cursor in a word-processing application: If you insert a section of a song or a loop from the Clipboard, it appears at the current location of the playhead. (More on copying and inserting loops later, so don't panic.)

- **New Track button:** Click this button to add a new track to your song.

- **Track Info button:** If you need to display the instrument used in a track, click the track to select it and then click this button. You can also control settings, such as Echo and Reverb, from the Edit pane of the Track Info display.

- **View/Hide Loop Browser button:** Click the button with the striking eye icon to display the Loop Browser at the bottom of the window; click the button again to close the Loop Browser. You can see more of your tracks at a time without scrolling by closing the Loop Browser.

✔ **View/Hide Media Browser button:** Click this button (which bears icons of a filmstrip, slide, and musical note) to display the Media Browser at the right side of the window; click it again to close it. By closing the Media Browser, you can see more of your tracks. If you're already familiar with iMovie, you recognize this pane in the GarageBand window; it allows you to add media (in this case, digital song files, still images, or video clips) to your GarageBand project for use in a podcast or as ringtones.

✔ **Return to Beginning button:** Clicking this button immediately moves the playhead back to the beginning of the timeline.

✔ **Back/Forward One Measure buttons:** To move quickly through your song by jumping to the previous or next measure, click the corresponding button.

✔ **Play button:** Hey, old friend! At last, a control that you've probably used countless times — and it works just like the same control on your audio CD player. Click Play, and GarageBand begins playing your entire song. Notice that the Play button turns blue. To pause the music, click Play again; the button loses that sexy blue sheen and the playhead stops immediately. (If playback is paused, it begins again at the playhead position when you next click Play.)

✔ **Time/Tempo display:** This cool-looking LCD display shows you the current playhead position in seconds.

You can click the icon at the left of the display to choose other modes, such as

- *Measures* (to display the current measure and mark the beat)

- *Chord* (to display note and chord names)

- *Project* (to show or change the key, tempo, and signature for the song)

✔ **Volume slider:** Here's another familiar face. Just drag the slider to raise or lower the volume.

Of course, more controls are scattered around the GarageBand window, but these are the main controls used to compose a song . . . which is the next stop!

Composing and Podcasting Made Easy

In this section, I cover the basics of composition in GarageBand, working from the very beginning. Follow along with this running example:

1. Close all existing GarageBand windows.

GarageBand displays the top-level New Project dialog.

2. In the list at the left, click New Project.

3. **Click the Piano icon and then click Choose.**

   GarageBand displays the New Project dialog, as shown in Figure 17-2.

   By choosing the Piano icon, my new GarageBand project will have one track already in place — a grand piano. If you choose Electric Guitar or Voice, you'll have a project automatically created with an electric guitar track or male and female voice tracks. To create a completely empty project that you populate with tracks yourself, choose Loops.

4. **Type a name for your new song, and then drag the Tempo slider to select the beats per minute (bpm).**

   A GarageBand song can have only one *tempo* (or speed) throughout, expressed as beats per minute.

5. **If you want to adjust the settings for your song, you can select the**

   - **Time signature** (a GarageBand can have only one signature, expressed as beats per measure in the Time box)

   - **Key** (the Key box)

   If you're new to music *theory* (the rules and syntax by which music is created and written), just use the defaults. Most of the toe-tappin' tunes that you and I are familiar with fit right in with these settings.

6. **Click the Create button.**

   You see the window shown earlier in Figure 17-1. (The Blue Jazz Piano 01 loop in Figure 17-1 — which I show you how to add in the next section — is an example of a typical loop.)

Figure 17-2: Start creating your new song here.

Adding tracks

Although I'm not a musician, I am a music lover, and I know that many classical composers approached a new work in the same way you approach a new song in GarageBand: by envisioning the instruments that they wanted to hear. (I imagine Mozart and Beethoven would've been thrilled to use GarageBand, but I think they did a decent job with quill and paper, too.)

In fact, GarageBand includes a *Songwriting* project (also available from the top-level New Project dialog). When you choose the Songwriting project, GarageBand presents you with a full set of four instrument tracks, plus a real instrument track for your voice. (More on software versus real instrument tracks in a page or two.) You're instantly ready to start adding loops and recording your own voice!

If you've followed along to this point, you've noticed two issues with your GarageBand window:

- ✔ **You find no keyboard.** You can record the contents of a software instrument track by "playing" the keyboard, clicking the keys by tapping your trackpad. (As you might imagine, this isn't the best solution.) If you're a musician, the best method of recording your own notes is with a USB MIDI instrument, which I discuss later in the chapter in the sidebar "Join in and jam . . . or talk!". For now, you can display the keyboard window by pressing ⌘+K. If the keyboard window is on the screen and you don't need it, banish the window by clicking the Close button.

  Even if you're not interested in the point-and-click keyboard, GarageBand offers a musical typing keyboard, where you press the keys on your keyboard to simulate the keys on a musical keyboard. (Hey, if you don't have a MIDI instrument, at least it's better than nothing.) To display the musical typing keyboard window, press Shift+⌘+K.

- ✔ **The example song has only one track.** If you want to write the next classical masterpiece for Grand Piano, that's fine. Otherwise, on the GarageBand menu bar, choose Track➪Delete Track to start with a clean slate. (I know, I could have started with a Loops project, but this way you get to see how to delete a track.)

You can use the following five kinds of tracks in GarageBand:

- ✔ **Software instrument tracks:** These tracks aren't audio recordings. Rather, they're mathematically precise algorithms that your laptop *renders* (or builds) to fit your needs. If you have a MIDI instrument connected to your MacBook, you can create your own software instrument tracks. (More on MIDI instruments later in this chapter.)

  In this chapter, I focus on software instrument tracks, which are the easiest for a nonmusician to use.

✔ **Real instrument tracks:** A real instrument track is an actual audio recording, such as your voice or a physical instrument without a MIDI connection. (Think microphone.)

✔ **Electric Guitar tracks:** GarageBand includes a real instrument track, especially made for an electric guitar, that allows you to use one of five different amplifiers and a number of stomp boxes (those effect pedals that guitarists are always poking with their foot to change the sound of their instruments).

✔ **Podcast artwork track:** You get only one of these; it holds photos that will appear in a video iPod (or a window on your website) when your podcast is playing.

✔ **Video tracks:** The video sound track appears if you're *scoring* (adding music to) an iMovie movie. Along with the video sound track, you get a cool, companion video track that shows the clips in your movie. (More on this in the "Look, I'm John Williams!" sidebar, later in this chapter.)

It's time to add a software instrument track of your very own. Follow these steps:

1. **Click the Create a New Track button (which carries a plus sign), labeled and shown earlier in Figure 17-1.**

   GarageBand displays the New Track dialog.

2. **Click the Software Instrument radio button, and then click Create.**

   See all those great instruments in the Track Info pane on the right?

3. **Select the general instrument category by clicking it.**

   I chose Drum Kits.

4. **From the right column, choose your specific style of weapon, such as Rock Kit for an arena sound.**

   Figure 17-3 illustrates the new track that appears in your list when you follow these steps.

If you're creating a podcast and you want to add a series of still images that will appear on a video iPod's screen (or on your web page), follow these steps:

1. **Click the View Media Browser button (labeled and shown earlier in Figure 17-1).**

2. **Click the Photos button.**

   GarageBand displays all the photos in your iPhoto Library and events.

3. **Drag an image from your iPhoto Library in the Media Browser to the Track list.**

   The Podcast track appears at the top of the Track list, and you can add and move images in the list at any time, just like the loops that you add to your instrument tracks. (More on adding and rearranging the contents of a track in the following sections.)

Figure 17-3:
The new
track
appears,
ready to
rock.

Choosing loops

When you have a new, empty track, you can add loops to build your song.
You do that by listening to loops and making selections from the Loop
Browser — Apple provides you with thousands of loops to choose from,
along with more you can buy — and photos from your Media Browser. (As I
mention earlier, think of loops as snippets of a specific instrument that you
hear in a song, such as a bass line or a drumbeat.) Click the Loop Browser
button (which bears the loop symbol, somewhat like a roller coaster) to display your collection, as shown in Figure 17-4.

If your Loop Browser looks different from what you see in Figure 17-4, you're
using another view mode, just like the different view modes available for a
Finder window. The three-icon button in the upper-left corner of the Loop
Browser toggles the browser display among Column, Musical Button, and
Podcast Sounds views. Click the middle of the three buttons to switch to
Button mode.

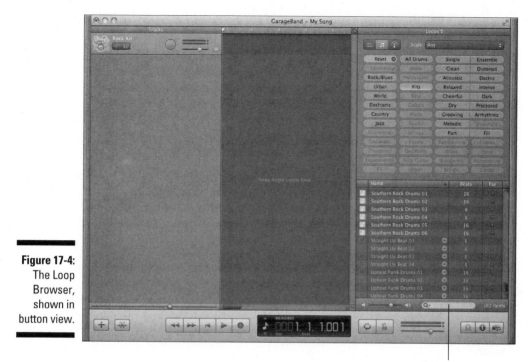

Figure 17-4:
The Loop
Browser,
shown in
button view.

Search box

Looking for just the right loop

The track in this running example uses a Rock drum kit, but you haven't
added a loop yet. (Refer to Figure 17-3.) Follow these steps to search through
your loop library for just the right rhythm:

1. **Click the button that corresponds to the instrument you're using.**

   In this example, I chose the Kits button in the Loop Browser. Click it, and
   a list of different beats appears in the pane at the bottom of the Loop
   Browser window. (Refer to Figure 17-4 for a gander at the Loop Browser.)

2. **Click one of the loops with a green musical-note icon.**

   Go ahead; this is where things get fun! GarageBand begins playing the loop
   nonstop, allowing you to get a feel for how that particular loop sounds.

   When you use only software instruments in a track (as I am throughout
   this chapter), choose only software instrument loops, which are identified by a green musical-note icon.

3. **Click another entry in the list, and the application switches immediately to that loop.**

Now you're beginning to understand why GarageBand is so cool for both musicians and the note-impaired. It's like having your own band, with members who never get tired and who play whatever you want while you're composing. (Mozart would've *loved* this.)

If you want to search for a particular instrument, click the Search box (labeled in Figure 17-4) and type the text you want to match. GarageBand returns the search results in the list.

4. **Scroll down the list and continue to sample the different loops until you find one that fits like a glove.**

For this reporter, it's Southern Rock Drums 01.

5. **Drag the entry to your Rock Kit track and drop it at the very beginning of the timeline (as indicated by the playhead).**

Your window looks like Figure 17-5.

If you want that same beat throughout the song, you don't need to add any more loops to that track. (More on extending that beat in the next section.) However, if you want the drum's beat to change later in the song, you would add a second loop after the first one in the *same* track. For now, leave this track as is.

Figure 17-5:
A track
with a loop
added.

Whoops! Did you do something that you regret? Don't forget that you can undo most actions in GarageBand by pressing the old standby — ⌘+Z — immediately afterward.

Second verse, same as the first

When you compose, you can add tracks for each instrument that you want in your song:

- ✔ Each track can have more than one loop.

- ✔ Loops *don't* have to start at the beginning; you can drop a loop anywhere in the timeline.

For example, in Figure 17-6, you can see that my drum kit kicks in first, but my bass line doesn't begin until some time later (for a funkier opening).

You put loops on separate tracks so that they can play simultaneously on different instruments. If all your loops in a song are added on the same track, you hear only one loop at any one time, and all the loops use the same software instrument. By creating multiple tracks, you give yourself the elbowroom to bring in the entire band at the same time. It's über-convenient to compose your song when you can see each instrument's loops and where they fall in the song.

Click the Reset button in the Loop Browser to choose another instrument or genre category.

Figure 17-6:
My timeline with a synth and an electric bass on-board. Let's rock!

Look, I'm John Williams!

You, too, can be a famous composer of soundtracks . . . well, perhaps not quite as famous as Mr. Williams, but even he had to start somewhere. To add a GarageBand score to an iMovie, click the Track menu in GarageBand and then click Show Movie Track to display the Movie track. Choose a movie to score from the familiar confines of the Media Browser, and drag it to the Movie track.

At this point, you add and modify instrument tracks and loops just as you would any other GarageBand project. The existing sound for the iMovie project appears in the Movie Sound track. A Video Preview pane appears on top of the Track Info pane on the right side of the GarageBand window. When you click the Play button, the video is shown as well so that you can check your work and tweak settings (as I describe later in the chapter).

After you finish composing, click Share on the menu bar to export your work as a QuickTime movie directly to your hard drive or as a movie to iTunes. You can't return to iMovie with your project after you do this, though, so scoring should be the final step in the production of your movie.

Resizing, repeating, and moving loops

If you haven't already tried listening to your entire song, try it now. You can click Play at any time without wreaking havoc on your carefully created tracks. Sounds pretty good, doesn't it?

But wait: I bet the song stopped after about five seconds, right? (You can watch the passing seconds, using either the Time/Tempo display or the second rule that appears at the very top of the timeline.) I'm sure that you want your song to last more than five seconds! After the playhead moves past the end of the last loop, your song is over. Click Play again to pause the playback; then click the Return to Beginning button (labeled and shown earlier in Figure 17-1) to move the playhead back to the beginning of the song.

The music stops so soon because your loops are only so long. Most are five seconds; others are even shorter. To keep the groove going, you have to do one of three things:

 ✔ **Resize the loop:** Hover your cursor over either the left or right edge of most loops, and your cursor changes to a vertical line with an arrow pointing away from the loop. That change is your cue to click and drag — and as you drag, most loops expand to fill the space you're making, repeating the beats in perfect time. You can drag the loop's edge as long as you like.

✔ **Repeat the loop:** Depending on the loop that you chose, you might find that resizing it doesn't repeat the measure. Instead, the new part of the loop is simply dead air. (This empty space is why I keep reminding you that the length of most loops is limited to five seconds.) If you move your cursor over the side of a loop that you want to extend, however, the cursor turns into a vertical line with a circular arrow, which tells you that you can click and *repeat* the loop. GarageBand adds multiple copies of the same loop automatically, for as far as you drag the loop. In Figure 17-7, I've repeated the bass loop that you see in Figure 17-6.

✔ **Add a new loop:** You can switch to a different loop to change the flow of the music. The instrument stays the same, but there's no reason you can't use a horn-riff loop in your violin track (as long as it sounds good played by a violin!). To GarageBand, a software instrument track is compatible with *any* software instrument loop that you add from the Loop Browser (as long as that loop is marked with our old friend, the green musical note).

TIP

You can also use the familiar keyboard shortcuts of cut (⌘+X), copy (⌘+C), and paste (⌘+V) to cut, copy, and paste loops from place to place — both on the timeline and from track to track. And you can click a loop and drag it anywhere.

Figure 17-7:
By repeating the bass loop, you can keep the thump flowing.

Each track can be adjusted so that you can listen to the interplay between two or more tracks or hear how your song sounds without a specific track:

- ✓ Click the tiny Speaker button under the track name in the list, and the button turns blue to indicate that the track is muted. To turn off the mute, click the Speaker button again.

- ✓ You can change the volume or balance of each individual track by using the mixer that appears next to the track name. This comes in handy if you want an instrument to sound louder or to confine that instrument to the left or right speaker.

A track doesn't have to be filled for every second with one loop or another. Most of my songs have a number of repeating loops with empty space between them as different instruments perform solo.

Using the Arrange track

GarageBand includes another method you can use to monkey with your music: The *Arrange track* can be used to define specific sections of a song, allowing you to reorganize things by selecting, moving, and copying entire sections. For example, you're probably familiar with the chorus (or refrain) of a song and how often it appears during the course of the tune. With the Arrange track, you can reposition the entire chorus — including all its loops and settings — within your song! If you need another chorus, just copy that arrangement.

To use the Arrange track, display it by choosing Track➪Show Arrange Track. The Arrange track then appears as a thin strip at the top of the Track list. Click the Add Region button in the Arrange track (which carries a plus sign) and you see a new, untitled region (as shown in Figure 17-8). You can drag the right side of the Arrangement region to resize it, or drag it to move it anywhere in the song.

Who wants an arrangement full of regions named "untitled"? To rename an Arrangement region, click the word *untitled* to select it (the Arrange track turns blue), and then click the title again to display a text box. Type a new name for the region and press Return.

Now, here's where Arrangement regions get *cool:*

- ✓ To move an entire Arrangement region, click the region's title in the Arrange track and then drag it anywhere you like in the song.

- ✓ To copy an Arrangement region, hold down the Option key and drag the desired region's title to the spot where you want the copy to appear.

- ✓ To delete an Arrangement region, select it and press ⌘+Option+Delete.

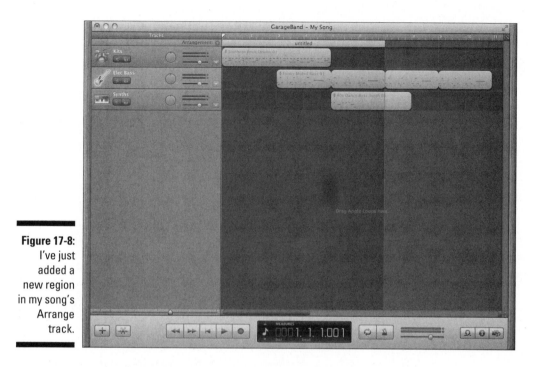

Figure 17-8:
I've just
added a
new region
in my song's
Arrange
track.

✔ To replace the contents of an Arrangement region with those of another Arrangement region, hold down the ⌘ key and drag the desired region's title on top of the offending region's title.

✔ To switch two Arrangement regions in your song — swapping the contents completely — drag one of the Arrangement region titles on top of the other and lift your finger from the trackpad.

Tweaking the settings for a track

You don't think that John Mayer or U2 just "play and walk away," do you? No, they spend hours after the recording session is over, tweaking their music in the studio and on the mixing board until every note sounds just as it should. You can adjust the settings for a track, too. The tweaks that you can perform include adding effects (pull a Hendrix and add echo and reverb to your electric guitar track) and kicking in an equalizer (for fine-tuning the sound of your background horns).

To make adjustments to a track, follow these steps:

1. **In the Track list, click the desired track to select it.**

2. **Click the Track Info button (labeled and shown earlier in Figure 17-1).**

3. **Click the Edit tab to display the settings shown in Figure 17-9.**

4. **Click the button next to each effect you want to enable. (The button glows green when enabled.)**

   Each of the effects has a modifier setting. For example, you can adjust the amount of echo to add by dragging its slider.

   GarageBand offers a Visual Equalizer window that you can use to create a custom equalizer setting for each track. You can display the Visual EQ window by clicking the animated button next to the Visual EQ control on the Edit pane. To change the Bass, Low Mid, High Mid, or Treble setting for a track, click and drag the equalizer waveform in the desired direction. And yep, you can do this while your song is playing, so you can use both your eyes *and* ears to define the perfect settings!

5. **To save the instrument as a new custom instrument, click the Save Instrument button.**

   Now you can use the instrument the next time you add a track.

6. **Click the Track Info button again to return to GarageBand.**

Figure 17-9:
Finesse your tune by tweaking the sound of a specific track.

Join in and jam . . . or talk!

As I mention elsewhere in this chapter, GarageBand is even more fun if you happen to play an instrument! (And yes, I'm envious, no matter how much I enjoy the techno and jazz music that I create. After all, take away my MacBook, and I'm back to playing the kazoo . . . at least until I absorb all the Learn to Play lessons for the guitar. More on this feature in the sidebar, "Hey, GarageBand, teach me how to play!")

Most musicians use MIDI instruments to play music on the computer. That pleasant-sounding acronym stands for *Musical Instrument Digital Interface.* A wide variety of MIDI instruments is available these days, from traditional MIDI keyboards to more exotic fun, such as MIDI saxophones.

For example, Apple sells a 49-key MIDI keyboard from M-Audio for around $100. Alternatively, the highly recommended Casio CTX-3000 offers 61 keys and is available online for about $130. (Both keyboards connect to your iMac via a USB cable.)

If you have an older instrument with traditional MIDI ports — they're round, so you'll never confuse them with USB connectors — you need a USB-to-MIDI converter. You can find this type of converter on the Apple website for

around $50. (If you're recording your voice for a podcast, things are easier because you can use your MacBook's built-in microphone; however, most podcasting professionals opt for an external microphone, which offers better fidelity and doesn't force you to sit directly in front of your screen to record.)

After your instrument is connected, you can record tracks using any software instrument. Create a new software instrument track as I demonstrate in this chapter, select it, and then play a few notes. Suddenly you're playing the instrument you chose! (If nothing happens, check the MIDI status light — which appears in the time display — to see whether it blinks with each note you play. If not, check the installation of your MIDI connection and make sure that you've loaded any required drivers, as well as configured your MIDI settings in QuickTime and the input settings in the System Preferences Sound pane.)

Drag the playhead to a beat or two before the spot in the timeline where you want your recording to start to give yourself time to match the beat. Then click the big red Record button and start jamming or speaking! When you finish, click the Play button to stop recording.

MARK'S MAXIM

Save your work often in GarageBand, just as you do in other iLife applications. One power blackout, and you'll never forgive yourself. Press ⌘+S frequently for peace of mind, and use Time Machine with an external backup drive for good measure!™

Automatic Composition with Magic GarageBand

In a hurry? Too rushed to snag loops and tweak effects? Never fear, GarageBand can even compose a song *automatically!* The Magic GarageBand feature (shown in Figure 17-10) provides nine genres of music to choose from — everything from blues to reggae to funk and rock.

To create a song automatically, follow these steps:

1. **Close all GarageBand windows.**

   If you're currently working on a song, GarageBand prompts you to save it before closing the window.

2. **Click the Magic GarageBand button in the New Project dialog.**

3. **Click the desired genre button, and then click Choose.**

   Hover your cursor over a genre button to get a preview of the song for that genre.

4. **To hear the entire song with the default instruments, click Entire Song and then click the Play button.**

   Alternatively, to hear a short sample of the song, click Snippet and then click the Play button.

   In Figure 17-10, you see each instrument onstage. To choose a different musical style for an instrument (or a variation of the instrument), click it and then select the desired sound from the menu below the stage.

Figure 17-10: Creating my own arena-rock classic with Magic GarageBand.

You'd like to join in and jam with Magic GarageBand? Click the instrument that appears at the front center of the stage to highlight it. GarageBand displays the My Instrument settings on the menu below the stage. Click My Instrument (the empty space in the middle of the stage) to add your own voice or instrumental, using a microphone or MIDI instrument.

5. **When the song satisfies your inner muse, click the Open in GarageBand button to open the song as a project in GarageBand.**

Now you can edit and tweak the song to your heart's delight as you can any other GarageBand project, adding other software or real instrument tracks as necessary.

Sharing Your Songs and Podcasts

After you finish your song, you can play it whenever you like through GarageBand. But then again, that isn't really what you want, is it? You want to share your music with others with an audio CD or download it to your iPod so that you can enjoy it yourself while walking through the mall!

Hey, GarageBand, teach me how to play!

In the early days of GarageBand, you were limited to creating music — and if you were a nonmusician like yours truly, GarageBand had no practical use as a tool for teaching yourself how to actually *play* an instrument.

Ah, but Apple's addition of Learn to Play turns GarageBand into your private video tutor for basic piano and guitar! From the New Project dialog, click the Learn to Play heading to display your lessons. Right out of the box, you have an introduction to both instruments, but you can download more free lessons for each instrument from the Lesson Store — and they cover more advanced topics such as fingering and chords. Your on-screen instructor can even record what you play.

GarageBand also includes the How Did I Play feature, which can pinpoint the portions of a lesson that you played correctly and which spots in the song you need to work on. (I'm told musicians call such trouble spots *flubs* — having no musical

talent whatsoever, anything I attempt to play would be one giant flub.) To try How Did I Play, open your favorite lesson, move your pointer to the left side of the window, and then click the Play button that appears. Click the Record button (with the red dot in the center) and begin playing. To stop recording, click the Play button. Now you can see the portions of the song that you played correctly (where the notation area is green) and those spots where you flubbed (the notation area turns red). Oh, and make sure that your instrument is in tune because even correct notes played on an out-of-tune instrument produce errors for How Did I Play!

If you find the free Learn to Play lessons valuable, you can move up to the Artist lessons, which are taught by famous musicians (including favorites of mine such as Alex Lifeson, John Fogerty and Sting, who actually teaches you how to play "Roxanne"). Each Artist lesson is $4.99 — well worth the price.

iTunes to the rescue! As with the other iLife applications that I cover in this book, GarageBand can share the music you make through the digital hub that is your Mac.

Creating MP3 and AAC files and ringtones

You can create an MP3 or AAC file (or an M4R file for a Mac, an iPhone, an iPod touch, or an iPad ringtone) from your song or podcast project in just a few simple steps:

1. **Open the song that you want to share.**

2. **Choose Share⮑Send Song to iTunes.**

   GarageBand displays the settings you see in Figure 17-11.

   To create a ringtone and send it to iTunes, choose Share⮑Send Ringtone to iTunes.

3. **Click in each of the four text boxes to type the playlist, artist name, composer name, and album name, respectively, for the tracks you create.**

   You can leave the defaults as they are, if you prefer. Each track that you export is named after the song's name in GarageBand.

Figure 17-11: Tweaking settings for iTunes song files.

   4. **Click the Compress Using pop-up menu and choose the encoder GarageBand should use to compress your song file.**

   The default is AAC, but you can also choose MP3 encoding for wider device compatibility.

   5. **Click the Audio Settings pop-up menu and select the proper audio quality for the finished file.**

   The higher the quality, the larger the file. GarageBand displays the approximate file size and finished file information in the description box.

   6. **Click Share.**

After a second or two of hard work, your MacBook opens the iTunes window and highlights the new (or existing) playlist that contains your new song.

Sending a podcast to iTunes

If you prepare a new podcast episode in GarageBand, you can send it automatically to iTunes by following these steps:

   1. **Open the podcast that you want to export.**

   Make sure that the Podcast track is displayed. If necessary, choose Track⇨Show Podcast Track to display it.

   2. **Choose Share⇨Send Podcast to iTunes.**

   3. **Click the Compress Using pop-up menu, and then choose the encoder that GarageBand should use to compress your podcast file.**

   Your choices are the AAC and MP3 formats.

   4. **Click the Audio Settings pop-up menu and select the proper audio quality for the finished file.**

   5. **Click Share.**

Burning an audio CD

Ready to create a demo CD with your latest GarageBand creation? Follow these steps to burn an audio disc from within GarageBand:

   1. **Open the song that you want to record to disc.**

   2. **Choose Share⇨Burn Song to CD.**

   3. **Load a blank disc into your optical drive.**

Note that the CD you create has only one track, and by *track* I mean one song (not like a track within a song). To include more songs on the CD, add the song to your iTunes Library (as described previously in the section "Creating MP3 and AAC files and ringtones"), create a playlist containing the song, and burn that playlist in iTunes.

Part V
Getting Productive with iWork

The 5th Wave   By Rich Tennant

Oh come on — how fatal can it be?

FATAL ERROR

In this part . . .

Who needs that *other* office productivity suite? If you've invested in Apple's iWork applications, these chapters will provide all the basics you need to use Pages, Numbers, and Keynote to produce eye-popping printed documents, spreadsheets, and professional-grade presentations!

Chapter 18

Desktop Publishing with Pages

· ·

In This Chapter

▶ Creating a Pages document

▶ Entering, editing, and formatting text

▶ Inserting tables and graphics

▶ Adding a shape as a background

▶ Checking your spelling

▶ Printing Pages documents

▶ Sharing your work

· ·

*W*hat's the difference between word processing and desktop publishing? In a nutshell, the difference is in how you *design* your document. Most folks use a word processor like an old-fashioned typewriter. (Yawn.)

A desktop-publishing application allows far more creativity in choosing where to place text, how to align graphics, and how to edit formats. I think desktop publishing is more visual and intuitive, allowing your imagination a free hand at creating a document.

In this chapter, I show you how to set your inner designer free from the tedious constraints of word processing! Whether you need a simple letter, a stunning brochure, or a multipage newsletter, Pages can handle the job with ease — and you'll be surprised at how simple it is to use.

Creating a New Pages Document

To create a new Pages document from scratch, follow these steps:

1. **Click the Launchpad icon in the Dock.**

2. **Click the Pages icon.**

   Pages displays the Template Chooser window that you see in Figure 18-1.

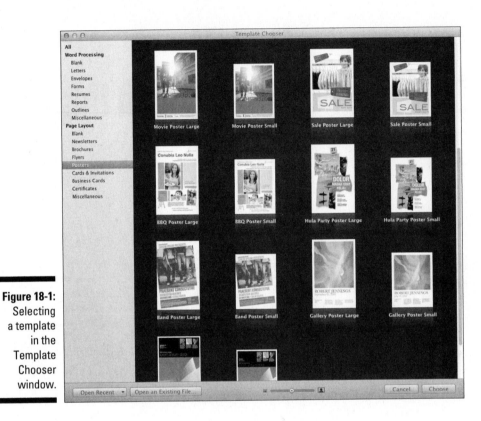

Figure 18-1:
Selecting
a template
in the
Template
Chooser
window.

3. **Click the type of document you want to create in the list to the left.**

   The thumbnails on the right are updated with templates that match your choice.

4. **Click the template that most closely matches your needs.**

5. **Click the Choose button to create a new document using the template you selected.**

Opening an Existing Pages Document

Of course, you can always open an existing Pages document from a Finder window — just double-click the document icon. (Mountain Lion's All My Files location in the Finder window sidebar makes it crazy-easy to track down a document.) However, you can also open a Pages document from within the program. Follow these steps:

1. **From Launchpad, click the Pages icon to run the program.**

2. **Press ⌘+O to display the Open dialog.**

   The Open dialog operates much the same as a Finder window in icon, list, column, or Cover Flow view mode.

3. **Click the desired drive in the Devices list at the left of the dialog and then click folders and subfolders until you've located the Pages document.**

   You can also click in the Search box at the top of the Open dialog and type a portion of the document name or its contents.

4. **Double-click the filename to load it.**

If you want to open a Pages document that you've edited in the recent past, things get even easier! Just choose File⇨Open Recent, and you can open the document with a single click from the submenu that appears.

Saving Your Work

Although Pages fully supports Mountain Lion's Auto Save feature, you may feel the need to manually save your work after you finish it (or to take a break while designing). Follow these steps to save a document for the first time:

1. **With the Pages document open, press ⌘+S.**

   If you're saving a document that hasn't yet been saved, the familiar Save sheet appears.

2. **Type a filename for your new document.**

3. **Click the Where pop-up menu and choose a location to save the document.**

   To save your document directly to Apple's iCloud, choose iCloud as your destination — you can open your iCloud documents from another Mac or from any iOS device running iWork for iOS 1.61 or later. (Naturally, you'll need to enter the same Apple ID on any device before using it to access the documents stored in your iCloud space.)

   If you choose a location other than iCloud, you can click the button sporting the down arrow to expand the Save sheet. This allows you to navigate to a different location or to create a new folder to store this Pages project.

4. **Click Save.**

After you save a Pages document to your drive for the first time, you can create a version of that document by choosing File➪Save a Version. To revert the current document to an older version, choose File➪Revert Document. Pages gives you the option of reverting to the last saved version, or you can click Older Version to browse multiple versions of the document and choose one of those to revert to.

Touring the Pages Window

Before you dive into any real work, let me show you around the Pages window! You'll find the following major components and controls, shown in Figure 18-2:

- ✔ **Pages list:** This thumbnail list displays all the pages you've created in your document. (For a single-page document, of course, the Pages list will contain only a single thumbnail.) You can switch instantly between different pages in your document by clicking the desired thumbnail in the list.

Toolbar

Format bar Pages list Layout pane

Styles drawer

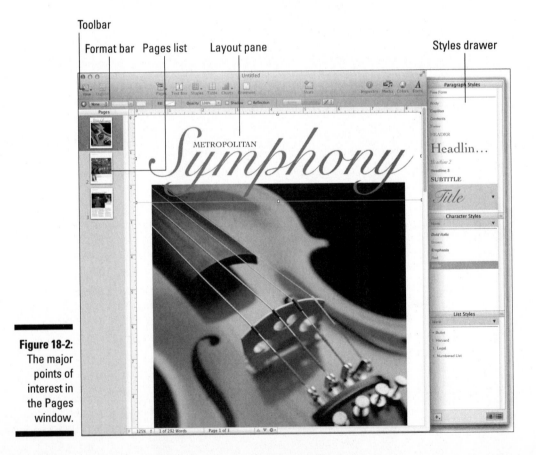

Figure 18-2:
The major points of interest in the Pages window.

✔ **Layout pane:** This section takes up most of the Pages window — it's where you design and edit each page in your document.

✔ **Toolbar:** Yep, Pages has its own toolbar. The toolbar keeps all the most common application controls within easy, one-click reach.

✔ **Styles drawer:** This window extension allows you to quickly switch the appearance of selected paragraphs, characters, and lists. You can hide and display the Styles drawer from the View menu or from the View drop-down menu on the toolbar.

✔ **Format Bar:** This button strip runs under the Pages toolbar. Use it to format selected text, paragraphs, and lists on-the-fly.

Entering and Editing Text

If you've used a modern word-processing program, you'll feel right at home typing within Pages. Just in case you're not familiar with word processing, however, review the high points:

✔ The bar-shaped text cursor, which looks like a capital letter *I,* indicates where the text you enter will appear in a Pages document.

✔ To enter text, simply begin typing. Your characters appear at the text cursor.

✔ To edit text in your Pages document, click the insertion cursor at any point in the text and drag the cursor across the characters to highlight them. Type the replacement text, and Pages automatically replaces the existing characters with the ones you typed.

✔ To delete text, click and drag across the characters to highlight them, and then press Delete.

Using Text and Graphics Boxes

In Pages, text and graphics appear in *boxes,* which can be resized by clicking and dragging on one of the handles that appear around the edges of the box. (Hover your cursor over one of the square handles, and you'll see that it changes to a double-sided arrow, indicating that Pages is ready to resize the box.)

You can also move a box, including all the stuff it contains, to another location in the Layout pane. Click in the center of the box and drag the box to the desired spot, or hold down the Option key while you drag to create a copy in the new location. Note that Pages displays blue alignment lines to help you align the box with other elements around it (or with regular divisions of the page, such as the vertical center of a poster or flyer). Figure 18-3 illustrates a box containing text that I'm moving; note the vertical alignment line that automatically appears.

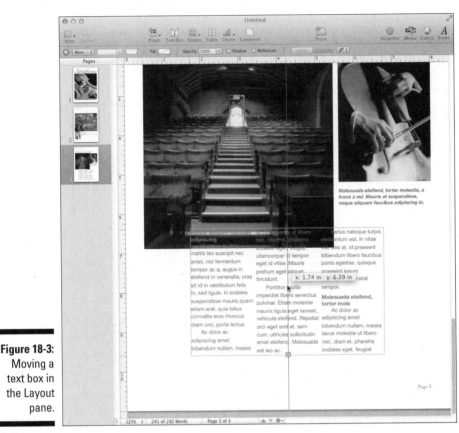

Figure 18-3:
Moving a
text box in
the Layout
pane.

To select text or graphics in a box, you must first click the box to select it and then click again on the line of text or the graphic that you want to change.

The Three Amigos: Cut, Copy, and Paste

"Hang on, Mark, you've covered moving stuff, but what if you want to *copy* a block of text or a photo to a second location? Or how about cutting something from a document open in another application?" Good questions, dear reader! That's when you can call on the power of the cut, copy, and paste features in Pages. The next few sections explain how you do these actions.

Cutting stuff

Cutting selected text or graphics removes the selection from your Pages document and places that material in your Clipboard. (Think of the Clipboard as a holding area for snippets of text and graphics that you want to manipulate.) To cut text or graphics, select some material and choose Edit⇔Cut or press ⌘+X.

Copying text and images

When you copy text or graphics, the original selection remains untouched, but a copy of the selection is placed in the Clipboard. Select some text or graphics and choose Edit⇔Copy or press ⌘+C.

Like copying a box and all its contents, you can also copy selected items by dragging — hold down the Option key while you drag the items to their destination.

If you cut or copy a new selection to the Clipboard, it erases what was there. In other words, the Clipboard holds only the latest material you cut or copied.

Pasting from the Clipboard

Are you wondering what you can do with the stuff that's stored in your Clipboard? Pasting the contents of the Clipboard places the material at the current location of the insertion cursor. You must paste the contents before you cut or copy again to avoid losing what's in the Clipboard.

To paste the Clipboard contents, click the insertion cursor at the location you want and choose Edit⇔Paste or press ⌘+V.

Formatting Text the Easy Way

If you feel that some (or all) text in your Pages document needs a facelift, you can format that text any way you like. Formatting lets you change the color, font family, character size, and attributes as necessary.

After the text is selected, you can apply basic formatting in two ways:

- ✔ **Use the Format bar.** The Format bar appears directly below the Pages toolbar (refer Figure 18-2). Click to select a font control to display a pop-up menu and then click your choice. For example, click the Font Family button and change the font family from Arial to a more daring font. You can also select characteristics such as the font's background color (perfect for highlighting key information) or choose italics or bold. The Format bar also provides buttons for text alignment (Align Left, Center, Align Right, and Justify).

- ✔ **Use the Format menu.** Most controls on the Format bar are available also on the Format menu. Click Format and hover the cursor over the Font menu item, and you can then apply bold, italics, and underlining to the selected text. You can also make the text bigger or smaller. To change the alignment from the Format menu, click Format and hover the cursor over the Text menu item.

Adding a Spiffy Table

In the world of word processing, a *table* is a grid of cells that holds text or graphics for easy comparison. You can create a custom table layout in Pages with a few simple taps on the old trackpad!

Follow these steps:

1. **Click the insertion cursor at the location where you want the table to appear.**

2. **Click the Table button on the Pages toolbar.**

   Pages inserts a simple table and displays the Table Inspector, shown on the right in Figure 18-4.

   By default, Pages creates a table with three rows and three columns, with an extra row for headings at the top. You can change this layout from the Table Inspector — just click in the Body Rows or Body Columns box and type a number.

3. **Click in a cell in the table to enter text.**

   The table cell automatically resizes and wraps the text to fit.

   You can paste material from the Clipboard into a table. See the earlier section "Pasting from the Clipboard" for details on pasting.

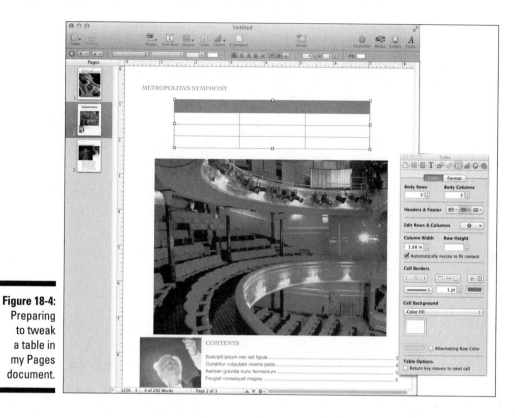

Figure 18-4:
Preparing
to tweak
a table in
my Pages
document.

4. To change the borders on a cell, click the cell to select it and then click one of the Cell Borders buttons to change the border.

Select a range of multiple cells in a table by holding down Shift as you click. Hold down the ⌘ key and click to select multiple cells that aren't contiguous.

5. To add a background color (or even fill cells with an image for a background), click the Cell Background pop-up menu and choose a type of background.

Adding Alluring Photos

You can choose from two methods for adding a picture in your Pages document: as a *floating* object (meaning that you can place the image in a particular spot and it doesn't move, even if you make changes to the text) or as an *inline* object (which flows with the surrounding text as you make layout changes). Here's the lowdown on adding these objects:

- ✔ **Add a floating object.** Drag an image file from a Finder window and place it where you want it in your document. Alternatively, you can click the Media button on the toolbar, click Photos, navigate to the location where the file is saved, and drag the image thumbnail to the spot where you want it in the document. Figure 18-5 illustrates the Media Browser in action.

    Note that a floating object (such as a shape or an image) can be sent to the *background,* where text will not wrap around it. (Think shaded background shape or an image as a background.) To bring a background object back as a regular floating object, click the object to select it and choose Arrange⇨Bring Background Objects to Front. (More about background objects later in this chapter.)

Figure 18-5: Hey, isn't that the Pages Media Browser?

To resize an image object, click the image to select it and then drag one of the selection handles that appears along the border of the image. (The handles look like tiny squares.) The side-selection handles drag only that edge of the frame. The corner-selection handles resize both adjoining edges of the selection frame. To avoid distortion, hold down the Shift key so that the vertical and horizontal proportions remain fixed. You can also flip images — click Arrange on the Pages menu bar to flip the image horizontally or vertically.

✔ **Add an inline object.** Hold down the ⌘ key as you drag an image file from a Finder window and place it where you want it in your document. You can also click the Media toolbar button and then click Photos to display the Media Browser. Navigate to the location where the file is saved, hold down the ⌘ key, and drag the image thumbnail to the spot where you want it in the document.

To move either type of object to another spot on the page, click it to select it (handles will appear around the object) and then click in the center of the object and drag it to the new position.

Adding a Background Shape

To add a shape (such as a rectangle or circle) as a background for your text, follow these steps:

1. **Click the insertion cursor in the location you want.**

2. **Click the Shapes button on the Pages toolbar and choose a shape.**

   The shape appears in your document.

3. **Click the center of the shape and drag it to a new spot.**

   Shapes can be resized or moved in the same manner as object boxes.

4. **Before you can type over a shape, remember to select it and choose Arrange⇨Send Object to Background.**

Are You Sure about That Spelling?

Pages can check spelling as you type (the default setting) or after you complete your document. If you find automatic spell-checking distracting, you should definitely choose the latter method.

As my technical editor reminds us, spell-checking confirms only that a sequence of characters is a correctly spelled word — *not* that it's the right word for the job! If you've ever *red* a document that someone else *rote,* you know what he means, *deer* reader.

To check spelling as you type, follow these steps:

1. **Click Edit and hover the cursor over the Spelling menu item.**

2. **Click Check Spelling As You Type in the submenu that appears.**

   If a possible misspelling is found, Pages underlines the word with a red, dashed line.

3. **Right-click the word to choose a possible correct spelling from the list, or ignore the word if it's spelled correctly.**

To turn off automatic spell-checking, click the Check Spelling As You Type menu item again to deselect it.

To check spelling manually, follow these steps:

1. **Click in the document to place the text insertion cursor where the spell check should begin.**

2. **Click Edit and hover the cursor over the Spelling menu item, then choose Check Spelling from the submenu that appears.**

3. **Right-click any possible misspellings. Then choose the correct spelling or choose Ignore if the word is spelled correctly.**

Printing Your Pages Documents

Ready to start the presses? You can print your Pages document on real paper, of course, but don't forget that you can also save a tree by creating an electronic, PDF-format document instead of a printout — you'll find the PDF button in the standard Mountain Lion Print dialog.

To print your Pages document on old-fashioned paper, follow these steps:

1. **In Pages, choose File⇨Print.**

   Pages displays the Print sheet.

2. **Click in the Copies field and enter the number of copies you need.**

3. **Select the pages to print:**

   - To print the entire document, select All.

   - To print a range of selected pages, select the From radio button and enter the starting and ending pages.

4. **Click the Print button to send the document to your printer.**

Sharing That Poster with Others

Besides printing — which is, after all, so passé — you can choose to share your Pages document electronically in a number of ways:

- ✔ **Share on iCloud.** As mentioned, you can share your Pages documents among all your Macs and iOS devices by saving them to your iCloud space.

- ✔ **Share through e-mail.** Choose Share⇨Send via Mail and select one of the following formats to add your Pages document to a Mail message: as a native Pages document file, as a Word format document, or as a PDF file. After you've selected a format, Pages obligingly launches Apple Mail and creates a new message, ready for you to address and send! (Remember, most Internet service providers have a maximum message size, so if your document is too large, it will likely be rejected by the recipient's mail server.)

- ✔ **Export.** Don't forget that Pages can export your work in one of four formats: a PDF document; a Word format document; an RTF (Rich Text Format) file; or even plain text. Choose Share⇨Export, choose your format, click Next, and then select the location where Pages should save the file. Click Export and sit back while your favorite desktop- publishing application does all the work.

To keep your document as close to how it appears in Pages as possible, I recommend selecting either PDF or Word. Your document will retain far more of your original formatting than an RTF or a plain-text document would.

Chapter 19

Creating Spreadsheets with Numbers

*A*re you downright afraid of spreadsheets? Does the idea of building a budget with charts and all sorts of fancy graphics send you running for the safety of the hall closet? Well, good MacBook owner, Apple has once again taken something that everyone else considers super-complex and turned it into something that normal human beings can use! (Much as Apple did with video editing, songwriting, and desktop publishing — heck, is there *any* type of software that Apple designers can't make intuitive and easy to use?)

In this chapter, I get to demonstrate how Numbers can help you organize data, analyze important financial decisions, and yes, even maintain a household budget! You'll soon see why the Numbers spreadsheet program is specifically designed with the home Mac owner in mind.

Before You Launch Numbers . . .

Just in case you're not familiar with applications such as Numbers and Microsoft Excel — and the documents they create — let me provide you with a little background information.

A *spreadsheet* organizes and calculates numbers of all kinds (including dates, times, and currency) by using a grid system of rows and columns. The intersection of each row and column is a *cell,* and cells can hold either text or numeric values (along with calculations that are usually linked to the contents of surrounding cells).

Spreadsheets are wonderful tools for making decisions and comparisons because they let you "plug in" different numbers — such as interest rates or your monthly insurance premium — and instantly see the results. Some of my favorite spreadsheets that I use regularly include

- ✔ Car and mortgage loan comparisons
- ✔ A college planner
- ✔ My household budget (not that I pay any attention to it)

Creating a New Numbers Document

Like Pages, Apple's desktop-publishing application, Numbers ships with a selection of templates that you can modify quickly to create a new spreadsheet. (For example, after a few modifications, you can easily use the Budget, Loan Comparison, and Mortgage templates to create your own spreadsheets.)

To create a spreadsheet project file, follow these steps:

1. **Click the Launchpad icon in the Dock.**

2. **Click the Numbers icon.**

   Numbers displays the Template Chooser window you see in Figure 19-1.

3. **Click the type of document you want to create in the list to the left.**

   The document thumbnails on the right are updated with templates that match your choice.

4. **Click the template that most closely matches your needs.**

5. **Click Choose to open a new document using the template you selected.**

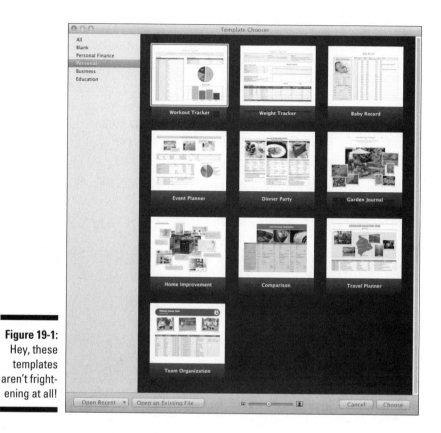

Figure 19-1:
Hey, these
templates
aren't fright-
ening at all!

Opening an Existing Spreadsheet File

If a Numbers document appears in a Finder window (or you use Spotlight
to search for it or it's included in the All My Files location), you can just
double-click the Document icon to open it; Numbers automatically loads
and displays the spreadsheet. However, it's equally easy to open a Numbers
document from within the program. Follow these steps:

1. **From Launchpad, click the Numbers icon to run the program.**

2. **Press ⌘+O to display the Open dialog.**

3. **Click the desired drive in the Devices list at the left of the dialog and
   then click folders and subfolders to drill down until you've located
   the desired Numbers document.**

If you're unsure of where the document is, click the Search box at the top-right corner of the Open dialog and type a portion of the document name or even a word or two of text it contains (using the pop-up menu that appears).

4. **Double-click the spreadsheet to load it.**

If you want to open a spreadsheet you've been working on over the last few days, choose File➪Open Recent to display Numbers documents that you've worked with recently.

The Template Chooser window also sports both an Open Recent button and an Open Existing File button. Convenience is A Good Thing!

Save Those Spreadsheets!

With the Auto Save feature built into Mountain Lion, you're no longer required to save on a regular basis — however, if you a fan of not retyping any data at all, I recommend that you save your spreadsheets often (just in case of a power failure or a coworker's mistake). Follow these steps the first time you save your spreadsheet to your hard drive:

1. **Press ⌘+S.**

   If you're saving a document that hasn't yet been saved, the Save As sheet appears.

2. **Type a filename for your new spreadsheet.**

3. **Click the Where pop-up menu and choose a location to save the file.**

To save your document directly to Apple's iCloud, choose iCloud as your destination — you can open your iCloud documents from another Mac or from any iOS device running iWork for iOS 1.61 or later. (Naturally, you'll need to enter the same Apple ID on any device before using it to access the documents stored in your iCloud space.)

If you choose a location other than iCloud, you can click a common location, such as your desktop, Documents folder, or Home folder.

If the location you want isn't listed in the Where pop-up menu, you can also click the down-arrow button next to the Save As text box to display the full Save As dialog. Click the desired drive in the Devices list at the left of the dialog and then click folders and subfolders to drill down until you reach the desired location. You can also create a new folder in the full Save As dialog.

4. **Click Save.**

After you save a Numbers document for the first time, you can create a version of that document by choosing File➪Save a Version. To revert the current document to an older version, choose File➪Revert Document. You can choose to revert to the last saved version, or you can click Older Version to browse multiple versions of the document and choose one of those to revert to.

Exploring the Numbers Window

Apple did a great job of minimizing the complexity of the Numbers window, as you can see in Figure 19-2.

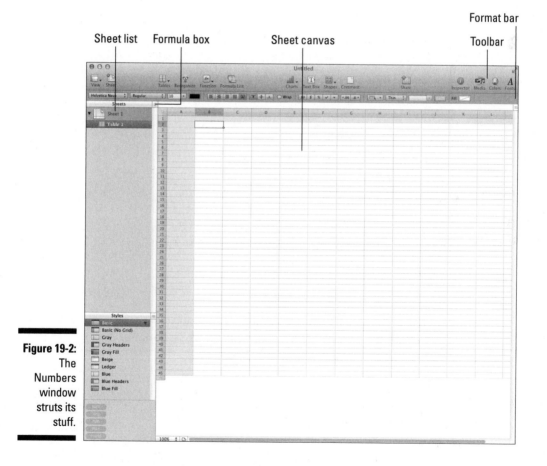

Figure 19-2: The Numbers window struts its stuff.

Following are the major points of interest:

- ✔ **Sheets list:** Because a Numbers project can contain multiple spreadsheets, they're displayed in the Sheets list at the left of the window. To switch between spreadsheets in a project, click the top-level headings (each of which has a spreadsheet icon).

- ✔ **Sheet canvas:** Numbers displays the rows and columns of your spreadsheet in this section of the window; you enter and edit cell values within the sheet canvas.

- ✔ **Toolbar:** The Numbers toolbar keeps the most common commands you use within easy reach.

- ✔ **Formula box:** You use the Formula box to enter formulas into a cell, allowing Numbers to automatically perform calculations based on the contents of other cells.

- ✔ **Format bar:** Located directly below the toolbar, the Format bar displays editing controls for the object that's currently selected. (If you enter an equal sign into the Formula box, the Format bar changes into the Formula bar. No, I'm not making this up.) My goodness, this is starting to sound like that classic movie about the chocolate tycoon and those kids!

Navigate and Select Cells in a Spreadsheet

You can use the scroll bars to move around in your spreadsheet, but when you enter data in cells, moving your fingers from the keyboard is a hassle. For this reason, Numbers has various movement shortcut keys that you can use to navigate, and I list them in Table 19-1. After you commit these keys to memory, your productivity shoots straight to the top.

Table 19-1	Movement Shortcut Keys in Numbers
Key or Key Combination	*Where the Cursor Moves*
Left arrow (←)	One cell to the left
Right arrow (→)	One cell to the right
Up arrow (↑)	One cell up
Down arrow (↓)	One cell down
Home	To the beginning of the active worksheet
End	To the end of the active worksheet
Page Down	Down one screen

Key or Key Combination	Where the Cursor Moves
Page Up	Up one screen
Return	One cell down (also works within a selection)
Tab	One cell to the right (also works within a selection)
Shift+Enter	One cell up (also works within a selection)
Shift+Tab	One cell to the left (also works within a selection)

You can use the trackpad to select cells in a spreadsheet:

✔ To select a *single* cell, click it.

✔ To select a *range* of multiple adjacent cells, click a cell at any corner of the range you want and then drag in the direction you want.

✔ To select a *column* of cells, click the alphabetic heading button at the top of the column.

✔ To select a *row* of cells, click the numeric heading button on the far left side of the row.

Entering and Editing Data in a Spreadsheet

After you navigate to the cell in which you want to enter data, you're ready to type your data. Follow these steps to enter That Important Stuff:

1. **Either click the cell or press the spacebar.**

   A cursor appears, indicating that the cell is ready to hold any data you type.

2. **Type your data.**

   Spreadsheets can use both numbers and text in a cell — either type of information is considered data in the Spreadsheet World.

3. **To edit data, click in the cell that contains the data to select it and then click the cell again to display the insertion cursor. Drag the insertion cursor across the characters to highlight them and then type the replacement data.**

4. **To simply delete characters, highlight the characters and press Delete.**

5. **When you're ready to move on, press Return (to save the data and move one cell down) or press Tab (to save the data and move one cell to the right).**

Selecting the Correct Number Format

After your data has been entered in a cell, row, or column, you still might need to format it before it appears correctly. Numbers gives you a healthy selection of formatting possibilities. *Number formatting* determines how a cell displays a number, such as a dollar amount, a percentage, or a date.

Characters and formatting rules, such as decimal places, commas, and dollar and percentage notation, are included in number formatting. So, if your spreadsheet contains units of currency, such as dollars, format it as such. Then all you need to do is type the numbers, and the currency formatting is applied automatically.

To specify a number format, follow these steps:

1. **Select the cells, rows, or columns you want to format.**

2. **Click the Inspector toolbar button.**

3. **Click the Cells Inspector button on the Inspector toolbar to display the settings you see in Figure 19-3.**

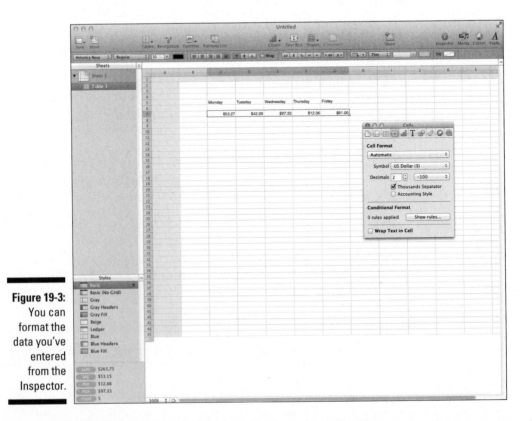

Figure 19-3: You can format the data you've entered from the Inspector.

4. **Click the Cell Format pop-up menu and click the type of formatting you want to apply.**

Aligning Cell Text Just So

You can also change the alignment of text in the selected cells. (The default alignment is flush left for text and flush right for numeric data.) Follow these steps:

1. **Select the cells, rows, or columns you want to format.**

   See "Navigate and Select Cells in a Spreadsheet," earlier in this chapter, for tips on selecting stuff.

2. **Click the Inspector toolbar button.**

3. **Click the Text Inspector button on the Inspector toolbar to display the settings you see in Figure 19-4.**

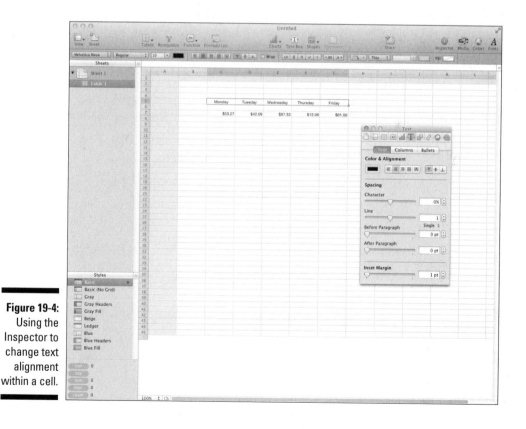

Figure 19-4:
Using the
Inspector to
change text
alignment
within a cell.

4. **Click the corresponding alignment button to choose the type of formatting you want to apply.**

   You can choose left, right, center, justified, and text left and numbers right. Text can also be aligned at the top, center, or bottom of a cell.

You can also select the cells you want to align and click the appropriate alignment button in the Format bar.

Do you need to set apart the contents of some cells? For example, you might need to create text headings for some columns and rows or to highlight the totals in a spreadsheet. To change the formatting of the data displayed in selected cells, select the cells, rows, or columns you want to format and then click the Font Family, Font Size, or Font Color buttons on the Format bar.

Format with Shading

Shading the contents of a cell, row, or column is helpful when your spreadsheet contains subtotals or logical divisions. Follow these steps to shade cells, rows, or columns:

1. **Select the cells, rows, or columns you want to format.**

2. **Click the Inspector toolbar button.**

3. **Click the Graphic Inspector button on the Inspector toolbar.**

   Numbers displays the settings you see in Figure 19-5.

4. **Click the Fill pop-up menu to select a shading option.**

5. **Click the color box to select a color for your shading.**

   Numbers displays a color picker (also shown in Figure 19-5).

6. **Click to select a color.**

7. **After you achieve the right effect, click the Close button in the color picker.**

8. **Click the Inspector's Close button to return to your spreadsheet.**

The Fill function is also available on the Format bar.

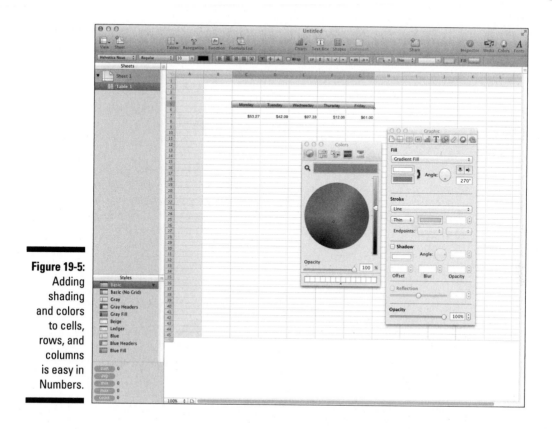

Figure 19-5:
Adding
shading
and colors
to cells,
rows, and
columns
is easy in
Numbers.

Insert and Delete Rows and Columns

What's that? You forgot to add a row and now you're three pages into your data entry? No problem. You can easily add or delete rows and columns. First, select the row or column that you want to delete or that you want to insert a row or column next to, and do one of the following:

- ✔ **For a row:** Right-click and choose Add Row Above, Add Row Below, or Delete Row from the shortcut menu that appears.

- ✔ **For a column:** Right-click and choose Add Columns Before, Add Columns After, or Delete Column from the shortcut menu that appears.

If you select multiple rows or columns and choose Add, Numbers inserts the same number of new rows or columns as you originally selected.

You can also insert rows and columns using the Table menu.

The Formula Is Your Friend

Sorry, but it's time to talk about *formulas.* These equations calculate values based on the contents of cells you specify in your spreadsheet. For example, if you designate cell A1 (the cell in column A at row 1) to hold your yearly salary and cell B1 to hold the number 12, you can divide the contents of cell A1 by cell B1 (to calculate your monthly salary) by typing this formula into any other cell:

> **=A1/B1**

By the way, formulas in Numbers always start with an equal sign (=).

"So what's the big deal, Mark? Why not use a calculator?" Sure, but maybe you want to calculate your weekly salary. Rather than grab a pencil and paper, you can simply change the contents of cell B1 to 52, and — boom! — the spreadsheet is updated to display your weekly salary.

That's a simple example, of course, but it demonstrates the basis of using formulas (and the reason why spreadsheets are often used to predict trends and forecast budgets). A spreadsheet is the "what if?" tool of choice for everyone who works with numeric data.

To add a simple formula in your spreadsheet, follow these steps:

1. **Select the cell that will hold the result of your calculation.**

2. **Click the Formula box and type = (equal sign).**

   The Formula box appears to the right of the Sheets heading, directly under the Button bar (refer to Figure 19-2). Note that the Format bar changes to show a set of formula controls (a.k.a. the Formula bar).

3. **Click the Function Browser button, which bears the *fx* label.**

   The Function Browser button appears next to the red Cancel button on the Formula bar.

4. **In the window that appears, as shown in Figure 19-6, click the desired formula and then click Insert Function to add the formula to the Formula box.**

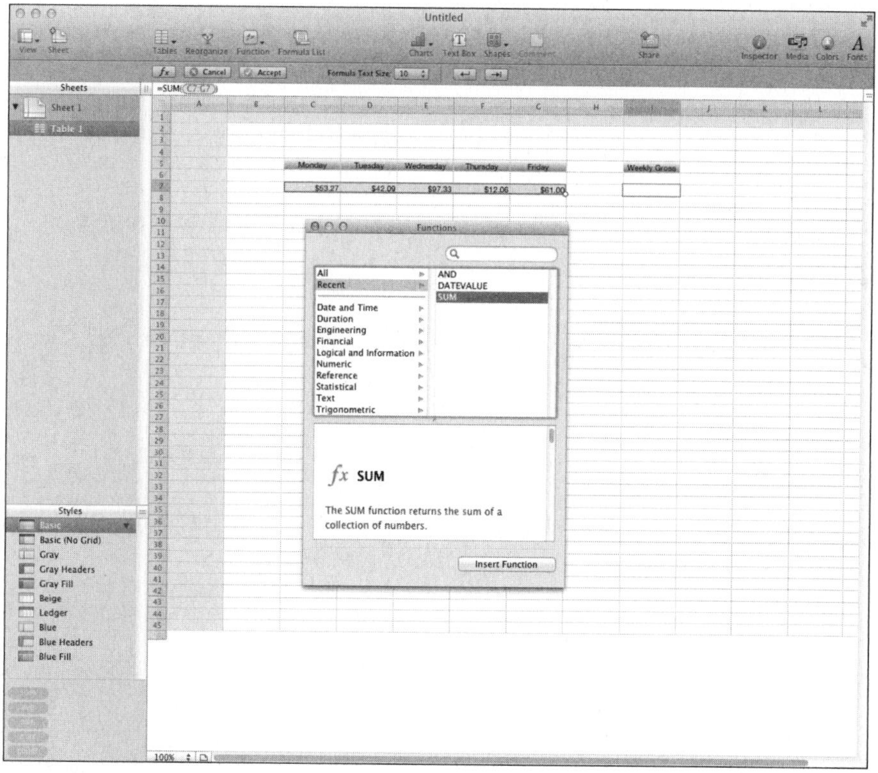

Figure 19-6:
If you have
to use
formulas,
at least
Numbers
can enter
them for
you.

5. **Click one of the rounded argument buttons in the formula and click the cell that contains the corresponding data.**

   Numbers automatically adds the cell you indicated to the formula. Repeat this for each argument in the formula.

6. **When you're finished, click the Accept button to add the formula to the cell.**

That's it! Your formula is now ready to work behind the scenes, doing math for you so that the correct numbers appear in the cell you specified.

To display all the formulas that you've added to a sheet, click the Formula List button on the toolbar.

Adding Visual Punch with a Chart

Sometimes you just have to see something to believe it — hence the capability to use the data you add to a spreadsheet to generate a professional-looking chart! Follow these steps to create a chart:

1. **Select the adjacent cells you want to chart by dragging.**

   To choose individual cells that aren't adjacent, hold down the ⌘ key as you click.

2. **Click the Charts button on the Numbers toolbar. The Charts button bears the symbol of a bar graph.**

   Numbers displays a thumbnail menu.

3. **Click the thumbnail for the chart type you want.**

   Numbers inserts the chart as an object in your spreadsheet so that you can move the chart. You can drag using the handles that appear on the outside of the object box to resize your chart. Figure 19-7 illustrates the 3-D chart I generated with just a couple of clicks.

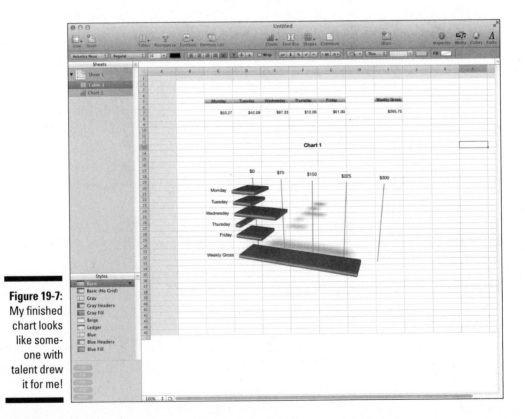

Figure 19-7: My finished chart looks like someone with talent drew it for me!

Click the Inspector toolbar button and switch to the Chart Inspector dialog, where you can change the colors and add (or remove) the chart title and legend.

4. **To change the default title, click the title box once to select it; click it again to edit the text.**

After you've added your chart to the sheet, it appears in the Sheets list, as shown in Figure 19-7. To edit the chart at any time, just click the corresponding entry in the Sheets list.

Chapter 20

Building Presentations with Keynote

*I*t seems like only yesterday that I was giving business presentations with a clunky overhead projector and black-and-white acetate transparencies. Fancy color gradients and animation were unheard of, and the only sound my presentations made was the droning of the projector's fan. I might as well have been using tree bark and chalk.

Thank goodness those days are gone forever, because cutting-edge presentation software such as Keynote makes slide creation easy and — believe it or not — *fun!* This is the application that Steve Jobs designed and used for his Macworld keynotes every year, and there's so much visual candy available that you'll never need to shout to wake your audience again.

In this chapter, I demonstrate how simple it is to build a stunning Keynote presentation, and how to start and control your slide display from your MacBook's keyboard (or even your iPhone, iPad, or iPod touch). Heck, you can even print your slides and notes so that your audience can keep a copy of your brilliant work!

Creating a New Keynote Project

As do the other applications in the iWork suite, Keynote begins the document creation process with a Template Chooser window. To create a new presentation project, follow these steps:

1. **Click the Launchpad icon in the Dock.**

2. **Click the Keynote icon.**

   The Template Chooser window that you see in Figure 20-1 appears. (I have to say that these are the most stunning visual building blocks I've ever seen in a presentation application.)

3. **Click the Slide Size pop-up menu at the bottom of the screen to select the resolution for your completed slides.**

   Although you don't necessarily need to select an exact match for your laptop's screen resolution, it's a good idea to select the closest value to the maximum resolution of your projector. (If someone else is providing the projector, the default value of 1024 x 768 is a good standard to use.) If you're using a second monitor during your presentation, select the native resolution for that monitor instead.

Figure 20-1: Selecting a template from the Template Chooser window.

4. **Click the template that most closely matches your needs.**

5. **Click Choose to open a new document by using the template you selected.**

Opening a Keynote Presentation

If an existing Keynote presentation file is visible in a Finder window, you can double-click the document icon to open the project. If Keynote is already running, however, follow these steps to load a project:

1. **Press ⌘+O to display the Open dialog.**

2. **Click the desired drive in the Devices list at the left of the dialog, and then click to drill down through folders and subfolders until you've located the Keynote project.**

   You can also use the Search box at the top of the Open dialog to locate the document by name or by some of the text it contains, or click the All My Files location in the Open dialog sidebar to display your documents.

3. **Double-click the filename to load it.**

If you want to open a Keynote document that you've edited in the recent past, things get even easier! Just choose File➪Open Recent and you can open the document with a single click from the submenu that appears. (Note that the Template Chooser window has both Open Recent and Open Existing File buttons as well.)

Saving Your Presentation

Because Keynote provides full support for Mountain Lion's Auto Save feature, you no longer need to manually save your presentation every few minutes. But if you're the prudent type and want to safeguard your work in a world of power failures, follow these steps the first time you save a presentation:

1. **Press ⌘+S.**

   If you're saving a document that hasn't yet been saved, the familiar Save As sheet appears.

2. **Type a filename for your new document.**

3. **Click the Where pop-up menu and then choose a location to save the document.**

By default, Keynote will save your presentation directly to Apple's iCloud, allowing you to open it from another Mac or from any iOS device running Keynote for iOS 1.61 or later. (You have to enter the same Apple ID on any device before using it to access the documents stored in your iCloud space.)

To select a location not on the Where pop-up menu (such as a specific folder on your drive), choose the volume or drive on the Where menu, and then click the button with the down arrow symbol to expand the sheet. You can also create a new folder from the expanded sheet.

4. Click Save.

After you save a Keynote presentation for the first time, you can create a version of that document by choosing File⇨Save a Version. To revert the current presentation to an older version, choose File⇨Revert to Saved. Keynote gives you the option of reverting to the last saved version, or you can click Older Version to browse multiple versions of the presentation and choose one of those to revert to.

Putting Keynote to Work

Ready for the 5-cent tour of the Keynote window? Launch the application and create or load a project, and you'll see the tourist attractions shown in Figure 20-2:

 ✔ **Slides list:** Use this thumbnail list of all the slides in your project to help you navigate quickly. Click a thumbnail to switch instantly to that slide.

The Slides list can also display your project in outline format, allowing you to check all your discussion points. (This is a great way to ferret out any "holes" in your presentation's flow.) While viewing the Slides list in outline mode, you can still jump directly to any slide by clicking the slide's title in the outline. To display the outline, choose View⇨Outline. You can switch back to the default Navigator Slides list by choosing View⇨Navigator.

 ✔ **Layout pane:** Your slide appears in its entirety in this pane. You can add elements and edit the content of the slide from the Layout pane.

 ✔ **Toolbar:** Keynote's toolbar, like the toolbars in Pages and Numbers, makes it easy to find the most common controls you'll use while designing and editing your slides. Clicking an icon on the toolbar performs an action, just as selecting a menu item does.

 ✔ **Notes pane:** If you decide to add notes to one or more slides (either for your own use or to print as additional information for your audience), choose View⇨Show Presenter Notes to open the Notes pane. The Notes pane (which is really just a glorified text box) appears under the Layout pane.

 ✔ **Format bar:** Keynote displays this button strip below the Keynote toolbar, allowing you to format selected text, paragraphs, and lists on-the-fly.

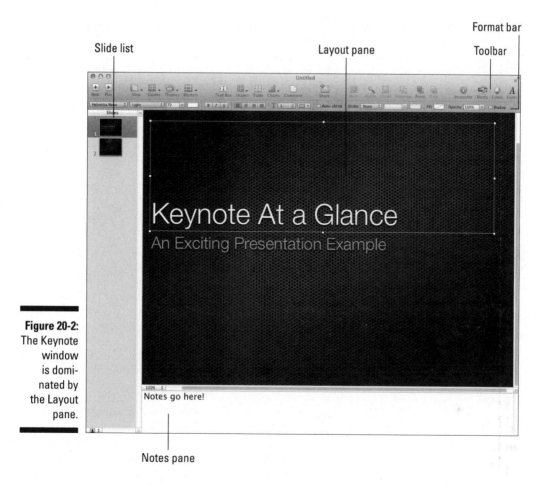

Format bar

Slide list   Layout pane   Toolbar

Notes pane

Figure 20-2:
The Keynote
window
is domi-
nated by
the Layout
pane.

Adding Slides

Sure, Keynote creates a single Title slide when you first create a project, but not many presentations are complete with just a single slide! To add more slides to your project, use one of these methods:

- Click the New button on the Keynote toolbar.
- Choose Slide➪New Slide.
- Press ⌘+Shift+N.
- Right-click (or Control-click) in the Slides list and choose New Slide from the shortcut menu.

Keynote adds the new slide to your Slides list and automatically switches to the new slide in the Layout pane.

Need a slide that's similar to an existing slide you've already designed? Right-click the existing slide and choose Duplicate to create a new slide just like it. (Consider it cloning without the science.) Now you can edit the duplicate!

To move slides to different positions in the Slides list (and therefore a different order in your Keynote slideshow), drag each slide thumbnail to the desired spot in the list.

Working with Text and Graphics Boxes

You've probably noticed that all the text in your first Title slide appears in boxes. Keynote uses boxes to manipulate text and graphics. You can resize a box (and its contents) by clicking and dragging one of the handles that appears around the edges of the box. (Your cursor changes into a double-sided arrow when you're "in the zone.") The side-selection handles drag only that edge of the frame, whereas the corner-selection handles resize both adjoining edges of the selection frame.

To keep the proportions of the box constrained, hold down the Shift key while dragging the corner handles.

Boxes make it easy to move text and graphics together (as a unit) to another location in the Layout pane. Click in the center of the box and drag the box to the desired spot; Keynote displays alignment lines to help you align the box with other elements around it (or with regular divisions of the slide, such as horizontal center). As you can see in Figure 20-3, I'm moving a box on the slide to a new location, and Keynote has supplied alignment lines to help me place it correctly.

To select text or graphics in a box, double-click the box.

If you're resizing a photo in a box, don't forget to hold down the Shift key as you drag the frame. That way, Keynote preserves the aspect ratio of the image so that the vertical and horizontal proportions remain fixed. You can also flip images horizontally or vertically from the Arrange menu.

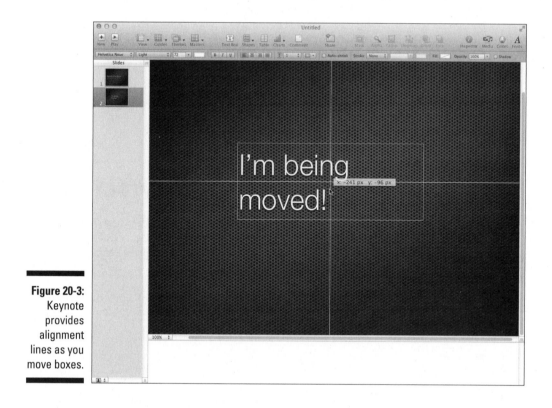

Figure 20-3:
Keynote
provides
alignment
lines as you
move boxes.

Adding and Editing Slide Text

As with Pages and Numbers, which also use boxes for text layout, Keynote allows you to add or edit text with ease. For example, double-click in a box with the text `Double-click to edit`, and the placeholder text disappears, leaving the field ready to accept new text. Any new text you type appears at the blinking cursor in the box.

To edit existing text in your Keynote document, click using the bar-shaped cursor to select just the right spot in the text, and drag the insertion cursor across the characters to highlight them. Type the replacement text, and Keynote obligingly replaces the text that was there with the text you type.

If you want to delete existing text, click and drag across the characters to highlight them and then press Delete. You can also delete an entire box and all its contents: Right-click (or Control-click) the offending box and choose Delete from the menu that appears.

When the contents of a box are just right and you've finished entering or editing text, click anywhere outside the box to hide it from view. You can always click the text again to display the box later.

Formatting Slide Text for the Perfect Look

Keynote doesn't restrict you to the default fonts for the theme you choose. It's easy to format the text in your slides — you can choose a different font family, font color, text alignment, and text attributes such as bold and italics on-the-fly, whenever you like.

Select the desired text by double-clicking a box and then dragging the text cursor to highlight the characters. Now apply your formatting using one of these two methods:

- **The Format bar:** The font controls on the Format bar work just like the controls on the toolbar. You click a font control to display a pop-up menu or click a button to immediately perform an action. Clicking the Font Size pop-up menu, for example, displays a range of sizes for the selected text. A single click on the B (bold) button adds the bold attribute to the highlighted characters.

- **The Format menu:** The controls on the Format menu generally mirror those on the Format bar. To change the alignment from the Format menu, click Format and hover the cursor over the Text menu item. To change text attributes, click Format and hover your cursor over the Font menu.

Using Notes in Your Project

As mentioned, you can type text notes in the Notes pane — I use them for displaying alternate topic points while presenting my slideshow. However, you can also print the notes for a project along with the slides; therefore, notes are great for including reminders and to-do points for your audience in handouts.

To type your notes, just click in the Notes pane; if the pane is hidden, choose View⇨Show Presenter Notes. When you've finished adding notes, click in the Slides list or the Layout pane to return to editing mode.

TIP

To display your notes while practicing, use Keynote's Rehearsal feature. Click Play and choose Rehearse Slideshow, and you can scroll through the notes while the slideshow runs. (More on slideshows in a second.)

Every Good Presentation Needs Media

Adding audio, photos, and movies to a slide is drag-and-drop easy in Keynote! Simply drag the image, audio, or movie file from a Finder window and place it at the spot you want within your document. (Naturally, audio and movies won't appear in a presentation distributed on paper or as an Adobe PDF electronic document. Go figure.)

You can also use the Media Browser — click the Media button on the toolbar and then click the Audio, Photos, or Movies button to select the desired type. Keynote displays the contents of your various media collections — such as your iPhoto and iTunes libraries. You can also navigate to the file's location on your hard drive or type a filename in the Search box at the bottom of the browser. When you've found the file you want to add, drag it to the spot where you want it in the document. Figure 20-4 illustrates the Media Browser in action.

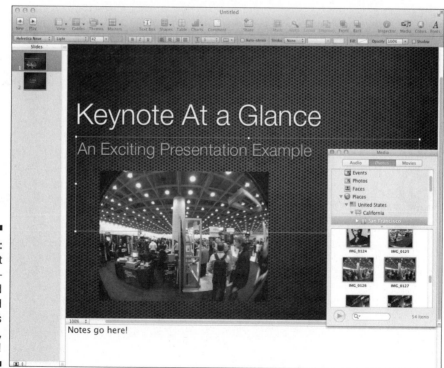

Figure 20-4:
It's not just photos — you can add audio and movie clips to a slide, too!

Adding a Background Shape

Text often stands out on a slide when it sits on top of a background shape. To add a shape (such as a rectangle or circle) as a background for your text, follow these steps:

1. **Click the insertion cursor in the location you want.**

2. **Click the Shapes button on the Keynote toolbar and then choose a shape.**

   The shape appears in your document. You can click in the Fill box on the Format bar to choose a different color and an opacity level.

3. **Click the center of the shape and drag it to a new spot.**

   Like image boxes, shapes can be resized or moved.

4. **When the shape is properly positioned and sized, select it and choose Arrange⇨Send to Back.**

Creating Your Keynote Slideshow

The heart of a Keynote presentation is the slideshow that you build from the slides you've created. A Keynote slideshow is typically presented as a full-screen presentation.

In its simplest form, you can always run a slideshow from a Keynote project by clicking the Play button on the toolbar or by choosing Play⇨Play Slideshow from the menu. You can advance to the next slide by tapping the trackpad or by pressing the right bracket key, which looks like this:].

If you'd prefer a presentation that runs automatically by itself (often called *kiosk mode*), click the Inspector icon on the toolbar and then click the Document button (which is the first button at the top of the Inspector). Now click the Presentation pop-up menu and choose Self-Playing. Click the Close button to close the Inspector window, and you're all set!

Of course, other controls are available besides just the ones that advance to the next slide! Table 20-1 illustrates the shortcuts you'll use most often during a slideshow.

Table 20-1	Keynote Slideshow Shortcut Keys
Key	*Action*
] (right bracket)	Next slide
P	Previous slide
Home	Jump to first slide
End	Jump to last slide
C	Show or hide the pointer
(number)	Jump to the corresponding slide in the Slides list
U	Scroll notes up
D	Scroll notes down
N	Show current slide number
H	Hide slideshow and display last application used (the presentation appears as a minimized icon in the Dock)
B	Pause slideshow and display a black screen (press any key to resume the slideshow)
Esc	Quit

Keynote offers a number of settings that you can tweak to fine-tune your slideshow. To display these settings, choose Keynote⇨Preferences and then click the Slideshow button in the Preferences window.

If you have an iPhone or iPod touch handy and you've installed the Apple Keynote Remote application on your device, display the Preferences window and click the Remote button to link your iPhone or iPod touch to your MacBook and Keynote. Now you can use your handheld device as a remote and use it during your slideshow!

Printing Your Slides and Notes

Okay, I'll be honest: I don't always print handouts for every presentation I give, just because some of the slideshows I run are short introductions to hands-on demonstrations. However, if you're presenting a lengthy slideshow with plenty of information that you'd like your audience to remember, nothing beats handouts that include scaled-down images of your slides (and, optionally, your presenter's notes).

You're not limited to just paper, though! You can also use Keynote to create an electronic PDF-format document instead of a printed handout, which your audience members can download from your website. Or, if you're an educator with access to an interactive whiteboard (such as the SMARTBoard), you can use this new technology with Keynote.

To print your slides and notes, follow these steps:

1. **In Keynote, choose File⇨Print.**

   Keynote displays the Print sheet you see in Figure 20-5. (Note that some printer-specific features may be different on your screen.)

2. **Click the desired format for printing your slides and notes.**

   - To print each slide on a separate page at full size, click Individual Slides.

   - To print each slide on a separate page with the presenter's notes for that slide, click Slides with Notes.

   - To print the contents of your Slides list in outline view, click Outline.

   - To print a handout with multiple slides per page (and, optionally, with presenter's notes), click Handout. Click the Slides per Page pop-up menu to specify the number of slides that Keynote should print on each page.

3. **Select the pages to print.**

   - To print the entire document, select All.

   - To print a range of selected slides, select the From radio button and enter the starting and ending pages.

4. **(Optional) Set specific options from the Options column.**

   You can include elements such as the date, borders around each slide, and the slide number as part of each page of the hard copy.

5. **Click the Print button to send the job to your printer.**

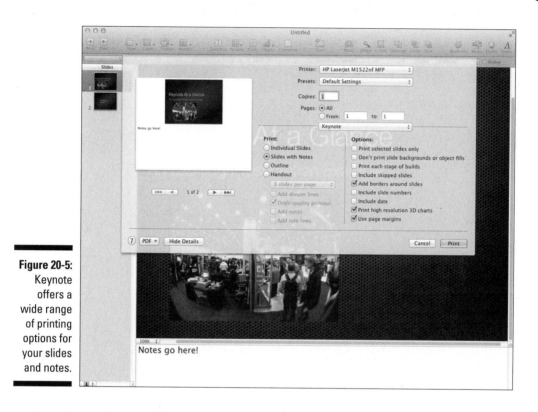

Figure 20-5:
Keynote
offers a
wide range
of printing
options for
your slides
and notes.

Part VI
Necessary Evils: Troubleshooting, Upgrading, Maintaining

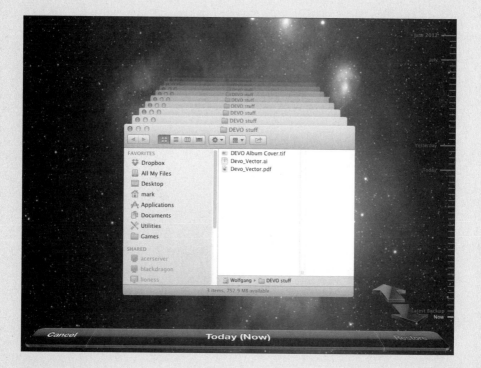

In this part . . .

No computer is *completely* trouble-free — and if your MacBook Pro, MacBook Air, or MacBook Pro Retina starts acting strangely, the troubleshooting tips you find in this part can help you get your favorite machine back to normal. I also provide you with all the guidance you need to maintain your MacBook properly as well as step-by-step instructions for upgrading your laptop with goodies such as additional RAM and external storage devices.

Chapter 21

When Good Mac Laptops Go Bad

1 wish you weren't reading this chapter.

Because you are, I can only surmise that you're having trouble with your MacBook, and that it needs fixing. (The other possibility — that you just like reading about solving computer problems — is more attractive but much more problematic.)

Consider this chapter a crash course in the logical puzzle that is computer *troubleshooting:* namely, the art of finding out What Needs Fixing. You also see what you can do when you just plain can't fix the problem by yourself.

Oh, and you're going to encounter a lot of Tips and Mark's Maxims in this chapter — all of them learned the hard way, so I recommend committing them to memory on the spot!

Repeat after Me: Yes, 1 Am a Tech!

Anyone can troubleshoot. Believe it, and put these common troubleshooting myths to rest:

> ✔ **It takes a college degree in computer science to troubleshoot.** Tell that to my troubleshooting kid. She'll think it's a hoot because she has an iMac in her room, as well as Apple computers in the classroom. You can follow all the steps in this chapter without any special training.

✔ **I'm to blame.** Ever heard of viruses? Failing hardware? Buggy software? Any of those things can be causing the problem. It's Mark's Maxim time:

Don't beat yourself up! Your laptop can be fixed.™

✔ **I need to buy expensive utility software.** Nope. You can certainly invest in a commercial testing and repair utility if you like. My favorite is TechTool Pro from Micromat (`www.micromat.com`), but a third-party utility isn't a requirement for troubleshooting. (I would, however, consider an antivirus application as a must-have, and you should have one already. Hint, hint.)

✔ **There's no hope if I can't fix it.** Sure, parts fail and computers crash, but your Apple Service Center can repair just about any problem. And (ahem) *if you backed up your laptop* (like I preach throughout this book), you'll keep that important data (even if a new hard drive is in your future).

✔ **It takes forever.** Wait until you read the number one rule in the next section; the first step takes but 10 seconds and often solves the problem. Naturally, not all problems can be fixed so quickly, but if you follow the procedures in this chapter, you should fix your laptop (or at least know that the problem requires outside help) in a single afternoon.

With those myths banished for good, you can get down to business and start feeling better soon.

Step-by-Step Laptop Troubleshooting

In the following sections, I walk you through my should-be-patented Troubleshooting Tree as well as the Mountain Lion built-in troubleshooting application, Disk Utility. I also introduce you to a number of keystrokes that can make your MacBook jump through hoops.

The number one rule: Reboot!

Yep, it sounds silly, but the fact is that rebooting your MacBook can often solve a number of problems. If you're encountering these types of strange behavior with your laptop, a reboot might be all you need to heal:

✔ Intermittent problems communicating over a network

✔ A garbled screen, strange colors, or screwed-up fonts

✔ The swirling Beach Ball of Doom that won't go away after several minutes

✔ An application that locks up

✔ An external device that seems to disappear or can't be opened

TECHNICAL STUFF

Why is rebooting so darned effective?

Rebooting fixes problems because it resets *everything.* Your network connection, for example, might be acting up or have timed out, and rebooting restores it. Rebooting also fixes problems due to brownouts or those notorious AC power flickerings that we all notice from time to time, which can even affect a laptop running on an AC adapter. Such interruptions in constant juice might not bother you or me (or your less-intelligent toaster), but they can play tricks on your laptop that rebooting can fix.

MARK'S MAXIM

To put it succinctly, here's a modest Mark's Maxim:

Always try a reboot before beginning to worry. *Always.*™

If you're in the middle of a program, try to save all your open documents before you reboot. That might not be possible, but try to save what you can.

As your first (and best) option for shutting down, click the Apple menu (🍎) and then choose Shut Down. If you need to force a *locked* application (one that's not responding) to quit so that you can reboot, follow these steps to squash that locked application:

1. **Click the Apple (🍎) menu and choose Force Quit.**

   The dialog shown in Figure 21-1 appears on your screen.

2. **Click the offending application, and then click the Force Quit button.**

When you get everything to quit, you should be able to click the Apple menu and choose Shut Down (not Restart) without a problem.

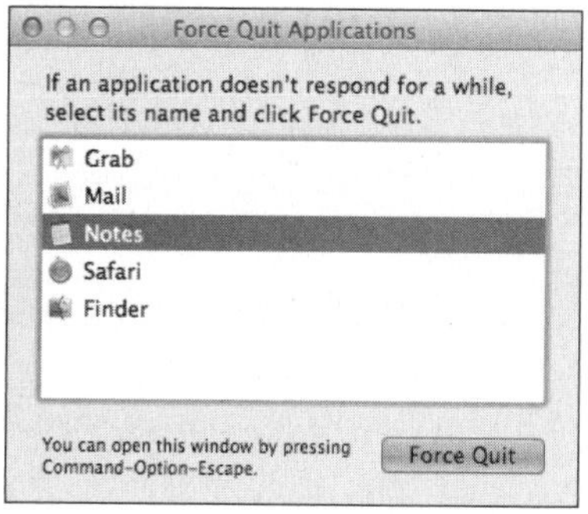

Figure 21-1:
Force a
recalcitrant
application
to take off.

	Force Quit Applications
If an application doesn't respond for a while, select its name and click Force Quit.	
Grab	
Mail	
Notes	
Safari	
Finder	
You can open this window by pressing Command-Option-Escape.	Force Quit

If your MacBook simply won't shut down (or you can't get the offending application to quit), do what must be done:

1. **Press and hold your laptop's Power button until it shuts itself off.**

   You have to wait about five seconds for your MacBook to turn itself off.

2. **Wait about ten seconds.**

3. **Press the Power button again to restart the computer.**

After everything is back up, check whether the problem is still apparent. If you use your laptop for an hour or two and the problem doesn't reoccur, you likely fixed it!

Special keys that can come in handy

A number of keys have special powers over your MacBook. No, I'm not kidding! These keys affect how your road warrior starts up, and they can really come in handy while troubleshooting.

Using Safe Boot mode

You can use Safe Boot mode to force Mountain Lion to run a directory check of your boot drive and disable any login items that might be interfering with Mountain Lion. Use the Shut Down menu item from the Apple () menu to completely turn off your laptop, press the Power button to restart the computer, and then press and hold down the Shift key immediately after you hear the start-up tone. After Mountain Lion completely boots, restart your MacBook again (this time without the Shift key) to return to normal operation.

Start-up keys

Table 21-1 provides the lowdown on start-up keys. Hold the indicated key down either *when you push your Power button* or *immediately after the screen blanks during a restart.* (As I just mentioned, the Shift key is the exception; it should be pressed and held down after you hear the start-up tone.)

Table 21-1	Start-up Keys and Their Tricks
Key	*Effect on Your MacBook*
C	Boots from the CD or DVD that's loaded in your optical drive (if you have one)
Media Eject	Ejects the CD or DVD in your optical drive (if you have one)
Option	Displays a system boot menu, allowing you to choose any bootable operating system on your laptop
Shift	Prevents your login items from running; runs a directory check

Key	Effect on Your MacBook
T	Starts your MacBook in FireWire Target Disk mode (except for the MacBook and MacBook Air, which have no FireWire port)
⌘+V	Shows OS X Console messages
⌘+R	Boots from Mountain Lion's Recovery HD volume
⌘+S	Starts your Mac in Single User mode
⌘+Option+P+R	Resets Parameter RAM (PRAM)

Some of the keys and combinations in Table 21-1 might never be necessary for your machine, but you might be instructed to use them by an Apple technician.

All hail Disk Utility, the troubleshooter's friend

Mountain Lion's *Disk Utility* is a handy tool for troubleshooting and repairing your MacBook's drive. You can find it in the Utilities folder in Launchpad.

Fire up Disk Utility and click the First Aid tab to open the rather powerful-looking window shown in Figure 21-2.

In the left column of the Disk Utility window, you can see

- ✔ The *physical* drives in your system (the actual hardware)
- ✔ The *volumes* (the data stored on the drives)

  You can always tell a volume because it's indented below the physical drive entry.

- ✔ Any CD or DVD loaded on your MacBook
- ✔ USB, Thunderbolt, or FireWire external drives

Danger, Will Robinson!

Many Disk Utility functions can actually *wipe your drives clean of data* instead of repairing them! These advanced functions aren't likely to help you with troubleshooting a problem with your existing volumes anyway.

Remember: Don't use the following Disk Utility functions unless an Apple technician *tells* you to use them:

- ✔ Partitioning and erasing drives
- ✔ Setting up RAID arrays
- ✔ Restoring files from disk images

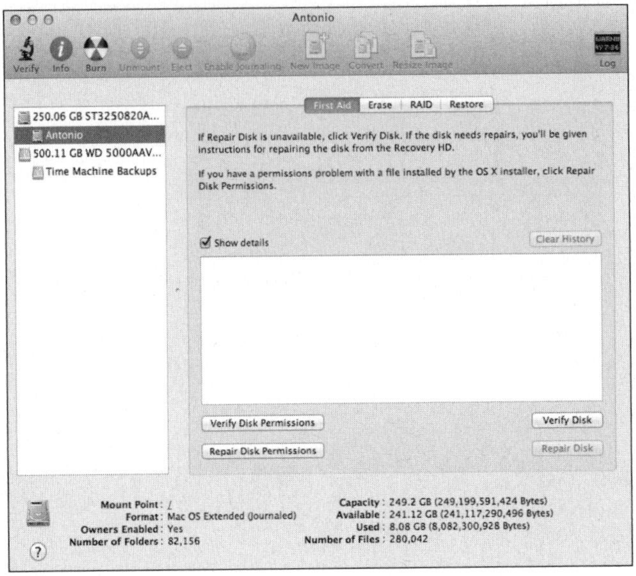

Figure 21-2:
The physician of drives — Mountain Lion's Disk Utility.

For example, referring to Figure 21-2, I have one internal drive (the 250.06GB entry) and one USB 3.0 external drive (the 500.11GB entry). The hard drive has one volume (Antonio), and the external drive has one volume (Time Machine Backups).

The information at the bottom of the Disk Utility window contains the specifications of the selected drive or volume — things such as capacity, free space, and the number of files and folders for a volume, or connection type and total capacity for a drive.

Repairing disk permissions

Because Mountain Lion is built on a UNIX base, lots of permissions can apply to the files on your drive — that is, who can open (or read or change) every application, folder, and document on your drive. Unfortunately, these permissions are often messed up by wayward applications or power glitches, or application installers that do a subpar job of cleaning up after themselves. And if the permissions on a file are changed, applications often lock up or refuse to run altogether.

I recommend repairing your disk permissions with Disk Utility once weekly. Figure 21-3 shows a permissions repair sweep on my internal hard drive's volume.

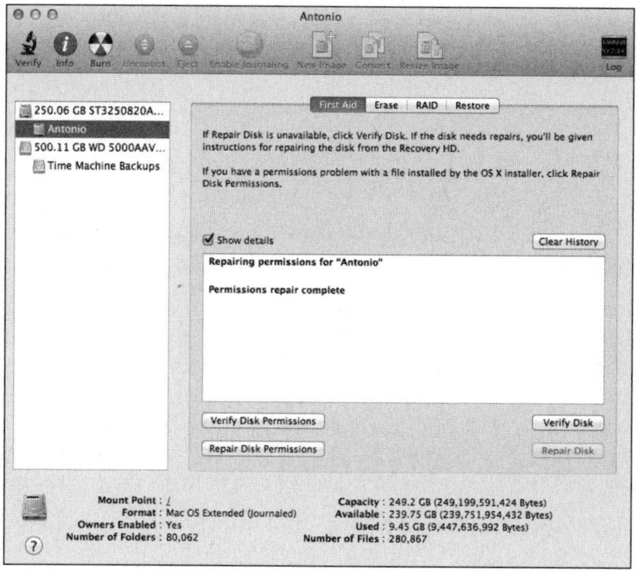

Figure 21-3:
A successful run, using Repair Disk Permissions.

Use these steps to repair permissions on your MacBook's hard drive:

1. **Make sure that you're logged in with an admin account.**

   Chapter 10 shows you how to log in as an admin user — most people who read this book use an admin account.

2. **Save and close any open documents.**

3. **Click the Launchpad icon in the Dock, click the Utilities folder, and then click the Disk Utility icon — from the keyboard, press ⌘+Shift+U.**

4. **Click the volume that you want to check.**

5. **Click the Repair Disk Permissions button.**

   I don't worry about verifying. If something's wrong, you end up clicking Repair Disk Permissions anyway. Just click Repair Disk Permissions; if nothing pops up, that's fine.

6. **To finish the process, always reboot after repairing permissions.**

   By rebooting, you see whether the problem has been corrected!

Repairing disks

Disk Utility can check the format and health of both drives and volumes with Verify Disk — and, if the problem can be corrected, fix any error by using Repair Disk.

Using Disk Utility to repair your hard drive carries a couple of caveats:

- ✔ **You can't repair the boot drive or the boot volume.** This limitation actually makes sense because you're using that drive and volume right now.

  To verify or repair your boot drive, boot your MacBook from the OS X Recovery HD volume. Reboot and hold down the ⌘+R keyboard shortcut immediately after you hear the start-up chord, and then run Disk Utility from the window that appears. Because you've booted your laptop from the Recovery HD volume, you can verify and repair problems with your start-up drive. (You should be able to select your boot hard drive or volume, and the Verify Disk and Repair Disk buttons should be enabled.)

- ✔ **You can't repair CDs and DVDs.** CDs and DVDs are read-only media and thus can't be repaired (at least by Disk Utility).

  If your MacBook is having trouble reading a CD or DVD, wipe the disc with a soft cloth to remove dust, oil, and fingerprints. Should that fail, invest in a disc-cleaning contrivance of some sort.

If you need to repair your boot drive and volume, save all your open documents and reboot from either an external drive or your OS X Recovery HD volume, as I describe earlier in this section. If you need to verify and repair a non-boot drive or volume, follow these steps:

Should I reinstall OS X?

The question of whether you should reinstall OS X seems to get a lot of attention on Mac-related Internet discussion boards and Usenet newsgroups — and the answer is a definitive *perhaps*. (I know. That's really helpful.)

Here's the explanation. You *shouldn't* lose a single byte of data by reinstalling OS X, so it's definitely okay to try it. However, reinstalling Mountain Lion isn't a universal balm that fixes all software errors because the problem that you're encountering might be due to a buggy application, a drive that's going critical, or a video card with faulty memory modules. If the trouble you're having is due to a corrupted OS X System folder, reinstalling Mountain Lion might or might not fix the problem.

Therefore, the debate rages on. I would certainly follow the MacBook Troubleshooting Tree all the way to the end and then, if necessary, contacti an Apple support technician via the Apple website before I would even consider reinstalling Mountain Lion.

1. **Click the Launchpad icon in the Dock, click the Utilities folder, and then click the Disk Utility icon (or press ⌘+Shift+U).**

2. **In the list at the left side of the Disk Utility window, click the drive or volume that you want to check.**

3. **Click the Repair Disk button.**

4. **If changes were made (or if you had to boot from the OS X Recovery HD volume), reboot after repairs have been made.**

Mark's MacBook Troubleshooting Tree

As the hip-hop artists say, "All right, kick it." And that's just what my MacBook Troubleshooting Tree is here for. If rebooting your laptop hasn't solved the problem, follow these steps in order (until either the solution is found or you run out of steps — more on that in the next section).

Step 1: Investigate recent changes

The first step is a simple one that many novice MacBook owners forget. Simply retrace your steps and consider what changes you made recently to your system. Here are the most common culprits:

✔ **Did you just finish installing a new application?** Try uninstalling it by removing the application directory and any support files that it might have added to your system. (And keep your applications current with the most recent patches and updates from the developer's website.)

From time to time, an application's *preference file* — which stores all the custom settings you make — can become corrupted. Although the application itself is okay, it might act strangely or refuse to launch. To check your preference files for signs of corruption, try scanning your applications with Preferential Treatment, a freeware AppleScript utility by Jonathan Nathan, available from his website at www.jonn8.com/html/pt.html. (Preferential Treatment can flag any dicey preference files, setting them up for a quick trip to the Trash.)

✔ **Did you just apply an update or a patch to an application?** Uninstall the application and reinstall it without applying the patch. If your MacBook suddenly works again, check the developer's website or contact the application's technical support department to report the problem.

✔ **Did you just update Mountain Lion by using Software Update?** Updating OS X can introduce problems in your applications that depend on specific routines and system files. Contact the developer of the application and look for updated patches that bring your software in line with the Mountain Lion updates.

✔ **Did you just make a change in System Preferences?** Return the options that you changed to their original settings; then consult Chapter 6 for information on what might have gone wrong. (If the setting in question isn't in Chapter 6, consider searching Mountain Lion's online Help or the Apple support website for more clues.)

✔ **Did you just connect (or reconnect) an external device?** Try unplugging the device and then rebooting to see whether the problem disappears. Remember that many peripherals need software drivers to run — and without those drivers installed, they don't work correctly. Check the device's manual or visit the company's website to search for software that you might need.

If you didn't make any significant changes to your system before you encountered the problem, proceed to the next step.

Step 2: Run Disk Utility

The next step is to run Disk Utility. The section "Repairing disk permissions," earlier in this chapter, shows how to complete this task on your Mountain Lion boot drive.

If you're experiencing hard drive problems, consider booting from your OS X Installation DVD to run a full-blown Repair Disk checkup on your boot volume.

Step 3: Check your cables

Cables work themselves loose, and they fail from time to time. Check all your cables to your external devices — make sure that they're snug — and verify that everything's plugged in and turned on. (Oh, and don't forget to check for crimps in your cables or even Fluffy's teeth marks.)

If a FireWire, Thunderbolt, or USB device acts up, swap cables around to find whether you have a bad one. A faulty cable can leave you pulling your hair out in no time.

Step 4: Check your Trash

Check the contents of your Trash to see whether you recently deleted files or folders by accident. Click the Trash icon in the Dock once to display the contents. If something's been deleted by mistake, drag it back to its original folder and try running the application again.

I know this one from personal experience. A slight miscalculation while selecting files to delete made an application freeze every time I launched it.

Step 5: Check your Internet and network connections

Now that always-on DSL and cable modem connections to the Internet are the norm, don't forget an obvious problem: Your laptop can't reach the Internet because your ISP is down, or your network is no longer working!

A quick visual check of your DSL or cable modem can usually indicate whether a connection problem exists between your modem and your ISP. For example, my modem has an informative activity light that I always glance at first. However, if your laptop is connected to the Internet through a larger home or office network and you can't check the modem visually, you can check your Internet connection by pinging www.apple.com:

1. **Run Launchpad and click the Utilities folder.**

2. **Click the Network Utility icon.**

3. **Click the Ping button.**

4. **Enter www.apple.com in the Address box.**

5. **Click Ping.**

    You should see successful ping messages. If you don't get a successful ping *and* you can still reach other computers on your network, your cable modem, DSL modem, or ISP is likely experiencing problems. If you can't reach your network at all, the problem lies in your network hardware or configuration.

Step 6: Think virus

If you made it to this point, it's time to run a full virus scan — and make sure that your antivirus application has the latest updated data files, too. My antivirus application of choice is Virus Barrier X6 from Intego (www.intego.com). If you don't want to invest in a commercial antivirus application, I can also recommend the excellent freeware ClamXav 2 (http://clamxav.com).

If a virus is detected and your antivirus application can't remove it, try *quarantining* it instead. This basically disables the virus-ridden application and prevents it from infecting other files.

Step 7: Disable your login items

OS X might encounter problems with applications that you've marked as login items in System Preferences. In this step, I show you how to identify login problems and how to fix 'em.

It's time to use another nifty start-up key (refer to Table 21-1). This time, hold down the Shift key after you hear the start-up tone.

This trick disables your account's login items, which are run automatically every time you log in to your MacBook. If one of these login items is to blame for your laptop's problems, your laptop will simply encounter trouble every time you log in.

If your laptop works fine with your login items disabled, follow this procedure for each item in the login items list:

1. **Open System Preferences, click Users & Groups, and then click the Login Items button.**

2. **Delete the item from the list.**

   You can delete the selected item by clicking the Delete button, which bears a minus sign.

3. **Reboot normally.**

4. **If your laptop is still misbehaving, repeat Steps 2 and 3 and disable a new login item.**

5. **When your MacBook starts up normally with login items enabled, you discovered the perpetrator. You'll likely need to delete that application and reinstall it. Don't forget to add each of the *working* login items back to the Login Items list!**

Step 8: Turn off your screen saver

The next step is to turn off your screen saver. This remedy is a long shot, but it isn't unheard of to discover that a faulty, bug-ridden screen saver has locked up your MacBook. (If you aren't running one of the Apple-supplied screen savers and your computer never wakes up from Sleep mode or hangs while displaying the screen saver, you found your prime suspect.)

Reboot your MacBook (if necessary), open System Preferences, click Desktop & Screen Saver, and then click the Screen Saver button. Then do one of the following:

 ✔ Switch to an Apple screen saver.

 ✔ Drag the Start Screen Saver slider to Never.

Step 9: Run System Information

Ouch. You reached Step 9, and you still haven't uncovered the culprit. At this point, you narrowed the possibilities to a serious problem, such as bad hardware or corrupted files in your OS X System folder. Fortunately, Mountain Lion provides the System Information utility, which displays real-time information on the hardware in your system. To start System Information, click the Launchpad icon in the Dock, click the Utilities folder icon, and then click the System Information icon. Alternatively, click the Apple menu and choose About This Mac, click More Info, and then click the System Report button. Click each one of the Hardware categories in turn, double-checking to make sure that everything looks okay.

You don't have to understand all the technical hieroglyphics. If a Hardware category doesn't return what you expect or displays an error message, though, that's suspicious. (If your MacBook doesn't have a specific type of hardware onboard — including an optical drive or Fibre Channel hardware — you won't get information from those categories.)

Diagnostics shows whether your MacBook passed the Power On self-test.

Okay, I Kicked It, and It Still Won't Work

Don't worry, friendly reader. Just because you've reached the end of my MacBook Troubleshooting Tree doesn't mean you're out of luck. In the following sections, I discuss the online help available in OS X and on the Apple website as well as local help in your own town.

Local service, at your service

In case you need to take in your MacBook for service, an Apple Store or Apple Authorized Service Provider is probably in your area. To find the closest service, launch Safari and visit www.apple.com/buy/locator/service, which is the Service Locator page on the Apple website. You can search by city and state or zip code. The results are complete with the provider's mailing address, website address, telephone number, and even a map of the location!

Always call your Apple service provider before you lug your (albeit lightweight) laptop all the way to the shop. Make sure that you know your MacBook's serial number (which you can display in System Information) and which version of OS X you're using.

The OS X Help Center

Although most OS X owners tend to blow off the Help Center when the troubleshooting gets tough, that's never the best course of action. Always take a few moments to search the contents of the Help Center — click Help on the Finder menu — to see whether any mention is made of the problem that you've encountered.

Apple Help Online

If you haven't visited the Apple MacBook Support site yet, run — don't walk — to www.apple.com/support/macbook, where you can find

- **The latest patches, updates, and how-to tutorials** for the MacBook line

- **MacBook and OS X discussion boards,** moderated by Apple

- **Tools** for ordering spare parts, checking on your remaining warranty coverage, and searching the Apple knowledge base

- **Do-it-yourself instructions** (PDF files) that you can follow to repair or upgrade your MacBook

Chapter 22

Adding New Stuff to Your Laptop

*"N*o laptop is an island." Somebody famous wrote that, I'm sure.

Without getting too philosophical — or invoking the all-powerful Internet yet again — the old saying really does make sense. All computer owners usually add at least one *peripheral* (external device), such as a printer, a joystick, an iPod, a backup drive, or a scanner. I talk about the ports on your MacBook in Chapter 1. Those holes aren't there to just add visual interest to the sides of your treasured laptop. Therefore, I cover your ports (and what you can plug into them) in detail in this chapter.

Ah, but what about the stuff *inside* your road warrior? That's where things get both interesting and scary at the same time. In this chapter, I describe what you can add to the innards of your computer as well as how to get inside there if you work up the courage to go exploring.

More Memory Will Help

Every computer will benefit from more memory — and no, there's no *however* stuck on the end! For once, I'm happy to report, there's no exception, no matter what type of computer you own. Hard as it is to believe, just keep in mind this Mark's Maxim:

More memory helps.™

Period. End of statement. No matter what type of computer you own, how old it is, or what operating system you use, adding more memory to your system (to the maximum it supports) significantly improves the performance of your operating system (and practically every application that you run).

Memory maximizes the power of your computer. The more memory you have, the less data your laptop has to temporarily store on its drive. Without getting into virtual memory and other techno-gunk, just consider that extra memory as extra elbowroom for your applications and your documents. Believe me, both OS X and Windows 7 and 8 efficiently make use of every kilobyte of memory that you can provide.

If your MacBook is already stuffed full with the maximum amount of memory it can hold, you can skip this section.

Owners of the MacBook Air and MacBook Pro Retina can skip this section as well, because these models can't be upgraded. (These laptops are sealed units — literally — and you must visit your local Apple hardware technician if your laptop's memory malfunctions and needs replacing. The same is true for both the Air's and the Retina's battery.)

If you have a MacBook Pro (or if you're using an older MacBook with upgradeable memory), read on!

Figuring out how much memory you have

To see how much memory you have in your computer, click the Apple menu (⌘) and choose About This Mac. In the dialog that appears, click the More Info button, and then click the Memory toolbar button.

Click the Memory Upgrade Instructions link at the bottom of the dialog, and OS X Mountain Lion automatically opens a Safari browser window with online instructions on how to upgrade the RAM in your specific MacBook model. If you're confident about your technical skills, you can use this documentation as a guide to removing and installing memory modules, along with the step-by-step procedure I cover later in the chapter.

While you're within the confines of the About This Mac dialog, click the Overview toolbar button to display both the machine speed (processor speed) and the common identifier that Apple uses to refer to your specific model. For example, my MacBook Air has a 1.8 GHz Intel Core i5 processor, and it's identified as a mid-2012 model. Write these two figures down — we're starting a handy-dandy list to help you while ordering your memory!

At the time of this writing, a mid-2012 MacBook Pro has sockets for two DDR3 SDRAM memory modules. (Don't fret over what all the abbreviations mean. Rest assured that this memory type is fast.) These modules are available with up to 4GB of memory, so you can install as much as 8GB of total memory in your MacBook Pro.

How you plan memory upgrades depends on how much memory you want. Most MacBook Pro owners simply opt to install the maximum amount of memory possible, so if your 4GB MacBook Pro uses the two default 2GB modules supplied by Apple, you can add 4GB of additional RAM by replacing the existing memory modules with two 4GB memory modules. At the time of this writing, a 4GB memory module should set you back less than $40.

I should note that the default 4GB of memory is certainly acceptable for running applications from the iLife and iWork suites as well as any of the applications bundled with Mountain Lion. With that said, these applications will run significantly faster with 8GB instead!

If your primary applications include video editing, game playing, or image editing, you can use all the memory your laptop can hold.

Unfortunately, Apple's prices for upgrade RAM are, well, *outrageous* (as in, "Boy, Howdy, I can't afford that!") Therefore, I can heartily recommend any one of these online sources that cater to Mac owners:

- ✔ **MacMall:** www.macmall.com
- ✔ **CDW:** www.cdw.com/content/brands/apple/default.aspx
- ✔ **Newegg:** www.newegg.com

Installing memory modules

I'm happy to report that adding extra memory to your system is one of the easiest internal upgrades that you can perform. Therefore, I recommend that you add memory yourself unless you simply don't want to mess with your laptop's internal organs. Your local Apple service specialist will be happy to install new RAM modules for you (for a price).

If you have a knowledgeable friend or family member who can help you install your hardware, buy that individual the proverbial NSD (short for *Nice Steak Dinner*) and enlist him or her in your cause. Even if you still do the work yourself, it's always better to have a second pair of experienced eyes watching, especially if you're a little nervous.

Climbing inside your Mac laptop

This section on laptop upgrades is short for a reason: Laptops simply aren't *meant* to be disassembled. As I mention several times in this book, internal expansion in your MacBook Pro is severely limited. Basically, you can add extra memory and swap out your drive. Adding memory is easy, but swapping out your hard drive requires more work and considerable preparation. And you can't make *any* internal modifications to the MacBook Air or the MacBook Pro Retina, which are sealed units. (Breaking in will likely void your warranty.)

Therefore, I always recommend that you seek professional servicing when you need to repair your laptop. For example, if your laptop's LED screen is cracked or broken, do *not* try to fix it yourself! Sure, you might see a number of used LED panels on eBay, but these parts aren't designed to be easily swapped out, like a desktop computer's video card. Besides, if you make a mistake when trying to fix something deep in the bowels of your laptop, you might end up causing more damage than you repair.

The moral of the story? Let your local Apple dealer's service technicians perform major surgery on your laptop, and buy an AppleCare Protection Plan that can cover your laptop like a blanket for up to three years!

Read more about swapping out drives in the upcoming section, "Gotta have internal."

To add memory modules to a MacBook Pro, follow these steps:

1. **Get ready to operate.**

    a. *Spread a clean towel on a stable work surface, such as your kitchen table.*

    The towel helps protect your screen from scratches.

    b. *Find a Phillips screwdriver.*

    c. *Shut down your laptop and wait at least ten minutes for it to cool down.*

    d. *Unplug all cables from the computer.*

2. **Close the computer and flip it over on top of the towel.**

3. **Ground thyself!**

    Check out the nearby "Let's get grounded!" sidebar.

4. **Remove the screws and bottom cover.**

    Depending on the model, you may have up to 10 screws to remove before the cover can be put aside. Note that some screws may be longer than others — if so, they must be replaced in the same locations. Place the screws in a handy plastic bowl for safekeeping. Tah-dah! That wasn't much of a challenge, was it? Here's your chance to gaze with rapt fascination at a portion of the bare innards of your favorite computer.

5. **Locate the memory modules in your Mac's svelte chassis.**

6. **If you're replacing an existing memory module, remove it.**

   To remove a memory module, gently spread the two tabs at the ends of the socket apart (as shown in Figure 22-1) and then lift and slide the module away from the socket.

   Save the old module in the static-free packaging that held the new module. Your old RAM (which you can now sell on eBay) will be protected from static electricity.

7. **Position the new module in the socket.**

   a. *Line up the module's gold connectors toward the socket, at a 25-degree angle.*

   b. *Line up the notch in the module with the matching spacer in the socket.*

   See what I mean in Figure 22-2.

8. **Press gently (but firmly) on both ends of the module until the module's tabs click into place on both ends of the socket.**

   Figure 22-3 shows the direction you should press on the module.

9. **Replace the bottom covers and screws.**

   To replace the bottom cover, just reverse the steps at the beginning of this list. (Rather like changing the oil in my Dad's 1970 Ford pickup truck.)

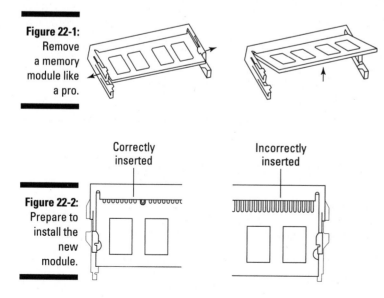

Figure 22-1: Remove a memory module like a pro.

Correctly inserted   Incorrectly inserted

Figure 22-2: Prepare to install the new module.

Figure 22-3:
Press the
new RAM
module into
place until it
locks.

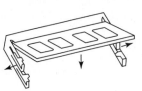

Congratulations! You've done it — you're now a MacBook Pro memory guru! To verify that all is well with your road warrior, boot the computer, click the Apple menu, and choose About This Mac. Your laptop should report the additional memory.

Let's get grounded!

Follow one cardinal rule when the unguarded insides of any computer are in easy reach: *Always ground yourself before you touch anything!* Your body can carry enough static electricity to damage the circuitry and chips that make up the brains of your MacBook Pro, and touching those parts without grounding yourself is an invitation for disaster.

Grounding yourself is easy to do: Just touch a conductive metal surface (preferably steel) around your workplace for a few seconds before you dig in. (Don't use something inside your laptop; use a metal surface outside your

MacBook Pro's case.) After you ground yourself, you can then safely handle both the internal components of your laptop and any new hardware components that you might be installing (such as memory modules or a hard drive).

If you walk anywhere in the room — hunting for a screwdriver, perhaps, or taking a sip of liquid reinforcement that you've stashed a comfortable distance away — you *must* ground yourself again before you get back to work. *Remember:* You can pick up a static charge by simply walking. Go figure.

Considering a Hard Drive Upgrade?

Asking whether you can upgrade your hard drive is a trick question. Yes, you certainly can upgrade your hard drive. But before you start cruisin' the Internet for a 1TB monster, though, I have two suggestions:

✔ Don't upgrade your internal hard drive yourself.

✔ Be sure you *really need* a hard drive upgrade.

And, all in all, Apple's pretty generous when configuring drive storage for its base systems — current models run with anywhere from a 64GB solid-state drive to a 1TB magnetic hard drive.

Most folks simply don't need more than 128GB or 500GB of drive space (even with Windows loaded in a separate partition for use with Boot Camp, which I discuss in Chapter 2). You're likely to find that you still have plenty of elbow-room on your drive for a typical family's needs unless you're heavily into

- ✔ Digital video (DV)
- ✔ Cutting-edge video games
- ✔ Tons of digital audio or digital photos

If you're short on drive space, clean up your existing drive by deleting all the crud you don't need, such as game and application demos, duplicate or work copies of images and documents, archived files you downloaded from the Internet, and the contents of your Trash. You can read how in Chapter 23.

If you decide that you *do* need to upgrade your MacBook's internal drive, I strongly recommend that you don't install your new hard drive yourself. Call on the services of an Apple technician to upgrade your drive!

Consider your external options

If you *do* need additional hard drive space, I recommend using an external drive! Use a high-speed Thunderbolt, FireWire, or USB port to connect a second hard drive the quick and easy way. (If your MacBook model isn't equipped with a FireWire port, you can concentrate on USB or Thunderbolt.)

Most of today's external peripherals don't even require the driver software that Mac old-timers remember with such hatred. You simply plug in a FireWire, Thunderbolt, or USB device, and it works. You can move your external drive between different Macs with a minimum of fuss and bother. A typical external USB 3.0 hard drive that holds 1TB will cost less than $100.

An external hard drive can do anything that your internal hard drive can do. You can boot from it, for example, or install a different version of OS X (great for beta testers like me). External optical drives work just the same as internal models; Apple sells an external USB SuperDrive optical drive for the MacBook Air and MacBook Pro Retina for about $80.

Apple's Time Capsule unit is an external hard drive with a difference: It stores the huge Time Machine backup files created by the Macs running Mountain Lion on your network, and it uses a wireless connection to transfer data! (In fact, if you're thinking of adding a wireless base station to your wired network, your Time Capsule actually acts as a full AirPort Extreme Base Station, complete with USB port for connecting a USB printer.) At the time of this writing, Time Capsule is available with either a 2TB ($299) or 3TB ($499) drive.

Here's one problem with external drives: Data typically transfers more slowly over a USB or FireWire connection than via an internal drive. (A Thunderbolt external drive can actually deliver transfer speeds comparable to your internal drive, but at the time of this writing they're far more expensive than USB or FireWire hardware.) That's why most Mac owners use their external drives for storing lesser-used documents and applications or for Time Machine backups. Their favorite applications and often-used documents are housed on the faster internal drive.

Putting a port to work

A MacBook can carry up to three kinds of high-speed ports, any of which is a good match for connecting any external device.

USB 2.0/3.0

The USB standard is popular because it's just as common in the PC world as in the Mac world. (Most PCs don't have a FireWire port.) Your laptop carries at least two USB 3.0 ports on the sides of the case, and older MacBook models that can run Mountain Lion will have at least one USB 2.0 port. Hardware manufacturers can make one USB device that works on both types of computers.

Naturally, USB 3.0 offers faster data transfer speeds than the older USB 2.0 standard, so if your MacBook model sports USB 3.0 ports, you should buy only USB 3.0 external hard drives, CD/DVD recorders, or flash drives. 'Nuff said.

FireWire 800

The faster FireWire 800 port has now replaced the older FireWire 400 port (also called *IEEE 1394*) on today's MacBook Pro models. However, with an adapter, you can use your FireWire 800 port for connecting older FireWire 400 external devices to your MacBook.

The physical FireWire 800 connector is shaped differently than the FireWire 400 port, so don't try to force the wrong connector into the wrong port!

Thunderbolt

A Thunderbolt external drive offers much better performance than either a FireWire 800 or a USB 3.0 drive, and today's shiny Thunderbolt drives are getting cheaper every day. All current MacBook models proudly sport a Thunderbolt port on the side.

The MacBook's mystery slot

If you're wondering what that inch-long slot is for on the side of your MacBook, you'll be pleased to hear that it's called an SD (or, on the MacBook Pro, SDXC) card slot. Why the glee? Well, this slot allows your MacBook to directly accept the storage cards used by many of today's digital cameras and mass-storage video camcorders, without requiring an external device or a cable connection to your camera!

Some MacBook owners also use SDC/SDXC cards for storage, much like a USB flash drive. I find that a USB flash drive offers far more storage for less cost (as well as being compatible with other Macs and PCs), but if you have a large number of SDC/SDXC cards collecting dust in your drawer, why not use them?

Connecting an external drive

With FireWire, Thunderbolt, or USB, you can install an external hard drive without opening your laptop's case. With your MacBook turned on, follow these steps:

1. **Connect the FireWire, Thunderbolt, or USB cable betwixt the drive and your computer.**

2. **Plug the external drive into a convenient surge protector or uninterruptible power supply (if necessary).**

   Note that some external devices are *bus-powered,* meaning that they don't need a separate power supply. These devices draw their power directly from the port.

3. **Switch on the external drive.**

4. **If the drive is unformatted (or formatted for use in Windows), partition and format the external drive.**

   The drive comes with instructions or software for you to do this. (Don't worry; your external drive comes from the factory completely empty, and you won't damage anything by formatting it.) Partitioning divides the new drive into one (or more) volumes, each of which is displayed as a separate hard drive in Mountain Lion.

   If the drive comes preformatted for use with a Windows PC, I strongly suggest reformatting it for use with OS X — doing so will result in faster performance and more efficient use of space.

After the drive is formatted and partitioned, it immediately appears on the desktop. Shazam!

Gotta have internal

If you decide that you must upgrade your existing internal drive — or if your internal drive fails and needs to be replaced — you should always take your MacBook to an authorized Apple service center and allow the techs there to sell you a drive and make the swap. Here are four darned good reasons why:

- ✔ **Warranty:** You're very likely to void your laptop's warranty by attempting a drive upgrade yourself.

- ✔ **Selection:** If you're worried about choosing the proper drive, your friendly neighborhood Apple technician can order the correct type and size of drive for you.

- ✔ **Difficulty:** Swapping a drive in your Mac laptop isn't anywhere near as easy as adding RAM modules in the MacBook Pro.

- ✔ **Backup:** That very same Apple service technician can back up all the data on your existing drive, format the new drive, and move all your data to its new mansion, so you won't lose a single document. That will save you time and possible angst.

To those who *truly* won't be satisfied with their lives until they upgrade an internal drive in a MacBook: Yes, I'm sure you can find a magazine article that purports to show you how. Even better, I've seen many how-to articles on the web that can lead you down a rosy path to a hard drive upgrade. Here's my take on those savvy instructions: You're walking into a field of land mines with someone else's map, so you had better have *complete* faith in your tech skills. (And a darn good backup.)

A List of Dreamy Laptop Add-Ons

The USB and FireWire toys I cover in the following sections might add a cable or two to your collection at the side of your road warrior, but they're well worth the investment. And they can really revolutionize how you look at technologies, such as television, digital audio, and computer gaming.

Game controllers

If you're ready to take a shot at the enemies — whether they be Nazi soldiers, chittering aliens, or the latest jet fighters — you'll likely find your keyboard and mouse somewhat lacking. (And if that enemy happens to be a friend of yours playing across the Internet, you'll be ruthlessly mocked while you're fumbling for the right key combination.) Instead, either pick up a USB joystick (for flying games) or a gamepad (for arcade and first-person shooting games)!

Video controllers

For armchair directors, specialized USB digital video controllers make editing easier. The ShuttleXpress from Contour Design (http://www.contourde sign.com) provides a five-button jog control that can be configured to match any DV editor. For $60, you get the same type of editing controller as dedicated video-editing stations costing several thousand dollars.

Audio hardware

Ready to put GarageBand to the test with your favorite version of *Chopsticks?* You'll need a USB piano keyboard, and I recommend the KeyRig 49 from M-Audio (www.m-audio.com), which retails for a mere $130. It provides 49 keys and uses a USB connection.

Chapter 23

Tackling the Housekeeping

In This Chapter

▶ Cleaning unnecessary stuff off your drive

▶ Backing up your data with Time Machine

▶ Fixing permission errors

▶ Automating tasks in Mountain Lion

▶ Updating OS X automatically

*N*othing runs better than a well-oiled machine, and your laptop is no exception. (Well, you don't have to oil it, but you know what I mean.) With a little Mountain Lion maintenance, you can ensure that your MacBook is performing as efficiently as possible (which translates into longer battery life).

In this chapter, I demonstrate how you can make good use of every byte of storage space provided by your drive, as well as how to back up and restore that hard drive to an external drive, using Time Machine. Your MacBook's drive also benefits from a periodic scan for permission errors.

Mountain Lion's Automator application is a great housekeeping tool. It allows your laptop to perform tasks automatically that used to require your attention. I show you how you can create Automator applications and set them up to run by themselves. (It sounds a little spooky, but you'll have a ball!)

And it's important to never forget about updating OS X itself. But then again, with Software Update configured correctly, you can live life free and easy, surfing the web and eating ice cream (or yogurt — your pick).

Cleaning Unseemly Data Deposits

Criminy! Where does all this stuff *come* from? Suddenly that spacious 512GB solid-state drive has 19GB left, and you start feeling pinched.

Before you consider buying a new internal or external drive (which you can read about in Chapter 22), take the smart step: Sweep your laptop's drive clean of unnecessary and space-hogging software and temporary files.

Getting dirty (Or, cleaning things the manual way)

If you're willing to dig into your data a little, you have no reason to buy additional software to help you clean up your hard drive. All you really need is the willpower to announce, "I simply don't need this application any longer." (And, sometimes, that's tougher than it might seem.)

Unnecessary files and unneeded folders

Consider all the stuff that you probably don't really need:

- ✔ Game demos and shareware that you no longer play (or even remember)
- ✔ Movie trailers and other QuickTime video files that have long since passed into obscurity
- ✔ Temporary files that you created and promptly forgot
- ✔ Log files that chronicle application installations and errors
- ✔ ZIP and StuffIt archives that you downloaded and no longer covet
- ✔ iTunes music and videos that no longer appeal to your eye and ear

How hard is it to clean this stuff off your drive? Easier than you might think!

- ✔ You can easily delete files.
- ✔ You can move seldom used files and folders to external storage (such as a USB flash drive, an external hard drive, or a DVD) to free up space on your laptop's internal drive.
- ✔ You can uninstall applications purchased from the App Store using Launchpad — from the Launchpad display, click and hold down the icon until it wiggles. If an X button appears on the icon, you can click the X to remove the application from your MacBook.
- ✔ You can get rid of an unnecessary application by deleting its application folder that was created during the installation process.

Always check the application's README file and documentation for any special instructions before you manually delete any application's folder! If you created any documents in that folder that you want to keep, don't forget to move them before you trash the folder and its contents. In fact, some applications may come complete with their own uninstall utility, so checking the README file and documentation may save you unnecessary steps.

Removing an application or a file from your drive is usually two simple steps:

1. **Display the file or application folder in a Finder window.**

2. **Delete the file or folder with one of these steps:**

   • Drag the icon to the Trash.

   • Press ⌘+Delete.

   • Right-click the icon and choose Move to Trash.

   • Select the icon and click the Delete button on the Finder toolbar (if you added one).

Truly, no big whoop.

Don't forget to actually *empty* the Trash, or you'll wonder why you aren't regaining any drive space. (Mountain Lion works hard to store the contents of the Trash until you manually delete it, just in case you want to undelete something.) To get rid of that stuff permanently and reclaim the space, follow these steps:

1. **Right-click the Trash icon in the Dock.**

2. **Choose Empty Trash from the pop-up menu that appears.**

Associated files in other folders

Some applications install files in different locations across your drive. (Applications in this category include Microsoft Office and Photoshop.) How can you clear out these orphan files after you delete the application folder?

The process is a little more involved than deleting a single folder, but it's still no big whoop. Here's the procedure:

1. **Click the Search text box in a Finder window.**

   You can read more about Search and Finder windows in Chapter 7.

2. **Type the name of the application in the Search text box.**

   Figure 23-1 shows a typical search. I want to remove orphan files associated with Adobe Illustrator — by searching for the words *Adobe Illustrator*, I found a number of files created in other folders, such as project files, PDF files, and the font files that appear in the system Fonts folder.

3. **Decide which of these files belong to the to-be-deleted application.**

   Be sure that the files you choose to delete are part of the deleted application. For example, a Keynote presentation with the name *Instructions on Building with Adobe* might not be part of Adobe Illustrator.

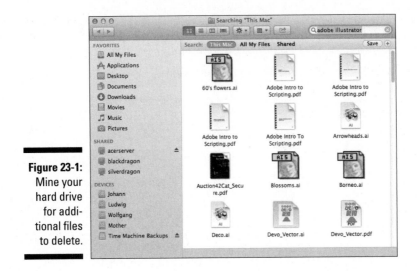

Figure 23-1:
Mine your hard drive for additional files to delete.

Many associated files either

- Have the same icon as the parent application
- Are in the Preferences, Caches, or Application Support folders

4. In the Search Results window, click the associated file(s) that you want to delete and just drag them to the Trash.

Don't empty the Trash immediately after you delete these files. Wait a few hours or a day. That way, if you realize that you deleted a file that you truly need, you can easily restore it from the Trash.

Using a commercial cleanup tool

If you'd rather use a commercial application to help you clean up your drive, a number of them are available but most are shareware and perform only one task. For example, Tidy Up! 3 from Hyperbolic Software (`www.hyperbolic software.com`) finds only duplicate files on your drive, matching by criteria such as filename, size, content, and extension. It's a good tool at $30.

For keeping your MacBook's drive slim and trim, I recommend CCleaner for Mac, from Piriform (`www.piriform.com/mac/ccleaner`). This great utility (shown in Figure 23-2) can clean everything from Internet crud (browser cookies and your surfing history) to the OS X system caches that can grow so doggone huge, and you can easily fine-tune what CCleaner for Mac will remove. The utility can also uninstall many applications for you with a single click. Oh, and did I mention that it's free? I *really* like free!

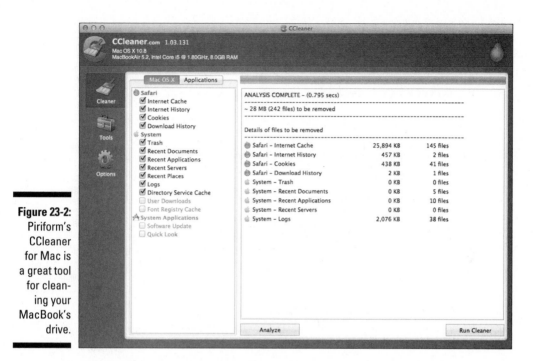

Backing Up Your Treasure

Do it. I'm not going to lecture you about backing up your drive . . . well, perhaps just for a moment. Imagine what it feels like to lose *everything* — names,
numbers, letters, reports, presentations, saved games, photographs, and
music. Then ask yourself, "Self, isn't all that irreplaceable stuff worth just a
couple of hours every month?" Time for a Mark's Maxim:

Back up your hard drive. On a regular basis.™

You can back up your files either by saving them to external media or by
using Mountain Lion's awesome Time Machine feature.

Saving files

The simplest method of backing up files is simply to copy the files and folders to an external hard drive, a USB flash drive, a CD, or a DVD. Nothing
fancy, but it works.

Backing up to an external hard drive or USB flash drive

If you use an external hard drive with your MacBook, you can easily drag backup files to it from your internal hard drive. Follow these steps:

1. **Open separate Finder windows for**

   - The external drive

   - The internal drive

2. **Select the desired files and folders that you want to back up from your internal drive.**

3. **Drag the selected files to the external drive window.**

Backing up to CD and DVD

You can burn backup files to a recordable CD or DVD. Owners of the MacBook Air and MacBook Pro Retina will need to use an external SuperDrive or third-party recorder, however.

Burning backups from the Finder

To use the Finder's Burn feature with a CD or DVD, follow these steps:

1. **Load a blank disc into your MacBook's optical drive.**

   If you're using the default settings in the CDs & DVDs pane in System Preferences, a dialog asks you for a disc name.

2. **Drag the files and folders that you want to back up into the disc's Finder window.**

   They can be organized any way you like. Don't forget that the total amount of data shouldn't exceed 700MB on a CD. You should also stick within 4GB or so (on a standard recordable DVD) or 8GB (on a dual-layer recordable DVD). You can see how much free space remains on the disc at the bottom of the disc's Finder window.

3. **Click File, and then choose Burn Disc from the menu.**

   You can also click the Burn button on the Recordable DVD bar — it appears at the top of the disc's Finder window.

4. **Choose the fastest recording speed possible.**

5. **Click Burn.**

Burning backups from other recording applications

If you've invested in Toast Titanium from Roxio (http://www.roxio.com) or another CD/DVD recording application, you can create a new disc layout to burn the same files to your backup disc in the future. (Think of a layout as a "road map" that indicates which files and folders Toast should store on the backup.)

Putting things right with Time Machine

If you enable backups via Mountain Lion's Time Machine feature, you can literally move backward through the contents of your MacBook's hard drive, selecting and restoring all sorts of data. Files and folders are ridiculously easy to restore — and I mean easier than *any* restore you've ever performed, no matter what the operating system or backup program. Time Machine can even handle such deleted items as Contacts cards or photos you sent to the Trash from iPhoto!

Because Time Machine should be an important and integral part of every Mac owner's existence, the Time Machine icon is included in the Dock. (Apple is not messing around!)

Apple's Time Capsule device is designed as a wireless storage drive for your Time Machine backup files. If you're interested in a single Time Machine backup location for multiple Macs across your wireless network, Time Capsule is a great addition to your home or office. Note, however, that the Time Capsule drive isn't meant to be mobile, so while you're on the road, you still need an external USB, Thunderbolt, or FireWire drive to safeguard your data.

Before you can use Time Machine, it must be enabled in the Time Machine pane in System Preferences. I cover the Time Machine configuration settings (and how to turn the feature on) in more detail in Chapter 6.

Here's how you can turn back time, step by step, to restore a file that you deleted or replaced in a folder:

1. **From a Finder window, open the folder that contained the file you want to restore.**

2. **Click the Time Machine icon in the Dock (which bears a rather funky clock with a counterclockwise arrow).**

   The oh-so-ultra-cool Time Machine background appears behind your folder, complete with its own set of buttons at the bottom of the screen (as shown in Figure 23-3). On the right, you see a timeline that corresponds to the different days and months included in the backups that Mountain Lion has made.

3. **Click within the timeline to jump directly to a date (displaying the folder's contents on that date).**

   Alternatively, use the Forward and Back arrows at the right to move through the folder's contents through time. (You should see the faces of Windows users when you riffle through your folders to locate something you deleted several weeks ago!)

   The backup date of the items you're viewing appears in the button bar at the bottom of the screen.

Timeline

Figure 23-3:
Yes, Time
Machine
really *does*
look like
this!

4. **After you locate the file you want to restore, click it to select it.**

5. **Click the Restore button at the right side of the Time Machine button bar.**

   If you want to restore all the contents of the folder, click the Restore All button instead.

Time Machine returns you to the Finder, with the newly restored file now appearing in the folder. Out-*standing!*

To restore specific data from your contacts or images from iPhoto, launch the desired application first and then launch Time Machine. Instead of riffling through a Finder window, you can move through time in the application window.

For robust backup and restore protection, Time Machine has everything that a typical Mac owner at home is likely to ever need. Therefore, an easy Mark's Maxim to predict:

Connect an external hard drive and turn on Time Machine. *Do it now*. Don't make a humongous mistake.™

Maintaining Hard Drive Health

Shifty-eyed, sneaky, irritating little problems can bother your hard drive: *permissions errors*. Incorrect disk and file permissions can

- ✔ Make your MacBook lock up
- ✔ Make applications act screwy (or refuse to run at all)
- ✔ Cause weird behavior in a Finder window or System Preferences

To keep Mountain Lion running at its best, I recommend that you fix permissions errors at least once per week.

To fix any permissions errors on your system, follow these steps:

1. **Click the Launchpad icon in the Dock, and then click the Utilities folder.**
2. **Click the Disk Utility icon.**
3. **Click the volume at the left (which in this case is a named partition, such as Macintosh HD, which appears under your physical hard drive) that you want to check.**
4. **Click the Repair Disk Permissions button.**

   Disk Utility does the rest and then displays a message about whatever it has to fix. (When will someone invent a *car* with a Repair Me button?)

Automating Those Mundane Chores

One popular feature in Mountain Lion — Automator — can save you a tremendous amount of time behind the keyboard. You use Automator (as shown in Figure 23-4) to create applications with a relative of AppleScript called *AppleEvents*. (In case you're not familiar with *AppleScript,* it's the simple programming language that you can use to automate tasks and applications within Mountain Lion.)

Of course, writing an application might sound daunting — akin to single-handedly building your own nuclear submarine over a long weekend — but Automator is actually easy to use. Heck, you might find it downright *fun!*

You can also create *workflows,* which are sequential (and repeatable) operations that are performed on the same files or data, and then your Automator application can automatically launch whatever applications are necessary to get the job done.

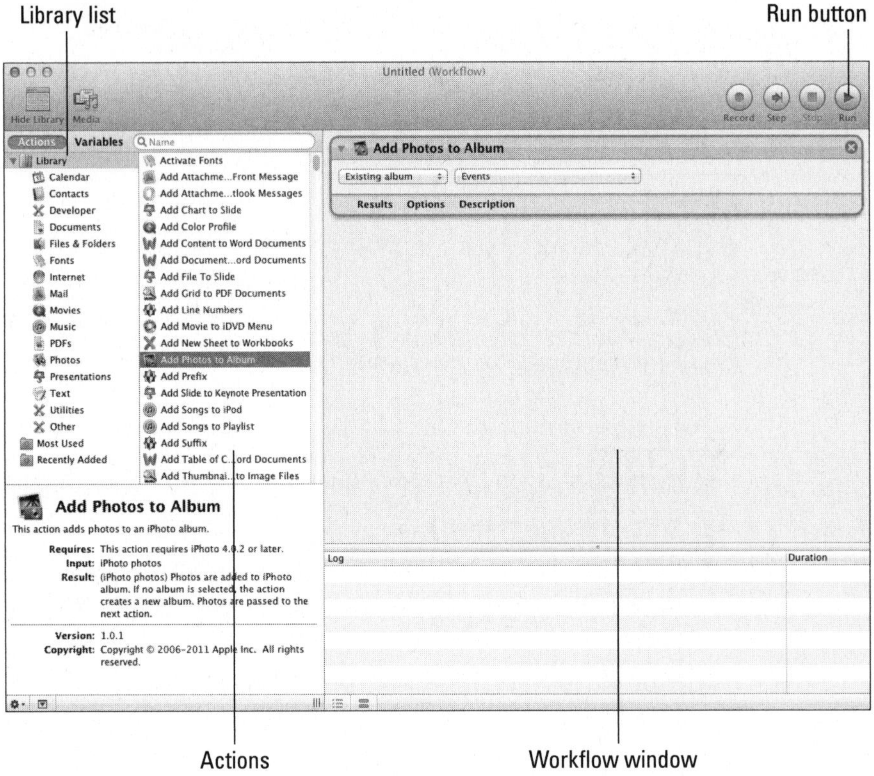

Library list

Run button

Figure 23-4:
Automator
is a dream
come true
for those
who hate
repetitive
tasks.

Actions

Workflow window

Here's a great example: You work with a service bureau that sends you a CD every week with new product shots for your company's marketing department. Unfortunately, these images are flat-out *huge* — taken with a 12-megapixel camera — and they're always in the wrong orientation. Before you move them to the Marketing folder on your server, you have to laboriously resize each image and rotate it, and then save the smaller version.

With help from Automator, though, you can build a custom application that automatically reads each image in the folder, resizes it, rotates it, and even generates a thumbnail image or prints the image, and then moves the massaged images to the proper folder. You'd normally have to manually launch Preview to perform the image operations and then use a Finder window to move the new files to the right location. But now, with Automator, a single double-click of your custom application icon does the trick.

You find Automator in the Utilities folder in Launchpad (or, from a Finder window, in your Applications folder). Currently, Automator can handle specific tasks in more than 80 applications (including the Finder), but both Apple and third-party developers can add new Automator task support to both new and existing applications.

To create a simple application with Automator, launch the application and follow these steps:

1. **Select Application and click Choose.**

2. **Click the desired application in the Library list.**

   Automator displays the actions available for that application.

3. **Drag the desired action from the Library window to the workflow window.**

4. **Modify any specific settings provided for the action you chose.**

5. **Repeat Steps 2–4 to complete the workflow.**

6. **Click Run (in the upper right) to test your script.**

   Use sample files while you're fine-tuning your application lest you accidentally do something deleterious to an original (and irreplaceable) file!

7. **When the application is working as you like, press ⌘+Shift+S to save it.**

8. **In the Save dialog that appears, type a name for your new application.**

9. **Click the Where pop-up menu and specify a location where the file should be saved.**

10. **Click the File Format pop-up menu and choose Application.**

11. **Click Save.**

   Your new Automator application icon includes the Automator robot standing on a document. Why, most normal human beings would call you a *programmer,* so make sure that you're inscrutable from now on! If you're going to use your new Automator application often, don't forget that you can make it more convenient to use by dragging the application icon to your Dock or to your desktop.

To find all the actions of a certain type in the Library list, click in the Search box at the top of the Library window and type a keyword, such as *save* or *burn.* You don't even need to press Return!

If your Automator application should run every time you log in — for example, the application tracks your time on a project — follow these steps to set up the application as a login item:

1. **Open System Preferences.**

2. **Display the Users & Groups pane.**

3. **Click the Login Items button.**

4. **Click the plus button at the bottom of the list.**

5. **Navigate to the location of your new Automator application.**

6. **Click Add.**

Now your Automator application is *really* automatic. Watch your significant other gape in amazement as your MacBook begins to work without you touching the keyboard! (If you've added the application icon to your Dock, you can also simply right-click the icon and choose Options⇨Open at Login from the right-click menu that appears. Either way, your MacBook gets the message.)

Updating OS X Automatically

I prefer my MacBook to take care of cleaning up after itself as much as possible, so updating Mountain Lion should be automatic as well. In OS X Mountain Lion, operating system updates are performed in the App Store, but you configure the update process from System Preferences.

Software Update uses the Internet, so you need an Internet connection to shake hands with the Apple server and download any updates.

Software Update can be found in two convenient spots:

- ✔ **The Apple menu:** Click the Apple menu (🍎) and then choose Software Update, which opens the App Store and alerts you to anything new that's available.

- ✔ **System Preferences:** Click the Software Update icon to display the Software Update pane.

 If you take the System Preferences route, you can set Software Update to check for critical system updates and install them automatically:

 a. *Select the Automatically Check for Updates check box to enable it.*

 b. *Select the Install System Data Files and Security Updates check box to enable it.*

You can even display any updates immediately from System Preferences (click the Show Updates button if it appears). That, dear reader, is just plain thoughtful design.

With automatic downloading disabled, OS X launches the Updates pane of the App Store and displays any available updates with short descriptions, and you can manually click the Update button next to a specific update. Mountain Lion also displays a Notification window alerting you to new updates — you can choose to continue with the update from the Notification window, or wait and update manually later.

If you're using the same Apple ID on more than one Mac, the applications you've purchased through the App Store on your other Macs can be automatically downloaded to this computer as well! Select the Automatically Download Apps Purchased on Other Macs check box to enable it, and then sit back and watch convenience happen.

Part VII
The Part of Tens

The 5th Wave   By Rich Tennant

JEEZ—YOU'D THINK THESE PEOPLE NEVER SAW A LAPTOP BEFORE!

GATE 9   GATE 8

In this part . . .

Ah, what book in the *For Dummies* series is truly complete without its Part of Tens? Here you find lots of this author's raw opinions: my best tips for Mac laptop road warriors as well as my infamous "Top Ten Things to Avoid Like the Plague."

Chapter 24

Top Ten Laptop Rules to Follow

. . . .

. . . .

Ah, the sedentary life of a desktop Mac — it sits there, like a bump on a log, comfortable and immobile. As long as you have a stable surface and an uninterrupted power supply, your iMac, Mac mini, or Mac Pro is a happy puppy.

But you, good reader, are *mobile!* Whether you're on campus or attending a convention, your Mac laptop is rarely running in the same spot, so it's susceptible to all sorts of road warrior pitfalls. In this chapter, I remind you of ten of the most important rules that every laptop owner should follow to prevent chaos and carnage while traveling.

Keep Your Laptop in a Bag

Sure, using a laptop case or bag *sounds* like common sense — but MacBooks are so doggone sexy that you'd be surprised how many people carry them around without any protection at all. These Mac owners hear phrases like "unibody construction" and "solid-state drive" and figure that their laptop can tackle a construction site, a college campus, or a hotel room with impunity.

Part of that is indeed true. Mac laptops are some of the toughest laptops ever made, but they're not immune to bumps, scratches, and the rare (I hope) fall. The moral? If you carry your MacBook from place to place without any protection, it'll soon look like a boxer after a bad fight.

If you're like me, you're proud that your computers remain in pristine condition, so use a laptop bag or case that offers ample padding and a convenient shoulder strap or carry handle. (My laptop bag even converts to a backpack, and it includes plenty of extra space for power supplies, discs, and all the assorted hoo-hah that you know you need to carry with you.) Spend an extra $30 on a laptop bag, and your $2,000 computer can weather the worst the world can dish out.

Many folks think that a traditional laptop bag draws too much attention — and to some extent, I agree. (That's one reason why no one totes an obvious 15-x-7 bag with a hardware manufacturer's logo emblazoned on the side these days.) If you're a member of this group, consider a *well-padded* laptop sleeve that allows you to carry your MacBook in your backpack, such as the BookBook cover I describe in Chapter 1 — the laptop always goes in on top of those heavy books, of course. Remember, though, that the padding is the important thing — without that extra cushion, you might as well just toss your unprotected laptop in with the rest of your books and must-have equipment.

Maximize Your RAM

Like any other computer running Windows or OS X, your MacBook will benefit from all the system RAM (memory) that you can squeeze onto it. (Chapter 22 describes how to add memory and the benefits of extra RAM.) However, additional memory is even *more* effective with a laptop using a traditional magnetic hard drive (such as the MacBook Pro), because your laptop's hard drive runs more slowly than the corresponding internal hard drive in a full-size desktop Mac. Therefore, the virtual memory functionality built into Mountain Lion (which I also describe in Chapter 22) will be even slower for a MacBook Pro with a magnetic hard drive, resulting in mediocre performance during memory-intensive tasks such as video and image editing.

With a full complement of RAM, your laptop's performance will rival the performance of a desktop computer with the same processor — and you'll be using it on the go!

Current MacBook models can be configured with anywhere from 4GB to 16GB of RAM at the time you order one from Apple, depending on the model. However, only an Apple technician can add extra memory to a MacBook Air or MacBook Pro Retina (and upgrading one of these models can be an expensive proposition). If you own a MacBook Pro, you can upgrade your laptop by following the steps I provide in Chapter 22.

Install a Tracker Application

The unthinkable happens: Your laptop is stolen while you're on vacation or on a business trip, and you know that the chances that it will be returned are next to nil. You've resigned yourself to replacing it (and all your data). But wait! What if I told you that you might just receive an e-mail message on your desktop computer that tells you the Internet (IP) address of the thief or perhaps even the telephone number he or she is using?

If this scenario sounds a little like a James Bond movie, you'll be surprised to discover that several *tracker applications* are available for Mountain Lion that can run invisibly on your laptop. A tracker application can turn your MacBook into a transmitting beacon, broadcasting to you its current location and all the Internet information it can get — allowing you to alert police and apprehend the crook (who might be in the middle of creating an iPhoto library).

In fact, Mountain Lion's *Find My Mac* feature is a tracker application in disguise! (Note that you must set up your iCloud account in the iCloud pane in System Preferences before you can use Find My Mac, as I cover in Chapter 9.) If your MacBook is lost or stolen, you can visit `www.icloud.com`, sign in with the same Apple ID, and click Find My iPhone. From the display that appears, you can choose to Remote Lock or Remote Wipe your MacBook.

If you prefer a commercial solution, check out LoJack for Laptops from Absolute Software (`www.xtool.com`), which invisibly sends a signal to the company's security center each time your laptop is connected to the Internet or a telephone line. LoJack for Laptops Standard edition costs about $40 per year, which is pocket change for a corporate road warrior or design professional who depends on both the laptop and the irreplaceable data it contains.

Keepest Thy Drive Encrypted

In Chapter 6, I discuss a number of System Preferences panes. The Security pane is particularly important to laptop users because it allows you to encrypt your drive. Encryption prevents just about anyone from accessing (or even *identifying*) any of the files you've stored on your MacBook. The robust encryption provided by Mountain Lion will certainly stymie just about anyone but the NSA and FBI. (I won't even go there.)

In System Preferences, click Security & Privacy, click the FileVault tab, and then click Turn On FileVault. You'll be given a recovery key that can unlock your MacBook's drive, just in case. (Your login account password is your primary password.) Mountain Lion takes care of automatically encrypting and decrypting files as necessary.

To take full advantage of an encrypted drive, you need the proper login mode (as I discuss in Chapter 10). Think about this possible security back door: From the Users & Groups pane, you've set your laptop to automatically log you in every time you boot your MacBook Air. This scenario is the very definition of Not Secure because your login account password automatically bypasses the FileVault encryption! Therefore, *make sure that you actually have to log in to access your account.* For the full scoop, see Chapter 10.

Brand Your MacBook

Put your brand on your laptop! Whether with an engraving tool on the bottom of the machine (my personal favorite) or a permanent metal tag, your MacBook deserves some sort of identifying information. After all, most of the people in the world are honest, and you might not need that tracking software that I mention earlier in this chapter. You might have left your laptop by accident, and someone would like to return it to you. (Don't forget to offer a reward!)

Some laptop owners want to include their name and address and other contact information, while other road warriors might feel more comfortable with just their name and e-mail address. Whatever information you choose to provide, branding your laptop is as important as backing it up.

Disable Your Wireless

Funny how we don't think about it, but wireless communications take juice, and that power comes straight from your laptop's battery! Because your Mac laptop comes with built-in Wi-Fi and Bluetooth hardware, you're constantly broadcasting — sending and receiving, or at least *trying* to exchange data with others.

And therein lies the rub: If you're not *connected* to a wireless network or a Bluetooth device, you're wasting your precious battery power. That's why Mountain Lion gives you the ability to turn off your Wi-Fi and Bluetooth hardware to save energy. And when you're sitting in a crowded auditorium without access to an AC socket or a wireless network, the energy savings you reap when you disable your wireless hardware can be significant.

In fact, you might *have* to disable your wireless connectivity in situations where cellphones are not allowed, such as on an airplane flight or in certain areas of a hospital. And, because I'm a security-conscious kind of guy, I always disable my wireless hardware whenever I'm not using it (even if I am in range of a wireless network). Call me overly careful, but none of my shared files have ever been sucked out of my MacBook without my permission!

To turn off your Wi-Fi hardware from the Mountain Lion menu bar, click the Wi-Fi status icon and choose Turn Wi-Fi Off from the menu. To turn off your Bluetooth hardware from the menu bar, click the Bluetooth icon and choose Turn Bluetooth Off.

Bring a Surge Protector with You

I'll be honest: I usually am not a huge supporter of surge protectors because I think they do only half the job. That job is protecting both your hardware *and* your data . . . and, as you probably know, a surge protector doesn't provide backup power in case of a brownout or total loss of power like a UPS (uninterruptible power supply) can.

Of course, many locales around the world offer a less-than-perfect power grid, which translates into a sudden loss of power — usually at exactly the wrong moment. (Think Great American Novel Takes a Nosedive.) Unlike a desktop, however, your MacBook is smart enough to immediately switch from AC current to its battery in case of a power failure (much like a UPS). So why am I suggesting a surge protector for your laptop, especially seeing as how it adds bulk and weight to your laptop bag or luggage?

- ✔ **The risk of a power spike:** A surge protector is good protection from a massive power spike, such as an overload or a lightning strike.

- ✔ **Extra sockets on tap:** Don't forget that you might need several more AC sockets for external devices, such as a hard drive, projector, and portable printer. A surge protector can provide the extra access to power, even when your host can't.

Naturally, if you're traveling to a country with different AC standards (and different socket configurations), invest in an AC plug adapter that's compatible with the standard used at your destination.

Use Power-Saving Features

Apple allows you considerable control over your MacBook's sleep schedule, which is a real boon to power-hungry laptop owners. In System Preferences, click Energy Saver to display the Battery and Power Adapter settings.

If your laptop is running on battery power and you need to conserve as much power as possible, click the Battery tab, and make sure that you move the Computer Sleep and Display Sleep sliders to 5 minutes or less. (If you're using a MacBook with a hard drive, you should also enable the Put Hard Disks to Sleep When Possible check box.) Now you're squeezing the maximum amount of computing time out of your remaining battery power.

If you're running your laptop while connected to an AC outlet, click the Power Adaptor tab — although power isn't a problem, I still don't recommend that you set the Computer Sleep and Display Sleep sliders to Never. (Sleep mode helps prolong the life of your MacBook's display, and a sleeping laptop generates practically no heat at all.) However, you can set both sliders for a much longer delay while connected to AC power, such as the 30 minutes I use for my display sleep!

Use an External Keyboard and Mouse

Does your laptop remain at your home, dorm room, or office for long periods of time? If so, I recommend that you invest in an external keyboard and an external mouse for two very good reasons:

- ✔ Adding external input devices helps lower the wear and tear on your laptop's keyboard and trackpad.
- ✔ External input devices are generally more comfortable and convenient to use than those offered by your MacBook, especially for gaming.

If price is no obstacle, a wireless keyboard and mouse allow you far more freedom of movement. Note, though, that a standard USB keyboard and mouse do just as fine a job and cost less.

In fact, you can have two external keyboards if you like: one to work with your laptop while you're running Mountain Lion (which has all the keys unique to an Apple keyboard) and one to use when you're running Windows under Boot Camp (with those gnarly Windows-specific keys). *Techno-suave.*

Not Again! What Is It with You and Backing Up?

Yes, it's one of the Top Ten Laptop Rules as well. I'm not kidding: If you think you don't need to back up on a regular basis, *you will eventually lose every byte of data you have.* Period. It's only a matter of time. Even if you have incredible luck and don't do something you regret with a Finder window, your MacBook is just a machine, and it will wear out in the long run. (Especially with the mobile life of a road warrior, with all the bumps and bruises of travel.) That's why hard drive manufacturers list MTBF — Mean Time Between *Failures* — figures for their hard drives.

Backing up your drive isn't difficult and doesn't take long. Chapter 23 explains everything you need to know. And after you finish your first full backup, drop me a line at mark@mlcbooks.com with the subject I've Got Laptop Peace of Mind! We can celebrate together!

Chapter 25

Ten Things to Avoid Like the Plague

*I*f you've read other books that I've written in the *Dummies* series, you might recognize the title of this chapter — it's a favorite Part of Tens subject of mine. I don't like to see any computer owner fall prey to pitfalls. Some pitfalls are minor (such as not keeping your laptop clean), and others are downright catastrophic (such as providing valuable information over the Internet to persons unknown).

All these potential mistakes, however, share one thing in common: They're *easy to prevent* with a little common sense — that is, as long as you're aware of them. And making you aware is my job. In this chapter, I fill in what you need to know. Consider these pages as experience gained easily!

USB 1.1 Storage Devices

Man, a USB 1.1 storage device is the very *definition* of sluggish. Only a creaking USB 1.1 external device such as a hard drive, hub, or CD-ROM drive could be as slow as a turtle on narcotics.

Unfortunately, you still find *countless* examples of USB 1.1 hardware hanging around. eBay is stuffed to the gills with USB 1.1 equipment, and your family and friends will certainly want to bestow that old 4x CD-RW drive to you as a gift. (This present, like your Aunt Harriet's fruitcake, is one that you should politely refuse immediately.) These drives were considered cool in the early days of the colorful iMac G3, when USB was a new technology. Today, a USB 1.1 hard drive is simply a slow-as-maple-syrup-in-January *embarrassment* (especially when it's hanging off your snazzy USB 3.0 port on your new MacBook).

I do admit that plenty of great USB 1.1 devices are still around these days, such as joysticks, keyboards, mice, and other controllers, along with printers that work just fine with slower transfer rates. However, if a peripheral's job is to store or move data quickly — including hard drives, network connections, hubs, CD-ROM drives, and USB flash drives — give a USB 1.1 device a wide berth, opting instead for a USB 2.0, USB 3.0, or FireWire device.

Phishing Operations

Phishing is no phun. No, that's not a misspelling. In Internet lingo, *phishing* refers to an attempt by unsavory characters to illegally obtain your personal information. If that sounds like an invitation to identity theft, it is — and thousands of sites have defrauded individuals like you and me (along with banks and credit card companies) out of billions of dollars. Unfortunately, the phishing industry has been growing like a weed, and more innocent folks are being ripped off every day. (The low-lifes running phishing operations are pond scum . . . and I'm being polite here because this will appear in print.)

A phishing scam works like this: You get an e-mail purporting to be from a major company or business, such as eBay, a government agency, or a big credit card company. The message looks genuine, with all the proper graphics and company information, but it warns you that you have to "update" your login or financial information to keep it current, or that you have to "validate" your information every so often — and even provides you with a convenient link to an official-looking web page. After you enter your oh-so-personal information on that bogus page, the info is piped directly to the bad guys, and they're off to the races.

Here's a Mark's Maxim that every Internet user should take to heart:

No *legitimate* company or agency will ever solicit your personal information through an e-mail message!™

Never respond to these messages. If you smell something phishy, open your web browser and visit the company's site (the *real* one) directly. Then contact the company's customer support personnel. They'll certainly want to know about the phishing expedition, and you can help by providing them with the e-mail and web addresses used in the scam.

In fact, sending any valuable financial information through unencrypted e-mail — even to those whom you know and trust — is a bad idea. E-mail messages can be intercepted or read from any e-mail server that stores your messages.

Oddly Shaped Optical Discs

Your MacBook Pro's optical drive (if you have one) is a marvel of precision — and it's doggone svelte to boot. Current MacBook optical drives (including the external drive available for the MacBook Air and MacBook Pro Retina) don't require a loading tray: Just slide your CD or DVD inside the drive, and it smoothly disappears from sight. Press the Media Eject key, right-click the disc icon on your desktop and choose Eject, or drag the disc icon to the Trash, and the disc appears like magic. No need to give the loading and ejecting procedures a second thought, right?

Well, good reader, that's true — but *only* if you're loading a standard 1.2mm-thick, 120mm *round* CD or DVD into your drive! Note that I didn't say

- **An 80mm minidisc:** Yes, they're cute. Yes, all sorts of devices use them these days, from DV camcorders to digital cameras. But no, they're not supported by many slot-loading drives, so there's a good chance one will refuse to eject.

- **A credit-card- or triangular-shaped disc:** Friends, these discs just aren't *natural!* Of course, that's part of their pizzazz for advertisers, who give them away in scads. A square disc works in a tray-loading drive, but a slot drive will likely get indigestion and refuse to eject it.

- **A super-thick disc:** Sure, a tray DVD drive can likely accept a disc with a thick, printed paper label, but if that disc is more than 1.5mm thick, it can actually damage your laptop's slot-loading drive. Consider these words: "Marge, it's stuck in there!" Now imagine how you would feel if *you* were the one saying that.

All three of these oddly shaped discs share one thing in common: *The damage you may cause by attempting to use one in your MacBook is not covered under your Apple warranty.* A weighty statement indeed.

If you do need to read or record a nonstandard disc size, I recommend that you pick up a USB or FireWire external tray-loading drive, which can easily handle any size disc you toss at it.

Submerged Keyboards

Do you *really* want a submerged keyboard? Your answer should be an unequivocal, "No!" And that's why everyone should make it a rule to keep all beverages well out of range of keyboards, trackpads, and external devices, such as speakers and mice — especially when kids or cats are in close proximity to your laptop.

If a soda spill comes in contact with your MacBook, you're likely to be visited with intermittent keyboard problems (or, in the worst-case scenario, a short in your laptop's motherboard). Suffice it to say that 12 inches of open space can make the difference between a simple cleanup and an expensive replacement!

Antiquated Utility Software

It's the upgrade game, and everyone's gotta play. If you're using OS X Mountain Lion, you must upgrade your older utility programs — such as an older copy of TechTool Pro from Micromat (www.micromat.com) that supports only Mac OS X Snow Leopard or Lion. I know that you spent good money on 'em, but these older disk utility applications can do more damage than good to a hard drive under OS X Mountain Lion. Of course, utility software designed for ancient versions of Mac OS X (such as Panther and Jaguar) should be strictly avoided (in fact, those antique applications probably won't even run with Mountain Lion)!

A number of things change when Apple makes the leap to a new version of OS X, including subtle changes to disk formats, memory management in applications, and the support provided for different types of hard drives and optical drives. If you use an older utility application, you could find yourself with corrupted data. Sometimes a complete operating system reinstall is necessary. (In fact, most utilities now refuse to run if they don't recognize the version of OS X you're running.)

Now that you're using OS X Mountain Lion, make sure that you diagnose and repair disk and file errors by using only a utility application specifically designed to run in Mountain Lion. Your laptop's drive will definitely thank you.

Software Piracy

Avoiding pirated software's a no-brainer: Don't endorse software piracy. Remember, Apple's overall market share among worldwide computer users currently weighs in at around 14 percent. Software developers know this, and they have to expect (and *receive*) a return on their investment, or they're going to find something more lucrative to do with their time. As a shareware author, I can attest to this firsthand.

Pirated software seems attractive — the price is right, no doubt about it — but if you use an application without buying it, you're cheating the developer, who will eventually find Macintosh programming no longer worth the time and trouble. Believe me, a MacBook is a great machine, and Mountain Lion is a great operating system, but the sexiest laptop and the best hardware won't make up for an absence of good applications.

Pay for what you use, and everyone benefits.

The Forbidden Account

You might never have encountered the *root,* or *System Administrator,* account in OS X — and that's always A Good Thing. Note that I'm not talking about a standard Administrator (or Admin) account here. Every Mac needs at least one Admin account (in fact, it might be the only visible account on your computer), and any Standard user account can be toggled between Standard and Admin status with no trouble at all.

The root account, though, is a different beast altogether, and that's why it's disabled by default. All UNIX systems have a root account. Mountain Lion is based on a UNIX foundation, so it has one, too. Anyone logging in with the root account can do *anything* on your system, including deleting or modifying files in the System folder (which no other account can normally access). Believe me, deliberately formatting your drive is about the only thing worse than screwing up the files in your System folder.

Luckily, no one can access the root/System Administrator account by accident. In fact, you can't assign the root account through System Preferences; you have to use the Directory Utility application located in your Utilities folder. Unless an Apple support technician tells you to enable and use it, you should promptly forget that the root account even exists.

Unsecured Wireless Connections

Okay, I like free Internet access as much as the next technology author — it's cool, it's convenient, and public-access wireless networks are popping up all over the world. Heck, a number of cities in the United States now offer city-wide free wireless Internet access.

However, just because something is *free* doesn't mean that it's *safe.* (Impromptu and overly trusting bungee jumpers, take note.) Unfortunately, the free public wireless access you're likely to encounter is not secure. Anyone can join, and the information you send and receive can be intercepted by any hacker worthy of the name. A public network uses no WEP or WPA key, so no encryption is involved, and therefore you have no guarantee that your private e-mail, your company's financial spreadsheets, and your Great American Novel aren't being intercepted while you're uploading and downloading them in the airport.

If you *must* use your laptop on an unsecured public network, make sure that the connection itself is secure instead. For example, don't check your e-mail by using a web browser unless your ISP or e-mail service offers an encrypted SSL (Secure Sockets Layer) connection. (Yep, I'm talking again about that little padlock that appears in Safari, which I discuss in Chapter 8. It's not just for ordering things online!) If you need to establish a secure connection with your home or office network, use an SSL-enabled Virtual Private Network (VPN) client, which allows you to transfer files and remotely operate a host computer with bulletproof security. Naturally, Mountain Lion includes a basic VPN client: Open System Preferences, click the Network icon, and then click the Add (plus sign) button. Click the Interface pop-up menu and choose VPN, and then select the correct VPN type and click Create.

Refurbished Hardware

Boy, howdy, do I hate refurbished stuff. Like my single-minded quest to rid the world of floppy disks, I likewise make it a point to dispel the myth that you're actually saving money when you buy a refurbished (or remanufactured) piece of hardware. To quote someone famous, "If the deal sounds too good to be true, it probably is."

Examine what you get when you buy a refurbished external hard drive. It's likely that the drive was returned as defective, of course, and was then sent back to the factory. There the manufacturer probably performed the most cursory of repairs (just enough to fix the known problem), perhaps tested the unit for a few seconds, and then packed it back up again. Legally, retailers can't resell the drive as a new item, so they have to cut the price so low that you're willing to take the chance.

Before you spend a dime on a bargain that's *remanufactured* — I can't get over that term — make sure that you find out how long a warranty you'll receive, if any. Consider that the hardware is likely to have crisscrossed the country at least once, picking up a few bumps and bruises during its travels. Also, you have no idea how well the repairs were tested or how thoroughly everything was inspected.

I don't buy refurbished computers or hardware, and most of the tales that I've heard of folks who do have ended badly (the exception is the Apple online store, where you can find a refurbished Mac with a full warranty). Take my advice: Spend the extra cash on trouble-free, new hardware that has a full warranty.

Dirty Laptops

Clean your machine. Every computer (and every piece of computer hardware) appreciates a weekly dusting.

Adding memory to your laptop? You have to open your MacBook Pro anyway, so take advantage of the opportunity to use a careful blast from that trusty can of compressed air.

On the outside of your laptop, your screen should be cleaned at least once every two or three days — that is, unless you like peering through a layer of dust, fingerprints, and smudges. Never spray anything directly on your screen or your MacBook's case. I highly recommend using premoistened LCD cleaning wipes typically used for notebook computers or monitors.

Your laptop's case really doesn't need a special cleaning agent — in fact, you shouldn't use any solvents — but a thorough wipe with a soft cloth should keep your MacBook's case in spotless shape.

Index

• Q •

• R •

• S •